SEX EQUITY IN EDUCATION

SEX EQUITY IN EDUCATION
Readings and Strategies

Edited by

ANNE O'BRIEN CARELLI, Ed.D.

Director
New York State Sex Equity
Technical Assistance and Resource Center
Regional Planning Center
Albany, New York

CHARLES C THOMAS • PUBLISHER
Springfield • Illinois • U.S.A.

Published and Distributed Throughout the World by

CHARLES C THOMAS • PUBLISHER
2600 South First Street
Springfield, Illinois 62794-9265

© *1988 by* CHARLES C THOMAS • PUBLISHER

ISBN 0-398-05415-0

Library of Congress Catalog Card Number:87-26942

Printed in the United States of America
SC-R-3

Library of Congress Cataloging-in-Publication Data

Sex equity in education: readings and strategies/edited by Anne
   O'Brien Carelli.
      p.   cm.
   Includes bibliographies and index.
   ISBN 0-398-05415-0
   1. Sex discrimination in education—United States.   2. Educational
equalization—United States.   I. Carelli, Anne O'Brien.
LC212.82.S49   1988
370.19′342—dc19   87-26942
                                                                        CIP

Carelli, Anne O'Brien

ABOUT THE AUTHORS

Barbara A. Bitters — Vocational Equity Consultant, Bureau for Equal Educational Opportunity, Wisconsin Department of Public Instruction; national consultant on sex equity in vocational education.

Ken Broadhurst — Staff Development Coordinator, Project VOICE/MOVE, Albany, New York; administrator/trainer, drug abuse prevention, youth leadership, equity issues.

Marylyn E. Calabrese — Chairperson, English Department, Conestoga Senior High School, Berwyn, Pennsylvania; educational consultant; Project Director, Becoming Sex Fair.

Anne O'Brien Carelli — Director, New York State Sex Equity Technical Assistance Center (Project VOICE/MOVE); Title IX consultant, compliance coordinator; graduate education instructor, gifted education, creativity, gender equity; author/consultant.

Jean R. Feldman — Instructor, Early Childhood Department, DeKalb Technical School, Atlanta, Georgia.

Craig Flood — Instructor, "Achieving Equity in Education," State University of New York at Albany; Director of Education, St. Coleman's School; staff development coordinator.

Cecelia H. Foxley — Associate Commissioner for Academic Affairs, Utah System of Higher Education; Professor of Psychology, Utah State University; instructor/ author.

Lynn Gangone — Director, Project SERVE — Resources for Vocational Equity, New Jersey; Coordinating Council, National Women's Studies Association.

Dolores (Dee) Grayson — Director, Educational Equity Center, Los Angeles County Office of Education; teacher, trainer, Title IX Specialist; founding member, National Coalition for Sex Equity in Education.

Marylyn A. Hulme — Assistant Director, Consortium for Educational Equity, Rutgers University; member, local board of education.

Margaret Jorgensen — Research Associate, Southern Regional Education Board, Atlanta, Georgia.

Sylvia Kramer — Executive Director, Women's Action Alliance, New York, New York; founder, Womanspace, Great Neck, New York; educator/co-author, *Equal Their Chances* (Prentice-Hall Publishers).

Eleanor Linn — Associate Director, Sex Equity in Schools, University of Michigan; consultant/trainer administrative policy, gender and race equity.

Mary D. Martin — Consultant, Proposal Center, Los Angeles City Office of Education;

co-developer of Empowering Leadership Program; originator, TESA (Teacher Effectiveness/Student Achievement) program.

Dorothy B. McKnight — Director, Athletic and Sport Consultants, Inc.; Executive Director, Educational Sport Institute; Women's Coordinator of Athletics, University of Maryland; Physical Education instructor and coach.

Christine O'Brien Palinski — Course Coordinator, Project MOVE (Maximizing Options in Vocational Education); co-author *Coping With Miscarriage* (Dial Press); guidance counselor.

Eve C. Poling — Director, Children's School, Atlanta, Georgia.

Gerald Porter — Instructor, "Achieving Equity in Education", State University of New York at Albany; Associate, New York State Education Department.

Barbara Healey Ring — Instructor, New York State Sex Equity Technical Assistance Center; Coordinator, Project Head Start.

Jo Sanders — Director, The Computer Equity Program, Women's Action Alliance, New York, New York; co-author *The Neuter Computer = Computers for Girls and Boys* (Neal-Schuman Publishers).

Cooper Thompson — Director, Education and Training for Health Care of Southeastern Massachusetts; Director, Resources for Change, Cambridge, Massachusetts.

Walteen Grady Truely — Sex Equity Coordinator, New York City Board of Education; Associate Director, Women's Educational Project; Program Officer, Education Equity Institute, American University.

Charles Vergon — Attorney; Associate Director of regional civil rights assistance center and adjunct associate professor of education law, University of Michigan.

Mary Ellen Verheyden-Hilliard — President, Equity Institute, Bethesda, Maryland; author/consultant gender equity, career education counseling.

Margaret Waterson — Editor, VOICE Newsletter, Albany, New York; Community Relations Coordinator, Cambridge Central School District, New York.

To
Eleanor Isabelle Johnson O'Brien
and
John Harrington O'Brien

PREFACE

The process of achieving sex equity in education involves the blending of equitable principles and strategies into curriculum, instruction, program development, policy, and evaluation. This text contains chapters on a number of topics relating to sex equity in education, followed by questions for discussion and suggestions for further reading. It has been prepared for use in undergraduate and graduate programs in the field of education. It has also been designed for use in staff development programs and other in-service activities conducted in educational institutions.

The issues related to gender equity in education should be discussed with every preservice and employed teacher, guidance counselor, and administrator. Separate courses in "equity" are unnecessary if every course includes aspects of the topic as routine subject matter. Sex equity can and should become an integral part of the educational process.

Grateful acknowledgement is made to the thousands of educators who strive to achieve equity every day with their students, colleagues, friends, and families. My respect for individuals who specialize in sex equity in education increased tenfold while preparing this text.

Special thanks goes to Betty Blanchet, the Staff of the New York State Sex Equity Technical Assistance Center (Project VOICE/MOVE), Pat Klimchak, Craig Flood, Jinne Welch, Gina Provenzano Culihan, Christine O'Brien Palinski, Frank Carelli, and my two-year old daughter, Caitlin, who thoroughly enjoyed "organizing" my files.

The author acknowledges permission to reprint the following material:

- Reprinted by permission of the Mid-Atlantic Center for Sex Equity Publications, "The Cost of Sex Bias in the Schools," Washington, D.C.
- "Winners and Losers," reprinted by permission of the author, Margaret Waterson.
- "Education and Masculinity," reprinted by permission of the Asso-

ciation for Supervision and Curriculum Development, Alexandria, Virginia.
• "What is Title IX?" and "Federal Anti-Discrimination Laws Pertaining to Schools," reprinted by permission of the New York State Education Department.

INTRODUCTION

You are a teacher. You are in your classroom. You are responsible for the academic, social, emotional, psychological, and physical well-being of thirty students. You may, indeed, be responsible for at least 100 students during one school day. You have to prepare interesting, challenging lessons to compete with television, MTV, and other media. You should be watching for signs of drug and alcohol abuse, or other potential student problems. You must be aware of the signals of possible suicide, pregnancy, physical abuse, drop-out, or signs of depression.

You are acutely aware of your paycheck, your status, and the demands of the community on your time and your psyche.

As you scan your classroom, you notice that one student seems to be withdrawing more and more each day. Today she is particularly morose, as is her boyfriend who is sitting nearby. You mentally record their names in your "better try to talk to those kids" file and toss out another question to the group.

In the faculty room you ask your colleagues if they have noticed anything different about the two students. Someone suggests that there is a rumor about the two of them considering dropping out—perhaps she is pregnant? You decide to leave a note with the guidance counselor —isn't there some new program for pregnant and parenting teens? You return to your classroom and try to get this lesson going like the last one.

You really are dedicated. You know that you are not paid as much as you should be, and that you do not necessarily command the respect that you deserve, but the job, on the whole, is a great job.

But now they want you to do "sex equity."

Regardless of how the above scenario seems to fit the attitude of the educators in a school, it would not be surprising if they groaned when told to "do equity." It can easily appear as just one more thing to do, another add-on to the school program. Once again, it seems that teachers, guidance counselors, and administrators must figure out a way to fit something else into the school day.

Since schools are being pressed to absorb more and more social responsibilities, many educators resist the suggestion that they should also include the elimination of sex bias as yet another responsibility. It is hard enough to decide what the school role should be in resolving social problems. It is hard enough to get through the school day without interruption. It is hard enough to listen to the community, indeed, the American public, consistently telling you how to do your job.

Yet, with just a slight introduction to the topic of sex equity, educators can begin to see that it is not a question of devising a new program, rewriting the curriculum, or preparing a system to handle complaints. It is not a "social problem" to be solved by educators. Sex equity, once understood, can quickly become an integral part of the school day. Once a school system understands the purpose and results of achieving equity, then equitable education can easily become part of the routine for educators and students alike. It is not *EXTRA* work, it is *DAILY* work. It is not *SOMETHING NEW,* a *PASSING FAD,* but something *STANDARD,* a *GIVEN* in the school program.

How can that be? Doesn't "sex equity" mean rights for women? Doesn't it apply to jobs and money? Isn't it watching what you say, listening to petty grievances, spending a lot of money on defending the athletic program, and paper compliance to legislation? Isn't it just more work because a few people are complaining?

The answer is no. Of course, any time a concept has to be contemplated, personalized, and applied, it is hard work. Any time there is a change in thinking or in process, there may be grievances, budget questions, and some paperwork. But educators who comprehend the meaning of sex equity in education consider those steps to be minor, compared to the positive, long-term consequences. The implementation of an equitable school climate can ultimately improve the lives of all students. If equity in education can expand the horizons of all children and help them to be productive, fulfilled, and contributing citizens, then it seems that it requires a closer look by all educators.

So what is "sex equity"? How can it be achieved in education so that it is not just another thing to add on to the responsibilities of educators? Compared to all of the other problems that schools currently have to contend with, how important can sex equity be?

WHAT IS MEANT BY THE TERM "SEX EQUITY"?

The term "sex equity" in education refers to the concepts of equal treatment and equal opportunity for all students, regardless of their sex. Sex equity pertains to both sexes, contrary to standard perceptions. Boys or girls are experiencing sex equity if they are *not limited* in their academic and career pursuits, social and emotional experiences, and leisure activities because of their gender.

The achievement of sex equity requires the elimination of three different forms of limitation by sex: *sex role stereotyping, sex bias,* and *sex discrimination.* Many inequitable rules and actions based on sex have been eliminated in schools either by choice or by law. But the subtle forms of stereotyping, bias, and discrimination can frustrate students and hinder their progress. Both boys and girls suffer when expectations and acceptable behavior are determined solely on the basis of gender. When educating students, the concept of sex equity should be an integral part of planning and instruction.

Sex Role Stereotyping

Whenever specific behaviors, abilities, interests, and values are attributed to one sex, then sex role stereotyping is taking place. The stereotypes are culturally defined, reinforced by parents, teachers, and the students themselves (Barnett, Baruch and Rivers, 1979). Stereotypes are generally conceptual in nature, therefore not necessarily observable. Stereotyping of boys, for example, conjures up images of strength, independence, achievement, and minimal emotional expression. The opposite of the characteristics traditionally applied to boys are often stereotypes of girls: weak, dependent, nonaggressive, and overly expressive emotionally.

The assumption that males and females each have specific characteristics leads to the determination of acceptable behaviors. *If the roles are established, then the rules are established.* Girls play jump rope, boys play football. Girls are good at creative writing; boys are good at science. The students know what is permitted according to their sex. But, by being pressured to adhere to their sex roles, students have limited opportunities to reject interests, behaviors, and values that do not suit them, and they rarely explore nontraditional roles (National Education Association, 1977).

Sex Bias

Behavior that results from the underlying belief in sex role stereotypes is referred to as "sex bias." In many cases sex bias is based on the assumption that one sex is superior to another sex (New York State Education Department, 1980). A teacher, for example, who believes in the stereotype that girls are not as capable in math as boys may exhibit biased behavior by providing girls less challenging math assignments, or by discouraging girls from pursuing math courses and careers.

The teacher may not be deliberately denying girls opportunities. Bias is often an unconscious action that results in severe limitations of choices and behaviors. As the stereotypes become reinforced through biased behaviors, both boy and girl students are being treated differently according to their sex. Smith (1977), writing for educators, states

> Understanding bias leads to understanding how we unconsciously shape our students and ourselves. We can analyze how we bend other people out of shape to meet our preconceptions and also learn how we develop positive traits, such as independence in boys and nurturance in girls, so that they can be extended to everyone. (p. 9)

Biased behavior on the part of educators has a powerful impact on the development of students' self-images and expectations, as well as their attitudes toward their own sex and the other sex. Restrictions by sex can cause students to become insecure about their abilities and interests, even at an early age (Aquila and Cohen, 1980; Kirschenbaum, 1980). The attributes of individual people, as opposed to "boys" and "girls," are often disregarded, especially if the characteristics tend to break a stereotype. The negative consequences of ignoring stereotypical sex roles and biasing influences can include criticism, labeling, and even ostracism. Sex bias can box students into roles that are uncomfortable and inhibitive. Pogrebin, in *Growing Up Free* (1980), challenges efforts to classify and confine children by sex role stereotyping and sex biased behavior. She writes to parents and educators

> After considering how various experts define "becoming" a girl or a boy as a healthy personality goal, I hope to persuade you that "being" a girl or boy is enough, and that the proper goal of childhood socialization is becoming human, as fully, gloriously, individually human as every child can be. (p. 302)

The extirpation of stereotypes would lead to the elimination of sex bias. Students could break out of the boxes that restrain them, and emphasis would instead be on the expansion of roles (Farris and Smith, 1980).

Sex Discrimination

Efforts to expand the roles of boys and girls are usually carried out voluntarily, with a commitment on the part of educators to eliminate sex role stereotyping and sex bias. In some cases, however, behavior changes are dictated by state and federal laws. Any action that specifically denies opportunities, privileges, or rewards to a person or a group because of their sex is termed "sex discrimination" if the action is against the law. Although "sex discrimination" is often referred to when sex biased behavior occurs, the advent of federal legislation such as Title VII of the Civil Rights Act of 1964 and Title IX of the Education Amendments of 1972 has caused sex discrimination to become more narrowly defined (Smith, 1977). Sandler (Aquila and Cohen, 1980) writes

> One of the problems encountered under Title IX and other civil rights laws as well is the answer to the question: What constitutes discrimination? Policies and practices that clearly and specifically apply to one sex are generally easy to assess as discriminatory. (p. 33)

Sex discrimination is often a conscious, deliberate action. Examples A and B demonstrates the interrelationships of sex role stereotyping, sex bias, and sex discrimination.

As the figure indicates, the three forms of limitation by sex are closely linked and in many cases overlap so significantly that one type is difficult to distinguish from another. The terminology, however, is less profound than the results of inequity in education.

SEX EQUITY AND THE SCHOOL PROGRAM

Sex equity, or equal treatment and equal opportunity regardless of gender, can be a significant part of planning and implementing educational programs for students. The development of potential in students requires a flexible school program that encourages exploration, inquiry, and risk-taking. If sex roles, and therefore opportunities, are predetermined, then the climate for learning is rigid and stultifying. If students are discouraged from investigating unconventional or nonstereotypical fields and interests, then they are being denied the chance to discover themselves and reach their full potential.

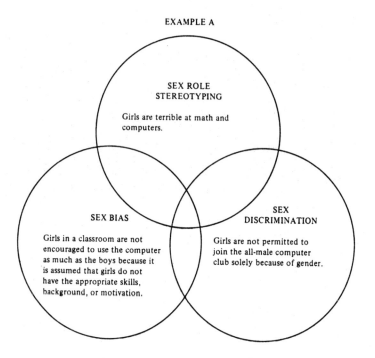

EXAMPLE A

SEX ROLE
STEREOTYPING

Girls are terrible at math and
computers.

SEX BIAS

Girls in a classroom are not
encouraged to use the computer
as much as the boys because it
is assumed that girls do not
have the appropriate skills,
background, or motivation.

SEX
DISCRIMINATION

Girls are not permitted to
join the all-male computer
club solely because of gender.

The First Step

The first step in achieving sex equity is to understand the need for individuals to have the opportunity to become self-fulfilled. It seems as if educators would be in a prime position to recognize this need in their students. Their job is, after all, to help children to grow and learn. Educators who are equitable in their approaches understand that growing and learning takes place when there is an expansion of experiences, not when there are restrictions.

Although the concept of freedom to grow and learn seems sensible and unarguable, it becomes complicated when SEX ROLE is confused with SEX IDENTITY. Obviously, boys and girls are different by virtue of their anatomy. They need to be able to identify with their sex for healthy psychological growth.

But those sex differences should not be translated to mean that one sex, as a group, is necessarily better than another sex. Or that one sex, as a group, is more successful at something than the other. Or that one sex,

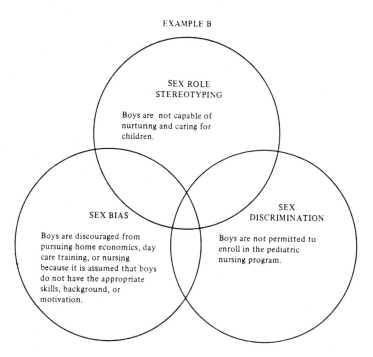

EXAMPLE B

SEX ROLE
STEREOTYPING

Boys are not capable of
nurturing and caring for
children.

SEX BIAS

Boys are discouraged from
pursuing home economics, day
care training, or nursing
because it is assumed that boys
do not have the appropriate
skills, background, or
motivation.

SEX
DISCRIMINATION

Boys are not permitted to
enroll in the pediatric
nursing program.

as a group, should be allowed to pursue an activity, and the other sex
excluded. Schau and Tittle (Klein, 1985) comment

> Most educators and psychologists believe that environmental and developmen-
> tal cognitive effects in conjunction with very small biological potentials con-
> tribute to the development of sex differences in roles. The development of sex
> roles and the tendency to sex-stereotype the behaviors, attitudes, and personal-
> ity characteristics expected of females and males in our culture have a strong
> and pervasive influence throughout all of our lives. (p. 88)

Socialization, permeated with sex role stereotyping, can result in auto-
matic limits and expectations that apply to the groups and may not relate
to the individual at all.

Landers (Kaser, Sadker and Sadker, 1982) states

> Although it's true that boys and girls may be somewhat different, it's also true
> that some boys are different from other boys and that some girls are different
> from other girls. Regarding physical abilities and skills, you'll find students of
> both sexes who are highly skilled, moderately skilled, and inadequately skilled.
> The differences between highly skilled boys and highly skilled girls is less
> than the differences between highly skilled and inadequately skilled boys or
> highly skilled and inadequately skilled girls. Thus, it makes more sense to

plan instruction based on the skills, abilities, and interests of the students rather than on their sex. (p. 95)

Take for example, a young boy in school who demonstrates exceptional musical ability. His gift, hopefully, would be encouraged. But not only has he received messages about his skills, but also messages about what is an acceptable instrument for a boy! Flutes and violins are generally regarded as the more "feminine" instruments, and are often discouraged for boys. Suddenly his ability has restrictions placed upon it by traditional, limiting views of acceptable sex role behavior.

Another example is a young girl who demonstrates ability in mathematical problem-solving. She is encouraged by her teachers and is even given early training on the computer so that she can experiment with the development of diagrams and other problem-solving activities. Then, as she approaches adolescence, she begins to notice that she is regarded as the "brain," and is not as popular with her peers as she would like to be. So she begins to release her time on the computer to some of the boys so that she does not appear to be too aggressive or brighter than they are. She loses valuable time and experience needed to build up her skills. Her sex role socialization as a girl begins to put limits on her capabilities.

In both examples, physiological sex differences between boys and girls are compounded by stereotypical images of both sexes as independent groups. Boys are viewed one way, girls another.

Palinski (1987) writes

> ... the profound and destructive manifestation of sexism in our society appears in the division of behaviors and characteristics into two separate lists, one labeled male and one labeled female. Because of the character of the lists, the impact is different for each group. *But each group is systematically prohibited from entry into a vast territory of experience and gratification.*
>
> The effect of this sex role division on women is heavily economic. Girls and women are conditioned to be dependent, compliant, and of secondary status in the home and workplace. Their energies are directed toward the affiliations rather than the potential achievements available to them. As adults they find themselves in lower paid, lower status employment. Boys and men are conditioned to be independent, autonomous, and to have achievement-oriented behavior. They are discouraged from developing the affective, nurturing side of their personalities. As adults they find themselves successful in varying degrees in the workplace but often lacking the skills and experience appropriate to forming satisfying, close relationships. Taking the position that women are victims while men are not is reinforcing the money and status ethic which is only half of the picture. It is devaluing the affective, nurturing, affiliating, caretaking side of life. (p. 1–2)

Perhaps these descriptions appear to be unrealistic in today's world. As educators look around their classrooms and school hallways, they may not see any overt evidence of sex role stereotyping, bias, or discrimination. Yet a closer look at statistics, enrollment figures, counseling records, and other documents indicates that there are still profound discrepancies between what is considered equal opportunity and what is actually accomplished by boys and girls in school. Educators who recognize that *all* students have a right to experience a full range of educational opportunities begin to include sex equity as standard procedure. Whenever this intervention takes place, then both the overt and covert biased activities can be reduced and the statistics begin to change (Klein, 1985).

The Second Step

The second step in achieving sex equity is to realize that the process of recognizing, implementing, and maintaining an equitable school climate is *good education.* If schools are striving to establish excellence in education, then they are also establishing equity in education. A fair education is an integral part of excellent schooling.

Schniedewind and Davidson write, "Students will know that equality is possible because they've experienced it. Such knowledge lasts a lifetime" (1983).

The Third Step

The third step in achieving sex equity is to incorporate it into all school programs. This requires a full comprehension of the value of a fair education for all students. Legislation cannot mandate a change in attitudes. It cannot dictate understanding of equity issues. Laws cannot force educators to recognize unintentionally biased behavior, or to stop perpetuating sex role stereotypes. Educators themselves have to determine how they can best assure students an equitable education. Increased awareness is the best route to assurance.

Students are influenced by daily interactions with teachers, the visible school environment (e.g., bulletin boards, athletic fields), written board policies, and extracurricular guidelines. They observe role models, study lessons, and participate in school athletic and social events. They repeatedly receive messages about what is expected and accepted for their gender. In an equitable school, the students are consistently treated as individuals with unique characteristics. They are given instructional materials that reflect a school philosophy of respect for the individual. They are not divided up by gender, assigned and grouped by gender, identified by gender, or expected to achieve on the basis of gender. They are permitted and directly encouraged to participate in a variety of school activities, depending on skill and interest.

Educators who are aware of the impact of disparate treatment of students realize that many biased actions are *unconsciously* carried out by teachers and other school personnel. For example, there is probably not a sign in an elementary classroom that says "The boys in this room are stronger than the girls." But the following may be occurring:

- The reading text describes workers as "he," especially if the job requires physical strength.
- Boys are assigned the job of moving chairs, carrying books, etc.
- Girls are not encouraged to participate in the rougher sports at recess.

The messages are subtle, but can be interpreted by *both* genders to mean that boys in that classroom are stronger than the girls. Teachers who are concerned about the welfare of students want to make the strong girl comfortable, and the not-so-strong boy comfortable, too. They want boys and girls to respect each other and to work and play together effectively. Slight changes in the classroom environment can eliminate the sex bias and increase the chance of improving the academic and social welfare of the class.

A gradual infusion of equity into all school programs can profoundly affect the tone and accomplishments of an educational institution. Barriers to learning and the development of potential are eliminated. Education is distributed fairly.

The Fourth Step

The fourth step in achieving equity is to understand that students and colleagues are affected *daily* by equity-related events that occur outside the school walls. Here are ten quick examples:

- Students are more than likely from homes with single parents, dual employed parents, or blended families.

Most textbooks and other instruction resources depict the traditional "nuclear" family. Students begin to believe that their family structure is not the norm, when, in fact, the nuclear family (father employed, mother at home, two children) is less than 5% of American families today. "Nuclear" now means many different types of family arrangements.

- Men are more prone to stress-related diseases and early death than women.

Sex role stereotyping of men may pressure them to concentrate on achievement, neglect personal health, and suppress emotional stress. The results are drug and alcohol abuse, few medical checkups, heart attacks, and other life-threatening events.

- Most working-age women are employed, for reasons of economic necessity, self-satisfaction and personal growth.

Changes in the American economy, coupled with the Women's Movement, have been instrumental in bringing women back into the work force to stay. Students not only witness this phenomenon, but must be prepared to participate in it in the future.

- Legislation, such as Title IX of the Education Amendments has been eroded since its passage in 1972.

Title IX legislation significantly altered the opportunities and experiences for girls in schools. Doors opened. Since its implementation, enforcement has decreased over time, and legislation to shore up Title IX has yet, as of 1987, to be passed.

- Adolescent pregnancy is rapidly on the rise.

Adolescent pregnancy is a national crisis. Pregnant and parenting teens frequently drop out of school. This move not only affects their personal well-being, but the American economy. Girls and boys need education that focuses on building self-esteem and communication skills and most importantly, preparing for the future.

- Child care, including after-school coverage, has become a critical national issue.

Schools are being viewed as a community solution for before- and after-school child care for students whose parents are employed. Educators themselves struggle with finding adequate coverage for their children. Solutions such as year-round schools and school-day extensions have been proposed, causing discussions of the appropriate role of education in solving this problem.

- Most fathers in 1986 assisted in the birth of their newborn.

    Fathers are becoming more involved in child rearing. Yet organizations, including schools, often do not recognize the father as a significant parent. Most employers do not have parental leave plans for fathers and do not support the father's need to stay home with children who are sick, attend school events, and so forth.

- Most television shows depict a "typical" family that no longer reflects American life.

    Students watch sitcoms, movies and game shows that repeatedly depict more men than women, the traditional "nuclear" family, and/or men and women employed in stereotypical jobs and activities. Students often use TV as a measure of real life.

- States are struggling with fair methods of providing pay equity (or comparable worth) to employees.

    Employers are beginning to recognize that many salaries were determined in the past on the basis of sex role stereotypes. Fair revisions in pay scales is a difficult, complicated process. Educators have generally been paid according to "steps" (years of experience), but pay equity may become an issue for some schools.

- Women who leave work to have a baby now have the security of knowing that they can legally return to the same or equivalent job.

    School districts are regularly affected by legislation and court decisions pertaining to employment. Recruitment, screening, interviewing, hiring practices, and leave policies are some of the personnel practices that require adherence to equity-related rulings.

These examples demonstrate that sex equity cannot be ignored. Everyone is experiencing the impact of equity issues in some capacity. The topics often require close personal and professional scrutiny. Review of attitudes and behaviors can be revealing, and some changes may need to occur. These changes can include participation in specific activities that counteract stereotyping, bias, and discrimination. Educators working towards an equitable educational system can strive for more positive (or "affirmative") action in the future.

HOW TO USE THE TEXT

The four steps towards achieving sex equity are actually conducted simultaneously as educators read about the issues, discuss and debate, and draw conclusions. Some topics will be easier than others to absorb and accept. Some will be a direct challenge to personal values and standards.

In this text:

- Each chapter has an Introduction, Discussion Questions, and Suggestions for Further Reading.
- The Discussion Questions are designed for contemplation and debate. They do not have a correct or appropriate response. Readers are encouraged to select additional resources from the suggestions associated with the article.
- A list of organizations pertaining to sex equity is at the back of the text. Newsletters, instructional materials, publications, and media may be ordered from these organizations.

Sex Equity in Education: Readings and Strategies, is designed to encourage educators to weigh facts, personal values and experiences, and to determine what activities can be carried out in order to achieve equity.

Whether you are teacher, guidance counselor, principal, superintendent, or school board member, the entire contents of the text are relevant to your role and responsibilities. Educators need to work hand-in-hand to understand and to establish sex equity in education.

Change seldom comes easy or fast. There are few quick and dirty tricks that will break down barriers that have existed for centuries. Identifying the problem is only the first step. In many ways, it is the easiest step to take. The real challenge and opportunity belong to educators.

When educators become aware of the nature and costs of sex bias in schools, they can make an important difference in the lives of their students . . . They can make sex equity become a reality for children in our schools. Then tomorrow's children, boys and girls, need not suffer from the limiting impact of sex-role stereotyping. (Equal Goals in Occupation, 1984, p. 8)

SUGGESTIONS FOR THE PROFESSIONAL LIBRARY

Brannon, R., & David, D.S. *The forty-nine percent majority: The male sex role.* Reading, Massachusetts: Addison-Wesley, 1976.

The Bureau of National Affairs, Inc. *Work & family: A changing dynamic.* Washington, D.C., 1986.

Klein, S.S. (Ed.). *Handbook for achieving equity through education.* Baltimore, Maryland: The Johns Hopkins University Press, 1985.

Schniedewind, N., & Davidson, E. *Open minds to equality — A sourcebook of learning activities to promote race, sex, class, and age equity.* Englewood Cliffs, New Jersey: Prentice-Hall, 1983.

Shapiro, J., Kramer, S., & Hunerberg, C. *Equal their chances — children's activities for non-sexist learning.* Englewood Cliffs, New Jersey: Prentice-Hall, 1981.

Available from Garland Publishing Company, Fall 1988:

Resources for Educational Equity, edited by Barbara Sprung and Merle Froschl, Co-Directors of Educational Equity Concepts, New York, New York. (address listed in General Resources)

REFERENCES

Aquila, F., & Cohen, R. (Eds.) *Monographs in urban and multicultural education-changing times: Sex desegregation and American education, Number one.* Indiana: Center for Urban and Multicultural Education, Indiana University, July, 1980.

Barnett, R., Baruch, G., & Rivers, C. *Beyond sugar and spice.* New York: G. Putnam's Sons, 1979.

Equal Goals in Occupations. *Sex equity goodies for the classroom.* Honolulu, Hawaii: Office of the State Director of Vocational Education, 1984.

Farris, C., & Smith, A. *Pioneering programs in sex equity: A teacher's guide.* Arlington, Virginia: American Vocational Association, 1980.

Kaser, J.S., Sadker, D., & Sadker, M. *Guide for sex equity trainers.* New York: Longman, 1982.

Kirchenbaum, R. Combating sexism in the preschool environment. *Roeper Review, 2* (3), February-March, 1980.

Klein, S.S. (Ed.) *Handbook for achieving equity through education.* Baltimore, Maryland: The Johns Hopkins University Press, 1985.

National Education Association. *Sex role stereotyping in the schools.* Washington, D.C., 1977.

New York State Education Department. *Actions for change.* New York: Office of Occupational and Continuing Education Special Programs Unit, 1980.

Palinski, C. Letter, April, 1987.

Pogrebin, L.C. *Growing up free — raising your child in the 80's.* New York: McGraw-Hill Book Company, 1980.

Schniedewind, N., & Davidson, E. *Open minds to equality: A sourcebook of learning activities to promote race, sex, class, and age equity.* Englewood Cliffs, New Jersey: Prentice-Hall, Inc., 1983.

Smith, A. (Ed.) *New pioneers—A program to expand sex role expectations in elementary and secondary education—seminar leader's handbook.* Washington, D.C.: Women's Education Association, 1977.

CONTENTS

SEX EQUITY IN EDUCATION

Chapter 1

SEX ROLE STEREOTYPING:
HOW IT HAPPENS AND HOW TO AVOID IT

Sylvia Kramer

INTRODUCTION

"That baby is really kicking. I bet it will be a boy!"

Sometimes before a child is even born, there are comments about expectations related to gender. Choice of colors, toys, baby equipment, even level
of activity are often determined once the sex of the child is known. From the
first day of a baby's life, expectations about the capabilities, life experiences,
and behaviors of the child begin to take shape. Although most hospitals have
switched from pink and blue blankets to different colors for all babies, the more
subtler messages about gender expectations still exist.

Observe how parents, relatives, and friends hold babies. How do they talk to
them, play with them, comment on their activity? Frequently boys are handled
casually, cuddled less often, left to cry longer, and pressed to demonstrate
movement. Comments such as "He's a real tough guy," "Looks like a line-
backer to me," are overheard. Tossing up in the air, lifting high, are examples of
interactions that occur with newborn boys.

Intentional bias? Probably not. No more than parents deliberately protect girl
babies, talk in high voices and comment on appearance more often than on
activity level and expectations for the future. "She's so sweet," is more familiar
than "Looks like she's going to be strong!" when newborn girls are discussed.

Boys and girls are different, simply by virtue of their anatomy. But individual
skills, interests, goals, likes and dislikes clearly cannot be determined by looking
at a week-old baby.

Yet as the months and years of development go by, the initial parental
interactions are compounded by messages from books, television, songs, and
people in the lives of children. The messages from these other influences,
although changing, are still gender based. More and more restrictions on
attitudes and feelings occur. Girls and boys begin to narrow down their choices
in activities and goals. Emotions become determined more by appropriate
gender reactions than by the incident that precipitated the motion. (If the
baseball hit your arm and hurt it, your gender determines whether you show
your tears or not. The pain becomes secondary.)

3

In addition, boys and girls become divided into gender factions. They learn about the expected characteristics of their own sex, but come to know little about the other sex. They often become suspect, even disdainful, of the other sex. Even though they will spend most of their working and family lives with the other gender, traditional upbringing allows them limited opportunities to get to know each other.

School experiences can counteract traditional sex role socialization. Classrooms that routinely encourage girls and boys to work and play together foster open communication, respect, and better understanding of the other gender. Activities that are open to all students encourage individual development, creativity, and achievement of full potential.

Kramer's chapter discusses how to counteract the development of sex role stereotyping in the lives of children. It is based on *Equal Their Chances,* by June Shapiro, Sylvia Kramer, and Catherine Hunerberg (Englewood Cliffs, New Jersey: Spectrum Books, 1981).

SEX ROLE STEREOTYPING:
HOW IT HAPPENS AND HOW TO AVOID IT

I need two strong boys to carry these books... Girls are so artistic... This is a book of space adventures you boys will really like... Whose mother can come on a trip with us?... I'd like some girls to bake cookies for the party... Would one of you boys help me with the computer?... Ask your father if we can borrow his hammer... Mary, you look so pretty today!

Repeated in thousands of different ways, comments like these shape children's learning about what it means to be a female or a male in our society. In countless ways, adults teach children that how they should think, feel, and act depends on their gender. This sexism is so deeply embedded in our thinking that teachers and parents are often unaware of how children get sexist ideas about life that channel them into "appropriate" sex roles.

Sex role stereotypes of males and females are rigid beliefs in and applications of sex roles to all females and males in all cultures, held to be universally true and biologically natural, and usually accepted without question. At an unconscious level of thinking, we know what a male should be: strong, logical, brave, aggressive, competitive, striving, unemotional, and a "good" family provider. A female should possess an entirely different set of characteristics: dependent, intuitive, emotional, unassertive, nurturing, talkative, patient, passive, illogical, and kind.

Actually, no man or woman is expected to fit the ideal male or female image exactly. Nevertheless, the further away people are from the accepted sex stereotypes, the more likely it is that something about them will be felt to be strange, either by their social group or by the people themselves.

Stereotyped ideas of female and male attributes are always unreal, unfair, and most important, limiting to the full development of an individual. They become particularly oppressive in periods of rapid social change when life requires a more expansive and flexible view of one's behavior and capabilities.

The last two decades have seen economic and social changes that have profoundly altered our lives. The family, the basic unit of our society, has changed greatly from our parents' generation. Only 5 percent of today's families are composed of the traditional breadwinner father, homemaker mother, and two children. In fact, only one of every ten girls in school today will become a full-time homeworker. Since World War II, women have joined the work force in unprecedented numbers, accounting for nearly 62 percent of the entire labor force in 1985. At that time, about 70 percent of women in the prime work age of 25 to 54 were working for pay (U. S. Department of Labor, 1985).

As more women work outside the home, more men are doing some of the work inside it. While a number of them find that housework conflicts with their male self-image, others derive great satisfaction in being able to share the life of the family more than before. These and other changes in economic and social patterns require a closer look at the way we educate children to meet a future that is in important respects different from the one we thought we would experience when we became adults.

More than a decade has passed since Congress, in an unprecedented move to address the issues of sex discrimination, mandated that schools provide equal educational opportunities to both sexes by passing Title IX. This 1972 educational law used the power of federal funds to support the American commitment to equal education for all children. Schools found themselves required to evaluate all aspects of school life covered under the regulations for sex equity or risk losing federal funds channeled into their systems. Physical education classes, extracurricular athletics, guidance, treatment of students and staff, employment, course enrollments and titles, and school regulations came under scrutiny. In many schools significant changes were made.

Recently the coverage of Title IX has been limited to only those programs or activities in the schools which directly receive federal funds. Although legislation has been proposed to reaffirm Title IX, some people have assumed that inequitable education is an issue of the past, and that it is time to turn our attention to other national priorities.

But while some aspects of school life have changed, we have not yet achieved sex equity in education. Research tells us that although there has been some improvement, females are not yet receiving the same educational opportunities and services as males. For example, girls still take fewer math, science, and computer courses than boys. Girls are overrepresented in vocational courses leading to low-paying careers. There is some evidence that teachers unintentionally pay less constructive attention to girls than to boys in the classroom and that boys are pressured to achieve in several domains simply because they are boys, and expectations are high. Stereotypic ideas about males and females still influence the way we prepare our students for their future.

No teacher or parent gives children deliberate lectures or lessons in how to restrict the full flowering of their personalities according to gender, yet the message comes through nevertheless. It comes through clearly in the ordinary comments adults make to children that began this chapter. The message, as inadvertent as it may be, comes through on television, in children's books, in rock music, in friends' houses . . . indeed, everywhere.

How Sex Role Stereotyping Happens

Teachers, parents and others who work with students do not consciously limit possibilities for growth. They may, however, use practices and materials in the school and the home that are sex biased and reinforce discriminatory stereotypes and attitudes. They need a new perspective on the way boys and girls are treated: how do ordinary events contribute to the sexism that children learn?

Parental Influence

The first and extremely powerful step in the socialization process is the one accomplished by parents. Despite the fact that research has shown that there is little difference in the behavior of infant girls and boys, adults interact with them differently.

In a classic 1974 study, researchers looked at the reactions of mothers and fathers within a day of the birth of their first children (Luria, Provenzano, and Rubin, 1974). The babies were in fact evenly matched in terms of birth length, birth weight, and Apgar scores (general health ratings). Nevertheless, both parents rated daughters as significantly softer, finer featured, smaller, more awkward, more inattentive, weaker, and more delicate than sons. Sons were rated by both parents as firmer, larger featured, coordinated, alert, stronger, and hardier than daughters. In general, fathers perceived greater sex differences in the infants than mothers. One can only assume that parents proceeded to treat their babies differently at home.

There are other studies that look at parental attitudes and behavior with toddler children. One found that parents reacted considerably more favorably to a toddler when he or she was engaged in sex stereotypical behavior, such as adult oriented or dependent behavior for girls, and active or large motor activities for boys (Fagot, 1978). Another study found that thirteen-month-old boys and girls were equal in assertiveness and in their attempts to communicate with adults, but the adults responded more to the assertive behavior of boys than that of girls, and more to the communication attempts of girls than those of boys. Eleven months later, the children showed sex-typed behavior that matched the adults' treatment of them: boys were more assertive and girls talked more to the adults (Dronsberg et al., 1985).

> Through differential treatment, through the provision of play materials, through the dressing in sex typed clothing, and through the observation of the role of gender in society, the child at the close of infancy is well equipped to acquire a sex role identity. (Brooks-Gunn & Matthews, 1979, p. 19)

As time passes, mothers talk more to female toddlers and encourage them to stay nearby when they play. Boys are allowed to explore, wander farther away from their parents, manipulate objects longer without disapproval, and exhibit more aggression than girls. When an accident occurs, boys who are hurt receive brief comfort and then are sent back to "try it again"; in a similar situation girls are cuddled extensively and warned not to try it again. Girls' passivity and dependency are further encouraged by the fact that they receive more help on tasks than boys.

It isn't long before children fit themselves into sex-appropriate patterns. They notice who does what in their family and how mommy and daddy and sister and brother behave differently. They naturally believe that what they observe in their own home is true for everybody. They start to generalize.

Their peers are, in all likelihood, learning the same lessons in their own homes. When children are old enough to play together, there will be agreement about what is appropriate. Children's assumptions that proper gender activities are strengthened by the seemingly universal acceptance of the same attitudes all around them, and by their desire to be like the other children in the neighborhood.

The Influence of Television

Young children spend enormous amounts of time in front of the TV set, watching a steady stream of shows that reinforce stereotypic views of men and women. This is even true of cartoons: try to imagine Bugs Bunny as a woman! Every Muppet is also recognizably female or male. Superhero cartoon characters are almost always exclusively male.

TV programs made ten, twenty, or even twenty-five years ago still dominate children's afternoon TV schedules. Parents may not realize the attitudes and values that these old shows pass on to children. Gilligan's Island, I Dream of Jeannie, The Brady Bunch, and I Love Lucy are a daily dose of stereotyping in many youngster's lives. While these reruns entertain children, they also instill outmoded concepts of men's and women's lives that can be even more powerful than the reality around them. One four year old whose pediatrician was female nevertheless insisted—on the authority of these old TV programs—that doctors are always men.

Commercials also provide children with a picture of the lives of adult women. Women are supposed to be beautiful and greatly concerned with products that improve their appearance to help them serve their family better. Dirt, in any form, distresses them. The impression children get is that women are absorbed in the drudgery surrounding cleaning and cooking, while men have fun or are involved with serious matters such as cars, insurance, "work," and business travel. Both the man who patiently instructs the helpless women housekeeper and the male voice-over in the cosmetics commercial reinforce the idea of authority as masculine. Children learn again that the male-female relationship is an unequal one, with each sex relegated to traditional gender-related roles.

A recent study found that television commercials for toys strongly influences children's sex role attitudes (Balaban, Cooper, and Rugle, 1981). Four- to six-year-old children were shown one of two commercials for the same sex-neutral toy (a Fisher-Price Movie Viewer). One version had two girls playing with the toy and the other had two boys playing with it, but otherwise the two versions were identical. The researchers found that those children with a strong sense of themselves as either female or male were much likelier to reject the toy if they had seen the opposite sex commercial. What is even more remarkable is that a single viewing of a thirty-second commercial produced such a striking effect.

Children can't help but notice that the majority of important people in news programs are men. The political, military, and economic events that TV reports often reinforce the idea that women are secondary or of little consequence. One encouraging trend, though, is that TV stations have begun to use more women on news programs as reporters and, more significantly, as newscasters and anchors. As children watch women in these roles, they have an opportunity to see females as competent, thinking, and important people.

Progress in eliminating sex stereotyping in prime-time TV is taking place, but it is very slow. Recent shows and television movies have portrayed men as involved, caring parents, and exhibiting a full range of emotions. Women are increasingly shown as workers outside the home, their lives no longer exclusively focused on marriage, or linked to kitchens, nurseries, and laundries. Sometimes they are even strong, determined, and smart. But most of the shows still characterize women primarily as dependent, inferior, and subordinate to men and portray men as aggressive, stoic perpetrators of violent and selfish acts. Women are shown as responsible for home, husband, and children, and the responsibility for financial support belongs to men. Women are rarely shown as having power or prestige equal to a man. In the home, the household chores men do are mostly the ones women aren't supposed to be capable of handling.

The Influence of Children's Books

The books we read to young children are yet another important influence in the socialization process. Around 1970 they began to be examined for sexism, and the discoveries remain important since the old books are still very much in use. Books written by Dr. Seuss, for example, are full of the kind of boy who is active, clever, willing to take risks, leads an interesting life, and is able to cope effectively with any problem. Such girls are almost nonexistent in his work. The popular Richard Scarry books are filled with an enormous variety of male workers and just a few women who are invariably shown doing "women's work".

Even in many modern preschool books, very few girls do anything interesting or exciting; they play it safe and stay close to home. Girls rely on boys to help them with their problems. The few women in the stories are teachers, nurses, or mommies, while boys learn that the whole world of work is open to them.

Traditional fairy tales also reinforce the stereotyped view of males and females. The young man is adventurous, brave, and achieving, whereas the young woman is considered the "prize" whose main attributes are beauty, patience, and a trusting nature. Her role is to wait for help or rescue by a handsome young man. The mature woman is often a mean stepmother, a witch, or a wicked queen, while the mature man is held in affection and respect. While fairy tales tell girls to wait for love and the blissful dependence (and permanence) of marriage, they tell boys to accomplish their goals by striving and competing, being clever and smart.

Fortunately, other kinds of books are available today. Every public library has listings of excellent nonsexist children's books that show girls as well as boys who lead interesting lives, boys as well as girls who have real feelings. But many new stereotyped books continue to be published, purchased, and used with children every year.

The Influence of Toys

Parents, relatives, and friends often choose toys for girls and boys based on what they feel children's interests should be rather than what they are. The idea of buying an "opposite sex" toy for a child, a toy truck for a girl, a doll for a boy, makes most adults uncomfortable. For this reason, toy sellers tend to ask about a child's gender before making recommendations.

Children's own choices are hardly unaffected. We have already mentioned the television toy commercial study. Packaging is another clue children pick up quickly. With few exceptions, blocks, cars, trains, manipulative games, chemistry sets, doctor's kits, work tools, building games, and of course balls of all kinds show boys on the package. Dolls, kitchen or cleaning toys, needlework or sewing equipment, and nurse's kits show girls on the package.

The comments "Girls aren't supposed to play with trucks" and "Boys don't play with toy stoves" results from a long history of children playing with gender-restricted toys.

Other Influences

As children grow older, they may notice that their religions value males and females differently. Men are the ministers, priests, and rabbis who tell people what is right and wrong. Women play a secondary role in religious literature as well. Bible stories are primarily concerned with males and present endless examples of stereotyped thinking about women and men. The stories foster the idea that gender roles are part of an eternal plan rather than a condition imposed on men and women by the time and society in which they live.

Boys and girls learn nursery rhymes and children's songs and enjoy singing the little tunes over and over again. While doing so, they absorb information about sex roles and gender related attributes. They sing about what little girls and little boys are made of, about Polly putting the kettle on and daddy who has to go a-hunting. Johnnie travels to a fair, but Susannah has to wait while a young man goes to Louisiana.

Rock music and other popular songs that children hear tend to reinforce stereotyped ideas about males and females. Women are expected to be able to tolerate any form of male behavior and remain patient and understanding. Songs suggest that happiness for women depends on their ability to handle men and accept the helpmate role. Men in songs, on the other hand, are more active and are interested in other things besides their emotional relations with the opposite sex.

Not to be neglected is the cumulative effect of the images flowing from other media. Movies, comics, and advertisements in magazines and on radio and billboards all enter children's lives regularly. The socialization process continues in all of them, and the sex stereotyped message is drilled again and again into the heads of young children.

Complicating the effects of differential early socialization is the role of the self-fulfilling prophecy: when we expect to see a certain behavior we tend to act in ways that encourage its occurence, and we are then confirmed in our expectation. The classic experiment was reported in 1968, when researchers told teachers that several of their students had been identified as academically gifted (Jacobson and Rosenthal, 1968). In reality, the targeted students had been randomly chosen. Nevertheless, subsequent testing revealed that these students did indeed score higher in academic tests than others. Apparently the teachers' expectation alone created the outcome. This study suggests that our expectations of sex role differences among children may in fact cause differences in behavior and attitudes.

Dealing With Sex Role Stereotyping In School

Given all these influences, it is not surprising that by the time a child enters school, teachers observe many differences in boys' and girls' behavior. Children have already spent several years in learning their "proper" roles.

Teachers see young boys as more active and aggressive and girls as quieter, more passive, and dependent. They often feel that boys are more difficult to control, whereas girls are more eager to please. They believe that girls' and boys' interests and skills are "obviously" different: boys work hard at developing their ball-throwing arm, and girls enjoy art, creative tasks, and jumping rope. Girls read better in the early grades, have a better command of language, and are better socialized to accept the role of student.

It is easy to understand how these sex differences are thought to be natural, perhaps even "innate": their origins are so common and everyday as to be invisible. People who study sex differences now suggest, however, that we cannot be sure that boys and girls are just "born that way." The treatment and messages that children receive in all those years before they enter school have influenced them, and much more research is needed to distinguish the truly innate differences from those that socialization has created.

The powerful early forces that create different sex roles for boys and girls might make it seem that it is too late to try to equalize opportunities for them once they enter school. But people grow and change throughout their lives, and schools are in a position to exert a strong positive influence. Attitudes about sex roles can be introduced, modified, or changed at any educational level, but the earlier the process is begun the less time children have to become rigid in their sex stereotyped beliefs. Elementary school teachers and parents are of vital importance in expanding children's sex stereotyped notions of appropriate behavior and goals. The result will be children who grow up to lead fuller and more satisfying lives.

How can we do this?

1. Help Children Become More Aware of Sex Role Stereotyping and of the Variety of Forces That Influence Attitudes, Thinking and Behavior.

Children generally have beliefs without questioning how they arrived at them. Before young people can change their attitudes about sex role stereotyping, they need to think about the foundations of their beliefs. Adults can help them recognize when they are responding in stereotyped or biased ways.

Teachers' and parents' own commitment to the elimination of sexism and sex stereotyping can be shown in the incidental events that take place in daily life. Many important lessons can be learned by using unexpected remarks or chance occurrences, such as the following comments from children: "Girls can't do that." "I don't want to sit with the boys." "Oooh, he's on the girls' line." "What a sissy." These can be handled on the spot by answering, "Of course, girls can do that. All people can." "We all cry. It makes us feel better." At other times, using the remark as the basis of a discussion is more effective.

Children's views are strongly affected by their teachers' and parents' opinions. A teacher's strong positive feeling toward sex fairness can permeate life in a classroom, and contributes to children's awareness of the existence and injustice of sexism. Your spontaneous reactions to classroom occurrences carry weight: "No, you can't have two strong boys to carry those boxes. How would you like two strong people?" "Of course, the boys can play in that game. It's only fair." "In this class, boys and girls sit together."

Teachers and other adults can focus children's attention on how their opinions about many issues are influenced by TV, movies, books, and people they know. Children can participate in "original" research that explores the sexism in textbooks, TV, and other areas. As these are analyzed and discussed, children become aware of stereotyping and how it affects people. Children can also interview parents or other community members to see how they feel about particular issues involving sexism, followed by discussions to help clarify their own points of view.

Once children are aware of sexism and how it affects them, analyzing their own feelings is next. Discussions that grow out of their explorations and interviews can be instrumental in "thinking out" their feelings. No real change in attitude can occur unless basic feelings are touched. Avoidance, laughter, teasing, defensiveness, and anger are all mechanisms for resisting change: "I hate boys—they're so mean." "Why should we let them play? They only spoil our game." "Ugh, I'm not going to sew that. That's girls' stuff."

These are common expressions of strong feelings, and challenging them requires a great deal of patience on the adult's part. Adults should not be discouraged if the change appears slowly, since modification of beliefs often takes a long time. Moreover, some children will continue to maintain sexist views, and some will be touched only superficially and revert to sexism later. Other children, however, do get the point, and one can never be sure which discussion, experience, project, or assignment is the one that makes a significant difference in attitudes years later.

One indication that a new attitude has formed is the desire to do something about it. Fortunately, the classroom provides many opportunities for children to put their new convictions into action. Developing a skill previously reserved to the opposite sex, forming a "people line" for the first time, and writing protests to publishers of sexist books are just a few of the avenues available. When children reach the action stage, they themselves will often suggest other things to do.

2. Change School Practices that Contribute to the Separation and Stereotyping of Children by Gender.

Rules, casual remarks, adult assumptions, what children get rewarded or reprimanded for, and all the other day-to-day experiences in school constitute a hidden curriculum with great power. It influences children throughout the day on the playground and in the cafeteria, auditorium, and hallways. Although barely noticed, it is one of the most effective ways schools transmit society's expectations to young girls and boys.

Separating children by sex is one of the most common hallmarks of the hidden curriculum that reinforces sexism. By its nature, the technique emphasizes the differences between girls and boys. Because we are so used to it, it may not at first glance seem harmful. Nevertheless, we must ask ourselves whether we would use race as the basis to organize children ("White children in this line, black children in that one") or disability ("Handicapped children have 5th period lunch; able-bodied children have 6th period lunch"). We wince at those formulations because we have learned, in the language of the Supreme Court outlawing school segregation, that "separate is inherently unequal." Segregation by sex is no less harmful to children.

As teachers and other adults become sensitized to the issue of sex equity in education, they begin to recognize many practices that need changing. Here are a few practices that bear examining:

- Children are often separated, arranged, or given directions by sex.

Examples	*Suggested Alternatives*
"Boys, be quiet."	"Children, be quiet."
"You'll have to go sit with the girls if you don't behave."	"Sitting by yourself may give you time to calm down."
"The girls can go first."	"The children at this table can go first."

- Classroom or school jobs are assigned on the basis of sex.

Examples	*Suggested Alternatives*
Housekeeping chores and secretarial work assigned solely to girls; only boys assigned to carrying equipment, operating classroom machines, or membership in an AV squad.	Set up a job chart that rotates all jobs, both in the classroom and for the entire school. Arrange for instruction in the use of AV equipment for all children.

- In conversation or in disciplinary comments, adults perpetuate stereotyping.

"How pretty you look today, Sara."   Look for opportunities to compli-

	ment a boy's appearance or clothing if this is what you do with girls.
"You're such a strong boy."	Comment on girls' physical ability too.
"Boys shouldn't be so rough with girls," or "Girls shouldn't behave like that."	Eliminate statements that characterize behavior as belonging to one gender or the other.

- Teachers allow unnecessarily sex-stereotyped results when children choose facilities, materials, and other children to work and play with.

Only boys choose blocks.	"John, Mary, and Jim can work with the blocks today. Robert, Sally, and Peter are in the house corner. Tomorrow we'll switch."
Only girls choose cooking.	"This half of the room will make the applesauce today, and tomorrow that half will make the cookies."
Woodworking is for boys.	"Mary, you made such a nice design. Would you help the group at the workbench to make . . . ?"
Children play in same-sex groups on the playground.	"On Monday every playground group must have at least one person with hazel eyes, on Tuesday at least one person with black hair, on Wednesday at least one person with a brightly colored shirt . . . "

- Adults have different expectations for girls and boys, both in achievement and in behavior.

Girls are quieter, get better grades, and are neater. Boys are better at math, can't sit still long, and don't cry.	Develop gender-blind standards.

- Sexist (condescending, improperly intimate) terms are used.

Darling, dish, doll, cutie, honey, sweetie, wimp, sissy, mama's boy, etc.	Stop!
Referring to an adult woman as a girl (or its diminutive, "gal").	If she's old enough to work or have children of her own, refer to her as a woman.

- Adults create needless competition between the sexes.

Examples	*Suggested Alternatives*
The boys against the girls in athletics and in classroom activities such as card drills and spelling bees.	Divide children by alphabet or color of clothing or favorite song or number of letters in first name or means other than by gender.
"Who will finish their work first, the boys or the girls?" or "The girls did their homework so neatly!"	Eliminate sex based statements of comparison, in fact, any group comparisons are questionable.

- Adults assume that children participate in sex stereotyped activities at home.

"Why don't the girls bake cookies for our party?"	"Who would like to make cookies for our party?" or "Robert, would you and Jane make the cookies for our party?"
"Did you boys watch the Yankee game last night?"	"Who watched the Yankee game last night?"

- School personnel assume that mothers and fathers live sex stereotyped lives.

Activities are scheduled during the day, making it difficult for working parents to attend.	Arrange for more activities to take place in the evening.
"I'm sure your mother will want to see our show."	"I'm sure your parents will want to see our show."
"Would you ask your mother to bake a cake (or make a costume) for our party?"	"Would you ask one of your parents to bake a cake (or make a costume) for our party?"
"We need a class mother to go on the trip with us."	"We need a class parent to go on the trip with us."

3. Help Children See that Sex Role Definitions Change with Time and Vary in Different Cultures.

Children tend to think that the world they see around them is the only way it can be. Adults can do a great deal to expand that limited view. Sex roles have changed over time, and they also vary by culture.

For instance, farming in the United States is thought of as men's work; in

China it's largely women's work. Elementary school teachers, secretaries, and bookkeepers in American used to be men, but now these jobs are usually performed by women. Pottery making used to be a man's craft but is now more frequently done by women, at least in the United States; in India it is still almost exclusively a male skill. Street cleaning in U.S. cities is done by "sanitation men," but in the Soviet Union it is performed primarily by women. Comparisons such as these expand children's sense of how societies determine sex roles differently. How each culture views hair length or who wears skirts (Scotsmen) or pants (Chinese women) or who walks behind or ahead are other illustrations of how sex roles vary from country to country and from time to time.

Children should also be taught about the changing patterns in men's lives. Participation in the nurturing, emotional, and esthetic aspects of life is as important to boys as to girls. These may be difficult, even threatening concepts for boys brought up in a macho culture, who see themselves as part of the privileged group in our society. Modifying current gender roles may strike them as undesirable. Too young to realize the incalculable benefits of being a real father to one's children or relating to women (especially wives) as equals rather than as superior to inferior, many boys think that being allowed to cry is scant reward for having to do the dishes at home or sharing a playing field at school.

Children seem to acknowledge the importance of being fair. Teachers and parents can build on this attitude to help them accept that stereotyping, bias, and discrimination are unfair and hurt people. The pledge of allegiance, for instance ("with liberty and justice for all"), can be used as an example of people wanting to be fair to others. Its application not only to females and males, but to blacks and whites, young and old, disabled and able-bodied, and poor and rich can be discussed. Because of the cultural diversity that exists in our country, children will have many viewpoints about sex roles. Race, religion, country of origin, and educational and social levels of parents all influence their attitudes. Sensitivity, tact, and care in the choice of discussions, activities, and goals are therefore important.

Educators who are helping children cope with men's and women's changed vocational and domestic roles find that in this time of transition, not all members of the community, nor all teachers, agree that the school should become involved in anything but instruction in "basic" subject matter. Despite possible opposition to promoting sex equity, boys and girls do need help in preparing for the real changes that are already taking place in our society.

4. Help Children Understand that There Is a Difference Between Sex Roles, Gender Identity, and Sexual Preference.

Some people fear that modifying the roles previously assigned strictly to one gender or the other will affect people's gender identity as well as their sexual behavior. However, for a woman to be assertive or a man to be nurturing has nothing to do with a person's "maleness" or "femaleness." Characteristics, skills, and feelings do not belong uniquely to one gender, nor do they affect an individual's heterosexuality or homosexuality. Sex roles are culturally assigned behavior that vary according to time and place, and indeed overlap in the capabilities and traits of men and women. Today, without fear of losing their gender identity or their interest in the other sex, many people have begun to explore new roles and assume new tasks.

Teachers and others who work with children can transmit the concept of expanding sex roles and allay any fears children (or their parents) may have. Photographs of men engaged in activities such as knitting, housework, or caring for a baby, or photos of women active in sports or working in nontraditional jobs (such as carpentry, construction work) can convey that message. Parents and other visitors to the classroom can talk about the many new opportunities open to them. Whatever strategy is used, the task is to increase awareness and acceptance of the idea that individual attributes, not gender, determine what boys and girls can do and enjoy.

5. Encourage Children to Work and Play Together and Experience a Variety of Roles Within a Group.

A classroom can provide children with opportunities to learn many social skills. Casual situations create opportunities for children to interact in many different ways with their classmates. They learn how to work together cooperatively, be a leader as well as a follower, handle their anger, give and take criticism, and contribute to group decisions. Classroom interactions also teach children about the importance and responsibilities of friendship, what it means to be part of a group, and the need to respect the rights and opinions of others.

Not all social skills can be learned through casual interaction, nor can all children be expected to practice certain behaviors without some teacher intervention. Children's experiences before they arrive in the classroom have influenced their ability to handle different social skills. Some will almost automatically become leaders; others will be fearful of such a role. Some will enjoy sharing in classroom discussions, whereas others either avoid involvement or demand the group's attention all the time.

Gender often determines whether a child will reach out for certain roles or cast them aside. Teachers can make a special effort to provide more encouragement, more opportunities, and more support for desirable skills or characteristics that boys and girls seem to be rejecting merely because of their gender. Girls may need help with experiencing leadership, particularly in situations where math, science, sports, and mechanics are involved. They can also benefit from activities that involve competitive teamwork. Boys, on the other hand, may need support as they try to express feelings and engage in cooperative teamwork.

Children start at a very early age to avoid work and play situations that involve members of the other sex ("Ugh—'girl' or 'boy' germs!"). It is essential that males and females interact, help each other, and practice and enjoy doing things together. Unless children already accept integrated groups as the norm, student choice should not be used as the only way of choosing groups. Although it is not possible (or advisable) to insist that every activity be organized as a mixed group, teachers will initially have to assign children to many activities to encourage such groupings.

Children may complain in the beginning about playing and working together. This usually does not continue, though, if the teacher is firm and sure that sex equality in the classroom must take place. Timidity, hesitation, or apologetic explanations reveal a teacher's doubt about such organizational patterns, so firmly stated assignments are in order. If necessary, a statement that "In this class we're all equal and we are not going to separate people," or "We are going to learn to work together because we will be doing that for the rest of our lives" can be used to convince children to accept the idea of playing and working with all the children in the class. If we can change the way boys and girls interact from kindergarten on, we may be able to reduce the sense of separateness and the need for the "battle of the sexes" in adolescence and beyond.

REFERENCES

Balaban, T., Cooper, J., & Ruble, D. Gender constancy and the effects of sex-typed televised toy commercials. *Child Development,* 1981, *52,* 667–73.

Brooks-Gunn, J., & Matthews, W.S. *He and she: How children develop their sex-role identity.* Englewood Cliffs, New Jersey: Prentice-Hall, 1979.

Dronsberg, S., Fagot, B., Hagan, R., & Leinbach, M.D. Differential reactions to assertive and communicative acts of toddler boys and girls. *Child Development,* 1985, *56,* 1499–1505.

Fagot, B. The influence of sex of child on parental reactions to toddler children. *Child Development,* 1978, *49,* 459–65.

Jacobson, L., & Rosenthal, R. *Pygmalion in the classroom.* New York: Rinehart and Winston, 1968.

Luria, Z., Provenzano, F., & Rubin, J. The eye of the beholder: Parents' views on sex of newborns. *Americal Journal of Orthopsychiatry,* 1974, *44* (4), 512–519.

U.S. Department of Labor. *Facts on women workers.* Washington, D.C., 1985.

The following statements are designed for the exploration of personal reactions to the chapter, as well as for the review of the contents of the chapter. Emphasis in discussions should be on exploring issues in depth, rather than on determining the correct or appropriate responses.

FOR DISCUSSION:

1. Are traditional expectations of boys and girls harmful or helpful for their personal development?
2. Describe a recent example of unintentional bias when an adult interacted with a young child. Describe an alternative interaction that is not stereotypical.
3. How does classroom grouping by sex affect students interacting with the other sex when they are adults?
4. Discuss the statement, "I group by sex because the students prefer to be with children of their own sex."
5. Evaluate television shows that attempt to provide role models free of sex role stereotypes.
6. Discuss the author's statement: "Before young people can change their attitudes about sex role stereotyping, they need to think about the foundations of their beliefs."
7. How would you respond if you heard a student make disdainful comments about the other sex?
8. The author states: "Help Children Understand That There Is a Difference Between Sex Roles, Gender Identity, and Sexual Preference." Review the author's discussion and determine how you would share definitions of the above with students.

SUGGESTIONS FOR FURTHER READING

Best, R. *We've all got scars: What boys and girls learn in elementary school.* Bloomington, Indiana: Indiana University Press, 1983.

Bracken, J., & Wigutoff, S. *Books for today's children: An annotated bibliography of non-stereotyped picture books.* New York: The Feminist Press, 1970.

Center for Vocational Education. *Sugar and spice: A parent handbook on the career implications of sex stereotyping.* Columbus, Ohio, 1977.

Fiarotta, N., & Fiarotta, P. *Be what you want to be!* New York: Workman Publishing Company, 1977.

Jenkins, J., & MacDonald, P. *Growing up equal—activities and resources for parents and teachers of young children.* Englewood Cliffs, New Jersey: Prentice-Hall, 1979.

Michigan Department of Education. *Home activities packet.* Lansing, Michigan, 1983.

Pogrebin, L.C. *Growing up free—raising your child in the 80's.* New York: McGraw-Hill Book Company, 1980.

Rivers, C., Barnett, R., & Baruch, G. *Beyond sugar and spice: How women grow, learn and thrive.* New York: G. Putnam's Sons, 1979.

Shapiro, J., Kramer, S., & Hunerberg, C. *Equal their chances—children's activities for non-sexist learning.* Englewood Cliffs, New Jersey: Prentice-Hall, 1981.

Sprung, B. (Ed.). *Perspectives on non-sexist early childhood education.* New York: Teachers College Press, 1978.

Chapter 2

COST OF SEX BIAS IN SCHOOLS:
THE REPORT CARD*

MID-ATLANTIC CENTER FOR SEX EQUITY

GIRLS   *BOYS*

ACADEMIC

- Girls start out ahead of boys in speaking, reading, and counting. In the early grades, their academic performance is equal to boys in math and science. However, as they progress through school, their achievement test scores show significant decline. The scores of boys, on the other hand, continue to rise and eventually reach and surpass those of their female counterparts, particularly in the areas of math and science.

- In spite of performance decline on standardized achievement tests, girls frequently receive better grades in school. This may be one of the rewards they get for being more quiet and docile in the classroom. However, this may be at the cost of independence and self-reliance.

- Girls are more likely to be invisible members of the classrooms. They

- Boys are more likely to be scolded and reprimanded in classrooms, even when the observed conduct and behavior of boys and girls do not differ. Also, boys are more likely to be referred to school authorities for disciplinary action than are girls.

- Boys are far more likely to be identified as exhibiting learning disabilities, reading problems, and mental retardation.

- Not only are boys identified as having learning and reading disabilities, they also receive lower grades, are more likely to be grade repeaters, and are less likely to complete high school.

---

*Reprinted with permission from Mid-Atlantic Center for Sex Equity Publications Washington, D.C.

receive fewer academic contacts, less praise, fewer complex and abstract questions, and less instruction on how to do things for themselves.

• Girls who are gifted in mathematics are far less likely to be identified than are gifted boys. Those girls who are identified as gifted, are far less likely to participate in special or accelerated math classes to develop this special talent.

• Girls who suffer from learning disabilities are also less likely to be identified or to participate in special education programs than are learning-disabled boys.

PSYCHOLOGICAL AND PHYSICAL

• Although women achieve better grades than men, they are less likely to believe that they can do college work. In fact, of the brightest high school graduates who do not go on to college, 70 to 90 percent are women.

• Learned helplessness exists when failure is perceived as insurmountable. Girls are more likely than boys to exhibit this pattern. They attribute failure to internal factors, such as ability, rather than to external factors, such as luck or effort. Girls who exhibit learned helplessness avoid failure situations—they stop trying. Research indicates that teacher interaction patterns may contribute to the learned helplessness exhibited by female students.

• By high school, young women demonstrate a decline in career commitment. This decline is related to their feeling that boys disapprove of a woman using her intelligence.

• Society socializes boys into an active, independent, and aggressive role. But such behavior is incongruent with school norms and rituals that stress quiet behavior and docility. This results in a pattern of role conflict for boys, particularly during the elementary years.

• Hyperactivity is estimated to be nine times more prevalent in boys than in girls. Boys are more likely to be identified as having emotional problems, and statistics indicate a higher male suicide rate.

• Boys are taught stereotyped behaviors earlier and more harshly than girls; there is a 20 percent greater probability that such stereotyped behavior will stay with them for life.

• Conforming to the male sex role stereotype takes a psychological toll. Boys who score high on sex-appropriate behavior tests also score highest on anxiety tests.

- Tests reveal that the majority of female and male college students report that the characteristics traditionally associated with masculinity are more valuable and more socially desirable than those characteristics associated with femininity.

- In athletics, females also suffer from sex bias. For example, women's athletic budgets in the nation's colleges are equal to approximately 18 percent of the men's budgets.

- Males are less likely than females to be close friends with one another. When asked, most males identify females as their closest friends.

- The strain and anxiety associated with conforming to the male sex stereotype also affects boys physically. Males are more likely to succumb to serious disease and to be victims of accidents or violence. The average life expectancy of men is eight years shorter than of women.

CAREER AND FAMILY RELATIONSHIPS

- When elementary school girls are asked to describe what they want to do when they grow up, they are able to identify only a limited number of career options, and even these fit stereotypic patterns. The majority identify only two careers, teaching and nursing. Boys, on the other hand, are able to identify many more potential occupations.

- The majority of girls enter college without completing four years of high school mathematics. This lack of preparation in math serves as a "critical filter," inhibiting or preventing girls from any science, math, and technologically related careers.

- The preparation and counseling girls receive in school contribute to the economic penalties that they encounter in the workplace. Although over 90 percent of the girls in our classrooms will work in the paid labor force for all or part of their lives, the following statistics reveal the cost of the bias that they encounter.

- Teachers and counselors advise boys to enter sex stereotyped careers and limit their potential in occupations like kindergarten teacher, nurse, or secretary.

- Many boys build career expectations that are higher than their abilities. This results in later compromise, disappointment, and frustration.

- Both at school and at home, boys are taught to hide or suppress their emotions; as men they may find it difficult or impossible to show feelings towards their family and friends.

- Boys are actively discouraged from playing with dolls (except those that play sports or wage war). Few schools provide programs that encourage boys to learn about the skills of parenting. Many men, through absence and apathy, become not so much parents as "transparents." In fact, the typical father spends only 12 minutes a day interacting with his children.

- More than a third of families headed by women live below the poverty level.

- A woman with a college degree will typically earn less than a male who is a high school dropout.

- Women must work nine days to earn what men get paid for five days of work.

- In contrast to the popular belief that things are getting better for female workers, since 1954 the gap between the wages earned by men and women has not gotten smaller.

- A majority of women work not for "extra" cash, but because of economic necessity. Nearly two-thirds of all women in the labor force are single, widowed, divorced, or separated, or are married to spouses earning less than $10,000 a year.

- Men and women differ in their beliefs of the important aspects of a father's role. Men emphasize the need for the father to earn a good income and to provide solutions to family problems. Women, on the other hand, stress the need for fathers to assist in caring for children and responding to the emotional needs of the family. These differing perceptions of fatherhood lead to family strain and anxiety.

Chapter 3

EARLY CHILDHOOD SEX ROLE SOCIALIZATION

BARBARA RING

INTRODUCTION

"That's for girls!" "Boys don't do that!"

As babies become more cognizant of their environment they begin to try to place themselves somewhere in that environment. They test their physical limits. They explore activities that seem to get a reaction from the people around them. They observe and imitate their parents, siblings, and peers.

Often as soon as babies become running, chattering toddlers, they have determined both their *gender identity* and *gender role.* They can classify themselves and others as boy and girl. A crucial developmental phase encourages them to identify closely with the characteristics of their gender.

At the same time they begin to classify behaviors that are gender appropriate. Although this classification may not be related to sexual identity, the classification is conducted anyway. Outside reinforcement, whether it be intentional or not, reaffirms the classification.

Very early in their development, children will tell you what boys can do and what girls can do. Their decisions are not based on the anatomy of boys and girls, but on daily observations. Because the classification of the environment is an important activity to children (dangerous, safe; taller, shorter; for grownups, for children, etc.), it is only natural that they categorize BOYS and GIRLS. Unfortunately, they are, therefore, categorizing their own capabilities. Despite observations that may refute the rigid classification system they have developed, they begin to identify certain activities with a specific gender.

A three-year-old child can be looking directly at a man who is a nurse, and make the statement, "Only girls are nurses." Visible evidence cannot necessarily overcome their need to devise separate columns with no room for cross-over.

Recognizing that gender identity is obviously crucial to mental health, it becomes difficult for adults when children move from gender identity to sex *role* identity. Suddenly "I am a girl" becomes "I am a girl so I can do...." The classification system becomes a method of limiting options and experiences.

The home and classroom environments can relay the message that each gender is valued and that each gender has a long list of options in life. Without contradicting the need for children to classify, information can be continuously provided that encourages children to explore all possibilities.

Barbara Ring describes early influences on children, and gives suggestions for expanding experiences for very young children.

EARLY CHILDHOOD SEX ROLE SOCIALIZATION

At the moment of a baby's birth, parents' earliest welcomes to their newborn usually include a rush of expectations and feelings such as enthusiasm, love, and early bonding. Preference for one sex or another will usually be forgotten with the arrival of a healthy baby. At the same time, parents' identification with their own gender roles imposes itself on this new being; and each parent consciously and unconsciously interacts with his or her baby in ways that reinforce male/female stereotypes that are defined by the social environment. Thus begins the process of sex role learning or sex role socialization in Western society whereby boy/girl genital differences are translated into boy/girl behavioral and aspirational differences.

Early Influences

Parents begin this process of sex role learning soon after the sex of the baby is known. Research indicates that male babies are handled more by fathers than are female babies. Boys are held and played with more roughly, with more physical jostling and playfulness than female babies — by both parents. Girls, conversely, are handled more gently, delicately and are perceived as more vulnerable by both parents (Frieze, et al., 1978). Female babies are talked to more by mothers than male babies, but both parents spend more time interacting with boy babies (Wesley and Wesley, 1977). This, in spite of the fact that there are no sex differences in sturdiness, strength, or response in early infancy.

Infants begin to perceive themselves as separate beings from the primary caretaker at about 7 or 8 months of age. In this process of self-identification they begin to see themselves as a makeup of color, size, family structure, as well as gender. The critical period for *gender identity*, (i.e., "I am a girl," "I am a boy") is thought to be between 18 months and 3 years of age (Pogrebin, 1980). During this same period of time as children learn to identify themselves as boys or girls, they also identify with the stereotypes of the culture and they make decisions about their own place in their social world of experience. Thus, sex role socialization accompanies sexual identity. The latter is a given; the former is a social construct.

31

Letty Cottin Pogrebin's description of the development of gender *role* identity is one of the clearest:

> Because children have to decode two sex roles, the one to play and the one to avoid, each sex must be familiar with the approved "norms" for the other sex ... by 2½ or 3 both girls and boys know which toys "belong to each sex" and which tools, appliances, clothing, and activities go with mommies and daddies ... They each seek clues and labels and embellishments to help clarify their discovery (I am a girl: I am a boy) and establish that there are others in the world like them. (p. 33)

From the expectations and guidance communicated by parents early on, children can see in time that one set of characteristics is desirable for females and another set is preferred in males. Their peers are receiving similar messages. These messages are reinforced by toys, books, advertising, television, and extended family and friends. In short, sex role expectations pervade the social environment of babies and children from birth.

At the same time that they are learning their expected place, they are also learning the relative value of that place. Both boys and girls in our society learn that boys are valued differently than girls, that this has consequences for both of them. For example, the behavioral characteristics encouraged in boys (assertiveness, roughhouse, aggression, noise) demand more attention than those encouraged in girls (passivity, demureness, dependence, quiet). The activities provided boys in our culture, particularly athletics and team play, provide public opportunities to test and develop skills—so their role is, quite early, more visible than the role of females. So are male role models: coaches, religious leaders, professionals in authority such as physicians, school principals, newscasters, game show hosts, professional athletes, statesmen, war heroes, etc. These role models are deemed valuable by this society. All are more highly salaried, have more status, authority, and respect than female role models such as child care professionals, flight attendants, nurses, secretaries, teachers, and so forth.

Stereotypical masculine behavioral characteristics such as independence, assertiveness, self-confidence, responsibility, analytical judgment, achievement, risk taking, and fearlessness are almost synonymous with those associated with adult mental health and maturity. Stereotypically feminine characteristics such as dependence, nurturing, passivity, timidity, and emotional expression are not. Gilligan (1982) asserts that this male standard for human development ignores the value of caring and of sensitivity to the needs of others; traits associated with feminine adulthood:

The stereotypes suggest a splitting of love and work that relegates expressive capacities to women while placing instrumental abilities in the masculine domain. Yet looked at from a different perspective, these stereotypes reflect a conception of adulthood that is itself out of balance, favoring the separateness of the individual self over connection to others, and leaning more toward an autonomous life of work than toward the interdependence of love and care. (p. 17)

Infants and very young children, of course, are not aware of these social stereotypes. Early awareness of a worth differential may be simply related to adult sex differences in size, voice quality, and availability. We can observe, for example, a young toddler gathering all the blocks to herself and making a tower higher: taller is more, more is better, taller is better. Or curiosity about an absent parent (e.g., the parent who is at work all day) may imbue that parent with higher value for an infant. We can observe babies dissolve into devoted delight when an absent parent returns to their company. As a child grows, these early sensory impressions may become connected with male/female worth and are not contradicted by the social environment. Indeed, they are reinforced and embellished as the child continues her/his cognitive development.

Classification by Gender

As infants become toddlers, they pursue the task of categorization. It enables children to cope with the experiences encountered as they engage in exploratory behavior and to construct and test reality through verbal expression and practice. As they decide where events, conditions, and people fit in this cognitive framework of classification, they naturally translate what girls do, and what boys do, what Mothers and Daddies do, into gender role definition (Pitcher and Schultz, 1983). It is easier for children to work out a rigid system than to deal with a lot of variation. Generally, the child's social contacts will gently correct other mistaken notions of reality such as "all furry, four legged creatures are dogs." But stereotyped notions of maleness and femaleness, are frequently accepted or ignored. So while children eventually grow out of limited notions of "furriness" and animal identity, they are often not given the kind of corrective input that will enable them to grow out of stereotyped notions of gender and behavior, and, perhaps more importantly, gender and worth. Joseph Pleck suggests that this early childhood stage is an excellent opportunity for a gentle expansion of role appropriateness (1975). If our expectations as parents, teachers and other caregivers are that children will outgrow rigid gender role prescriptions, then that is what is likely to happen at a very early age. This would enable parents and other caring adults to respond to children as individuals, encouraging behaviors and traits that are valuable regardless of the sex of the child. Children of both sexes could be encouraged in art, roughhouse, interdependence, listening, helpfulness, skill development, sensitivity, fair play, leadership, quietude, and invited to experiment with all kinds of valuable activities.

This kind of expansion of the accepted behavioral repertoire of boys and girls should result in freeing up their energies which are currently directed toward learning and maintaining prescriptions for behavior that may go against their particular grain. For example, the prescription for male children includes a strong prohibition against being anything like the stereotyped female. Boys who prefer quiet activities and resist rough and tumble play may receive negative responses from parents or peers. Adolescent boys whose appearance and interests deviate from the notions pervading teen and young adult culture must struggle with similar pressures. We teach boys to tough it out when they encounter physical and emotional pain. We do not tell them, though, that the long-term consequences of this habit may include a real loss of emotional experiencing. The internal conflict for boys created by this pressure provides fertile ground for behavior problems, learning difficulties and other problems associated with many developmental tasks of childhood, adolescence, and adulthood.

The prescription for feminine behavior is associated with the development of learned helplessness (Dowling, 1981). Girls grow up expecting and receiving help and are not encouraged as boys are to explore, to risk, to make mistakes and self-correct. This would seem to be the opposite of "learned mastery" which is characteristic of boys' expectations of themselves. In turn, the characteristics of "learned helplessness," coupled with internal conflict about being helpless, could result in low achievement, limited goals, and low self-esteem.

The prescribed limitations, imposed by the social structure on girls and boys at an early age, can stifle their personal development and well-being.

It is interesting to look at these differing prescriptions in light of Burton White's research presented in his book *The First Three Years of Life* (1975). He describes the early childhood period from ten months to three years of age as a critical period for the development of a sense of competence as a learner and doer; a child's realization that he or she is a capable person, able to perform many tasks, to enjoy the approval of significant "others," to learn how to approach new tasks such as climbing up a slide, helping with chores, following directions, trying a new food, and so forth. Society's prescriptions of gender-appropriate behavior provide the conditions likely to result in "learned helplessness" for girls and "learned mastery" for boys (Dowling, 1981). If we viewed these outcomes as lines on a continuum, boys and girls are likely to cluster at opposite ends. Understanding this "competent-self continuum" gives us a basis for looking at this critical period as an opportunity for providing experiences and expectations that are likely to help children of both sexes to see themselves as masterful: able to affect the physical and social environment within limits of responsible behavior, and to express emotions as they are felt (i.e., emotionally competent). Obviously, where a child fits on a "competent-self continuum" can color every aspect of a child's approach to the social, emotional, and physical environment and is likely to color the responses of that environment as well.

Care Giving

The goal of child rearing should be to help children to grow up with a persistent capacity for well-being. Well-being is, for this writer, that elusive core of identity that literally enables individuals to choose, to risk, to grow, to share, to produce, and to love. Access to this core is more likely if we expand each child's experiences during early childhood to foster a "competent me" role rather than a particular sex role. Activities for both boys and girls such as doll play, throwing, jungle gym climbing, truck "driving," car racing, hero modeling, clay pounding, nail banging, screw loosening, dancing, dish washing, weighing and measuring, cuddling, and risking may help.

Caregiving for this age group provides continuous opportunities to interrupt society's role prescriptions and provide models for alternative patterns of behavior. Daily, repetitive events such as feeding, diapering, bathing, folding laundry, excursions to the store, can be experienced regularly with both parents. Nurturing behavior then becomes associated by the child with both sexes. While fathers as a group are taking a much larger role in early childhood caregiving than has traditionally been the case, they are often unavailable during workdays. Business, industry, and other institutions which provide jobs to parents do not usually provide flexibility in work hours, part-time positions or on-site child care that would result in opportunities for parents to spend time with children during the day. There are also very few male professional child care workers. Hence, babies and young children usually identify nurturing and child care as female activities even when the mother is employed outside the home. Full involvement of fathers (and other males) in infant and child care would provide a vital balance in how boys and girls understand their own place in the social scheme of things.

Take, for example, the daily ritual of diapering a baby. Diapering is an intimate engagement of parent and child, because it involves the adult fully in the comfort and well-being of a dependent other. The repetition of this task changes both participants: the adult becoming a nurturer, the child bonding to this adult individual who relieves distress and brings satisfaction. The regular process of changing a diaper forces an adult/infant encounter and often results in close personal interactions. Participating regularly in this process forges a relationship; a bond which is a profound basis for participation of the adult in later developmental leaps of the child. For example, toilet training is accompanied by emancipation of both parent and child—but only the parents who have been primary in this avenue of care are intimate partners in this emancipation.

It may be difficult for the reader to imagine this aspect of infant care as a source of intimacy and satisfaction. We are accustomed to viewing diapering negatively and often do not pay attention to it as a source of growth for both participants. Feeding and comforting translate more easily into intimacy and satisfaction and are accepted more readily by fathers participating in child care. But this writer suggests that avoiding the drudgery of diapering is a missed opportunity for understanding and expressing love and intimacy for both father and child.

Caring for toddlers provides minute by minute opportunities for parents and other caregivers to support exploration, imaginative play, manipulation of the environment, involvement in home and family maintenance, and expression of emotion. The dance required between parent and child calls for spontaneity and flexibility in the adult, and adaptation and assertion in both. The nature of the child's daily life interacts with an inner pressure to establish an identity: a sense of "Who am I? What can I do? How do I do it? What do I feel? Why do I feel it? What do I will *to do?* and, What do I will *not to do?* What I like, etc." How the social environment responds to these decisions helps the child to temporarily solidify his or her identity. The child is anxious to establish these limits and so is naturally drawn to sex role prescriptions. The caregiver can interrupt this by providing materials, experiences, and verbal communication that expands the child's notions of what is acceptable for him or her to do. For example, children of both genders using trucks and building materials together can be coaxed to take this seriously together on equal terms. With a little encouragement females can involve themselves in traffic activity (including crashes and other excesses) and boys may then become accustomed to female participation in this activity, losing consciousness of gender appropriateness. This kind of encouragement and other invitations to appealing "other sex" activities may help children relax their own learned, inner barriers. Researchers agree that boys are especially susceptible to peer reinforcement of rigid sex role definitions (Best, 1987; Pitcher, 1983). Therefore, including peers in frequent nonstereotypical tasks in play groups, and in nursery school may help to interrupt self-imposed restrictions on behavior.

Theory and Practice

The origins of sex role acquisitions are described extensively by development theorists (Maccoby, 1966). Most agree that both cognitive mechanisms and social learning processes interact in sex role acquisition. Research indicates that children appear to imitate behaviors and develop preferences that are congruent with their sex role identity. In addition, parental responses and children's expectancies of parental responses also affect children's sex role acquisition (Frieze et al. 1978).

The inner propensity in each child to categorize and to stereotype is a powerful phenomenon. This process and the influences of socialization agents such as parents, peers, and television form the basis for a child's creation of sex role stereotypes (Frieze et al. 1978). Efforts to broaden each child's male and female schema would need to include changes in a " . . . so far taken for granted condition of our existence: that the auspices under which human infancy and early childhood are lived out are predominantly female auspices" (Dinnerstein, 1976, p. 8). Women as the primary caretakers of young children model the female role for boys and girls. All activities associated with nurturing and child care are therefore identified as female activities. This one-sidedness of nurturing by women increases the likelihood that females will see their primary identities as mothers; with other developmental challenges such as life partner and breadwinner taking a back set. Changing this pattern of socialization would expand each child's notions of who he or she is or might be. The writer believes that this expansion will diminish internal conflicts related to sex role acquisition and enhance each individual's persistent capacity for well-being.

Readers are invited to add their own ideas to those that follow for lessening the adherence to rigid sex roles during the early childhood stage of development. The writer suggests that we:

- Value fathercare equally with mothercare. Men who allow themselves the tenderness required in the nurture and care of infants and young children have so much to offer. Children can gain a model (for maleness) which includes struggling with new tasks, and responding with spontaneity, imagination, and warmth as a counterpoint to the cultural stereotype. In the process, men who risk emotional involvement with children are likely to become people who are more concerned with familial, international, and environmental issues connecting their children's well-being with family and world health.

- Help parents, teachers, and other caregivers to become aware of the stereotyping and bias displayed in toys, storybooks, advertising, entertainment, products and services; and help them see how these influences can limit emotional, intellectual, educational, and occupational possibilities for boys and girls.

- Recognize that the early childhood stage of rigid sex role conformity is a necessary and temporary developmental passage that contributes to each child's identity formation in a culture constrained by stereotyping and rigid sex roles. Without such constraints "boys can do" and "girls can do" pronouncements would change into "I can do" and "Let's do." In the meantime, if caregivers expect that children are capable of growing out of these perceptions just as they grow out of excessive rebelliousness associated with being two years old, then we can use this natural interest in role appropriateness and provide experimentation in the activities culturally associated with the other sex.

- Separate sex role behaviors, activities, and expectations from sexual identity. Gender is a fact; sex roles are invented (Pogrebin, 1980). If exposure to or reinforcement of a specific skill or self-definition is judged as "good" by the culture for one sex (i.e., boys need experience with team sports, and with winning and losing; girls need experiences that cultivate nurturing behaviors) then should it not also be considered "good" for the other sex?

- Welcome human capacities and contributions according to the talents and interests of each individual without regard to gender, color or other identifying characteristics traditionally used to limit access to full participation in the human endeavor.

Society's gender role prescriptions are promoted in our parenting and socialization theories and traditions. We socialize our children to behave and aspire according to a definition of their identity rooted in gender. We begin this engendering process at birth thereby masking any talents, proclivities, and potentialities inherent in the child that social custom allows only the other gender. This article looked at the components of the engendering process, the costs to individual boys, girls, men, women, and society, and the opportunities inherent in infancy and early childhood for expanding children's notions of who they might become and how they might best make their way in the world.

REFERENCES

Bell, D.H. *Being a man.* Lexington, Massachusetts: The Lewis Publishing Company, 1982.

Bergman, A., Mahler, M.S., & Pine, F. *The psychological birth of the infant.* New York: Basic Books, 1975.

Best, R. *We've all got scars: What boys and girls learn in elementary school.* Bloomington, Indiana: Indiana University Press, 1983.

Brownmiller, S. *Femininity.* New York: London Express, Simon & Schuster, 1984.

Carney, C.G., & McMahon, S.L. *Exploring contemporary male and female roles.* LaJolla, California: University Associates, 1977.

Chodorow, N. *The reproduction of mothering: psychoanalysis and the sociology of gender.* Berkley, California: University of California Press, 1974.

David, D.S., & Brannon, R. (Eds.). *The forty nine percent majority.* Reading, Massachusetts: Addison-Wesley Publishing Co., 1976.

Dinnerstein, D. *The mermaid and the minotaur.* New York: Harper Colophon Books, 1976.

Dowling, C. *The Cinderella complex.* New York: Pocket Books, 1981.

Frieze, I.H., Johnson, P.B., Parsons, J.E., Ruble, D.N., & Zellman, G.L. *Women and sex roles — a social psychological perspective.* New York: W.W. Norton, 1978.

Gilligan, C. *In a different voice.* Boston, Massachusetts: Harvard University Press, 1972.

Komarovsky, M. *Dilemmas of masculinity.* New York: Norton, 1976.

Maccoby, E. (Ed.). *The development of sex differences.* California: Stanford University Press, 1966.

Pitcher, E.G., & Shultz, L.H. *Boys and girls at play.* New York: Praeger Special Studies, Bergin and Garvey Publishers, Inc., 1983.

Pleck, J. Masculinity-femininity: Current and alternative paradigms. *Sex roles,* 1975, *1* (2), 173.

Pogrebin, L.C. *Growing up free.* New York: Bantam Books, 1980.

Wesley, C., & Wesley, F. *Sex role psychology.* New York: Human Sciences Press, 1977.

White, B.L. *The first three years of life.* Englewood Cliffs, New Jersey: Prentice-Hall, Inc., 1975.

The following statements are designed for the exploration of personal reactions to the chapter, as well as for the review of the contents of the chapter. Emphasis in discussions should be on exploring issues in depth, rather than on determining the correct or appropriate responses.

FOR DISCUSSION:

1. What is "gender identity" as compared to "gender role identity"?
2. Discuss the statement: "Gender is a fact, sex roles are invented."
3. Discuss the author's statement: "The prescription for male children includes a strong prohibition against being anything like the female."
4. Should adults encourage children to expand their notions of rigid sex role conformity, particularly when the children are in the midst of this apparent developmental phase?
5. How does block building, nail banging, or cuddling pertain to early childhood sex role socialization?
6. Discuss how girls develop "learned helplessness."
7. Is diapering a baby "difficult to imagine . . . as a source of intimacy and satisfaction"?
8. As the author suggests, add your own ideas for "lessening the adherence to rigid sex roles during the early childhood stages of development."

SUGGESTIONS FOR FURTHER READING

Carmichael, C. *Non-sexist childraising: How you can help your children grow up free to be themselves.* Boston, Massachusetts: Beacon Press, 1977.

Corsi, P.M. *A just beginning.* Newton, Massachusetts: EDC/WEEA Publishing Center, 1981.

Greenleaf, P.T. *Liberating young children from sex roles.* Somerville, Massachusetts: New England Free Press, 1972.

Klagsbrun, F. (Ed.). *Free to be-you and me.* New York: McGraw-Hill Book Company, 1974. (Record and film also available.)

New York State Education Department Division of Civil Rights and Intercultural Relations. *Multicultural early childhood guide.* Albany, New York, 1983.

Romer, N. *The sex-role cycle: Socialization from infancy to old age.* New York: McGraw-Hill Book Company, 1981.

Sprung, B. *Maximizing young children's potential: A non-sexist manual for early childhood trainers.* Newton, Massachusetts: EDC/WEEA Publishing Center, 1980.

Sprung, B. *Non-sexist education for young children—a practical guide.* New York: Citation Press, 1975.

Stockard, J., & Johnson, M. *Sex roles, sex inequality, and sex role development.* Englewood Cliffs, New Jersey: Prentice-Hall, 1980.

Chapter 4

WINNERS AND LOSERS?

Margaret Waterson

EDUCATION AND MASCULINITY

Cooper Thompson

INTRODUCTION

"Boys will be boys!"

As little boys cross the threshold into their kindergarten class, they begin to get messages that differ from their preschool years. Suddenly climbing, tumbling, getting dirty, shedding tears, and playing with girls becomes sitting still, staying neat, biting lips, and choosing games limited to boys. The messages are confusing to boys as they try to sort out what is expected and what is accepted. Eventually they learn that they are to excel in three domains: the classroom (good grades, good job), the athletic field (make the cut, get off the bench), and in interpersonal relationships (call her up, pay her way, be in charge).

Choices become increasingly more limited for boys as they progress through school. For boys?! Sex equity concentrates on limited opportunities for girls, not for their male peers! Boys are not counseled out of advanced classes, discouraged from pursuing vocational programs, left out of the athletic curriculum, or denied scholarships and awards. How can education be biased against boys?

Begin by looking at the expectations of all boys, and consider the number of male students (or children, peers, relatives) who simply do not meet the traditional standards. Look at boys who are average athletes, or not even intrigued with the thought of participating in sports. Consider boys who play the flute or violin, or excel in dramatics and the arts. Or consider boys who openly care about children, or express emotions overtly (even tears!).

What about the boys who actively pursue all of the three domains? They star on the team, keep up the grades, and escort the girls. The pressure to maintain the status of the best and brightest can often be too much.

Boys drop out of school, attempt suicide (and succeed), fail coursework, and abuse drug and alcohol more than girls. Perhaps because they are

43

socialized to take risks, handle anything, never show weakness, and be in constant control, they are unable to say no. Perhaps because they are discouraged from expressing fear, depression, anxiety, or stress, they resolve problems with external, damaging means. Perhaps not much attention is paid to the emotional well-being of boys because they are not supposed to be in need, or because they cannot let their needs be known.

Sex equity for boys means equal opportunities and experiences, just as it does for girls. Students, male and female, deserve the freedom to develop themselves without restrictions. Although many of the restrictions for girls are different than those for boys, the type of inhibitor is irrelevant. Boys will be boys; the boy they choose to be, not the boy created by a rigid definition of masculinity. Margaret Waterson provides a short, thought-provoking piece on the socialization of boys. Cooper Thompson explores the role of education in traditional male socialization, with suggestions as to how to include boys when attempting to provide education that is sensitive and fair.

WINNERS AND LOSERS?*

When boys first enter kindergarten, they have already been through five years of "male socialization." Family and friends, thoroughly socialized themselves, have been busy reinforcing "appropriate" male behaviors. Perpetual motion, aggression, avoidance of quiet activities, and suppression of emotion have been tolerated to a high degree.

Then, suddenly, the rules seem to change. The "boys-will-be-boys" acceptance of these traits gives way during the school day to a much more structured environment. The resulting conflicts for male students may be causing significant academic and emotional difficulties.

It has long been noted that boys number disproportionately high among discipline problems, grade repeaters, dropouts, remedial program participants, and abusers of drugs and alcohol. Admittedly, it is difficult to document specific causes among the many variables of school experience. Common sense tells us, however, that conflicting expectations must contribute to these problems.

At the same time that these conflicts are developing, another set of stereotypes seems to emerge: the "winners" and the "losers." In the winner role, boys are expected to achieve academically, begin preparation for high career (and earning) goals, and excel in competitive sports. The role of winner is fraught with pressure to succeed.

In the role of "losers," certain boys are expected to have problems academically, socially, and emotionally. Their identities become tied up with academic failure and acting-out behaviors. The role of loser is fraught with conflict and sense of failure.

The common thread in both roles is unwillingness to show emotion or signs of weakness and self-doubt.

Obviously, many boys do not fit naturally into either of these roles. They should fall somewhere in between. But that is the trouble with stereotypes: they set up expectations to be met and push individuals into roles that may not really fit.

As educators, we certainly cannot eliminate the effects of male stereo-

---

*(Reprinted from the VOICE Newsletter, Regional Planning Center, Albany-Schoharie-Schenectady BOCES, Volume VIII, Number 1, October 1986, Margaret Waterson, Editor)

types on our students. We need to be conscious, though, of how these stereotypes affect both student behavior and our own expectations. Our efforts to respond to the actual interests and abilities of each student can go a long way toward reducing the negative effects of stereotypes.

EDUCATION AND MASCULINITY

I was once asked by a teacher in a suburban high school to give a guest presentation on male roles. She hoped that I might help her deal with four boys who exercised extraordinary control over the other boys in the class. Using ridicule and their status as physically imposing athletes, these four wrestlers had succeeded in stifling the participation of the other boys, who were reluctant to comment in class discussions.

As a class, we talked about how boys got status in that school and how they were put down by others. I was told that the most humiliating put-down was being called a "fag." The list of behaviors that could elicit ridicule filled two large chalkboards; the boys in the school were conforming to rigid, narrow standards of masculinity to avoid being called a fag. I, too, felt this pressure and became very conscious of my mannerisms in front of the group. Partly from exasperation, I decided to test the seriousness of these assertions. Since one of the four boys had some streaks of pink in his shirt, and since he had told me that wearing pink was grounds for being called a fag, I told him that I thought *he* was a fag. Instead of laughing, he said, "I'm going to kill you."

He obviously didn't and, in retrospect, I think that what I said was inappropriate. But, in that moment, I understood how frightening it is for a boy to have his masculinity challenged, and I realized that the pressure to be masculine was higher than I ever would have expected. This was, after all, a boy who was a popular and successful athlete, whose masculinity was presumably established in the eyes of his peers; yet because of that single remark from me, he experienced a destruction of his self-image as a male.

Equally distressing was my realization that these boys defined masculinity by what it isn't—a set of "prohibited" feminine behaviors. As I studied their list, it became clear that "fag" was used to describe behaviors stereotypically attributed to girls and displayed by boys who were perceived as feminized males. The targeted behaviors were almost never sexual, so the reference was to sex roles, not sexual orientation, with the not-so-subtle message that gay men ("fags") are simply feminized males. The other message was clear: being masculine means avoiding all "feminine" behaviors. The unfortunate consequence of this view is that it locks out a whole range of behaviors from the male experience.

Traditional masculinity stresses attributes such as independence, pride, resiliency, self-control, and physical strength. To some extent, these are desirable attributes for both boys and girls. But masculinity tends to take these attributes to the extreme, and turns them into dominance, toughness, aggression, and even violence in some settings—qualities that are the antithesis of traditional femininity. In this definition of masculinity, there is no room for positive, traditionally feminine values such as nurturance, cooperation, emotional expression, and resolving conflicts in nonaggressive, noncompetitive ways.

Women Scorned

I have come to believe that this one aspect of masculinity—"avoid anything feminine"—accurately summarizes all other values associated with masculinity and directly supports two critical socializing forces in boys' lives—*homophobia* and *misogyny*. Homophobia is the fear of being perceived as homosexual (in boys' experience, being feminized) as well as the fear and hatred of homosexuals. Misogyny is the hatred of women. The two forces appear to be targeted at different classes of victims, but they are really just flip sides of the same coin. Homophobia is the hatred of feminine qualities in men, while misogyny is the hatred of feminine qualities in women. The boy who is called a fag is the target of other boys' homophobia. While the overt message is the absolute need to avoid being feminized, the implication is that females—and all that they represent—are contemptible.

The pressure of homophobia and misogyny in boys' lives is poignantly demonstrated to me each time I repeat a simple yet provocative activity with students. I ask them to answer the question, "If you woke up tomorrow and discovered that you were the opposite sex from the one you are now, how would you and your life be different?" Girls consistently indicate that there are clear advantages to being a boy—from increased independence and career opportunities to decreased risks of physical and sexual assault—and eagerly answer the question. But boys often express disgust at this possibility and may even refuse to answer the question. In her reports of a broad-based survey using this question, Alice Baumgartner of the Institute for Equality in Education, Denver, Colorado reports the following responses as typical of boys: "If I were a girl, I'd be stupid and weak as a string"; "I would have to wear makeup, cook, be a mother, and other yukky stuff like that"; "I would have to hate snakes. Everything would be miserable"; and "If I were a girl, I'd kill myself."

The costs associated with this view of masculinity are enormous, and the damage occurs at both personal and societal levels. The belief that a boy should be tough (aggressive, competitive, and daring) can create emotional pain for him. While a few boys experience short-term success for their toughness, there is little security in the long run. Instead, it leads to a series of challenges that few boys ultimately win. There is no security at the top when so many other boys are competing for the same status. Toughness also leads to increased chances of stress, physical injury, and even early death. It is considered manly to take extreme physical risks and voluntarily engage in combative, hostile activities.

On the other hand, nurturance is not a quality perceived as masculine, and thus is not valued. Because of this, boys and men experience greater emotional distance from other people and fewer opportunities to participate in rewarding interpersonal relationships. Studies consistently show that fathers spend very little time interacting with their children. In addition, men report that they seldom form intimate relationships, a reflection in part of their homophobia. They are afraid of getting too close and don't know how to take down the walls that they have built around themselves.

As boys become older and accept adult roles, the larger social costs of masculinity clearly emerge. Most women experience male resistance to an expansion of women's roles; one of the assumptions of traditional masculinity is the belief that women should be subordinate to men (an example of men's misogyny). Consequently, men are often not willing to accept females as equal, competent partners in personal and professional settings. Whether the setting is a sexual relationship, the family, the streets, or the battlefield, men are continuously engaged in efforts to dominate.

Resocialization for Males

Masculinity, like many other human traits, is determined by both biological and environmental factors. While there is extensive research indicating biological factors as significant in shaping some masculine behavior, there is undeniable evidence that cultural and environmental factors are strong enough to override biological impulses. What, then, could we be teaching boys about being men?

- To accept their vulnerability, express a range of emotions such as fear and sadness, and ask for help and support in appropriate situations.
- To be gentle, nurturant, cooperative, and communicative, and, in particular, learn nonviolent means of resolving conflicts.
- To accept those behaviors and attitudes that have traditionally been labeled "feminine" as necessary for full human development thereby reducing homophobia and misogyny.

Courage, physical strength, and independence are indeed positive qualities for males, provided they are not obsessive traits nor used to exploit or dominate others. It is not necessary to completely disregard or unlearn what is traditionally called "masculine." However, what is needed is a broader view of masculinity, one that is healthier for all people.

Where will this resocialization occur? Much of what boys learn about masculinity comes from the influences of parents, siblings, and role models portrayed on television. Even the school curriculum and environment provide powerful reinforcing images of traditional masculinity — through course content, teacher roles, and extracurricular activities, especially competitive sports.

School athletics are a microcosm of the socialization of male values. While participation in competitive activities can be enjoyable and healthy, it too easily becomes a lesson in the need for toughness, invulnerability, and dominance. Athletes learn to ignore their own injuries and pain, and instead try to inflict pain on others in their attempts to win, regardless of the cost to themselves or to their opponents. Yet such lessons are believed to be vital for full and complete masculine development and as a model for problem solving in other areas of life.

In addition to encouraging traditional male values, schools provide too few experiences in nurturance, cooperation, negotiation, nonviolent conflict resolution, and strategies for empathizing with and empowering others. School should become places where boys have the opportunity to learn these skills; clearly boys can't learn them on the streets, from peers, or on television.

While there is little formal curriculum on masculinity, educators can do a great deal to help students explore and expand their definitions of what it means to be male.

Students see few examples of nontraditional men, so positive role models matter. I think it's particularly important to have examples of men who share their feelings, who admit to making mistakes, and who listen to and trust women. These role models can be drawn from the male staff of the school (in which case it's important for the male staff to consider their *own* masculinity) or from examples in literature and popular media. (You may have to hunt for these examples, but they're there.) In general, you can use the media and popular literature to explore social expectations of men.

Sometimes I think that feelings in men and boys simply atrophy, like underused muscles. Boys may literally need to be given a vocabulary to talk about their feelings and encouragement to express their feelings. The world of male athletics would be a good place to examine how feelings *don't* get expressed; feelings are seldom specifically identified by sportscasters and athletes but are referred to simply as "emotions," as in, "There's a lot of emotion out there on the field."

Some educators have developed programs to teach nonviolent conflict resolution skills. This material is critical for boys, who may have learned that the only real way to resolve a conflict is by fighting. If you have responsibility for physical education programming, look carefully at the extent to which your programs encourage cooperation in addition to competition. Most programs stress single-sex competitive game play at the expense of single-sex or co-sexual cooperative games and social play. Take up the study of nonviolence as an academic pursuit. There is a rich history of heroic, nonviolent action in social change movements. And explore the impact of "war" toys with your students, using, perhaps, material developed by the various national and regional organizations working on the issue of violence in children's toys.

Be willing to talk openly—and affirmatively—about homophobia and the experiences of lesbian women and gay men. This will indicate to students that it is safe to talk with you about affectional preference and sexual orientation. Make sure that school policies and classroom norms on name calling include sanctions against labeling someone a "fag" or "dyke" or similar homophobic put-downs. Provide accurate information on sexuality and sexual orientation and consider having a gay man or lesbian woman come to talk to your students. Seeing a healthy and proud gay person can have a major impact on students' attitudes towards gay men and lesbian women.

In classroom discussions of social intolerance and oppression, link homophobia to sexism, racism, classism, etc. As a way to help students understand the treatment of subordinate groups, talk about ageism and its impact on young people. Your students will easily provide examples of their treatment as members of this targeted group and you can draw on this experience to help them understand the experience of being members of other oppressed groups.

Most history curriculum is filled with the achievements of a few famous white men; include the achievements of ordinary men and women of all races and classes, as well as the achievements of famous men and women. This history is important for all students; it gives girls a sense of potential and pride as women and it gives boys the knowledge that women are capable, strong, and intelligent. Encourage cross-sex interaction in classroom activities and social play; this will give boys a richer sense of girls' abilities and the opportunity to cooperate with them. And explore the dynamics of male-female relationships, focusing particularly on issues of sexual harassment and coercion and date rape. Boys need information to challenge the prevailing stereotypes of the sexually aggressive male and skills at communicating with and understanding the needs of their sexual partners.

A New Vision

I think back to the four wrestlers and the stifling culture of masculinity in which they live. In a new vision of masculinity, those boys would be able to express a full range of behaviors and emotions without fear of being chastized. They would be permitted and encouraged to cry, to be afraid, to show joy, and to express love in a gentle fashion. Extreme concern for career goals would be replaced by efforts to fulfill needs for recreation, health, and meaningful work. Older boys would be encouraged to tutor and play with younger students. They would receive as much recognition for artistic talents as they do for athletics, and value recreational activities as highly as competitive sports.

In a system where maleness and femaleness were equally valued, boys might no longer feel that they have to prove themselves to other boys; they would simply accept the worth of each person and value the differences. Few boys would boast about beating up another boy; name-calling would diminish. Boys would realize that it is possible to admit failure. Relationships between boys would reflect their care for one another, rather than their mutual fear and distrust.

Relationships between boys and girls would no longer be based on limited roles, but would become expressions of two individuals learning from and supporting one another. Boys would seek out opportunities to learn from girls and women. Emotional support would become common-place, and it would no longer be seen as the role of the female to provide the support. Aggressive styles of resolving conflicts would be the exception, rather than the norm.

The development of a new conception of masculinity based on this vision is an ambitious task, but an essential one for the health and safety of both men and women. Traditional definitions of masculinity will only lead to widening the gaps that currently separate men from women and men from each other. It is time to begin healing these wounds. The change can begin with a rethinking of how we teach about masculinity.

The following statements are designed for the exploration of personal reactions to the chapter, as well as for the review of the contents of the chapter. Emphasis in discussions should be on exploring issues in depth, rather than on determining the correct or appropriate responses.

FOR DISCUSSION:

1. How did the student with the pink shirt experience "a destruction of his self-image as a male"?
2. What does the author mean when he states, "... nurturance is not a quality perceived as masculine, and thus not valued."
3. List stereotypical images of boys and men (e.g., leader, math ability, drives fast, etc.). Review the characteristics and consider the positive and negative aspects of each. Include related issues such as health, psychological well-being, success, and relationships with men and women.
4. Should expression of feelings be encouraged in boys and men?
5. Are there social costs to masculinity?
6. Describe ways that educators teach about masculinity.
7. How can boys be "given a vocabulary to talk about their feelings?"
8. How do your male students (or sons, nephews, brothers, and other male relatives) fit the "new vision of masculinity" described by the author? How would they respond to this article, particularly to the discussion of homophobia and misogyny?

SUGGESTIONS FOR FURTHER READING

August, E.R. *Men's studies*. Littleton, Colorado: Libraries Unlimited, Inc., 1985.

Brannon, R., & David, D. (Eds.). *The forty-nine percent majority: The male sex role*. Reading, Massachusetts: Addison-Wesley Publishing Company, 1976.

Ehrenreich, B. *The hearts of men: American dreams and the flight from commitment*. New York: Anchor Press, 1984.

Farrell, W. *The liberated man*. New York: Bantam Books, 1979.

Farrell, W. *Why men are the way they are*. New York: McGraw-Hill Book Company, 1986.

Gerzon, M. *A choice of heros*. Boston, Massachusetts: Houghton-Mifflin, 1982.

Goldberg, H. *The new male-female relationship*. New York: William Morrow and Company, 1983.

NOW Legal Defense and Education Fund. *Ties that bind: The price of pursuing the male mystique*. Washington, D.C.: Project on Equal Education Rights, 1981.

Pleck, J. *The myth of masculinity*. Cambridge, Massachusetts: MIT Press, 1981.

Radical teacher—Gay and lesbian studies issue #24. Cambridge, Massachusetts.

Staples, R. *Black masculinity*. San Francisco, California: The Black Scholar Press, 1982.

Thompson, D. *As boys become men: Learning new male roles*. Cambridge, Massachusetts: Resources for Change, 1981.

Chapter 5

EDUCATIONAL RESPONSE
TO CONTEMPORARY FAMILIES

Christine O'Brien Palinski

INTRODUCTION

"Honey! I'm home!"

A quick survey of America's classrooms reveals that students are more than likely from dual working households, or from homes with single parents. Children of the 80s are not from the "traditional nuclear" family. In fact, the contemporary "nuclear" family is made up of several configurations.

The 1950s family structure was, in fact, limited to the 1950s. Although it is a strong image that still persists (grey-suited dad, happy homemaker mom, older son, younger daughter, and a pet dog), the so-called "traditional" family was not a tradition at all. Economics, the Civil Rights Movement, the Women's Movement, and other enormously significant social events impacted on the 1950s model to mold and change the composition of the American family. By the 1970s the picture began to show blended families, shared custody, single moms and single dads, and other nonrelated caretakers. Children began growing up in families that differed from others on their block, rather than carbon copies of everyone else in town.

Families became an equity issue because roles within the family structure began to change. The traditional patriarchal, father-at-a-distance evolved into a LaMaze coach, diaper changer, "involved" dad. The traditional stay-at-home, "nonworking" mom became an employed "woman in the work force." Concomitant issues such as quality child care, equitable pay scales, and rights of fathers became questions clearly falling into the sex equity domain.

It was inevitable that the schools would become more and more involved in family concerns. Supervision outside of school hours, parental involvement in activities, and other issues emerged quickly for schools to consider. While educators themselves grappled with their own changing family structures, they were finding it necessary to recognize the family lives of their students as well. Assumptions could no longer be made that:

- Johnny's mother will be a "room mother" again this year.
- Suzie's mom and dad will both attend the 2 p.m. teacher conference.

55

- Billy will see dad and mom in the audience during the morning presentation of his school play.
- Carol will arrive home greeted by mom, milk and cookies.
- Jack will take the same bus route to and from his house to the school every day.

Assumptions can also no longer be made that:

- Parents are working so they cannot or will not be involved in school functions. In fact, they often need employer permission, and advance notice, so that they can juggle and share what used to be simple tasks.
- Children are miserable without their after-school sugar cookies. In fact, most "latch-key" children are self-reliant, supervised, and welcome a short period of time to themselves.
- Students feel confused, and harried about changing schedules. In fact, it appears that this way of life is normal for the children. It is the adults that are having trouble adjusting.

The changing contemporary family demands the recognition and acceptance of educators. Christine O'Brien Palinski discusses the impact of the modern family on educational institutions.

EDUCATIONAL RESPONSE TO CONTEMPORARY FAMILIES

Most sentient adults are aware that the American family looks quite different today than it did twenty or thirty years ago. Media attention to the transformation has been particularly intense in recent years. Because we are all part of this transformation, however, it may be difficult to notice the scope of the change without quantifying some of our observations.

Some Key Statistics About Families Today

- In almost 50 percent of married couples with infants 1 year old or under, both parents are working for pay.
- Between 64 and 71 percent of these children at school age have "working" Moms; 91 percent have "working" Dads. (U.S. Census Bureau, 1986.)
- The number of one parent households increased by 107 percent between 1960 and 1983.
- In 1985, there were more than 10.5 million families principally supported by women. This means almost 17 percent of all families in the United States.
- 80 percent of the employed women maintaining families in 1985 worked at full time jobs. (National Commission on Working Women, 1986.)
- Estimates of the number of "latchkey children" who spend at least 3 hours a day in self- or sibling-care range from 2 to 7 million. (Kahn and Kammerman, 1987.)

In short, Dick and Jane and Mother and Father no longer live in stereotyped bliss on some friendly, tree lined street in small town America. Exit Ozzie and Harriet, the Cleavers, Father Knows Best, etc. If those snapshots of Americana ever represented an accurate picture of "us" (and they probably did not), they do not now. They did, however, play an important part in our cultural imagery. Those of us who look back on childhoods in the 1950s and 60s remember the comfort and clarity this imagery projected.

"Family" was squeaky clean; Mom had cookies warm from the oven when the school bus rolled up Maple Street. Dad breezed in at dinner time to solve a few minor family problems while reading the paper in his easy chair. Missy and Junior knew their respective places; so did Spot and Puff. Everyone seemed to be having a good time.

What About Reality?

Certainly most of us didn't live that way. Some of us were poor or non-Caucasian or urban dwellers or from different ethnic groups. Some of us lived in factory towns or in cities with high crime rates. Some of us lived with only one parent. Some of us wore keys on chains around our necks for after school. Some of us were children of alcoholics.

Someone has said, "Nostalgia isn't what it used to be." It is important to recall that even those of us who lived the traditional of family image may not have attained the fulfillment that comes at the end of a thirty-minute sitcom.

This is not to deny the important impact of the Cleavers. They looked familiar to some of us and some of us wished we looked more like them. That was the fifties and part of the sixties but the imagery dies hard. We've passed through the seventies, and most of the eighties, still trying to overcome that narrow restrictive imagery. It is not only old and entrenched, it is filled with cozy sentiment and imbued with something of the sacred. For some of us it continues to hold substantial appeal and for that reason, it is important to distinguish between the reality and the "wish."

We are witness in the eighties to many diverse ideologies claiming affiliation and protector status toward "the family." Sociologist Andrew Cherlin calls it "Politicizing the Family" (1987). Democrats and Republicans, Fundamentalists and Agnostics, Conservatives and Liberals all identify themselves as "pro family," but embrace contrasting visions and agendas.

We are all entitled, of course, to our choice of "vision." As educators, however, it is our responsibility to know the facts, whether that knowledge enhances or detracts from that "vision." The statistics listed earlier outline some of the facts. Let's elaborate a bit further. A few more statistics:

- Fewer than 10 percent of the families of our current students resemble the Cleavers (employed father, homemaker mother, and children).
- The majority of students live in families with employed mothers.

- Almost 20 percent of students live with one parent (usually the mother).
- Approximately half of today's students by age 18 will have divorced parents.
- One child in 6 lives in a second marriage family (with a biological parent and a step parent). (U. S. Census Bureau, 1986).

A Classroom Profile

These startling statistics may well add to our "data banks" and help us make quantitative mental revisions. Statistics create a problem for many of us, however, in their coldness. In an effort to breathe life into them, to "warm them up," we'll look at an actual classroom profile. The school this is drawn from is an old one, as is the "neighborhood." It is one of the "outer reach" suburbs of a mid-sized city, including approximately 20 percent rural area. These are not the suburbs of CEOs and expensive European cars. It is probably thought of as lower middle to middle class. Approximately 65 percent of the high school's graduates go on to further education.

Mr. Jones's third grade class numbers twenty-four. Five of the children live with single custodial Moms or Moms and siblings. Four of these Moms are separated or divorced; one never married. One of the children lives with a single, custodial Dad. Of the eighteen remaining students, four live in blended families with one biological and one step-parent, fourteen live with both biological parents and siblings. (Two of them still will experience separation or divorce during the school year according to parental reports.)

In this class of 24, eight students have one full-time at home parent. Five of the families of the eight students contain one or more infants or toddlers. (One is a home care Mother, who cares for three pre-school children in addition to her own.)

The sixteen remaining children demonstrate an astonishing number of work/home configurations. Ten live with two full-time employed parents. Five of these couples represent a fairly conventional pattern of working hours (in the 9 to 5 vicinity). Two of the other Dads are long distance truckers who are away from home in six-out-of-eight-day patterns. Two of the other Moms are nurses who work rotating schedules (7:00 a.m. to 3:00 p.m., 3:00 p.m. to 11:00 p.m., 11:00 p.m. to 7:00 a.m.). The other two Dads work two jobs and are effectively absent from their homes for all of the families' waking hours except Sundays.

There are six children who have one full-time employed parent and one part-timer. Two of the Moms are workers in the school cafeteria, thus able to go home at dismissal time with their children. Two Dads are self-employed and frequently available for daytime parenting activity. Two other Moms are bakery workers who start their day at 4:00 a.m., returning home shortly after the children leave for school.

Eight of the children spend weekends, vacations, and occasional school nights at their "other home" with a noncustodial parent. One family is currently negotiating a shared residence arrangement, which will involve weekly moves for children alternating residence with each parent.

This information was difficult to collect, awkward to report, and undoubtedly confusing to read. Think of the impact these variables have on the lives of each student and the challenge they create for teachers trying to respond to individual needs.

Let's draw back from this complicated and confusing classroom profile. It is reasonable to ask why this information is included here. Some would say that the teacher is hired to instruct, not to do case work. This extra information does not appear to be instructional; it is social data.

So how are children's lives affected by the demographic characteristics we've described?

Enormously. For instance, of Mr. Jones's twenty-four students, eight arrive at school and return home to one or both parents on a regular school bus route daily. Six children arrive at school on one bus, but leave on another bus which takes them to the home of a baby-sitter daily. Three go to the home of a baby-sitter two or three afternoons a week. Three others meet an older sibling or neighbor child who is responsible for their care after school. The remaining four children demonstrate no recognizable pattern of before or after school care. The teacher assumes that they spend considerable time without adult supervision.

Add to this the fact that the early morning "before school" care issue is barely acknowledged, and we begin to see a pattern of considerable stress for families. Several of the children in the above survey have parents whose morning departures for work precede the arrival of the school bus. Three parents choose to drive children to school on their way to work. These children wait on school grounds (largely unattended) for teachers and other children to arrive. Other children are brought to the homes of baby-sitters and friends in the morning to pass the time between parental departure and the beginning of the school day. A few children spend some time each morning alone or with siblings not much older than they awaiting the school bus.

The logistics of child care and travel make a powerful statement about the complexity of the lives of today's students. The question of where the children are (before and after school) is a relatively new consideration for many of us. The brief sketch here suggests its import. Notice, however, that we've only looked at the logistics of *getting them there and here*. We've not even approached any evaluation of quality of care.

An additional feature to assimilate in this sketch is its fluidity. These arrangements are not characterized by their endurance. Mr. Jones reports that the majority of families' arrangements for before and after school care change at least once in the year. In some cases, there are several changes in the course of the school year. Illness of any of the people involved (child, caretaker, caretaker's children, even another "cared for" child) devastate almost any arrangements.

Some of the effects of the complexity of children's lives are not so easy to observe. Most of the children in Mr. Jones's class are described in school records as well-adjusted, normal, good group members. These children seem to be faring well in their "Eighties" family styles. There is at least nothing obvious in their behavior that indicates a negative reaction to their situations. They are, on the whole, achieving and producing satisfactorily in school. Mr. Jones reports that he observes three children suffering from severe family stress situations, including one recent divorce, and one severe employment reversal. He is appropriately reticent about suggesting causal relationships between family circumstances and academic achievement, but points sadly to the diminishing number of parents he is able to draw into the classroom during the school day.

The majority of the children, obviously, have limited access to their parents during the day. They spend a good portion of their "free" time in the company of other adults and children. Their parents are not frequent visitors to the school environment. Parents are not, for the most part, chaperoning field trips or volunteering in the library.

Significantly, Mr. Jones reports very little dissatisfaction with this pattern among his students. When students are asked what they would change in their families, they tend to point to what appears to be less fundamental issues, like bedtime hour, or luxury products they'd like to own. This "new" family system, despite all its complexities and stresses, is the one they know and accept.

Child Care—A Major Factor

One of the most complicated pieces of the eighties family picture is child care. A review of the credible research and discussion in the literature regarding child care suggests that there is no categorical evaluation that holds up. Age of the child and the form of care (large group, family care setting, parent substitute) are extremely significant variables. Children who spend all their time in the family unit do not appear to be more secure, intelligent, or successful than those whose parents are unavailable to them during the day. Each individual care situation must be evaluated in its own unique terms. A critical variable seems to be parental satisfaction with the care.

It has not been easy for families to feel satisfaction with child care arrangements for myriad of reasons. The cultural imagery discussed earlier, which promotes the employed father/homemaker mother as the "American Way" causes families that do not match the image to question their adequacy. This persists in spite of the fact that the "Leave It to Beaver" group represents fewer than 10 percent of American families.

As a society, we are only beginning to look at the possibilities for collaborating on child care. In the past, the child care dilemma has been one that families were forced to resolve in isolation. This has not been the case in Europe (or many other industrialized nations), where comprehensive child care systems have existed since the labor shortages following World War II. There are models in those countries that have endured the tests of time. They include day care, before and after school programming, paid and unpaid parental leave and subsidies, leave for care of sick children, and more.

In the late 1980s, we are seeing in this country, movement toward such policies (Mercers, 1985). Some evidence of this movement is in continuing legislative efforts to extend disability benefits to include a parenting component. Organized labor has also assumed a role in creating benefits packages that acknowledge the family needs of workers (child care, alternative work schedules, employee assistance plans, etc.). The Reagan Administration has heavily promoted private sector involvement in child care provision. In fact, a recent national survey by *Ms. Magazine* indicates that a sizable majority of Americans want employer supported child care programs (Rubin, 1987).

Child care service providers and advocacy groups indicate that the private sector cannot be expected to fulfill this responsibility without a major government commitment as well. Information from the Children's Defense Fund suggests that approximately 2,500 out of six million employers offer any child care assistance to their employees, and this includes a large number who offer such supports as noontime seminars on parenting (1982). As government policy moves toward an investment in family issues and a commitment to its articulated "pro family" stance, a mutual effort will emerge as in tax incentives for family-related employee benefits, government subsidies for research and development in what has been called the "families industry," and more.

The interest of employers in this country in family and child care has been aroused. Studies of companies which have child care programs indicate that the investment is worthwhile. Perhaps even more significant are the studies which indicate that problems and concerns with child care are the most significant predictors of absenteeism and unproductive time at work for women and men (Cherlin, A. 1987).

There is growing societal recognition that families are in need of support. Children's lives *are* significantly affected by shifts in the work force and the economy. Perhaps the first institution to see these effects up close is the school.

How are Teachers Lives Affected by the Changes in Family Life Styles Described Here?

Earlier, we looked at a description of children's travel arrangements to and from school. This complicated, multivariable picture surely impacts the teachers' day as well. Most of Mr. Jones's students are eight years old. They must have parental and school clearance in order to make any change in their travel patterns. Hence, Mr. Jones handles an average of six travel-related notes from parents daily. He also checks at dismissal time to be sure that the children remember and execute the travel alterations that they've requested. Mr. Jones reports an average of four travel related "glitches" weekly. These include lost and forgotten notes and last-minute changes phoned in by parents, which he must interpret to the children. Of course, there is the inevitable kid who "slips through the cracks" in his vigilance and ends up on the wrong bus only to be returned to the school an hour later by a disgruntled bus driver (who is probably worried about getting home to her own waiting children). Mr. Jones usually drives that child home himself after the necessary calls are made.

As any teacher of young children knows, a great deal of time is consumed in tending to these arrangements. Mr. Jones speaks of it as "housekeeping." There has always been school-related housekeeping (scheduling "make-up" work, special instructional time for some of the students, visits to the nurse, etc.). Teachers report increased home-related house-keeping as well. Travel arrangements are the tip of a "growing" iceberg.

Scheduling the two formal parent-teacher conferences required for elementary students is an extremely difficult and frustrating task. Few parents are available during the afternoon hours that the district frees for conferences. In fact, the early dismissal for children on conference days in many cases translates to a child care burden for their parents. Family schedules already stretched to include more than fits comfortably, must be juggled to cover several extra child hours, plus an appointment at school. Teachers make themselves available in the evening to accom-modate these working parents, but it's not much of a surprise to find a high incidence of cancelled appointments. It's even less surprising to see how rare is the conference that includes both parents.

Mr. Jones makes a practice of inviting noncustodial parents and step-parents, or any other significant adults in the children's lives, to partici-pate in these conferences. This policy in itself, represents a substantial "housekeeping" chore for him. He also encourages all of these adults to maintain frequent, informal contact with him. Although he devotes a great deal of energy to the planning and execution of the formal con-ference, it is his belief that the most important parent-teacher contacts occur when a question or issue arises with an individual child and the teacher and family are able to consult immediately. Unfortunately, the busy schedules of many of his students' parents preclude the fluid kind of interaction that this philosophy demands.

In addition to the planned and spontaneous conferences regarding individual children's development and progress, there is much to be gained all around from parental involvement in general classroom activi-ties. In fact, studies conducted at preschool, elementary, and secondary levels all point up a relationship between parental involvement and student achievement. In an extensive review of the literature regarding teacher-parent relationships, Hauser-Cram reports that frequency or intensity of parent involvement correlates significantly with student achievement, especially in the area of reading (1983).

In September, Mr. Jones establishes an "open door" policy for parents and "significant others." He encourages them to drop in when they find time and observe or join whatever class activity is happening. He urges those who can to participate on a regular basis. Although he reports very few drop-ins, he does have two parents who read aloud to the children on a weekly basis. Four other parents (and step-parents) are planning to join the class for particular lessons which connect with their career areas.

Educators have long struggled with the challenge of involving the parents of their students in the educational process. There are many factors which influence parent involvement, not the least of which is the parents' own school experience. Teachers often work very hard and display remarkable creativity in attracting the reticent, the wary, the preoccupied. Mr. Jones reports that in spite of his most creative efforts, family circumstances have noticeably limited parent presence in his classroom. He is not alone. Many teachers point to similar difficulties.

Teachers understand the factors that hinder school involvement, because they are so often struggling with the same problems in their own families. Mr. Jones and many of his colleagues are themselves working parents. They are not available to spend much time in their own children's schools, for obvious reasons. When they are accommodating their students' parents with early morning and evening conference time, they are sacrificing time with their own children. And the beat goes on.

How Can Schools Respond to Societal Change?

We are all affected by the changes in families and work force discussed in this article. Our ideas and behavior, in fact our lives, take different form as these central institutions in our world shift. Because of their dependent status, children are impacted in an immediate way by the shifts. The impact is highly observable since children are all housed within the same institution, the school. This factor magnifies the role of school in society. No other institution houses or relates to an entire segment of the population in the unique, total, and long-term context of the school. In this capacity, schools are the first institutions to absorb the fallout from major societal change.

Absorbing the fallout means adjusting in various ways. It is increasingly clear that the major institutions in our society need to catch up with the circumstances of families. Schools are the paradigm. "Back to Basics" and curriculum coordinators notwithstanding, schools really are in the business of preparing children for adult life. That may happen by careful teacher design, or as a by-product of instruction.

It is possible to build into our curricula by careful teacher design a realistic picture of what students' adult lives will look like, including paid and unpaid work, parenting and family responsibilities, and more.

As paradigm, schools can also adjust in a variety of ways to match the lives of their students.

The School as Paradigm for Change

In accomplishing these adjustments and providing real glimpses of the future for students, schools model for other institutions in the community. They model after hours availability. Civil and governmental offices need to recognize the hours during which most adults are available and adjust their schedules to match. Professional services, medical services, even religious institutions can pattern after the schools' "evening hours." They can also follow the school's lead in acknowledging the variety of family circumstances, including dual worker households, single parents, etc. They can expect, and provide comfortable surroundings and diversions for them.

Beyond modeling for the rest of the community, there are many areas for school response. The format for parent contacts, with special emphasis on the involvement of fathers, evaluation of materials, the input of interested teachers into after school programming, and teacher awareness of career education potential are only a sampling of the approaches schools can take.

Parent Contacts

The short description earlier of Mr. Jones's involvement in students' travel to and from school is a good example of the school's accommodation to match students' needs. Teachers have had to take on this task, although it is a frustrating and time-consuming one. Other tasks which teachers can assume are less arduous and constant. The National Committee for Citizens in Education recommends a number of ways for schools to respond to the needs of single and working parents (VOICE, 1985). A primary recommendation focuses on teacher recognition of students' family situations. Reading students' records at the time of initial contact gives the teacher an abundance of individuating information. It also limits the possibility of embarrassing or disturbing students by erroneous assumptions that may be made about their homes. Names and relationships of parents, step-parents, guardians, and siblings can be clarified as well, enabling the teacher to make direct, personal contact with all the significant adults in students' lives early in the school year.

Scheduling for Parent Involvement

In observing Mr. Jones's class, the issue of scheduling for parent involvement is inescapable. His classroom is not the exception. Most adults work during the day, and are unable to leave work except in emergency situations. It is, therefore, essential that evening hours be made available for parent/teacher interaction. Additionally, parents need a substantial lead time to plan for evening conferences. They also may need more motivational assistance for participating in regular parent/teacher communication. They are not only tired and unaccustomed to school programming in the evening, they also have to think about child care arrangements. Some schools meet this problem with potluck suppers or other inexpensive dinner arrangements which include babysitting afterward so that parents can visit classrooms and talk with teachers.

Availability and flexibility of this nature can create a very difficult squeeze for teachers, who have to consider their own families' needs. Schools can surely investigate ways of compensating teachers for their time. Many of these working parents would be happy to exchange evening time for day time freedom from the classroom so that they could attend to some of their own family responsibilities. Others would prefer to be paid. Either way, the goal should be a payoff for families.

Materials

Another obvious arena for school response to families' needs is in the textbook and other resources presented to students. It is important that publications used in school reflect the kinds of varied family structures represented in the class. Single parent households, working parents, divorced parents, and blended families can be portrayed easily in text books and other materials. Seeing the family structure they live in is comforting and validating to children (and adults). On the other hand, seeing old, stereotyped images raises doubts and worries. It's a matter of buying from a publisher who is sensitive to these issues and there are an increasing number of such resources available.

Role of Fathers

Some of the central themes in family structure in the eighties is increased involvement of fathers in nurturing activities. If there is no full-time nurturer/homemaker, then hopefully, the slack is picked up by two part-timers. In some cases, of course, fathers are full-time homemakers and caretakers, and deserve that recognition. More often than not, however, in two-parent households, Mom and Dad are each involved in child care and homemaking as well as working for pay. Because some parts of the role are new, Dads may need some extra help in feeling comfortable in the school setting. Teachers have found it especially important to address all communication to both parents if they are living together, and to make sure each receives a copy if they are not. Making clear to the Dads how much their presence is valued is very important, especially in the early grades, which have traditionally been seen as "female" areas. Needless to say, a male teacher at the grade level is often a powerful influence in "dealing" fathers in. Including as many men as possible in any parent meetings (teachers, other staff, school board, administrators, etc.) can help fathers feel more at ease in the group. Making information about the importance of father involvement available to parents is another positive step that is recommended by The Fatherhood Project at Bank Street College of Education (Kinman & Kohl, 1983).

Teacher Involvement in After School Programs

An area of most visible deficit for families in the eighties is child care and specifically care during the before and after school hours. As discussed earlier in this article, parents have been on their own, coping with this critically important problem. Schools are probably the community resource most suited to assist in this area. In terms of physical plant and equipment, they are already appropriate for most of the population in question. Even the essential issue of safety has been ensured.

Staff expertise is also a significant available resource. Teachers and other school personnel are uniquely capable of dealing with the child care population. They are comfortable in the school setting and in many cases, already have established relationships with the children. This is not to suggest that they should be expected to fill these major social gaps, but they are a valuable, underutilized resource. It will require the collaborative efforts of many institutions in the community to respond comprehensively to the emerging needs of families.

Many teachers take on second jobs for economic reasons. In fact, youth recreation programs have been a common source of summer employment for teachers. Involvement in before or after school care programs at their own employment site might be a very attractive source of additional income for them. In any case, their input to design and formulation of programs makes sense from an educational viewpoint and more importantly, from a trust and confidence viewpoint.

Preparing Students for the Future

Research and writings pertaining to schools and the contemporary family tend to focus on logistical issues such as those discussed previously, but probably the most significant communication that happens between teacher and student is the subtle messages that the teacher sends about self-esteem and expectations. Teachers who concern themselves with the emotional and psychological development of their students inevitably consider the life of the student outside of the school environment.

Teachers are capable of interrupting patterns of disinterest and low academic achievement in families and in communities (Bronfenbrenner, 1974). Teacher belief can suggest possibilities formerly inconceivable to children. Most successful adults can look back into their school years and find one or more teachers whom they credit with inspiring and encouraging them to perform at levels they hadn't considered. Although teachers are aware of their impact on self-confidence and career goals, they are also aware that they are by no means the only input. Families, social environment, media, and a myriad of other variables all contribute to this piece of self for children. Teachers, however, are often a conscious, intervening influence in the messages that originate in the rest of society.

A logical extension of this influence exists in the teacher expectations about student lifestyles. Teachers can help students absorb the notion that they will have many important duties as adults. They will be employed with job related responsibilities. They will also have family and home tending responsibilities for which they need to prepare themselves.

Traditionally, these dual roles have been separated with boys expecting to take primary ownership of one and girls expecting primary ownership of the other. However, as the statistics we looked at earlier in this article indicated, such a breakdown is no longer an accurate picture of family life. More adults, in more households, experience a blending of these roles than not. Frequently, that blending is a source of confusion and stress, especially when it is unexpected.

This is where teacher influence can be paramount. As early as pre-school and kindergarten, teachers can encourage all the children to play with the full range of toys and games so that they can fully develop their interests and abilities. The teacher's expectation that boys will want to play with dolls and kitchens and the like, goes a long way toward removing social stigmas. Similarly, providing an environment that allows and encourages girls to involve themselves in building and structural play, ball games, and other team experiences is a major influence.

As children move into the "middle" years of grade school, teachers can help in a big way by encouraging boys and girls to play and work together. There is an overly simple tone to such a concept; the reality is anything but simple. By second grade, many boys and girls have absorbed the social message that they have little use for one another. This unfortunate notion lives on until adolescence, when they rediscover one another, and wonder why it's so difficult to work out meaningful relationships that are mutually rewarding.

But contemporary and future work/home life demands more than ever before that men and women share and communicate. Teachers who see the problems inherent in the traditionally devisive social system can structure their lessons and their classrooms in ways that minimize segregation. They can assign sex-integrated project teams. They can arrange seating, and various classroom responsibilities to enhance cooperative, friendly interaction among boys and girls. They can, of course, avoid sex segregation when it is avoidable, with the same concern that they might bring to the related issue of race segregation.

As children approach adolescence, teachers can continue to encourage male/female cooperation, and discourage the objectification that starts to mark the sexual awakening of these students. Active career planning starts in this time sequence, as students begin to have options in course work. It is essential that they be encouraged at this time, to consider all options, and to recognize the lifestyle that will probably be theirs. In some cases, this means "taking on" the stereotypes, in order to help the students see past them.

Career education, a much larger concept than the planning phase, happens over the whole of a student's school life (and earlier). In fact, the teacher's day-to-day impact on career education cannot be overstated. The ideas that teachers have about the way that students will live, the contributions that they will make, and the satisfactions that they will experience, constitute the richest input in this arena.

It is the daily interactions with students that will allow students to develop fully and feel strong and comfortable about their family configurations. Topics of discussion such as changing traditional schedules, rewording letters to homes, and evaluating testbooks are secondary to the topic of validating the current life experiences of students.

If a school district recognizes the changes in the American family, then they are tackling the problems inherent in the changing structure. For example, one district rearranged the bus schedule (a monumental task) so that older students arrived home before their younger siblings. A temporary solution to a national issue perhaps, but a major contribution to the safety and well-being of the children of the school and a strong recognition of parental concerns.

Schools are a critical piece in identifying and facing the issues concomitant with the reorganization of families. It is important that teachers take note, weigh the issues and suggest educational alternatives. Their students cannot help but be the better for it.

REFERENCES

Ashery, R. & Basen, M. *Guide for parents with careers.* Washington, D.C.: Acropolis Books Lts., 1986.

Beckwith, H., Miller, S., Morns, T., Sage, K. *Schools and the changing family,* Oneonta, New York: Teacher Center, 1985.

Bronfenbrenner, U. *Is early intervention effective? A report on longitudinal evaluations of pre-school programs.* Washington, D.C.: Department of Health Education and Welfare, 1974.

Cherlin, A., Politicizing the family. *Johns Hopkins Magazine,* Feb. 1987, *34* (1), 18–24.

Children's Defense Fund. *The child care handbook,* Washington, D.C., 1982.

Genovese, R. (Ed.) *Families and change.* South Hadley, Massachusetts: Bergin & Garvey, 1984.

Henderson, A., Merburger, C., Doms, T. *Beyond the bake sale,* Columbia, Maryland: The National Committee for Citizens in Education, 1986.

Kahn, A. & Kamerman, S. *Child care facing the hard choices,* Diver, Massachusetts: Auburn House Publishing Co., 1987.

Klinman, D. G. & Kohl, R. *Fatherhood USA.* New York: Garland Publishing, Inc., 1984.

Mercers, A. Child care finds a champion in the corporation. *New York Times,* 1985.

National Commission on Working Women, *Child care fact sheet,* Washington, D.C., 1986

Rich, D. *The forgotten factor in school success.* Washington, D.C.: The Home and School Institute, Inc., 1985.

Rubin, K. Whose job is child care? *Ms.,* March, 1987, *15* (9), 32–44.

Swap, S. *Enhancing parent involvement in schools,* New York: Teachers College Press, 1987.

U. S. Census Bureau, *Population profile of the United States 1984/85.* Washington, D. C.,
   1986.
U. S. Department of Labor, *Facts on U. S. working women,* Washington, D. C., 1986.
VOICE *School response to contemporary families,* Albany, N. Y., 1985.

The following statements are designed for the exploration of personal reactions to the article, as well as for the review of the contents of the article. Emphasis in discussions should be on exploring issues indepth, rather than on determining the correct or appropriate responses.

FOR DISCUSSION:

1. Are the educators in your institution aware of the family structures of most of their students? Does their awareness (or lack thereof) influence their classroom instruction?
2. How have the family configurations of you and your colleagues changed over the last five years?
3. Is it the responsibility of the schools to provide evening conferences, and after-school child care?
4. What efforts to respond to the American family have been made by your educational institution? What additional steps might be taken?
5. What do students believe is a "typical American family"? How does their view reflect their plans for future family life?
6. Respond to the author's statement: " . . . Dads may need some extra help in feeling comfortable in the school setting."
7. What efforts can be taken by educational institutions to prepare students for their future family roles?
8. Respond to the author's statement: "Either way, the expense is minimal when weighed against the payoff for families."

SUGGESTIONS FOR FURTHER READING

Bank Street College of Education. *Work and family life newsletter: Balancing job and personal responsibilities.* New York, 1987.

Baruch, G., Barnett, P., & Rivers, C. *Life prints: New patterns of love and work for today's women.* New York: New American Library, 1983.

Berg, B.J. *The crisis of the working mother: Resolving the conflict between family and work.* New York: Summit Books, 1986.

Bureau of National Affairs, Inc. *Work and family: A changing dynamic.* Washington, D.C., 1986.

Henderson, A., Marburger, C., & Ooms, T. *Beyond the bake sale: An educator's guide to working with parents.* Columbia, Maryland: National Committee for Citizens in Education, 1986.

Kamerman, S. *Parenting in an unresponsive society: Managing work and family life.* New York: Free Press, 1980.

Pogrebin, L.C. *Family politics: Love and power on an intimate frontier.* New York: McGraw-Hill Book Company, 1983.

Rich, D., & Mattox, B. *101 activities for building more effective school-community involvement.* Washington, D.C.: Home and School Institute, 1983.

Sayers, R. *Fathering: It's not the same.* Larkspur, California: The Nurturing Family School, 1983.

Seltzer, S., & Baden, K. *School-age child care: An action manual.* Dover, Massachusetts: Auburn House, 1982.

Sidel, R. *Women and children last: The plight of poor women in affluent America.* New York: Viking, 1986.

Staines, G., & Pleck, J. *The impact of work schedules on the family.* Ann Arbor, Michigan: Institute of Social Research, 1983.

Chapter 6

WHAT IS SEX FAIR EDUCATION?

MARYLYN E. CALABRESE

INTRODUCTION

"Sex fair education? You're going to have a sex fair?"

Just over a decade ago, terms such as "sexist," "sex equity" and "sex fair" were barely recognizable. Although they are often freely included in current conversations and literature, there are a multitude of definitions for them. All too often the terms have a negative connotation, full of criticism and assumptions. Are programs that are "non-sexist," "unbiased," "equitable," or "sex fair" for girls only? Designed to blame men? Reverse discrimination? Are they really sex education, secular humanism, women's studies, or some other controversial topic in education?

None of the above. Educators who pursue curriculum and instruction that is sex fair are recognizing that all students are different. Individual family circumstances, racial and ethnic background, socioeconomic class, and other factors in addition to gender create an individual with very personal needs. Sex fair education attempts to recognize the student's unique needs regardless of the derivation of those needs.

Educators who pursue curriculum and instruction that is sex fair are recognizing that all students are entitled to explore a variety of options during their school years. Class requirements, extracurricular activities, special programs, and other school activities are designed to encourage students to learn and grow. Sex fair education assures that no doors are closed, that no student who seeks another way to gather knowledge and thrive, can be turned away.

Educators who pursue curriculum and instruction that is sex fair are recognizing that contemporary educational institutions are generally inequitable. Through constant vigilance, education of colleagues, research, and open dialogue, schools can become affirmative in their actions to provide sex fair education.

Marylyn Calabrese provides a succinct definition to a component of the educational process that can be so easily misunderstood.

Suggestions for Further Reading follow the chapter "Sexism: Still An Issue in Education" by Cecelia H. Foxley.

75

WHAT IS SEX FAIR EDUCATION?

O ver the past twenty years the movement for sexual equality has had a considerable influence on public education in the United States. Pressure for change has come from various sources, including activist organizations, parent and community groups, and professional education associations. Many school districts have revised their policies and practices in response to this need. Although educators and parents may subscribe to the idea of equality in theory, many do not understand what the concept means in practice. This chapter will explore equity in education by describing many examples of its operations and by explaining its fundamental meaning.

Because sex fairness is so often misunderstood, basic definitions can be helpful.

Sexist: discriminating on the basis of a person's gender; assuming that because you know a person's gender, you automatically know something about her or his abilities, aspirations, strengths or shortcomings; measuring people by sex stereotypes.

Nonsexist: considering each person as an individual with particular talents, needs, hopes and weaknesses unrelated to gender; regarding sex stereotypes as meaningless restrictions upon people; the opposite of sexist; this term arose to denote what was devoid of sexism.

Sex Fair: used interchangeably with *nonsexist.* However, getting rid of unfairness may not be sufficient for providing equity. *Sex fairness* takes a more positive approach in setting out what should be provided rather than simply eliminating the negative.

Sex fairness in education refers to the entire operation of a public school district. This includes its hiring practices and policies, curricular offerings, textbooks and instructional materials, staff behaviors (especially a teacher's behavior in the classroom) the ways students are counseled in the guidance department, and the extracurricular programs that students may participate in. The terms "sex fair," or its opposite, "sexist," may be used to refer to the actions of teachers, administrators, parents, or students in any of these situations.

In each of these areas lies the potential for fairness and unfairness. Hence, a sex fair policy may stipulate that single sex awards are not permitted; thus, a local business club can name the "student of the month" but not the "boy of the month." Similarly, an example of an unfair practice would be male high school faculty members being asked to perform outdoor duty assignments while female faculty members are not given such assignments. An example of an unfair facility would be a vocational technical school in which male industrial arts students have ample locker, shower, and changing facilities while female students have a small closet for the same purpose. As far as observable staff behaviors are concerned, a sex fair teacher performs activities traditionally thought to be more easily done by the other sex, that is, if female, running audiovisual equipment and lifting boxes, if male, performing clerical duties and dusting shelves. In all of these examples, the potential both for fairness and unfairness is present.

It is interesting to note that such a potential exists on a continuum with some of the items having more potential than others. The behavior of a teacher has a great deal of potential, whereas a building, except in certain specified areas such as locker and bathroom facilities, has less potential. An elementary reading text has more potential for fairness or unfairness than a fourth grade math workbook. To the extent that the latter has pictures and word problems, the potential exists, in so far as people are referred to and portrayed.

Are there any aspects of a school's activities that lack this potential? Yes, the learning process itself does, particularly learning skills such as reading, writing, outlining, dividing, sewing, driving; none of these has the potential for either fairness or unfairness. However, it is important to note this potential exists in the context of how the skills may be taught. For example, if one sex is excluded or discouraged from learning advanced computational skills, then that is unfair treatment; if there are different standards of performance for either sex, or if the sexes are regarded differently for their performance, then the potential for unfairness becomes apparent. For example, the process of learning how to read lacks the potential, but the reading materials used for instruction may portray the sexes unfairly, and thus have this potential.

What exactly does it mean to be fair? One of the reasons why equity can be confusing is that there may be several different definitions operating simultaneously. First of all, "fair" can mean *neutral;* in other words, in most school situations it is simply irrelevant to recognize sex differences. For example, behind the old requirement that junior high girls take sewing and cooking and boys take shop was the presumption that boys are mechanical and girls are homemakers, an inaccurate presumption of some later life role, rather than the reality that all students will need a multitude of skills in their working and personal lives. Additional examples of this kind of unfairness would be discipline practices which differentiate girls from boys. Consider the two ten-year-old boys who are fighting on the school playground and receive a simple reprimand; two girls who are fighting in a similar fashion, however, are sent to the principal's office.

Other definitions of "fair" can mean *identical* treatment, such as providing the same treatment for both sexes. For example, in a public school district's interscholastic athletic programs, it is not fair for boys to have their uniforms laundered by the school, while the girls take care of this responsibility themselves. Or, "fair" in some instances, can mean *comparable;* consider a school that has eight interscholastic sports for boys and one for girls. Although identical treatment may not be possible, comparable treatment is. Or, "fair" can mean *differential;* perhaps recruitment or special encouragement is necessary to get boys into classes in family living, or girls onto the coed cross-country team. Because of years of past nonparticipation, differential treatment may be the only fair solution.

The final definition of "fairness" refers to how men and women are portrayed in texts and instructional materials. For example, if an elementary reader shows only boys and men as doing, thinking human beings without feelings and portrays only girls and women as nurturing, caring creatures who cry, worry, and, in general, stand on the sidelines of the action, we would call this depiction stereotyped or unfair. Such a portrayal is an incomplete representation of men and women as they actually exist, both groups fulfilling a variety of activities, roles and behaviors. Stereotyped depictions, then, are unfair because they fail to be *fully representational* of the diversity of real life.

Examples can be helpful in describing a sex fairness program or its reverse, a sexist one. Some common examples of sexism in school include the following: few women are in leadership positions, and few men teach in kindergarten or in the early elementary grades. Sporting events for girls are seldom promoted or publicized—no pep rallies or press coverage. An eighth grade American Cultures assignment asks students to write a report on an important American; the list of 50 names includes four women and two minorities. Students tease a young boy who prefers practicing the violin to playing baseball.

A teacher's behavior can prompt many examples: teachers who ask only boys to carry heavy books, who divide the girls and boys into competitive classroom teams; who punish the boys by making them sit with the girls; who meet a new class of students and assume the boys will be good in discussion and that the girls will be adept in taking notes; who are proud when a boy gets in a fight and upset when a girl does; who use "he" to refer to both boys and girls; who ask only girls to hostess at school functions instead of expecting boys to host as well, and who mark packages "boy" or "girl" in holiday gift exchanges.

Sometimes sexist behavior is unconscious and even well-intentioned. Consider the industrial arts teacher who welcomed girls into his classes, but then after presenting each class lesson, repeated it over again to the girls whom he had seated together, to give them "special help." By so doing, his behavior implied that he did not think the girls were capable enough to get the lesson the first time.

How does equity occur? A sex fair educational program grows out of a basic question: in what ways is education equitable for boys and girls in a school district? Sex fair education in an actual school district can refer to many different areas.

From the Superintendent and the School Board to every staff member, there is active commitment to the principles of equal educational opportunities for all students. This commitment did not occur overnight. It happened because the district revised and communicated school board policies on sex fairness and because the staff was trained to recognize what sexism is and how to change educational programs for sex fairness.

- All parts of the school program benefit children of both sexes since each child is treated as an individual with many educational and career options.
- The total curriculum has been reviewed and revised, where necessary, to remove sex bias.
- There may be sexist textbooks still used in some courses; however, the teachers using them have developed sex fair units and assignments to balance the texts. As books are replaced, sex fairness is one important criterion in their selection.
- Every course is open to students of both sexes. If a particular course—say Typing or Calculus—has been traditionally stereotyped, the district has taken action to remove the stigma and encourage interested students of both sexes to enroll in the course. The underlying philosophy is that everyone will need similar skills for earn-

ing a living, getting along with others, building a positive self-image, developing recreational interests, and managing in a complex world.

- By the same token, the extracurricular activities program is designed to encourage students of both sexes to join and take leadership roles.
- The media centers and libraries have a good selection of sex fair books, reference works and films for use by teachers and students.
- The guidance department counsels and encourages students on the basis of interest and ability, without regard to gender.
- Parents understand and support the program because the district established communications from the very beginning about the program's value to students of both sexes.
- Most students graduate understanding that outdated stereotypes need not restrict their futures in any way.
- Staffing patterns are changing so that there is a better balance of both sexes in teaching, administrative, and support positions.
- Such a program is founded on several basic principles which stand at the heart of sex fair education.

For Both Sexes. With a sex fair education, it is the individual—male or female—who stands at the center. In the past, countless students have been harmed by stereotypes—boys who considered themselves failures because they came in second or third or last; girls who skipped the more demanding courses because it wasn't the feminine thing to do; boys and girls who were encouraged to choose courses or careers on the basis of gender, without regard to interest or ability.

Different from Women's Studies. Although not synonymous with women's studies, sex fair education is based on the contributions feminist and women's studies scholars have made in all subject areas. Sex fair education should be always integrated into existing courses of study and not considered as an extra.

Focus on Professionalism. Sex fairness should be approached just as you would handle any other serious professional concern or educational change. Sex fairness is a serious responsibility for every educator and not a passing political fad. Even though most people are biased to some degree, educators should be able to separate personal bias from professional responsibilities.

Changing Behaviors and Attitudes. What is important is for educators to accept sex fairness as part of their professional behavior, regardless of what their personal beliefs might be. As people learn more about the principles of sex fair education, both behavior and attitudes can and do change. Facts, information, and understanding go a long way toward making sex fairness a meaningful part of school life.

Eliminating Bias Along With Discrimination. Opening all classes to both sexes is one way of getting rid of sex discrimination, which is against the law. Dealing with unconscious sexist attitudes of teachers and administrators is necessary for getting rid of sex bias.

Consideration of Minority Needs. Both short and long-term change are important. It's fairly easy to change course titles and open classes to children of both sexes. It may take longer, however, to make changes in behavior and attitudes. Just because there are girls present in Industrial Arts classes doesn't mean you automatically change the teacher's expectations of girls in that class.

In exploring the concept of sex fairness in education, it is essential to clarify basic definitions. If educators and parents do not fully comprehend fundamental purpose, as well as actual use, sex fair educational programs have little chance for being implemented by a district's staff and community. Only with complete understanding can confusion and resistance be minimized and equity provided. In the process of implementation, however, people's understanding of this complex topic may differ. Although some educators may understand the need for fairness in textbooks, they may have difficulty in recognizing bias in their own language and behavior. Others may realize how limiting stereotypes are for students, but they may miss the point of affirmative action. Part of the challenge of sex fair education is to get diverse types people working together and not insist that the sex fair educator be only one kind of person.

(Adapted from *Becoming Sex Fair*, the Tredyffrin/Easttown Sex Fairness Materials, developed and written by Marylyn E. Calabrese, Geraldine A. Edwards, and David H. Johnston).

The following statements are designed for the exploration of personal reactions to the chapter, as well as for the review of the contents of the chapter. Emphasis in discussions should be on exploring issues in depth, rather than on determining the correct or appropriate responses.

FOR DISCUSSION:

1. What is sex fair education?
2. Give additional examples for the different definitions of fair (i.e., neutral, identical, comparable, differential).
3. What does the author mean when she states that the learning process itself lacks the potential for fairness or unfairness?
4. Describe overt and covert examples of sex fair education in your institution.
5. Describe overt and covert examples of sex biased education in your institution. For each example, describe an alternative that is sex fair.
6. Evaluate an existing school activity that appears to be impossible to revise to become sex fair. Identify what characteristics of the activity need specific revision, and determine the goals and the necessary steps to make the activity sex fair. Include identification of key personnel, potential barriers to change, and sources of assistance.
7. What does the author mean by the closing statement: "Part of the challenge of sex fair education is to get diverse types of people working together and not insist that the sex fair educator be only one kind of person."
8. Can education ever be sex fair?

Chapter 7

WHAT IS TITLE IX?
AND FEDERAL ANTI-DISCRIMINATION LAWS
PERTAINING TO SCHOOLS

INTRODUCTION

"You have to do sex equity. It's the law."

In 1975 the regulations for Title IX of the Education Amendments of 1972 were published and disseminated to school districts and postsecondary institutions. For the first time, legislative guidelines pertaining to sex discrimination in education were specified for educators. The immediate reaction to the legislation was resistance on the part of many educational institutions (particularly because the legislation was not tied directly to sources of funding for carrying out the law), but compliance did occur, albeit sporadically. The law was intended to point out specific areas of possible discrimination in education, and to provide steps for remediation. As educational leaders became more informed about the legislation, concrete efforts were made to demonstrate compliance.

Recent court decisions have challenged the intent and content of Title IX. On February 28, 1984, the Supreme Court decided an important civil rights case: *Grove City College v. Bell.* The case significantly narrowed Title IX's prohibition against sex discrimination in any educational "program or activity receiving federal financial assistance."

When the Supreme Court handed down its *Grove City College v. Bell* decision on February 28, 1984, it, in effect, created a giant loophole through which institutions can now discriminate, even if they are receiving substantial contributions from the federal government. The Court ruled that since the student financial aid office was the only part of Grove City College which received direct federal funds it, alone, was subject to the anti-sex discrimination provisions of Title IX of the Education Amendments of 1972. Consequently, the rest of the college would be free to discriminate against women in any of its other programs and activities . . .

Immediately following the Grove City College decision, there was a strong, broad-based commitment to pass legislation to overturn the Court's decision. The Civil Rights Restoration Act of 1985, was introduced to do exactly what its title implies—to restore the principle that the entire institution receiving federal assistance must comply with the nondiscrimination requirements of federal law.

83

(NAACP Legal Defense and Educational Fund, Inc. Report, March 1986, p. 1, 6.)

A coalition of organizations representing minorities, women, the disabled, older Americans, and labor are continuing to work to secure the legislation's passage.

An antidiscrimination law, of course, does not guarantee gender equity in America's schools. Even if the law is obeyed and enforced, changes in attitudes and behaviors must occur before a school is truly equitable. An understanding of the negative effects of stereotyping and bias can lead to voluntary compliance with equity legislation. It can also lead to positive steps that assure participants in the educational system that they will have a fair and just educational experience.

The following chapter describes the basic information about the Title IX legislation. Specific resources for analyzing and fulfilling the legislative requirements are listed in Suggestions for Further Reading following the chapter.

WHAT IS TITLE IX?

Title IX of the Education Amendments of 1972 was the first comprehensive federal law to prohibit sex discrimination against students and employees of education institutions. It was passed after congressional hearings documented the widespread existence and consequences of sex discrimination in education.

According to the preamble to Title IX:

> No person in the United States shall, on the basis of sex, be excluded from participation in, be denied the benefits of, or be subjected to discrimination under any education program or activity receiving federal financial assistance.

Title IX is one of several federal and state antidiscrimination laws which define and ensure equality in education. It is patterned after Title VI of the Civil Rights Act of 1964 which prohibits discrimination on the basis of race, color, and national origin.

The language of Title IX generally makes it illegal to treat males and females differently or separately. In addition, districts are required to remedy the effects of past discrimination with affirmative measures when necessary. Without such remedial steps, equal access produces little real change in traditional patterns.

After a great deal of controversy and 10,000 written comments from citizens, the implementing regulations for Title IX were published in 1975. They prohibit discrimination, exclusion, denial, limitation, or separation based on gender. The regulations cover in detail the following areas relating to elementary and secondary schools:

- admissions and recruitment
- comparable facilities
- access to course offerings
- access to schools of vocational education
- counseling and counseling materials
- financial assistance
- student health and insurance benefits/services
- marital and parental status of students
- physical education and athletics
- education programs and activities
- employment

Several procedural requirements are also included in the regulations:
• designation of responsible employee(s)
• establishment of grievance procedure
• dissemination of nondiscrimination policy
• self-evaluation
• remedial and affirmative action

PROCEDURAL REQUIREMENTS

The following is a summary of the steps required for compliance with the legislation.

Self-Evaluation

Each education institution receiving federal funds (labeled recipient) should have evaluated its current policies and practices as to their compliance with the Title IX regulations by July 1976. Policies and practices that did not meet the requirements should have been modified, and remedial steps taken to eliminate the effects of discrimination. Self-evaluation should be an ongoing process. Ideally, self-evaluation would be conducted every school year to ensure continued compliance with the regulations.

Remedial and Affirmative Action

If a school system is found to have discriminated on the basis of sex, it can be required if it does not choose of its own initiative to take specific remedial steps to eliminate the discrimination and to overcome the effects of the discrimination.

A recipient is also allowed to take affirmative steps to increase participation of students in programs or activities where girls or boys have taken part only on a limited basis.

Designation of Responsible Employee

Every recipient must designate at least one employee to coordinate compliance efforts and investigate any complaints of sex discrimination. All students and employees must be notified of the name(s), office address(es), and telephone number(s) of the designated employee(s).

Grievance Procedure

Each recipient must adopt and publish grievance procedures to provide for prompt and equitable resolution of student and employee complaints of discrimination on the basis of sex. Utilization of these procedures is not necessary before a complainant seeks assistance from the federal Office for Civil Rights or files a formal complaint.

Dissemination of Policy

Each recipient must take specific and continuing steps to announce that it does not discriminate on the basis of sex. This notification must be made to applicants for admission, students, parents, and employees. It must also be sent to collective bargaining agencies and to those who may refer applicants for employment or admission.

The policy must be well-publicized and must include publication in local newspaper and school publications (including student newspapers) as well as in direct written communication with students, parents, and employees on at least a yearly basis.

Schools must carry a statement of nondiscrimination on the basis of sex in bulletins, handbooks, announcements, application forms, and any material which is used to recruit either students or employees.

Schools cannot use or distribute any material which suggests by words or pictures that students or employees are treated differently on the basis of sex.

All of these steps must be carried out on a continuing basis.

Public Announcement of Compliance

Title IX requires each school district identify the name(s), address(es), and telephone number(s) of the person(s) serving as the Title IX coordinator(s). Another federal law, Section 504 of the Rehabilitation Act of 1973, requires that similar public announcements be made to identify the Section 504 coordinator and the district's discrimination policy relating to handicapping conditions. In addition, the federal Office for Civil Rights issued Guidelines which require that school districts offer vocational education programs without regard to race, color, national origin, sex or handicap.

TREATMENT OF STUDENTS

The following is a summary of the eleven main components of the legislation.

Comparable Facilities

A recipient may provide separate toilet, locker, and shower facilities on the basis of sex; those provided for one sex must be comparable to those provided for the other.

Comparable facilities for physical education and athletics must be provided for all students.

Access to Course Offerings

Schools may neither require nor refuse participation in a course on the basis of sex. This prohibition includes physical education; health education; vocational and technical education; home economics, industrial, and business education; advanced placement courses; and adult education classes.

Students may be grouped by ability in physical education classes and activities as long as ability is assessed by objective standards developed and applied without regard to sex. Students may be separated by sex within physical education classes during participation in contact sports.

Portions of classes in elementary and secondary schools which deal exclusively with human sexuality may be conducted separately for males and females.

Recipient institutions may make requirements based on vocal range or quality which may result in choruses of one or predominantly one sex.

Access to Schools of Vocational Education

A local education agency may not exclude, on the basis of sex, any person from admission to a vocational education institution or any other school or unit operated by the agency.

Counseling and Counseling Materials

A recipient may not use assessment and counseling materials or methods that discriminate on the basis of sex. A recipient is required to ensure that materials are sex fair, including tests, pamphlets, and books on educational opportunities, careers, and occupations, and on many facets of personal growth and aspirations.

Recipients are also required to take steps to ensure that any disproportion in the numbers or percentages of males and females in classes is not due to discrimination on the basis of sex in counseling materials and practices.

Financial Assistance

Financial assistance to students may not be awarded on the basis of sex, with certain exceptions which are detailed in this section.

Although this section most frequently applies to colleges and universities that provide financial assistance in the form of tuition assistance, high school officials should also be mindful of its provisions. High schools are not allowed to solicit, list, approve, or assist any kind of financial aid which discriminates against students on the basis of their sex. For example, a school district may not provide monetary awards, or permit community organizations to use the school to promote such awards, for which gender is an eligibility criterion for receipt. Athletic scholarships offered only to members of single-sex teams are legal, but it then becomes the responsibility of the district to ensure availability of scholarships for athletes of the other sex, so that equality of opportunity is maintained.

The recipient may administer financial assistance established by legal instruments (e.g., trusts, wills) which require that awards be made to members of a specified sex provided that the overall effect of such sex-restricted awards does not discriminate on the basis of sex.

Employment Assistance

Before a school can assist an employer in seeking students for part-time or full-time work, the school must assure itself that the potential employer does not discriminate in employment on the basis of sex.

If a school itself offers employment to students, it must offer equal employment opportunities and equal pay to boys and girls.

Student Health Insurance Benefits and Services

The school district must make sure that its insurance policies provide the same full coverage for male and female students. If a school allows an insurance company to contact parents about purchasing insurance for students, these policies must also offer the same benefits for males and females.

Marital or Parental Status of Students

A district may not apply rules relating to parental, family, or marital status which treat students differently on the basis of sex. This regulation affects not only academic programs, but also any extracurricular activities or awards operated or sponsored by the school.

A student may not be excluded or treated differently because of pregnancy, childbirth, false pregnancy, termination of pregnancy, or recovery period. A pregnant student may not be kept out of any program, class, or extracurricular activity operated or sponsored by the school simply because she is pregnant or a parent.

Even if a district maintains a separate program for pregnant students, it cannot require pregnant students to attend the program. Such a program may be offered only on a completely voluntary basis.

Schools may not require notes from physicians before allowing pregnant students to take part in any program or activity, unless notes are required from all students who are seeing physicians for physical or emotional conditions.

Athletics

The general requirement of this section provides that no athletic programs or clubs, whether intermural or intramural, can be set up to exclude one sex or treat one sex differently from the other.

Within integrated programs, schools may have separate teams for girls and boys only if team members are chosen on the basis of competitive skills. Girls must be allowed to try out for the team in noncontact sports if the school does not sponsor a girls' team in the same sport and if athletic opportunities for girls at that school have been limited in the past. (Individual state educational policy boards, as well as court decisions, have determined specific interpretations of the Athletic component of Title IX. It is best to check with recent state guidelines for all aspects of the legislation.)

Where a school provides separate teams for male and female students in a particular sport, the regulation says that girls may compete on the boys' team with the approval of the school superintendent or principal, but that boys may not participate on teams organized for girls where a team for boys is also provided. This would be allowed where the level of competition on the girls' team would not be challenging to the girls desiring to play on the boys' team.

Equal opportunity is required for both sexes in interscholastic athletics, school clubs, and intramural games sponsored by the school.

Equal dollar for dollar expenditures on girls' and boys' separate athletic activities are not required, but failure to "provide necessary funds" will be taken into consideration when assessing equality of opportunity for members of each sex.

Education Programs and Activities

No person shall, on the basis of sex, be excluded from participation in, be denied the benefits of, or be subjected to discrimination under any academic, extracurricular, research, occupational training, or other education program or activity operated by a recipient which receives federal assistance. A recipient is also prohibited from cooperating with any agency, organization, or person that discriminates on the basis of sex in providing help, benefits, or services to students. Equal access and treatment of all students in educational programs is mandated by Title IX.

Employment

Discrimination on the basis of sex is prohibited in employment as well as employee recruitment and selection. The provisions apply to advertising, upgrading, promotion, tenure, layoffs, termination, rates of pay, job classification, collective bargaining, leave, fringe benefits, financial support for training, preemployment inquiries, pregnancy, marital or parental status, and employer-sponsored activities. The most common violation of Title IX concerns a district's failure to provide child care leave to males when it is offered to females and treatment of pregnancy differently than any other temporary disability.*

---

*Source: *A manual for Title IX coordinators: Sex equity in New York State schools.* Occupational Education Civil Rights Coordinating Unit, New York State Education Department, Albany, New York, 1987.

FEDERAL ANTI-DISCRIMINATION LAWS PERTAINING TO SCHOOLS

Law	Area of Discrimination	Covers	Enforced By*
14th Amendment of the U.S. Constitution, 1868	Rights of citizens	Employees and students	Office for Civil Rights
Equal Pay Act, 1963	Sex (in pay)	Employees	Dept. of Labor
Title VI, Civil Rights Act of 1964	Race, color, and national origin	Students	Office for Civil Rights
Title VII, Civil Rights Act of 1964	Race, sex, color, national origin and religion (in employment)	Employees	Equal Employment Opportunity Commission
Executive Order 11246 (as amended by E.O. 11375), 1968	Race, sex, color, national origin and religion	Employees	Office for Civil Rights
Title IX, Education Amendments of 1972	Sex	Employees and students	Office for Civil Rights
Rehabilitation Act, 1973 (Section 504)	Handicapped	Employees and students	Office for Civil Rights
Education for all Handicapped Children Act Public Law 94-142, 1976	Handicapped	Students	Office for Civil Rights
Pregnancy Discrimination Act, 1978	Sex (pregnancy)	Employees	Equal Employment Opportunity Commission
Age Discrimination in Employment Act, amended 1978	Age	Employees	Dept. of Labor and Office for Civil Rights
Guidelines for Eliminating Discrimination and Denial of Services on the Basis of Race, Color, National Origin, Sex and Handicap	Race, color, national origin, sex, and handicap	Employees and students	Office for Civilg Rights
Carl D. Perkins Vocational Education Act, 1984	Sex (also national origin and handicap)	Students	Office for Civil Rights

(Prepared by Michael J. Moon, Division of Civil Rights and Intercultural Relations, New York State Education Department.)

Chapter 8

SEXISM: STILL AN ISSUE IN EDUCATION

CECELIA H. FOXLEY

INTRODUCTION

"Sexism? Oh, that's been solved."

If recent national reports on the status of American education were to be used as the ultimate guide, sex equity would not be an educational issue. Even though sex role stereotyping, bias, and discrimination in education affect the personal success and well-being of most K–12 students, they were not considered to be of significant concern to evaluators of current educational systems. None of the reports issued over the last five years suggested that gender inequities in education can influence student attitudes, achievement, and actions in and out of school.

Despite the reports, sexism is still an issue in education. Schools are intended to be designed for the best opportunities to learn. If opportunities are diminished for *any* reason (e.g., safety, racism, finances, geographical setting) then those problems merit attention and solutions. If opportunities are limited because of gender, then sex equity as a solution deserves attention also.

But has not sex equity been achieved? After all, there was the Title IX legislation, the Women's Movement, a considerable amount of media attention, and several changes in school programs. It appears that the athletic fields, industrial arts classrooms, bus driver seats, and colleges are filled with women. These gains in representation of girls and women seem to provide evidence that inequality in education is no longer a problem.

But a review of classrooms and jobs reveals that, although several changes have occurred over the last decade, proof of achievement of equity cannot be shown. The math and science classrooms, the computer labs, and the technology courses are dominated by males. Employment related to those fields are, too. The textbooks, reading material, and instructional resources still stress archaic notions of women and men. Schools are managed primarily by men, and women dominate the elementary grades and the subject areas traditionally taught by women. Men rarely teach the primary grades, home economics, and subject areas traditionally taught by women.

Most importantly, the school experiences of boys and girls differ. Of course they must be in separate locker rooms, sex education classes, and even choirs if necessary. But beyond division for reasons of anatomy and privacy, students

95

should receive the same education. Their options, experiences, and expectations should match their skills and their interests. Overt and covert sexism stands in the way of equal education. It often is so pervasive, institutionalized, that it has become part of the educational system. Indeed, sex bias can be present, yet invisible to those who do not comprehend the forms of its existence. It certainly was invisible to the authors of recent education reports. Cecelia H. Foxley discusses how to recognize that sexism still exists and suggests how to eradicate the remaining barriers to complete sex equity.

SEXISM: STILL AN ISSUE IN EDUCATION

Focusing on sex equality in the schools has never been easy, even with strong legal backing. With diminished legal protection and little interest in sex equity shown by the Reagan administration, providing educational equity for students of both sexes continues to be an uphill struggle. This is especially true in light of other pressing problems and competing issues facing education today. Traditional concepts of educational quality and opportunity are being reevaluated. And political, judicial, and regulatory institutions are exerting new influence in educational decision-making.

In no other era in our history have so many public and private organizations issued reports recommending reform in American education. The release of the National Commission on Excellence in Education's report, *A Nation at Risk: The Imperative for Educational Reform* (1983), began an onslaught of major national reports calling for reform in education at all levels. These reports provided impetus for state governments and state education departments and commissions to draft reports of their own, all focusing on the need for increasing the quality of education.

With all of this attention on the need to increase the quality of American education, none of the major reports address in any substantive way the need to improve educational equity for male and female students. If the topic is mentioned at all, it is done very briefly.

And without some impetus and encouragement at the national level, few educators and administrators at the local level will bother to be concerned about sex equity. Indeed, declining numbers of students in public schools in several states have produced teacher surpluses and layoffs. Many teachers who were once aggressive in pushing for sex equity in schools are now much more complaisant and on the defensive as jobs are eliminated. In states where the student-age population is increasing, revenues supporting education are not keeping pace. Thus, larger class size and expanded teaching loads result, leaving teachers even less time to be concerned about issues such as differential treatment on the basis of sex.

Enough Progress? . . . Other More Pressing Problems?

There is an attitude among some educators and educational administrators that America has paid enough attention to sex equity issues in the 1970s during which time many gains were made, and it is now time to focus on other issues. Certainly, there are many other issues and problems which merit our attention: increased drug use among school-age population; increased violence in the schools; increased teenage pregnancies . . . and the list goes on. But these problems, as serious as they are, should not cause us to ignore other important problems, the solutions of which may have a positive impact on these other issues as well. It just may be that if the schools were viewed as environments which supported and valued all individuals regardless of their sex, race, ability/disability, etc., students might rely less on drugs and violence as ways of solving their problems.

Despite the sex equity problems which still exist, many forms of sex discriminatory policies and practices in education have been abolished, making way for equal opportunity in course selection, college admissions, and extracurricular activities. A good fifteen years have passed since restrictions for women existed in these areas. We now take these opportunities for granted.

All courses at all levels of education (with the exception of sex education courses in the public schools and contact sports classes in high schools and colleges) are open to students of both sexes. While it is no longer uncommon for girls to take courses in mechanical and industrial arts and boys to take courses in home economics and family life (National Advisory Council on Women's Educational Progress, 1981), there is still not a balanced distribution of males and females in courses which were once restricted to students on the basis of their sex.

Selection criteria for admissions are applied equally to men and women. This has made a marked difference in college enrollments. For the first time since World War II, women college students outnumbered men students in 1979, and have continued to do so. In 1982, 51.6 percent of all college students were women. In that same year the Census Bureau estimated that women accounted for 51.3 percent of the total U.S. population. Thus, it could be said that women have a more than proportionate representation in college enrollments (Magarrell, 1982). Their numbers have continued to increase; 1985 college enrollments were 52.5 percent female (*Chronicle of Higher Education,* 1986).

Of particular import is the influx of women into traditionally male fields such as business, engineering, medicine, and law, and the influx of men into traditionally female fields such as nursing, early childhood development education, and secretarial science. For example, from 1972 to 1982, the proportion of women in law school rose from 12 percent to 39 percent; in medical school, from 11 percent to 29 percent; in dental school, from 2 percent to 20 percent; and in veterinary school, from 12 percent to 46 percent (Sandler, 1984). The proportion of women among first-year business majors rose from 30 percent in 1967 to 52 percent in 1981; during the same time frame, first-year engineering majors increased from 2 percent to 17 percent (Fields, 1984). While the increase of men in traditionally female fields has not been as marked, it is still meaningful.

With these enrollment trends, it is not surprising that women are obtaining an increasing proportion of college degrees at every level. The chart below illustrates this progress.

Percentage of Degrees Earned by Women

	1971–72	*1979–80*	*1984–85*
B.A.	44%	49%	51%
M.A.	41%	50%	50%
Ph.D.	16%	30%	34%
Professional	6%	25%	33%

Source: U.S. Department of Education, National Center for Educational Statistics, 1973, 1981, 1986.

The gains made in degrees awarded to women in some of the traditionally male fields during the same time period (1972–1985) include: agriculture (6% to 31%), business and management (10% to 45%, engineering (1% to 15%), law (7% to 38%), medicine (9% to 30%), dentistry (1% to 21%), and veterinary science (9% to 45%).

Extracurricular programs and activities, including athletics, provide developmental opportunities for male and female students on a more equitable basis than ever before. More female students are elected into leadership positions at both the high school and college levels. There has also been increased participation of women students in sports activities.

In the decade from 1971 to 1981, the percentage of female participants in interscholastic high school sports increased from 7 percent to 35 percent. Similarly on the college level, women are now 30 percent of all participants in intercollegiate athletics programs, compared to less than 15 percent in the early 1970s (Women's Equity Action League, 1980).

Some authors have focused on the developmental advantages men have by participating in team sports when they were young. It is thought that this sense of "team effort" carries over into the organizational work setting (Henning and Jordin, 1977).

Problems Still Needing Attention

The gains in sex equity in education discussed above were not made easily. They represent years of struggle on the part of many people and considerable financial cost to educational institutions. While such progress is laudable, many problems still remain. But the problems still remaining will be even more difficult to overcome, either because they entail extensive attitude and behavior change, because the cost of solving them seems prohibitive, or because the federal government is currently viewed as not particularly supportive of sex equity issues. None of these reasons should keep us from addressing these problems, however.

With some exceptions, teacher preparation programs have not effectively included instruction and practicum experiences dealing with sexism and sex role stereotyping topics. We can point to examples of positive efforts being made due to several states requiring such instruction as part of a human relations component, or recommendations of accreditation teams, or special projects receiving outside funding. But the usual argument we hear for not instructing future teachers about sexism is the fact that teacher preparation programs are already packed full of education requirements and adding another requirement would mean something else would have to be excluded.

An analysis of teacher education textbooks published between 1973 and 1978 (Sadker and Sadker, 1979) illustrated that 23 of 24 tests devoted less than one percent of their space to the consideration of sex equity concerns—even those books which dealt with science and mathematics education, areas in which there are notable sex differences in student achievement. And not a single text in the study included strategies and resources designed to combat sex stereotyping and differential treatment in the classroom. Until teacher preparation programs and materials are updated to include the topic of sex role stereotyping and sexism, there is little chance of sending aware and informed teachers to the classroom.

More men are becoming elementary school teachers. Thirty years ago only one elementary school teacher in 14 was a man. Today, approximately one in five is male (U.S. Department of Education, 1981). Studies of students' problems in school (especially at the elementary level) consistently report the boys have more difficulties in classroom adjustment and learning. Some researchers feel these problems may be due in part or at least exacerbated by the male students' view of early school setting as a "feminized environment" with few male role models (Goldman and May, 1970; McFarland, 1968). If there is a relationship here, having more male elementary school teachers may help diminish some of the adjustment and learning problems of many male students.

While effort to bring more male teachers into the elementary schools has had some success, and there appears to be a rather equitable balance between male and female teachers at the secondary level, there is a clear sex demarcation in subjects taught. Approximately two-thirds of the teachers of industrial arts, agriculture, science, math, music, social studies are male (Stockard, et al., 1980). This differentiation by subject matter closely parallels occupations of men and women in the work force. We clearly need a better balance of staffing by subject matter to promote a wider range of role models for students.

A similar pattern is seen among the faculty in colleges and universities, with only 25 percent of the teaching staff being female (*Academe,* 1985). While university administrators have proudly pointed to their colleges of education as "proof" they hire women faculty (since many of their colleges have token female representatives or none at all) close scrutiny of individual colleges of education will show that most of the women faculty will be in elementary education, English education, home economics education, special education, or counselor education. Very few are in departments of educational administration, or higher education or specialty areas such as science education or math education. Also, despite over fifteen years of affirmative action efforts, the majority of the women faculty are still in the lower ranks of lecturer, instructor and assistant professor. Nationwide, only 10 percent of the full professors are female. Only 47 percent of women faculty are tenured, compared to 69 percent of the men. In addition, women faculty members earn only 85 percent of the salary earned by their male counterparts (Sandler, 1984, 1986).

The area in which women are most noticeably absent at all levels of education is administration. Less than 1 percent of the school superintendents are women. Only about 14 percent of school principals are women, and they are more likely to be in small elementary schools and in urban areas. This represents a severe decline from 55 percent of the elementary school principals in 1928 (Howard, 1980). This trend has a chance to be reversed as almost 30 percent of the Ph.D.s in educational administration and supervision are now earned by women. At the college level, only eight percent of the presidents, 12 percent of the academic vice presidents, and 18 percent of the deans are women. Women are less likely to be top level administrators at large, coeducational schools and in public institutions than at private schools with enrollments of fewer than 1,000 students (Howard, 1980). Approximately 90 percent of all college students attend institutions where the three top administrative officers—president, academic vice president, and dean— are male (Sandler, 1984).

Although considerable attention has been given the topics of math anxiety and science anxiety, and sex differences in motivation orientation and achievement in these subjects, males generally take more mathematics and science courses and tend to achieve at slightly higher levels than females in high school (Fox, Fennema, and Sherman, 1977; Steinkamp and Maehr, 1984).

Girls' equal participation in secondary school mathematics and science is discouraged by elementary math and science textbooks in which girls appear much less often than boys, by the infrequency of female role models teaching math and science in junior high and high school, and by the sex stereotyped perception of many teachers, counselors, parents, and peers that math and science are not important for female career patterns. Both male and female students perceive math and science as "male domains," and several studies show that while high school teachers of these subjects may intend to treat students of both sexes equitably, there are both quantitative and qualitative differences in how they interact with male and female students (Kreinberg, 1983). Perhaps because math and science teachers have different expectations for male and female students, they tend to interact more with male students, call on them more frequently to answer questions, ask them more difficult questions, and give them more individual help. In short, male students receive more encouragement for their work than do female students. There should be no surprise that male students fulfill their teachers' expectations and outperform the female students.

Ignatz (1982) found that boys and girls employ different cognitive styles when learning physics, but with equally successful results. As teachers become more aware of learning style differences and recognize their own and students' stereotypical attitudes regarding sex differences in math and science, we should expect to see more female students excel in these subjects. Several successful programs designed to facilitate this kind of awareness and training (Kreinberg, 1983) are: *Multiplying Options and Subtracting Bias, Expanding Your Horizons in Science and Mathematics,* and *Women and Mathematics.*

Upon entering college, women students' academic options are severely limited if they have had insufficient preparation in high school science and mathematics. Their entry into college majors and occupational education programs in scientific and technical fields is restricted by lack of appropriate academic preparation.

Far too few educators at all levels, kindergarten through college, are willing to take the necessary time and effort to analyze their own attitudes regarding sex roles and their behavior towards students which may indeed be stereotypic. Many well-meaning educators firmly believe in sex equity when it comes to educational opportunities, but still treat male and female students differently due to habit, fail to point out inequities and sexist elements in educational materials, and avoid pointing out sexist behaviors and attitudes in students and colleagues (Foxley, 1979). It takes conscious effort to do these things. And it's hard work. No change in school policy will cause these things to happen. No law can require it. And such personalized efforts would be impossible to monitor. Educators and educational administrators must want to make the effort because they believe it is right and because it will make them more effective in their work.

Solutions to Remaining Problems

Solving the remaining impediments to complete sex equity in education will not be easy, especially with the existing fiscal constraints and lessening federal backing on affirmative action issues. But there are some things all of us as educators and educational administrators at all levels can do. Those of us in higher education can ask: What kind of shape are our own colleges of education in regarding sex equity? With the few faculty vacancies we have in the next few years, we must endeavor to appoint women in areas and specialties where they are not now represented. We must encourage and help prepare more women for department heads and deanships. In the name of professional development, faculty renewal, and inservice training, we need to see that our own faculty members have ample opportunity for self-examination of sexist attitudes and behaviors. We need to examine our curricula for sexist content and ensure that those individuals now receiving their professional training become aware of sexist elements in the high schools and learn ways of combating sexism. We need to encourage and support special training and research projects dealing with sex inequities in education. We also need to continue to provide leadership in attending to the problems caused by sexism in education by working collaboratively with the public schools, parent and community groups, state departments of education, and state and national professional associations.

Regardless of our school setting (elementary, secondary, or higher education) we need to continually assess ourselves, our colleagues and our school systems by asking the following questions:

- Do I view my students in sex role stereotypic ways? Do I treat them differently on the basis of sex? Am I willing to change my own attitudes and behaviors?
- Do I observe other school personnel treating students or each other differently on the basis of sex?
- Are there any school policies or practices still existing which treat males and females differently? If so, can these be changed?
- Are instructional materials and curricula reviewed for sexism and replaced/corrected when resources allow?
- Does the staffing profile provide for a wide range of role models for students?
- Am I willing to speak up when I observe an incident which is contrary to the equal treatment of persons regardless of their sex?

If each of us is willing to ask these questions and then take actions to affirm our values of equality and fairness, we can collectively continue the progress made in this area. Some specific suggestions for facilitating increased self-awareness, improved classroom practices and behaviors, and improved school environments outside the classroom can be found in Colangelo, Dustin, and Foxley (1985). A collection of learning exercises and experiences designed for instructors and students are contained in Colangelo, Dustin, and Foxley (1982).

The goal of equal educational opportunity for female and male students can be reached, with the end result being the improved quality of education. But it will take all of us working in concert to do it.

REFERENCES

Colangelo, N., Dustin, R., & Foxley, C.H. *The human relations experience: Exercises in multicultural, nonsexist education.* Monterey, California: Brooks/Cole Publishers, 1982.

Colangelo, N., Dustin, R., & Foxley, C.H. (Eds.) *Multicultural nonsexist education: A human relations approach,* Revised Edition. Dubuque, Iowa: Kendall/Hunt Publishing Company, 1985.

Cordes, C. Rights of women, minorities threatened by Title IX ruling. *APA monitor,* April 1984, 2.

Education Commission on the States. *Action for excellence.* Denver, Colorado: Distribution Center, Education Commission of the States, 1983.

Fact-file—Fall 1985 enrollment. *Chronicle of higher education.* October 1986.

Fields, C.M. Big rise in female engineering majors found. *Chronicle of higher education,* May 9, 1984, 14.

Fox, L.H., Fennema, E., & Sherman, J. *Women and mathematics: Research perspectives for change.* Washington, D.C.: National Institute of Education, 1977.

Foxley, C.H. *Nonsexist counseling: Helping women and men redefine their roles.* Dubuque, Iowa: Kendall/Hunt Publishing Company, 1979.

Goldman, W.J., & May, A. Males: A minority group in the classroom. *Journal of learning disabilities,* 1970, *3,* 276–278.

Henning, M., & Jordin, A. *The managerial woman.* New York: Simon and Schuster, 1977.

Howard, S. *Fact sheet on women in educational administration.* Alexandria, Virginia: American Association of School Administrators, 1980.

Ignatz, M. Sex differences in predictive ability of tests of structure-of-intellect factors relative to a criterion examination of high school physics achievement. *Educational and psychological measurement,* Spring 1982, *42* (1), 353–360.

Kreinberg, N. Moving women and minorities into math. *Educational horizons,* Winter 1983, 61 (2), 57–67.

McFarland, W. Are girls really smarter? *Elementary school journal,* 1968, *70* (1), 14–19.

Magarrell, J. Student enrollment. *Chronicle of higher education,* November 1982, *1,* 7.

National Advisory Council on Women's Educational Progress, U.S. Department of Education. *Title IX: The half full, half empty glass.* Washington, D.C.: U.S. Government Printing Office, 1981.

National Commission on Excellence in Education. *A nation at risk: The imperative for educational reform,* Washington, D.C., April 1983.

Percent distribution of full-time faculty. *Academe,* 1984–85, November–December 1985.

Sadker, M., & Sadker, D. *Beyond pictures and pronouns: Sexism in teacher education textbooks.* Washington, D.C.: U.S. Government Printing Office, 1981.

Sandler, B.R. *The campus climate revisited: Chilly for women faculty, administrators, and graduate students.* Washington, D.C.: Association of American Colleges, Project on the Status and Education of Women, October 1986.

Sandler, B.R. The quiet revolution on campus: How sex discrimination has changed. *Chronicle of higher education,* February 29, 1984, 72.

Steinkamp, M.W., & Maehr, M.L. Gender differences in motivational orientations toward achievement in school science: A quantitative synthesis. *American educational research journal,* 1984 (21), 39–59.

Stockard, J., Schmuck, P.A., Kempner, K., Williams, P., Edison, S.K., & Smith, M.A. *Sex equity in education.* New York: Academic Press, 1980.

Twentieth Century Fund. *Report of the twentieth century fund task force on federal elementary and secondary education policy.* New York: New York: The Twentieth Century Fund, 1983.

U.S. Department of Education, National Center for Educational Statistics. *Digest of education statistics.* Washington, D.C.: U.S. Government Printing Office, 1973, 1981, 1986.

Women's Equity Action League Education and Legal Defense Fund. *SPRINT project: Evidence of growth in the participation of women in sports.* Washington, D.C., 1980.

The following statements are designed for the exploration of personal reactions to the chapter, as well as for the review of the contents of the chapter. Emphasis in discussions should be on exploring issues in depth, rather than on determining the correct or appropriate responses.

FOR DISCUSSION:

1. Would your colleagues agree with the author's premise that sexism still exists in education?
2. If possible, note the changes in your educational organization that have occurred as a result of attempts to achieve equity. What is your reaction to those changes?
3. How could pre-service teacher education and/or staff development experiences includes sex equity as part of the training?
4. Respond to the author's statement: "Far too few educators at all levels, kindergarten through college, are willing to take the necessary time and effort to analyze their own attitudes regarding sex roles and their behavior towards students which may indeed be stereotypic."
5. Do students express concern about sexism in education?
6. What does the author mean by "Certainly there are many other issues and problems which merit our attention . . . But these problems . . . should not cause us to ignore other important problems, the solutions of which may have a positive impact on these other issues as well"?
7. The author describes a "conscious effort" to eliminate inequities in education. Describe a situation(s) where you observed sexism. Describe possible actions to make the situation equitable. Discuss possible repercussions for any attempts at achieving equity.
8. What does the author mean by the statement: "No law can require (equity.)"

SUGGESTIONS FOR FURTHER READING

Constitutional Rights Foundation. *Bill of Rights in action.* Los Angeles, California, 1983.

Kaser, J. *It's your right!* Andover, Massachusetts: The Network, Inc., 1984.

Klinman, D. *Teacher skill guide for combatting sexism.* Newton, Massachusetts: EDC/WEEA Publishing Center, 1979.

Leadership Conference on Civil Rights. *Brief fact sheet on the bipartisan Civil Rights Restoration Act of 1985.* Washington, D.C., 1985.

The NAAC Legal Defense and Education Fund, Inc. *Justice denied: The loss of civil rights after the Grove City College decision.* Washington, D.C., 1986.

National Women's History Project. *Title IX student advocacy unit.* Santa Rosa, California, 1981.

Project on Equal Education Rights. *Beyond Title IX: PEER's state-by-state guide to women's educational equity laws.* Washington, D.C., 1985.

Project on Equal Education Rights. *Cracking the glass slipper: PEER's guide to ending sex bias in your schools.* Washington, D.C., 1978.

Project on Equal Education Rights. *Injustice under the law: The impact of the Grove City College decision on civil rights in America.* Washington, D.C., 1985.

Project on Equal Education Rights. *Summary of the regulation for Title IX Education Amendments of 1972.* Washington, D.C., 1978.

Project on the Status and Education of Women. *Title IX packet, Legal requirements packet, Title IX and sports packet.* Washington, D.C.: Association of American Colleges, 1975, 1985.

Project SERVE. *1986–87 catalog of resources.* Sacramento, California: Vocational and Occupational Information Center for Educators, 1987.

Reed, T. *Destination . . . sex-fair education.* Harrisburg, Pennsylvania: Vocational Education Equity Program, 1980.

Sargent, A. *Beyond sex roles* (2nd ed.). New York: West Publishing Company, 1985.

United States Department of Health, Education, and Welfare (Department of Education-Office for Civil Rights). *Final Title IX regulation implementing Education Amendments of 1972.* Washington, D.C., 1975.

Chapter 9

STEREOTYPING AND CLASSROOM INTERACTIONS

CRAIG FLOOD

INTRODUCTION

"But they like to sit by their friends!"

It could be quickly assumed that sex bias in an educational setting is created and perpetuated by the classroom instructor. Administrators set and influence policy, and guidance counselors advise and direct students, but it is the teacher who has constant daily interactions with boys and girls in the classroom. Teachers consistently participate in or lead peer-to-peer conversations, classroom debates, student-to-teacher questioning, class discussions, and other means of communication with students. Topics of discussion are rarely limited to academics only, and teachers profoundly influence student thoughts and behaviors.

The implication, therefore, can be that teachers manipulate, whether consciously or not, the type of communication that takes place. Through regular classroom interactions, it can be concluded that they alone can determine whether the environment is sex biased or not.

But a more sensible view of classroom interactions is that *both* the student and teacher are constantly creating, revising, perpetuating, and reducing sex bias. Each student crosses the threshold of the school with a foundation of learned stereotypes and biased observations, expectations, and experiences. Each teacher does the same. The range and type of notions about sex roles varies extensively amongst all of the participants in the educational process. Some students and teachers, for example, have had little experience in recognizing sex bias in American culture. Others have been exposed to readings, discussions, and lifestyles that attempt to reduce sex bias. This mixture of ideas, values, and knowledge is represented in a classroom setting.

To assume that the teacher alone is responsible for perpetuating bias in classroom interactions is to declare that the teacher has had control over the socialization of all of the students and of himself or herself. Like any issue in education, it is critical to understand that students come in many different forms, and it is up to the teacher to assess, intervene, and build on what is given to them. Teachers who understand their *own* viewpoints (and actions) related to sex equity can then recognize the same with their students. They will be caught in interactions that are simply a reflection of society. They should be encouraged to look more closely at the fairness of the interactions to determine if all students are treated equitably. If they are able to see that the activity in the classroom requires further attention and a different form of education, then they are able to reevaluate the interactions and convey strong bias-free messages.

Craig Flood discusses the many different factors that influence the potential for biased classroom interactions.

STEREOTYPING AND CLASSROOM INTERACTIONS

Most educators would agree with the premise that schools are meant to provide equal educational opportunity for all students: certainly the excellence in education movement is grounded, in part, by the principle. This is the notion that *all* students need to be "dealt" into the process of education in an equitable manner. As we have witnessed with the Civil Rights movement, the fruition of such a precept is far more easy to realize on paper than it is in practice. While not making the task at hand any easier, the issue of sex equity in the classroom may bring such efforts into sharper focus.

The classroom is a reflection of society in many respects. The pervasive quality of sex role stereotypes and expectations in our society precludes their presence in the classroom. Teachers and students alike bring into the classroom setting a lifetime of perceptions, attitudes, values, and behaviors, some of which are based on stereotypical notions about the roles of men and women, and boys and girls in our society. It is critical in understanding this chapter to recognize the fact that both teachers and students have been affected by these notions before entering the classroom. Though such a view brings to bear an overwhelming number of variables on the makeup of a classroom, it is the only honest way in which to view the social environment of the classroom; the interactions between students and teachers, students and students, and the organizational structure that is established through those interactions. To negate the presence of any of those variables in the social setting is simplistic and only serves to detract from the richness of that environment.

Such a view of the classroom and the recognition of the multiple variables found with respect to interactions also presumes that no one area is anymore responsible for the problems that arise in creating an equitable classroom environment. Nor is any one area lacking the need for a conscious response and effort on the parts of teachers and students to become more aware of the need to "deal all students into the game" in an equitable manner.

The research does indicate gender differences in the interactions and organizational structures that are found in classrooms. While this article does not intend to disregard any of the significant variables in the mix, it will isolate certain areas for the sake of a closer view. In reading the article and examining the various areas in isolation it is important to understand that the research and commentary should not be construed as blaming or "pointing the finger" at any one party, but rather is done for the sake of clarity.

Though teacher-student interactions have typically been a focus in looking at the issue of stereotyping in classrooms, such a view does not necessarily consider the "whole picture." While it may be easier to concentrate on teachers as the causes of specific problems cited in the research, it is quite another issue to expect those teachers, the receivers of this information, to understand and embrace any effort to effect lasting solutions to the problems while staring at a pointed finger. A more sensitive and meaningful approach is to consider such behavior as a reflection of the social constructs and expectations that frame much of our behavior in the general social setting.

Furthermore, it is quite clear that gender differences are not found only in teacher-student interactions, but, as previously stated, are only part of a complex set of variables that presumes a wide range of interactions, behaviors, and structural characteristics found in classrooms. This chapter will present an overview of those variables in order to develop a conceptual framework more accurately based on a global view of these patterns in classrooms. Finally, it will examine some proven intervention strategies and practical suggestions for encouraging more equitable approaches in classrooms.

The following areas will be considered in examining the issue of gender and classroom interaction:

- Stereotyping and interactions
- Teacher-student interactions
- Student-student interactions
- Intervention strategies

The article will focus on research as well as personal experience and anecdotal references. The intent is to present a practical examination of these issues as they relate to the needs of educators in understanding the integral role that they play in creating interventions that will have lasting effects in the development of a more equitable school environment for all students.

Stereotyping and Interaction: A Powerful Mix

Thus far the articles in this book have provided a comprehensive picture of the concepts of sex role stereotyping and bias. More specifically, readers have been shown how those concepts have formed the underpinnings of many of our notions about the kinds of behaviors that are expected of boys and girls, and men and women based on the stereotypes with which we are all familiar. So much of social interaction has relied on those ideas in order to frame and give some structure to the behavioral responses between men and women. It is one thing to be aware of sex role stereotyping and its effects in an objective sense, and most teachers with whom I have worked initially indicate an awareness of these issues. But many do question why it is still even an issue in our enlightened times. They generally have never taken a step beyond the awareness to assume a more active part in understanding, subjectively, their individual role in perpetuating or more importantly eliminating bias in their own behavior. Personal awareness is most assuredly the first step in that process, but it presumes the ability to look at one's own behavior and make judgements about the changes necessary to move toward a more equitable approach.

Perhaps it is necessary, by way of example, to look subjectively at the "power" of sex role stereotyping in guiding our behavior. Of importance here is the need to create an understanding of the fact that most individuals are not immune to acting on the basis of stereotyped notions. Consider the following confession.

I have worked for a statewide sex equity project for the past four years. My role in addition to keeping fully apprised of the issues involved in that field, has been to work directly with educators, through workshops and a graduate course, to assist them in recognizing the need for and ultimately in creating a more equitable school/classroom environment. My awareness of the concept of sex role stereotyping and its effects can be presumed to be intimate.

While driving to work recently I passed a construction site. Glancing briefly at the site, I noticed a woman operating an air hammer. Within seconds (the time it took to drive by the site) I realized that I had, in the recesses of my consciousness, listed a number of reasons why there was something "wrong" with that picture. Surely, it must just be a summer job for her; at least she doesn't see it as a career. What is she doing handling such dangerous and heavy equipment? She must know someone to have gotten the job. Why is an attractive young woman doing such a dirty job?

The list was longer. Once I was aware of what I was doing, I "hauled" the thoughts more squarely into my consciousness and spent the remainder of my ride marvelling at the "power" of my unconsciousness to frame such a response. Despite the fact that I "live and breathe" equity issues, my perceptions of situations can be/are still given to the unconscious power of sex role stereotypes.

The bright light in this observation is that I was able to "catch" myself in the act and examine my reaction before it ever became played out as biased behavior. However, can I be sure that I can catch all of those moments? Clearly, because of my increased awareness, I do catch more now than I did four years ago. Now consider for a moment how those thoughts might have played themselves out in some behavioral sense. What if I were a teacher in a vocational education center that was attempting to increase it's nontraditional enrollment in the construction trades? Think about yourself. Perhaps you can draw on a similar experience. Think about a stereotyped expectation you might have about a boy or girl in your class. Try to imagine that expectation being played out in your interaction with that student in the classroom setting.

I have obviously used this example to illustrate how, despite our best intentions, our perceptions of situations can be guided unconsciously by biased expectations and then ultimately may have some effect on the individuals with whom we interact. In trying to be equitable with our students, keep in mind the not-too-subtle power of sex role stereotypes. Because of the "opposite" nature of these stereotypes, what is stereotypically expected of one gender is necessarily not expected of the other gender. There is really no "grey-area": one group is automatically excluded if sex-role stereotypes are allowed to become biased practice in any social setting.

Now think about the number of interactions we have each day with other individuals. In classrooms alone it has been estimated that teachers have as many as 1000 interactions with students during the course of a day. This statistic is not meant to overwhelm, but more to place in some meaningful perspective the idea that many of our interactions (directives, responses, reactions, conversations, etc.) take place so often that we barely/rarely/or never have the time to consciously examine how we interact the way we do with students. If what we know about the power of stereotyping in framing our perceptions of situations and behavioral interactions with others has any validity, then it would be naive to assume that the interactions that take place within the classroom would be free of such bias. We need then to begin to recognize the "baggage" that we carry into the classroom and how it might effect our interactions with students.

Classroom Interactions

Classroom research over the past thirty years has established the existence of gender-based differences in teacher-student interaction and communication patterns. The research has specifically cited differential treatment of males and females in a broad range of classroom settings from preschool through to postsecondary levels (Meyer & Thompson, 1956: Hall, 1982; Sadker & Sadker, 1985; Brophy & Evertson, 1981; Brophy & Good, 1974). Additionally, these studies have discussed the possible effects that differential patterns may have on students such as: lowered self-esteem for girls (Sears, 1963; Brophy & Good, 1974); less participation of girls in high school math and science classes and gifted programs (Sadker & Sadker, 1985); differences between boys and girls achievement motivation patterns (Hall, 1982), and less commitment to careers on the part of girls (Sadker & Sadker, 1985).

The above overview, while understandably brief, does encapsulize the body of research that examines gender differences that presumably relate to teacher-student interaction patterns. Though less "hard research" based, Raphaela Best's ethnographic study *We've All Got Scars: What Boys and Girls Learn in Elementary School* (1983) takes a more focused look at the interactions in a classroom over a two-year period and their relationship to gender differences. She states:

> For some time social psychologists and students of human development have been greatly preoccupied with the processes of socialization that prepare boys and girls for appropriate gender roles. Thus, along with the first, or academic curriculum (reading, writing, and arithmetic) there was a second, or gender-role, curriculum in operation, which taught the children the traditional role behavior for sex. It taught little girls to be helpful and nurturant. It taught little boys to distance themselves from girls, to look down on them, and to accept as their due the help that little girls offered. Through its insistence that boys learn to be boys and girls learn to be girls, this second curriculum resulted in separate worlds for the two sexes within the classroom and on the playground . . . The second curriculum did an effective job of teaching each sex how to perform according to conventional gender norms . . . It was not as successful in teaching the boys and girls how to relate to one another. (p. 4–5)

While the research does show strong evidence of gender differences in the interactions between teachers and students, we should not lose sight of the fact that what takes place in classrooms is in part a reflection of society in general. It is an environment that largely operates on social constructs which draw on sex role stereotypes and expectations so much a part of us that they guide our behavior, as well as our students, at a subconscious level.

Perhaps it is time for another confession to help clarify this notion. A year after I began working for a sex equity project, my wife and I were blessed with the birth of twins—a boy and a girl. Was this to be some divine test of my mettle? Would I be able to practice what I "preached?" We had a three-year-old daughter who had, I felt, surely been nurtured and grown in an equitable family environment. Besides the obvious difficulties of caring for two infants, how could I not help but care and nurture them in the same manner? I found it fascinating to field the comments from friends and family who upon first seeing the babies would matter of factly make some of the most blatantly stereotyped comments about what they "saw" in each of the babies, often those who couldn't tell them apart (they were rarely dressed in pink and blue though on occasion I would do it in "reverse") would make a typical "boy" comment to the girl or vice versa. I always embraced the opportunity to do some "on the spot" equity training and feel that I even managed to open some eyes. However, several months later after the dust had settled, a routine established, and some of the novelty worn off, my wife, after some careful observation, pointed out to me that I was talking to each of the babies in different ways. The tone and the phrases I used with Meghan often were markedly different than those I used with Brandon. I was much softer and more gentle in my interactions with her. With Brandon, I was louder and somewhat more animated in my behavior. Though somewhat skeptical at first, I was able to "catch myself" in the act more than once. I began to consciously make myself aware of how I interacted with each of them. I began to take control of my interactions in that conscious state and tried to make sure that both Brandon and Meghan experienced the full range of behaviors and interactions from me. Understandably, I was in awe of the power of the stereotypes to unconsciously dictate my behavior with my own children.

By way of the above observation I hope that some understanding of the classroom implications of such interactions can be gained. The problem lies in the fact that such behaviors, as subtle as they are, may have a profound effect on our ability to equitably deal all students into the process of education and indeed life itself. There is no question that sex stereotyped behaviors and expectations limit a full range of possibilities and choices for any individual. Remember the "opposite" characteristic of sex role stereotyping discussed earlier; how acting on any of the stereotypes implicitly excludes one-half of the population.

There is also little doubt that children experience some of these "limits" long before they enter the classroom. Certainly, teachers are not the first adults nor are schools the first social settings that may impose such limits on children. However, schools are the first formal social settings whose charge it is to treat all the participants equitably, to deal everyone into the process, to maximize the range of choices and possibilities for all students. It is that concept alone that makes schools the special environments that they are and most importantly makes teachers the special individuals they are for our children. If inequities do exist in the general social setting and they do limit options, then it is imperative that classrooms and teachers become models of equity and not reflections of an inequitable system. Schools can serve to set a standard for a new set of social constructs that inherently consider all individuals. As we will see, the process of "dealing students in" is more an issue of controlling interactions in the classroom; it is one of being proactive about the desired behaviors as opposed to simply maintaining those behaviors that are limiting.

As we enter the classroom to examine the interactions between teachers and students we must keep in mind the "baggage" that both the students and we as educators bring into that setting. Not all of it, but surely some of it does serve to obstruct the possibility for an equitable learning experience for all students.

Teacher-Student Interactions

This section is not meant to be a review of the literature on teacher-student interactions. For excellent discussions of such research and its implications refer to Hall, (1982); Klein, (1985); Sadker & Sadker, (1985) and Wilkenson and Marrett (1985). The following examples should, however, be sufficient in having a foundation for examining the process of classroom interactions:

1. Girls tend to be called on if they sit within close proximity to the teacher; first row—right under his or her nose. Boys tend to be called on wherever they sit in the classroom. (Sadker & Sadker, 1985)

2. Teachers have been observed showing boys how to go about an activity then letting them "do it" on their own, while the teacher "does it" for the girls. (Serbin, 1973; Safilios-Rothschild, 1979)

3. Overall boys receive more positive and more negative teacher contacts than girls; on the average two and one half times more disapproving comments than girls. A higher proportion of the girls contacts are positive in nature. (Good & Brophy, 1973)

4. Girls receive more contacts in reading classes while boys get more in math classes. (Leinhart, Seewald & Engle, 1979)

5. One study examined teacher contact with various "achievement groups" in classrooms. It was found that contact time given to each "group" was ranked as follows: high achieving boys, low achieving girls, low achieving boys, high achieving girls. (Good & Brophy, 1973)

Some piece of each of these observations can be related, without much effort, to sex role expectations on the part of the teachers as well as sex typed behaviors displayed by the students. Who are generally the "active" members of the classroom and/or who are expected to be? How does that effect the contact with students/teachers: who commands the most time/contact from teachers? Who are the students who "follow the rules" in classrooms, in quiet fashion, or are expected to? How does that affect contact time? Once again we must recognize the existence of the interplay of teacher expectations based on sex roles as well as student behaviors which play out those roles.

Surely, it is important to understand the research; specifically that differential patterns exist in classrooms across both grade levels and subject areas. More salient to the discussion, however, is an examination of the process of interactions in classrooms; the dynamics of the teacher-student interactions, how and why they might take place and moreover how can more equitable patterns be introduced into that setting.

Interactions in classrooms (or anywhere) are minimally two-way requiring some initiating behavior and a response to that behavior. In classrooms, much teacher time is spent responding to student behaviors; behaviors/attitudes that they bring into the classroom. Important here is the fact that while there is, as Klein reports (1985):

... little evidence of academic differences between boys and girls in the classroom. There is, however, substantial evidence of behavioral differences: girls are less disruptive than boys and speak out less than boys. Should a teacher seek to lessen male disruptive behavior or to increase female verbal participation in class, the teacher might need to interact differently with the girls and boys in the classroom—calling on girls more than on boys, or selectively ignoring certain male behavior. Equality of treatment would be an inappropriate teacher response to differential student behavior. If student behavior were not sex differentiated, however, then sex-differentiated teacher response could lead to sex-differentiated student behavior. The matter is further complicated by considering teacher attention as a classroom resource to be evenly distributed to all students. In that case, teachers should attend to all students identically, without regard to student behavior. This suggestion, however, is not likely to be accepted by teachers who are concerned with maintaining control over disruptive students or who are eager to encourage the participation of reticent students. (p. 196)

No one ever said that this was going to be easy! This passage has been excerpted because it so articulately presents the complexity of the "mix" in any given classroom. This is not a simple picture. There is not a simple one-step solution. The classroom is three dimensional and any effort to reduce the dimensions to approach a solution is giving short shrift to the problem.

Early research as well as some of the textbook treatment of the topic of teacher-student interaction tended to focus on the teacher as a "causal" factor in differentiated behavior patterns in classrooms. However, researchers looking more closely at the patterns began to see that teacher-student interaction was as much a function of student initiated behavior as it was teacher to student interaction (Klein, 1985). Much of the research was citing greater activity on the part of boys in the classrooms; activities and behaviors to which teachers were compelled to react. In fact, to a great extent, the consistencies in the research pointed more to behaviors initiated by students than those initiated by teachers. These observations became an extremely important link to understanding the dynamics of the interaction process in classrooms. It seemed teachers were interacting more with males to a large degree because they were simply responding to their higher levels of activity, both positive and negative. Boys were seen as more active and as initiating more contact with those around them, particularly teachers. Boys in the classrooms observed were controlling the interactive environment of the classroom; they seemed to be setting the "tone" as opposed to having one set for them. Why? Though not thoroughly explained by the "squeaky wheel" theory, there is certainly some validity in considering that notion. So, if we compound boys higher level of activity in general with the expectation that "boys will be boys" we arrive at a situation in the classroom where those notions about how boys are "supposed to be" are a dictating factor in the environmental/interactional tone of the classroom. It is difficult to "point a finger" at the source in such a situation and it is certainly not as easy to point in the direction of the teacher. The real question becomes a matter of "who is in charge here?"

What is the Teacher's Role?

Klein (1985) suggests that research which controls for the students' role in differential treatment might provide a truer picture of the teacher's role. This research shows that while the frequency of contact might still be greater with boys, the teacher responses are not found to be consistently different toward boys and girls. But, it must be noted that simple frequency of interaction with one group more than another can understandably have profound effects on both the receivers and nonreceivers of responses. Whether direct or not there is a message being conveyed about the relative importance/value of one group over the other. It is still an issue of inequitable treatment, though perhaps not as blaming, as has been reported. The gender inequities, it would appear, might be more attributable to student rather than teacher behavior; or more to teacher nonbehavior in classrooms. Brophy and Eccles & Blumenfield (Wilkenson and Marrett, 1985) agree that a more realistic perspective on the teacher role in the classroom could be that rather than causing disparities in student experiences (e.g., gender differences) through interactions, teachers serve to maintain the differences that students bring to the classroom. It is clear that the focal point is not who is to blame or who is the cause. Again, the attitudes/behaviors are a reflection of society and no one "owns" them any more than another. The solution, then, becomes more an issue of becoming aware of how such attitudes/behaviors control the nature of classroom interactions and wresting that control so that a more equitable pattern of interactions can be established. Awareness of potential inequity and a concomittant proactive response would seem to be a more appropriate response; call it "proactive as opposed to reactive."

Student-Student Interaction

We have seen how teacher control of their own interaction patterns with students is understandably necessary to provide an equitable distribution of teacher attention to all students. This involves an awareness of both teacher and student initiated attitudes/behaviors that can inhibit that distribution. An understanding of one's role in interactions necessarily draws an individual (teacher or student) into closer observation of their own interactions; for teachers it facilitates taking control. The interactions in classrooms that take place between students, though somewhat more difficult to be aware of and thus to control, require considerable teacher attention.

Lockheed (1982) estimated that 29 percent of a student's classroom experience involves peer interactions. Those estimates can vary depending upon such factors as approach/philosophy to class activities, the subject area, class size, etc. Though they may escape the eye, these interactions can be significant sources of gender inequities. In fact, research indicates that most students, if given the opportunity, will tend to self segregate or group themselves along gender lines. Such behavior, again brought to the classroom by the students themselves can have a profoundly limiting effect on the range of experiences that a student can have in classrooms.

I recently took the opportunity to interview my six-year-old daughter about her perspective on what went on during "activity time" in her kindergarten class. This is a block of time where the students are expected to choose one activity from a possible five or six. The activities are typical for a kindergarten class—doll house corner, painting, blocks/trucks, story writing, computers, etc. What I was interested in, of course, was who was choosing what activities. Fortunately, the students had to choose a different activity at least every other day. However, the patterns she described were anything but surprising. For example, though she indicated that boys and girls both chose the "doll corner," it was usually more girls than boys and the boys often were made to sit out after their behavior had become inappropriate. Here we have the mix of both self-segregation and teacher reaction to behavior both of which create/ maintain inequitable grouping patterns. The "building corner" was usually more boys and they generally dominated or guided the course of the play in that activity. The "computer corner" was similar with boys dominating time at the keyboard while girls were not asserting their interest in equal time. Though hardly a scientific study, her observations clearly parallel though done by many researchers of peer interactions in elementary classrooms.

Klein and Lockheed (Klein, 1985) provide a thorough review of the research. In general they cite very little evidence of cross-sex interaction. These studies include examinations of seating arrangements, friendship choices, unstructured play, and work partner preferences. As with teacher-student interaction patterns, inequitable classroom grouping patterns are found from nursery school up through post-secondary levels. The research has shown that sex stereotyped behaviors tend to become more entrenched as students get older, and accordingly, so do the patterns of segregation, as well as male dominance of group work in classrooms. Once again, many of these patterns/behaviors go unnoticed and thus escape intervention. Intervention involves teacher awareness of inequitable patterns and taking a more active role in structuring the patterns of interaction so that students begin to experience the opportunity to interact, cooperate and learn in a full range of group settings.

Intervention

There is no real secret to intervening in the interactions that take place in classrooms between teachers and students. In fact many of you upon reading this chapter will walk into your classrooms tomorrow and begin to notice patterns that have, until now, gone unnoticed. So subtle are such patterns that teachers in the graduate course I teach often come back to class reporting a whole new view of their classroom and new found enthusiasm in their approach to teaching. Below are several suggestions, in sequential order, on how to begin to approach intervention in the classroom.

Awareness

This is understandably the first step in the process of intervention. Hopefully, this chapter, indeed this book, has provided some foundation in understanding sex role stereotyping/expectations and how they effect the patterns of interaction in classrooms. Go back to your classroom with a new set of eyes. Look for the subtleties and not so subtleties in your interactions with students and their interactions with each other. Who is controlling the "air time" in your classroom? How are students grouping themselves in structured as well as unstructured activities? Who is being consistently "left out" of the active learning process in the classroom? You should be able to generate your own list of questions based on your readings thus far. Spend a considerable amount of time looking at your classroom before intervening. You may want to visit a colleague's classroom to compare your observations. Take note of the "new" observations you make and choose one on which to focus your initial efforts at change. Don't attempt to do it all at once. Begin with easy changes. Identify those areas where you can take more control of the situation. Write them down and make priorities on a scale of easy to difficult.

Share Your Efforts With the Students

One way in which you can begin to have some effect on the behaviors/attitudes that students bring into the classroom is to share your observations with the students. Develop a unit on sex role stereotypes that is geared to the abilities of your students. Describe the patterns that you have observed and enlist your students as investigators themselves. This can have a "snowballing" effect on your efforts. Teachers have reported what a truly rewarding experience such a practice can be for all involved. There is no pay off in hiding your efforts from the students. Just as awareness is your first step in effecting change, the same case can be made for the students role in the process of change. Students will very quickly notice how they are grouping themselves during classroom activities. They may, as some of the research indicates, already be aware of inequitable patterns in your interactions with them. Allow them the opportunity to honestly and openly share their observations with you.

Take Control

If you follow the above suggestions, the process of taking control of interactions in your classroom will be much easier. Understandably, taking control will be a more complex process than the observations you make. The process of dealing all students into the process of learning involves a recognition of the multiple variables discussed in this chapter. Remember that schools need to create environments that effectively provide students with the full range of options available to them. Implicit here is the attempt to "control for" those situations, attitudes and behaviors that have traditionally excluded one group from access to significant portions of, in many cases half, of the range of options available. It is important to focus on the control factor in breaking down such effects and not on who is to blame for there is nothing to be gained in those waters. After all, it is your environment to control.

This chapter has focused on how individual teachers can begin to informally identify and change factors in their classroom environment that may limit students access to a full range of options. The following chapter describes a more formal approach in effecting such changes. GESA (Gender Expectation and Student Achievement) is a thoughtfully structured and comprehensive approach to creating an equitable classroom environment. It represents one of the first attempts to effect widespread change in the areas described in this chapter.

REFERENCES

Best, R. *We've all got scars; what boys and girls learn in elementary school.* Bloomington: Indiana University Press, 1983.

Brophy, J. E. & Evertson, C. M. *Student characteristics and teaching.* New York: Longman, 1981.

Brophy, J. E. & Good, T. L. *Teacher-student relationships: causes and consequences.* New York: Holt, Reinhardt and Winston, Inc., 1974.

Good, T. L. & Brophy, J. E. *Looking in classrooms.* New York: Harper and Rowe, 1973.

Hall, R. M. *The classroom climate: A chilly one for women?* Washington, D.C.: Project on the Status and Education of Women of the Association of American Colleges, 1982.

Klein, S. *Handbook for achieving sex equity through education.* Baltimore: Johns Hopkins University Press, 1985.

Kuhler, R. G. & Thompson, G. G. (Eds.) *Psychological studies of human development,* New York: Appleton-Century-Crafts, 1956.

Leinhardt, G.; Seewald, A. & Engel, M. Learning what's taught: sex differences in instruction. *Journal of ducational sychology,* 1979, *71,* 432–439.

Lockheed, M. E. *Sex equity in classroom interaction: An analysis of behavior chains.* Paper presented at the annual meeting of the American Educational Research A-sociation, New York, 1982.

McMillan, J. H. *The social psychology of school learning.* New York: Academic Press, 1980.

Sadker, M. P. & Sadker, D. M. *Between teacher and student: Overcoming bias in the classroom.* Unpublished report of the Non-Sexist Teacher Education Project of the Women's Educational Equity Act Program, U. S., DHEW, Office of Education, 1979.

Sadker, M. P. & Sadker, D. M., Bauchner, J. and Herbert L. *Year 2: Final report— Promoting effectiveness in classroom instruction.* Andover, Mass.: The Network, 1985.

Safilios-Rothschild, C. *Sex role socialization and sex discrimination: A synthesis and critique of the literature.* Washington, D. C.: National Institute of Education, 1979.

Sears, P. S. *The effect of classroom conditions on the strength of achievement motive and work output of elementary school children.* Cooperative Research Project No. OE-873, U. S. DHEW, Office of Education, 1963.

Serbin, L. A comparison of teacher response to the preacademic and problem behavior of boys and girls. *Child development,* 1973, *44,* 87–93.

Wilkenson, L. C. & Marrett, C. B. *Gender influences in classroom interaction.* New York: Academic Press, 1985.

The following statements are designed for the exploration of personal reactions to the chapter, as well as for the review of the contents of the chapter. Emphasis in discussions should be on exploring issues in depth, rather than on determining the correct or appropriate responses.

FOR DISCUSSION:

1. Discuss the author's statement: "Teachers and students alike bring into the classroom setting a lifetime of perceptions, attitudes, values and behaviors, some of which are based on stereotypical notions about the roles of men and women . . . in our society."
2. Discuss personal examples of the "power" of sex role stereotyping in guiding our behavior.
3. Discuss personal examples of the "power" of sex role stereotyping in guiding the behavior of teachers and of students.
4. Discuss the author's statement: "Though teacher-student interactions have typically been a focus in looking at the issue of stereotyping in classrooms, such a view does not necessarily consider the 'whole picture'."
5. Observe and discuss with students examples of peer interaction that perpetuates stereotypes. Report the results of the discussions to colleagues.
6. Identify biased teacher-student interactions (obvious and subtle) that you never noticed before, and determine appropriate intervention.
7. What does the author mean by "taking control" of the classroom?
8. If teachers are not to "blame" for sex bias in the classroom, then can they be the solution to the problem?

SUGGESTIONS FOR FURTHER READING

Bauchner, J., Hergert, L., Sadker, D., & Sadker, M. *Intersect (interactions for sex equity in classroom teaching)*. Andover, Massachusetts: The Network, Inc., 1985.

Chipman, S. F. *Women and mathematics: Balancing the equation.* Hillsdale, New Jersey: L. Erlbaum Associates, 1985.

Grayson, D. *Infusing an equity agenda into school districts.* Los Angeles, California: County Office of Education, 1984.

Grayson, D., & Martin, M. *Gender expectations and student achievement (GESA).* Los Angeles, California: Los Angeles County Office of Education, 1985.

Johnson, L., & Hall, R. *Selected activities using "The classroom climate: A chilly one for women?"* Washington, D.C.: Association of American Colleges, 1984.

Sadker, D., Sadker, M., & Thomas, D. *Non-sexist teaching: Overcoming sex bias in teacher-student interaction.* Washington, D.C.: Mid-Atlantic Center for Sex Equity, 1985.

Chapter 10

GENDER EXPECTATIONS AND STUDENT ACHIEVEMENT (GESA): A TEACHER TRAINING PROGRAM ADDRESSING GENDER DISPARITY IN THE CLASSROOM

DOLORES A. GRAYSON AND MARY D. MARTIN

INTRODUCTION

"If they raise their hands, I call on them. It's that simple."

There are a number of instructional programs that have been created for the express purpose of counteracting sex bias in the classroom. Special exercises, workbooks, school activities, and discussion topics aim at raising teacher and student awareness about issues related to sex equity. They are informative, useful, and often achieve the objective of changing attitudes and behaviors. The Gender Expectations and Student Achievement (GESA) Program focuses on student/teacher interaction in the classroom. Emphasis is on encouraging teachers of all grades and subject areas to look at the impact of gender bias on teaching and learning. Then teachers also discover the results of reducing sex bias in their classrooms.

Modeled after the well-established and successful Teacher Expectations and Student Achievement (TESA) Program, GESA is designed to address major areas of gender disparity in the classroom. After extensive testing, it is now offered as a teacher training program throughout the nation by the Los Angeles County Office of Education where the program was developed. The emphasis and potential outcomes of the program are described in the following article.

Teachers may wonder why a training program is necessary, especially if the teacher works hard at creating an equitable classroom environment. If teachers are prepared, responsive, and enthusiastic about teaching, they will treat all students as individuals. If students are prepared, responsive, and enthusiastic about learning, they will receive the attention in the classroom that they deserve.

Bur research as described in the GESA program does not bear this theory out. Apparently boys and girls are treated differently by both male and female teachers. Expectation, encouragement, attention, even discipline varies depending on the student's gender. The teacher, more than likely in an unconscious manner, perpetuates bias when verbally interacting with students, when setting

127

classroom policy, and when moving around the room. Most importantly, the seemingly minor teacher/student interactions can profoundly affect student achievement.

Teachers, of course, are not to blame. They do not deliberately treat boys and girls differently when teaching. In fact, many teachers go out of their way to provide a learning environment that is free of stereotypes. Yet they enter the classroom with their own socialization, their own classroom experiences, and their own preconceived notions about the capabilities and interests of boys and girls. The GESA program provides information to all teachers, even those who stress sex fair classroom interaction. Participants reinforce their skills, learn about new classroom strategies, and most significantly, watch their students gain in achievement.

The GESA program is summarized in this chapter, but educators can fully comprehend the content and impact of the program by reviewing the materials and participating in the program. A description of the program is included so that readers can discover and personally evaluate the program. (Discussion questions do not follow the chapter.)

For more information about the GESA program, contact the author at:

Division of Project Funding and Management
Room 246
Los Angeles County Office of Education
9300 East Imperial Highway
Downey, California 90242

GENDER EXPECTATIONS AND STUDENT ACHIEVEMENT (GESA): A TEACHER TRAINING PROGRAM ADDRESSING GENDER DISPARITY IN THE CLASSROOM

For more than a decade, researchers have accumulated evidence of differential treatment in classrooms resulting in different results for males and females (Sadker and Sadker, 1982 and 1985; Lockheed and Harris, 1982; Best, 1983; Hall and Sandler, 1982).

This research has added to a body of knowledge related to teacher's perceived expectations (Brophy and Good, 1970 and 1978). Repeatedly the studies have indicated a correlation between these perceived expectations and classroom interactions and their impact on academic achievement (Kerman, Kimball and Martin, 1980).

This difference in expectations, influencing interactions and impacting achievement, is manifested in some subject areas more than others. For example, Fennema states that "it appears reasonable to assume that some types of teacher-pupil interactions influence the development of one's internal motivational beliefs" (Fennema and Peterson, in press) contributing to gender related differences in mathematics.

A review of the literature indicates that gender bias influencing interaction patterns and achievement is evident in five major areas. These will be referred to as the areas of gender disparity and include the following: instructional contact, grouping and organization, classroom control, enhancing self-esteem, and evaluation of student performance. Parallel information related to ethnic and cultural diversity also surfaces within these categories.

GESA is designed to counter the areas of disparity with research based instructional strategies and motivational interactions. The objectives are to reduce the disparity in the frequency distribution of interactions with males and females by teachers; to reduce stereotyping by the teachers; to increase nonstereotypical interaction with students; and to produce increased achievement in mathematics and reading by girls and boys in classroom of teachers receiving GESA training. The conceptual framework includes the three primary factors generally accepted to effect academic achievement. These include the curriculum (content and materials), the learning environment and the classroom interactions.

Instructional Contact

Good and Brophy, after an extensive review of the research and numerous studies of classroom interaction, concluded that boys receive more instructional contact with their teachers than girls (1978). This conclusion is supported by classroom interaction data collected from thousands of classrooms during the ten years that the OLACSS* has conducted the Teacher Expectations and Student Achievement (TESA) project. Although TESA is concerned with the differences in teacher interaction with students perceived as high and low achievers, the data from classroom observations are analyzed by sex as well as by achievement level. Despite the fact that the TESA teachers know the observer is recording interaction with six low and six high achievers to determine whether supportive teaching behaviors are distributed equitably between the two groups, the boys consistently receive more attention. Recent studies by Myra and David Sadker show that male students in elementary, secondary, and postsecondary classrooms receive more teaching attention than female students. Female students were less likely to participate in classroom discussions and more likely to be invisible members of the classes (*Newsletter: Project Effect,* 1984).

The TESA data indicated that teachers are more apt to help boys individually, to ask them questions, to wait for their response, to delve if they have difficulty responding, and to ask them higher level questions. Good and Brophy found that boys were asked a higher percentage of process questions than girls, who were more apt to be asked product or choice questions (Good, Sikes, and Brophy, 1972). In a landmark study on motivation, Sears concluded that teachers orient academic activities to the superior boys (Sears, 1963).

Many studies have shown that the extent to which a student is involved in the instructional process correlates with achievement. The TESA findings prove that providing as much instructional support to low achievers as to high achievers results in increased learning among all students (Kerman, Kimball, and Martin, 1980). Clearly, the deficit in instructional attention experienced by girls contributes heavily to the decrease in the achievement level of girls as they move up through the grades.

Grouping and Organization

The Sadkers, in a National Institute of Education supported study, found that "one out of every three classrooms is segregated by sex. At other times, students segregate themselves through seating and lines of work and play activities" (*Newsletter Project Effect,* 1984). Anyone who has frequently observed classrooms knows that teachers most often are working with small groups of boys or organize the room so that a small cluster of boys surround the teacher's desk. Adams and Biddle (1970) videotaped sixteen classrooms at grade levels one, six, and eleven. In all classrooms, they found that the students most likely to be asked questions or to participate in discussions were seated in a T-shaped area directly in front of the teacher. Sixty-three percent of the time that a student spoke, that student was in one of the first three seats in the stem of the T.

Discipline

Boys receive more criticism and punishment for misbehavior than girls (Jackson and Lehaderne, 1967; Safilios-Rothschild, 1979). This both reflects and reinforces the stereotype of girls as docile and boys as aggressive. This contributes to the greater amount of teacher contact boys receive. Curiously enough, in one study, teachers admitted that they discouraged girls' aggressive behavior more than boys (and encouraged aggression more in boys) even though they perceived boys as more aggressive (Chasen, 1974). According to the Sadkers' studies, even when boys and girls are misbehaving equally, the boys are more likely to get harsher reprimands (Sadker and Sadker, 1982).

Self Concept

The classroom is a crucial force in shaping the self-concepts of boys and girls. The impact of this gender differentiation was earlier reported by Sears in her analysis of self-concept scores. More of the low-ability boys tended to give themselves a high self-concept than did girls; and more high-ability girls than boys tended to give themselves a low self-concept (Sears, 1963). Best (1983) also found that the differences between boys and girls in sex role socialization became especially marked in the fourth grade.

Baumgartner-Papageorgiou's (1982) study indicates that "both males and females are taught that being male is inherently better than being female."

Evaluation

Lee and Wolinsky (1973) found that boys were subject to more evaluation, i.e., feedback regarding their performance than girls, whether the feedback expressed approval or disapproval. Brophy and Good (1970) reported that boys were praised more frequently than girls after giving the correct answer. Boys were also criticized more often for incorrect responses or for failing to respond, which Safilios-Rothschild (1979) suggested places boys under greater pressure to succeed. In the TESA project, boys were more apt to be told whether their performance was acceptable, to be praised for good performance, and to be given reasons for such praise.

Many educators have long believed that public evaluation does not help girls in working toward academic goals but is facilitating for boys. As early as 1925, a careful study by Hurlock looked at the achievement of students who were praised, reproved, and ignored. Both boys and girls responded best to praise. The boys did respond slightly better than the girls to reproof. However, the ignored group achieved the least. Thus, the saliency that boys hold for teachers in both criticizing and praising places girls at a disadvantage.

Teacher Expectations and Student Achievement (TESA)

The GESA program is adapted from the inservice training model developed by OLACSS staff for the Teacher Expectations and Student Achievement (TESA) project. TESA addresses the differential expectations teachers hold for students labeled low achievers. Like TESA, GESA training is designed around monthly meetings where teacher behaviors which reflect expectations are discussed followed by the teachers observing and coding each other's interactions in the classroom. This provides an action research climate in which teams of teachers examine the impact of deliberately counteracting gender bias on their own and their students' behavior and on student learning.

The TESA model has been highly successful. TESA coordinator workshops are held monthly in four locations throughout the United States and the trained coordinators have conducted TESA teacher training in school districts in most states as well as in other countries, notably

Australia and Canada, and in Puerto Rico. TESA received a National Pacesetter Award in 1974 and is now recognized as one of the two or three most successful staff development programs in the nation.

GESA, designed to address the major areas of gender disparity in the classroom, is based on widely-held theories of change management and staff development. The basic concepts underlying GESA are as follows:

Expectations

Teachers' gender-based expectations are reflected in what and how they teach and often place limits on what students can learn. Therefore, the GESA training sessions focus on how gender-based expectations are reflected in the classroom.

Attitudinal Change

Attitudes are resistant to change. Repeated reinforcement over a span of time is required for attitudinal change. Therefore, the GESA training is organized in five monthly workshops with structured practice in the classroom between workshops.

Behavior Change

Attitudes are reflected in behavior. If that behavior is changed and the new behaviors are rewarded, attitudinal change is likely to follow. Therefore, the GESA participants are observed in the classroom demonstrating gender-free teacher/student interactions. Immediate feedback from the observer provides immediate reward. However, the TESA experience suggests that the most meaningful reward for the teachers is the responses of their students.

Climate for Change

Administrative support and a supportive network of colleagues create a climate in which change can occur. Therefore, GESA involves key administrators in cooperating school districts and teams of teachers at each participating school. GESA training sessions include ample time for sharing progress reports.

Ownership

Change is more likely to occur if the participants feel they are playing an important role in the process. Therefore, the teams of teachers participating in GESA also observe and code interactions in each other's classrooms. This gives each participant a crucial role in the training process.

Training*

The training content was identified and five training sessions about one month apart were planned. The accompanying chart (Fig. 10-1) shows the themes for each training session which are based on the five areas of gender disparity identified from the literature. The second column gives the teacher/student interactions which are defined and discussed in the workshop and become the basis for classroom observations following the workshop. The interactions were selected because the literature indicates that these are teaching behaviors which tend to reflect gender bias. (This literature is summarized in the GESA training materials.) The third column is the curriculum related concerns, which are also addressed in each workshop.

The training incorporates the three primary factors directly related to academic achievement. Curriculum, Learning Environment and Interactions.

Figure 10-1
Gender Expectations and Student Achievement (GESA).

Five Major Areas of Disparity (Working Themes)	Learning Climate (Interactions)	Instructional Management (Curriculum-Related)
I. Instructional Contact	Response Opportunities/ Acknowledgment	Evaluating Materials for Bias Bias
II. Grouping/Organization	Wait Time/Physical Closeness	Math/Science/Technology
III. Discipline	Touching/Reproof	Multicultural Resources
IV. Self-Concept	Probing/Listening	Gender Balance in History
V. Evaluation	High Level Questioning/ Analytical Feedback	Physical Activities

Grayson and Martin, 1984

---

*Office of the Los Angeles County School System

Process of GESA

As an example of the process of GESA training, nineteen elementary (3,4,5,6th grades) teachers attend monthly training sessions at the Los Angeles County Education Center. Following each workshop the teams of four teachers from a district observe teacher/student interaction in each other's classrooms a minimum of three times. Each observation session is 30 minutes. The observing teacher records the number of times a teacher interacts in the ways specified for that unit with girls and the number of times with boys. (At this time, we are experimenting with targeting particular students to be observed as is done in TESA compared to simply coding interaction with boys and girls. This permits dyadic coding (i.e., coding of interaction with a specific student) which enables the teacher to identify those students who are being ignored or treated differently from others. The observing teacher leaves the coding sheet with the demonstrating teacher to provide immediate feedback. Observation methods are discussed and practiced in the workshop, and the teachers are generally effective and accurate observers when evaluated by comparing coding of a teacher participant and a staff member. However, the observation data are for learning purposes, not for research or evaluation. The observations serve as an impetus for the demonstrating teacher to practice the interactions with students and provide a laboratory in which the observing teacher can examine the impact of teacher interaction on student behavior. Therefore, the occasional observer's lapse from objective coding (such as a teacher who, during Unit III, held up a paper on which she had scribbled, "Touch Elaine") does not impair the project.

Teachers report serendipitous outcomes of the observation process including adapting instructional and management procedures and becoming accustomed to having a visitor in the classroom.

At the following workshop, time is provided for teachers to share student reactions. As the training progresses and the teachers become aware of the changes in themselves and their students, this sharing process builds enthusiasm to a surprisingly high pitch.

Findings

Some of the following results are evidenced by comparison of pretraining observations, monthly summaries of coding sheets and responses to a mid-project survey:

1. Teachers participating in GESA training have reduced the disparities in their interactions with males and females.
2. All participating teachers have identified at least one curricular change implemented in their classrooms during the training period for the purpose of reducing gender bias.
3. All participating teachers report benefiting professionally from involvement in collegial observations and coding and have talked with their principals and other staff members about their involvement in GESA.
4. Most participating teachers report positive attitudinal changes in themselves and positive effects on their students, as a result of their participation in GESA.
5. All participating teachers have identified at least one major area of disparity and a specific interaction that has impacted their classroom and been most beneficial to them as a teacher.

The following are results from the pilot phase of 1984:

1. Students in classes taught by teachers participating in GESA achieved a mean gain of 2.1 percent in reading and 7.0 percent in math, as assessed by the California Test of Basic Skills (CTBS). (No comparison data was analyzed.)
2. The highest math gain recorded by students in classes taught by teachers participating in GESA was a mean gain of 18.7 percent in a class with a large population of English as a Second Language (ESL) students, predominantly Hispanic and Asian.
3. The highest reading gain recorded by students in classes taught by teachers participating in GESA was a mean gain of 7.4 percent in a class with a large population of Asian Pacific students.
4. All participating teachers report benefiting professionally from involvement in collegial observation and coding and have talked with their principals and other staff members about GESA.
5. All participating teachers have identified at least one area of disparity corrected by them, at least one specific interaction as most beneficial and a curricular change that they have implemented in their classroom.

Conclusions

Based on the preliminary data of the pilot, the following conclusions seem reasonable:

- Teachers who have participated in the GESA program have reduced the disparity in the frequency distribution of their interaction with males and females.
- Teachers who have participated in the GESA program report an increased use of nonstereotypical interactions, materials and activities.
- Preliminary data indicate that students in classes taught by teachers participating in GESA achieve significant gains in reading and math as assessed by the CTBS scores.

Whether or not the significant gains are higher than a comparison group remains to be analyzed from the field test data.

Finally, there is some indication that the areas of disparity may be generic and that GESA positively impacts other parallel factors subjected to past discrimination such as race, national origin, and cultural diversity.

In an April 24, 1987 paper presented at the American Educational Research Association Convention in Washington, D.C., the author presented up-to-date information on the impact of the GESA program. Specific research details are itemized in the report. A copy of the paper is available from the author at the address given in the introduction to this chapter.

REFERENCES

Adams, R., & Biddle, B. *Realities of teaching: Explorations with video tape.* New York: Holt, Rinehart and Winston, Inc., 1970.

Baumgartner-Papageorgiou, A. *"My Daddy might have loved me": Student perceptions of differences between being male and being female.* Institute for Equality in Education, Denver: University of Colorado, 1982.

Best, R. *We've all got scars: What boys and girls learn in elementary school.* Bloomington: Indiana University Press, 1983.

Brophy, J., & Good, T. Teachers' communication of differential expectations for children's classroom performance: Some behavioral data. *Journal of educational psychology,* 1970, *61,* 365–374.

Chasen, B. Sex role stereotyping and pre-kindergarten teachers. *Elementary school journal,* 1974, *72,* 220–235.

Fennema, E., & Peterson, P. Autonomous learning behavior: A possible explanation of gender-related differences in mathematics. *Gender related differences in class-room interaction.* Academic Press, in press.

Good, T., & Brophy, J. *Looking in classrooms.* New York: Harper & Row Publishers, 1978.

Good, T., Sikes, J., & Brophy, J. Effects of teacher sex, student sex, and student achievement on classroom interaction. *Technical report No. 61, Center for Research in Social Behavior.* Columbia: University of Missouri, 1972.

Hall, R., & Sandler, B. *The classroom climate: A chilly one for women?* Project on the Status and Education of Women, Association of American Colleges, Washington, D.C., 1982.

Hurlock, E. An evaluation of certain incentives used in schoolwork. *Journal of educational psychology,* 1925, *16,* 145–149.

Jackson, P., & Lahaderne, H. Inequalities of teacher-pupil contacts. *Psychology in schools,* 1967, *4,* 204–208.

Kerman, S., Kimball, T., & Martin, M. *Teacher expectations and student achievement.* Bloomington, Indiana: Phi Delta Kappa, 1980.

Lee, P., & Wolinsky, A. Male teachers of young children: A preliminary empirical study. *Young children,* 1973, *28,* 342–352.

Lockheed, M.E., & Harris, A.M. *"Classroom interaction and opportunities for cross-sex peer learning in science."* Paper presented at the Annual Meeting of the American Educational Research Association, New York, 1982.

Newsletter: Project Effect, 1, Washington, D.C., 1984.

Sadker, M., & Sadker, D. *Sex equity handbook for schools.* New York and London: Longman, Inc., 1982.

Sadker, M., & Sadker, D. *Sexism in the schoolroom of the `80's. Psychology today,* March, 1985, 54–57.

Safilios-Rothschild, C. *Sex role socialization and sex discrimination: A synthesis and critique of the literature.* Washington, D.C.: National Institute of Education (1979).

Schubert, J.G. *An interactive approach to infusing equity: A teacher model.* AERA paper, Montreal, 1983.

Sears, P. *The effect of classroom conditions on the strengths of achievement motive and work output of elementary school children.* Stanford: Stanford University, 1963.

Chapter 11

CHECKLIST OF
EQUITABLE TEACHING PRACTICES

One of the best ways for teachers to determine if their classrooms are free of sex bias is for them to quickly complete a checklist evaluation. The questions below should assist teachers in viewing their classrooms objectively. Although the checklist is by no means complete, it allows teachers to get a preliminary picture of the environment and interactions in their classrooms. Any checks marked in the NO column warrant further attention. Instructional resources are listed in SUGGESTIONS FOR FURTHER READING following the checklist.

CLASSROOM ORGANIZATION

Do you . . .   YES NO

Examine enrollment patterns to identify possible sex bias? □ □

Establish and apply the same grading system to students of both sexes? □ □

Set the same standards of behavior for all students in your classroom (e.g., attention, quiet, visiting, etc.)? □ □

Apply the same standards for use of tools and equipment to all students? □ □

Have the same safety rules for both boys and girls? □ □

Keep libraries well-stocked with catalogues of bias-free materials? □ □

Examine, replace and supplement biased materials? □ □

Assign classroom tasks (operating projector, notetaking) on the bias of skills and interest, not gender? □ □

Avoid separating boys and girls for seating, teams, lining up, etc.? □ □

Rearrange the classroom regularly so that you have a chance to move around the room and interact with different students? □ □

Arrange opportunities for boys and girls to work and play together? □ □

Encourage children to experience a variety of roles within a group? □ □

INSTRUCTIONAL TECHNIQUES

Address all students with the same tone of voice? □ □

Use gender-free terms and occupational titles? □ □

Make course descriptions and content appealing to all students, regardless of gender? □ □

Refrain from using terms such as "broken home", "latchkey child", and "child of a single parent"? □ □

Provide the same learning activities and projects for students (rather than different ones on the basis of sex as providing boys with more labs, girls with more seat work)? □ □

Expect the same work habits from both boys and girls? □ □

Evaluate standards and expectations to determine if differences are the result of sex role stereotyping? □ □

Pay close attention to classroom interaction patterns? □ □

Give equitable attention to students of both sexes (instead of more criticism for boys and more support for girls)? □ □

Use parallel terminology when addressing women and men students, or referring to men and women in examples (When the chemist works, she must . . .)? □ □

Ask both boys and girls divergent or opinion questions (e.g., explain the theory, describe your reaction)? □ □

STUDENT INTERACTION

	YES	NO
Encourage students to consider a broader range of program and career options?	☐	☐
Encourage use of all tools, toys, and equipment in the classroom?	☐	☐
Recognize skill areas that may require extra encouragement (e.g., math for girls, dramatics for boys)?	☐	☐
Avoid saying things that would make students think that boys must act one way and girls another way (e.g., "Boys will be boys," "Act like a lady")?	☐	☐
Give equivalent attention to students of both sexes (rather than more criticism for boys, support for the girls, etc.)?	☐	☐
Have the same health and dress guidelines for both sexes?	☐	☐
Recognize *all* athletic achievements and events?	☐	☐
Support students in behavior that is not limited by their sex role stereotype (e.g., boys who are sensitive, caring, artistic)?	☐	☐
Help students, boys and girls, to share feelings and cope with stress in a healthy manner?	☐	☐
Accept emotional expression from both sexes?	☐	☐
Support "pioneer" students who take a chance on fields of study that are not traditionally for their sex?	☐	☐
Set the same standards for behavior and administer the same disciplinary actions to boys and girls?	☐	☐
Avoid comparisons of boys and girls with respect to classroom behavior, attitudes and accomplishments?	☐	☐
Help students understand the difference between sex roles and gender identity?	☐	☐
Ask students to tell you when you are treating male and female students differently?	☐	☐

INFORMATION SHARING

	YES	NO
Make it clear to students that they do not have to conform to rigid sex roles, but to just be themselves?	☐	☐
Point out when textbooks, films, and other materials show men and women only in stereotyped ways?	☐	☐
Share information with both sexes about their future dual roles as worker/parent?	☐	☐
Provide children with nontraditional role models in books, displays, and guest speakers?	☐	☐

	YES	NO
Maintain a file on role models and volunteers who have worked with students?	☐	☐
Share information with students about the structure of the contemporary American family?	☐	☐

COLLEAGUES AND PARENTS

	YES	NO
Examine and change school practices that contribute to separation and stereotyping of children by gender?	☐	☐
Familiarize yourself and colleagues with sex equity legislation such as Title IX and the Carl Perkins Vocational Education Act?	☐	☐
Help to arrange staff training on issues of sex bias and sex equity?	☐	☐
Promote discussion of stereotyping and changing sex roles among students and colleagues?	☐	☐
Encourage the recruitment and hiring of women in administration, and teachers in nontraditional fields?	☐	☐
Respond to parents on the basis of their concerns, rather than their gender?	☐	☐
Recognize that a child from a single parent household does not necessarily imply a problem at home?	☐	☐
Include parents without custody in school memos and activities?	☐	☐
Review letters to home for bias?	☐	☐
Request parental involvement without specifying gender (room-mother, fathers to build a playground)?	☐	☐

SUGGESTIONS FOR FURTHER READING

Alexander, M.C. *Boys and girls together: non-sexist activities for elementary schools.* Holmes Beach, Florida: Learning Publications, 1980.

Council of Chief State School Officers. Resource Center on Educational Equity. *Increasing educational equity for disabled students.* Washington, D.C., 1984.

Farris, C. & Smith, A. *Pioneering programs in sex equity: A teacher's guide.* Arlington, Virginia: American Vocational Association, 1980.

Gabelko, N., & Michaels, J. *Reducing adolescent prejudice.* New York: Columbia University Press, 1981.

Hull, G., Scott, B., & Smith, B. *But some of us are brave: Black women's studies.* New York: The Feminist Press, 1982.

Kerr, B. *Smart girls, gifted women.* Columbus, Ohio: Ohio Psychology Publishing Company, 1985.

Lang, M.A. *Creating inclusive, nonstereotyping environments: The child with a disability.* New York: Educational Equity Concepts, Inc., 1984.

Mid-Atlantic Center for Race Equity. *Guidelines for effective teaching: Every child deserves a chance.* Washington, D.C., 1984.

Office of Sex Equity in Vocational Education. *Achieving sex equity through social studies grades 7-12.* District of Columbia, 1986.

Office of the State Director of Vocational Education. *Rainbow shave ice, crackseed, and other ono stuff: Sex equity goodies for the classroom.* Honolulu, Hawaii, 1985.

Pico de Hernandez, I. *Sexism in the classroom — For bilingual classes.* Newton, Massachusetts: EDC/WEEA Publishing Center, 1980.

Project on Sex Stereotyping in Education (Series of Subject Areas Packets). Atlanta, Georgia: Georgia State University, 1978.

Schniedewind, N., & Davidson, E. *Open minds to equality: A sourcebook of learning activities to promote race, sex, class, and age equity.* Englewood Cliffs, New Jersey: Prentice-Hall, 1983.

Section for Women in Public Administration. *The right word: Guidelines for avoiding sex-biased language.* McLean, Virginia, 1985.

Stein, D. *Thinking and doing: Overcoming sex-role stereotyping in education.* Honolulu, Hawaii: Hawaii Educational Equity Program, 1978.

Weiss, M. *People and places, USA.* Newton, Massachusetts: WEEA Publishing Center, 1981.

Chapter 12

SOLVING THE EXCLUSION PROBLEM: THE KEY TO SEX EQUITABLE EDUCATION IN MATH, SCIENCE, AND TECHNOLOGY

KENNETH BROADHURST

INTRODUCTION

"Why should I take more math? I'll never use it!"

Any well-informed educator with a modicum of observational skills, can see that the "age of technology" is not only upon us, but here to stay. Despite the attempts of many adults to resist the technological invasion (those "new-fangled machines"?), new scientific achievements have become a matter of routine in the office and household. Certainly everyone can point to the computer. But added to the obvious evidence of daily life (VCRs, laser discs, cellular phones, and so forth) are monumental advances in biomedical research, energy development, production techniques, even weaponry. Progress in these and other areas requires not only workers skilled in math and science, but citizens well versed in technological issues.

It is difficult to imagine the technological future for students. Many jobs will be related to information-sharing and production and will require a strong math and science background. Many decisions for voters (e.g., environmental, defense, and health concerns) will be based on an understanding of math and science issues.

Yet science and math remain the subject areas often viewed as mysterious, difficult, and tedious. Careers related to math, science, and technology are generally regarded as a male domain, requiring discipline, logic, spatial skills, and knowledge of tools—characteristics that are stereotypically male only. Math and science classrooms, and therefore fields of employment, are dominated by males. Despite the fact that knowledge of science has become a critical issue for Americans, a significant portion of the school population (i.e., girls) is being excluded from pursuing programs in math, science, and technology. Consider the statistics:

- Electrical and electronic $33,972 average   93% male
  engineers   1984 salary

- Of the nation's 2.7 million scientists, only 5% are female
  and 1.5% are black

- Data processing $24,000 average   90% male
  equipment repairers   1984 salary

Do these numbers reflect deliberate attempts on the part of educators and employers to leave girls and women out of future enterprises? Of course not. They reflect traditional views that have not caught up to rapidly changing demands for well-trained workers in fields of technology. Gender stereotypes still work against the creation of a broader field of scientific technicians, inventors and leaders. Ken Broadhurst discusses the exclusion problem, and suggests strategies to prepare more students for the technological future.

SOLVING THE EXCLUSION PROBLEM: THE KEY TO SEX EQUITABLE EDUCATION IN MATH, SCIENCE, AND TECHNOLOGY

Our society is in the midst of a crisis. The demand for skilled technical workers now exceeds the supply. Fingers are being pointed at our educational system for its failure to adequately prepare young people for today's job market. In response, educational organizations such as The National Science Foundation and the National Science Board have called for improvements in math, science, and technology education at all academic levels. Of particular concern for many educators is the gross underrepresentation of women and minorities in these fields, as illustrated by the following statistic: of the nation's 2.7 million scientists, only 5 percent are female and 1.5 percent are black (Campbell, 1986).

Historically, the number of women who have chosen careers in the math, science, and engineering fields are few. Without an adequate educational response, women will continue to be underrepresented in the pool of workers who are technologically literate. Since it is becoming increasingly clear that proficiency in the use of technology expands the career and life options of young people, it is imperative that educators address the root causes of this disparity. For both young men and women, technological literacy may mean the difference between a life of plenty and a life of poverty.

Although the reasons for the underrepresentation of women in these fields are complex and perhaps not fully understood, many experts agree that the stereotyping of math, science, and technology as a "male domain" is a contributing factor. This stereotype, in turn, leads to the systematic exclusion of women from informal and formal educational activities that foster technological literacy. Understanding these patterns of exclusion leads to strategies for systematically "including" all students in technology classrooms. (Technology classrooms could refer to pre-K or elementary classrooms as well as secondary level courses.) This chapter will focus on the exclusion issue, and will offer educational strategies that promote inclusion and sex equity.

Early Intervention

The stereotype of math, science, and technology being "male" subjects takes root during early childhood when boys are encouraged far more than girls by adults to play with toys that involve or simulate tools and machinery. Boys are more likely to explore their environment independent from close adult supervision, while girls are socialized to stay closer to parents and receive more encouragement by parents to engage in play activities that foster nurturing and social skills (Klein, 1985). Children see men much more often than women performing tasks that involve complex tools and machinery. In the absence of adult intervention, children tend to self-select activities that they feel competent at by the time they reach preschool classrooms. Through this process, girls begin to exclude *themselves* from activities that foster an understanding of, and an appreciation for technology. It is no wonder that researchers have found that the physical sciences are sex-typed as a "male" subject by students as early as the second grade (Klein, 1985).

Preschool and elementary classrooms do little to reverse this trend. In fact, technology education is systematically neglected at the preschool and elementary school levels. Although preschool classrooms usually offer rich, well-rounded learning environments to children, Barbara Sprung and her associates contend that the only "required" learning activities typically involve reading and writing preparatory skills (areas in which boys need the most remedial attention), while other activities, including those that foster math and science skills, are left open for self-selection by students (1985).

The final report of the *ACS 1984 Chemistry Education Planning Conference* identified the quantity and quality of science instruction, especially in the physical sciences, as an area needing vast improvement at the elementary school level nationwide. According to the report, biology and ecology receive the most attention in preschool and elementary classrooms, while the physical sciences receive little. Educators who are developing technology education programs must first turn their attention to the elementary and preschool classrooms in an effort to remediate the learning deficits of girls while systematically improving the level of math, science and technology instruction for all students.

Enrollment

Exclusion is also evident when one looks at female enrollment patterns in higher level math and science courses in high school. Researchers have found little difference between boys' and girls' achievement patterns in math and science until the junior high school, when both achievement and interest in these subjects begins to fall for girls. It is important to note that girls generally develop less confidence in their ability to perform in these subjects *before* their performance actually drops (Campbell, 1986). Girls, in general, have poorer attitudes about these subjects; they enroll less often in higher level coursework, demonstrate lower achievement at these subjects, and report having less experience using scientific materials and instruments than boys (Kahle, 1983). The "hard" or "physical" science courses are particularly prone to rejection or avoidance by girls.

Even when girls complete high school with a strong background in math and science, they are less apt to turn their expertise into advanced college degrees and/or employment in these fields than boys (Berryman, 1983). Although these patterns can be attributed to a host of factors, one can argue that the stereotype of math, science, and technology as a whole "male domain," in its institutionalized form, has contributed significantly to the decisions by girls to exclude themselves from participation in these subjects, and ultimately in related careers.

Classroom Environment

In addition to girls opting out of math, science, and technology because of their own stereotypical notions, the possibility exists that girls may find themselves excluded from active participation in classroom activities if the technology instructor does not take measures to ensure that they do actively participate. This exclusion or isolation may result from the following factors: the quantity and quality of attention given to female students by the instructor, the group dynamics that result when girls are vastly outnumbered by boys, and girls' lack of previous exposure to technology concepts.

The fact that many girls exclude themselves or are excluded from activities that involve tools and machinery at early ages because of socialization factors has been mentioned previously. As a result, girls may enter a technology course lacking basic skills and confidence. The chances, therefore, that girls will need compensatory help is greater than for boys. If the instructor does not evaluate all students, especially girls, for skill readiness at the beginning of the course, and provide remedial help early on, she or he may find a knowledge and interest gap between students who have basic skills and students who do not. This gap may cause students without basic skills to shy away from active participation in class activities.

A technology instructor faces another dilemma if only a handful of girls enroll in a course. Small and large group dynamics in this instance may make it nearly impossible for girls to participate on an equal basis with boys. In on-going classroom situations, researchers have found that boys are generally more active and influential in mixed-sex work groups (Klein, 1985). If there are less girls than boys in a work group, and if it is perceived that the girls have less ability regarding the subject matter, the likelihood that girls will have less influence on group talk and will contribute less to the groups goals increases. Girls also have a greater chance of being treated in a sex-stereotyped fashion by boys if they are not perceived as equals.

An instructor can effectively deal with an under-enrollment of girls by carefully structuring group activity so that all group roles and tasks are rotated and shared. Girls should be placed in work groups with equal numbers of boys. When possible, mixed-sex groups should involve members that have equal ability levels. Structured, cooperative mixed-sex group work has been identified as an effective, sex-equitable instructional strategy (Klein, 1985).

Finally, females may find themselves excluded from active classroom participation by the instructor's behavior towards them in class. Research has shown that teachers tend to expect boys and girls to act in a sex-stereotypic manner in classrooms. These often subtle expectations lead to differences in the way boys and girls are treated. For example, girls generally get less attention in classrooms than boys, and the attention they do get often reinforces stereotypic notions of helplessness and reliance on others (Weiner, 1980). Instructors, regardless of their gender, are more apt to complete problem-solving tasks for girls, while boys are given more latitude to solve problems themselves. Girls are praised for trying, while boys are told to try harder. These patterns are particularly counterproductive in a classroom where experimentation and calculated risk taking are essential ingredients for success.

Recognizing and counteracting sex-biased behavior is a complex task that requires time, energy, and commitment on the part of the technology instructor. Awareness of these patterns is the first step. Staff development programs designed to promote teacher awareness and behavioral change are described in the following discussion of educational approaches.

Strategies to Promote Inclusion and Sex Equity

The first priority for educators who approach technology with sex equity in mind is to address the exclusion problem as it is defined here. Strategies for the systematic inclusion of girls in technology education are outlined below. One should note that almost all of these strategies will benefit *all* students, not just female students. Some strategies are compensatory in nature, others involve common sense and effective teaching. Educators who adopt these strategies will be one step closer to the important goal of helping all students become technologically literate.

Curriculum:

1. *Start Young:* A pre-K–12 approach is essential.
2. *Be Interdisciplinary:* Understanding how technology has shaped our world, and how humans continue to shape technology can only be accomplished if it is discussed in relation to all basic subjects. For example, one can investigate the effect of the printing press on public education in a social studies class.
3. *Help Students Connect the Concept of Technology with Their World:* Everyone employs technology to solve problems. By personalizing this subject, students are less apt to be threatened or turned off to it.
4. *Provide Compensatory Help:* Plan to remediate the deficits that some students, especially girls, may have in this subject area. Remedial attention should focus particularly on visual-spatial and problem-solving skills, and on experimental deficits (e.g., with tools and machines).
5. *Educate Parents and Family Members:* Involve households in technology education by making them aware of equity issues, and by providing them with enrichment activities to use with their children. This strategy will be most effective at the pre-school and elementary levels.
6. *Teacher In-Service:* Many pre- and elementary school teachers confidence in their ability to teach applied mathematics, the physical sciences, and technology. In-service programs must be available to upgrade their skills and improve their confidence levels in these areas.

Instruction:

1. *Employ a "Discovery" or "Socratic" Format:* "Learn by doing" should be the rule for instruction. Students should be encouraged to solve real problems and take calculated risks. Merely providing information via a lecture format should be avoided.

2. *Promote Equity:* Be up front with students, especially older students, about your commitment to equity. Take the time to discuss stereotypes and the limitations that they impose on people. Point out bias as it surfaces in books, media, and during class discussion, and discuss equitable alternatives. Encourage students to be assertive about their feelings and needs.

3. *Use Activities That Promote Leadership and Teamwork:* Leadership and teamwork skills are essential for future employability. Structure activities to ensure that all students develop these skills. "Cooperative Learning" techniques that focus on cooperative, group work, and shared leadership may be particularly useful in a technology classroom. Ideally, the groups are mixed by gender.

4. *Use Role Models:* It is extremely important for career planning purposes that students have a chance to interact with female and male adults who have technology-related careers. Personalized demonstrations and field trips are useful strategies. Whenever possible, role models should be screened for their charisma and ability to relate to students in order to ensure successful adult-student contact.

5. *Teacher In-Service:* Teachers should be provided the opportunity to systematically review the way that they interact with students in order to discuss whether or not they treat students equitably, and to improve affective teaching skills. (Nationally recognized in-service program models of this nature are recommended in the resource section.)

Enrollment:

1. *Outreach:* Secondary level technology instructors should begin to encourage enrollment through outreach activities to fourth, fifth, and sixth-grade students. These students could take part in exploratory visits to technology labs that involve hands-on demonstration and guidance by older student "leaders." If carefully orchestrated, such activities give entering students the message that technology classrooms are exciting, fun places to be.

2. *Enrichment Programs:* Summer "activity camps" and enrichment programs have been used with great success to increase the achievement and interest levels of young adolescent girls and minority students in math, science, and computer literacy. Such programs have led to increased enrollments in secondary courses. (Model programs are listed in the resource section.)

3. *K-12 Guidance:* Teachers, counselors, administrators, and parents must be consistent in their encouragement of all students to take a full complement of science, and technology coursework. Technology instructors should play an active role in this process by sharing resources with colleagues, by taking part in community education efforts, and by using career pairs and other guidance activities as opportunities to promote technology education.

REFERENCES

American Chemical Society. *Priorities, partnerships, and plans: Chemistry education in schools.* Washington, D.C., 1984.

Berryman, S.E. *Who will do science? Trends and their causes, in minority and female representation among holders of advanced degrees in science and mathematics.* New York: The Rockefeller Foundation, 1983.

Campbell, P.B. What's a nice girl like you doing in a math class? *Phi Delta Kappan,* March 1986, *67* (7), 516–520.

Kahle, J.P. *The disadvantaged majority: Science education for women.* (Reprint of AETS Outstanding Paper for 1983.) Burlington, North Carolina: Carolina Biological Supply Company, 1983.

Klein, S.S. (Ed.). *Handbook for achieving sex equity through education.* Baltimore, Maryland: The Johns Hopkins University Press, 1985.

Melnick, S.L., Wheeler, C.W., & Gunnings, B.B. Can science teachers promote gender equity in their classrooms? How two teachers do it. *Journal of educational equity and leadership,* 1986, *6* (1), 5–25.

National Science Board. *Educating Americans for the 21st century.* Washington, D.C., 1983.

Sargent, A. (Ed.). *Beyond sex roles.* New York: West Publishing Company, 1977.

Sprung, B., Frosch, M., & Campbell, P.B. *What will happen if . . . young children and the scientific method.* Brooklyn, New York: Faculty Press, Inc., 1985.

Weiner, E.H. (Ed.). *Sex role stereotyping in the schools.* Washington, D.C.: National Education Association of the United States, 1980.

The following statements are designed for the exploration of personal reactions to the chapter, as well as for the review of the contents of the chapter. Emphasis in discussions should be on exploring issues in depth, rather than on determining the correct or appropriate responses.

FOR DISCUSSION:

1. Respond to the author's statement: "For both young men and women, technological literacy may mean the difference between a life of plenty and a life of poverty."
2. How is "technology" taught in your educational institution?
3. How does the author define the issue of "exclusion" from math, science, and technology education?
4. Do girls exclude themselves from "activities that foster an understanding of, and an appreciation for, technology"?
5. Respond to the author's statement: "Educators who are developing technology education programs must first turn their attention to the elementary and preschool classrooms..."
6. Describe strategies that may improve the attitude of *students* toward math, science, and technology education.
7. Describe strategies that may improve the attitude of *teachers* toward math, science, and technology education.
8. What steps should be taken in your educational setting to "adequately prepare young people for today's job market"?

SUGGESTIONS FOR FURTHER READING

Blum, L. *Expanding your horizons in science and mathematics: A handbook for planners.* Newton, Massachusetts: WEEA Publishing Company, 1980.

Brush, L. *Encouraging girls in mathematics: The problem and the solution.* Cambridge, Massachusetts: Abt Books, 1980.

Cheek, H. N. *Handbook for conducting equity activities on mathematics education.* Reston, Virginia: National Council of Teachers of Mathematics, 1981.

Fennema, E. *Multiplying options and subtracting bias.* Reston, Virginia: National Council of Teachers of Mathematics, 1981.

Humphreys, S. M. (Ed.). *Women and minorities in science: Strategies for increasing participation.* Boulder, Colorado: Westview Press, 1982.

Lemons, C. D. *Education and training for a technological world.* Columbus, Ohio: National Center for Research in Vocational Education, 1984.

Mathematics Department. *The invisible filter kit; Survive and succeed in math; Mathaphobia can cost you a career; Dropping math? Say good-bye to 82 jobs.* Toronto, Canada: Toronto Board of Education, 1985.

Office of Opportunities in Science. *Science, technology and women: A world perspective.* Washington, D.C.: American Association for the Advancement of Science, 1987.

Sharon, S., Hare, P., Hertz-Lazarowitz, & Webb, C. *Cooperation in education.* Brigham Young University Press, 1980.

Skolnick, J. *How to encourage girls in math and science: Strategies for parents and educators.* Englewood Cliffs, New Jersey: Prentice-Hall, 1982.

Sprung, B., Froschl, M., & Campbell, P. *What will happen if . . . young children and the scientific method.* New York: Beginning Math and Science Equitably Project, 1985.

Strauss, M.J. *Recommended resources for use in developing programs to achieve sex equity in mathematics, science & technology.* Baltimore: Maryland: Maryland State Department of Education, 1987.

Tobias, S. *Overcoming math anxiety.* New York: Houghton Mifflin, 1980.

Ysleta Independent School District. *Ysleta girls count!* El Paso, Texas, 1985.

Chapter 13

COMPUTER EQUITY FOR GIRLS

Jo Sanders

INTRODUCTION

"These computers are user friendly!"

Computer education appears to be the one area of education where equity is not a problem. Most schools have computers readily available in the classrooms, and computer labs, accessible to students and staff. Since classes in computer programming were created recently, educators were conscious of creating mixed gender classes. Some schools even require that all students take at least one semester of word processing so that all students are comfortable operating a computer. Boys and girls have often had hands-on experience since the primary grades. They accept that computers are and will continue to be an integral part of their personal and professional lives.

But something is wrong in this rosy picture. Girls have computers to use, but they are not using them. Girls are shying away from demonstrating any expertise on a computer. Girls have home computers, but do not seem to be learning and applying computer skills. They do not even participate in the entertainment of computer games.

Since the doors to the computer centers are more than likely not closed to girls, why are they staying away? Why are they stepping aside for their male peers to tackle a problem, work the keyboard, program a new lesson?

The answer appears to be a familiar theme, sex role stereotyping: the old biased image of girls who do not need or care about technical skills, girls who are not capable of solving problems, analyzing a program, translating information into symbols. This results in girls who are afraid to be as smart or smarter than the boys (particularly her potential boyfriends), and girls who are afraid to be assertive and demand equal time at the machine. Most importantly, it leads to girls who are uninformed about the impact of computer training on employment potential.

Sex role stereotyping has interfered with girls' attitudes about computers. It has also limited the view of educators about girls and computers. Most educators have appeared to have made the assumption that since computers are open to all, girls must choose not to learn the skills. On the surface it can easily appear as if the options are available and girls freely and deliberately opt out.

Jo Sanders provides information about the issues of "computer equity," and presents effective strategies that can assure girls more than just access to computers.

COMPUTER EQUITY FOR GIRLS

I have noticed that the subject of sex equity makes many people uncomfortable. They think the author is going to accuse them of sex bias and make them feel guilty for oppressing poor, defenseless little girls. Naturally, they'd rather avoid the whole thing.

But truly evil oppressors of little girls are really quite rare. Certainly with respect to computer equity, you won't find anybody hanging "No Girls Allowed" signs on the computer. On the contrary, a good many educators have noticed girls' reluctance with computers and have tried to do something about it. Often, they fail.

This chapter will describe the extent of the computer gender gap and why it matters, explore the factors that cause it, and present suggestions for educators on how to close it.

WHERE YOU SEE A COMPUTER GENDER GAP

Once you know how to look, you see it all over the place.

In School

There is a great deal of evidence that the computer gender gap usually starts becoming noticeable at the middle school level and that it typically widens as girls get older. It's best to look at optional computer use, such as enrollment in computer electives or free-time computer use: using a computer when you don't have to is the best barometer of genuine interest and involvement. Consider:

- In the Computer Equity Training Project (CETP) in 1983–86, described later in this chapter, it was found that girls were 26 percent of the optional computer users in the middle and junior high schools we worked with across the country.
- In 1982, researcher Lockheed found that 40 percent of the boys at Princeton High School used school computers in their free time, as compared with 8 percent of the girls (Kolata, 1984).
- Researcher Anderson reports that the gap between males and females taking programming courses actually widened somewhat between 1978 and 1982 (Anderson, Welch, and Harris, 1984).

159

- The Project on Equal Education Rights tells of surveys on computer course enrollments in California, Michigan, and Maryland. There was a 2:1 ratio in favor of boys (Lipken and Martin-McCormick, 1984).
- In 1984, Albuquerque Public Schools found that 37 percent of the boys had taught themselves how to use a computer. Only 20 percent of the girls did (Albuquerque Public Schools, 1984).
- It's the same in higher education. Nationally, in 1982 (the latest published figures), women earned 33 percent of the Bachelors degrees in Computer and Information Science, 23 percent of the Masters degrees, and 10 percent of the Ph.D.'s (National Center for Education Statistics, 1984). This is the most severe relative decline for women in any field of study except law, including mathematics, chemistry, and physics.

At Home

There is also a lot of evidence of a computer gender gap in American homes:

- The CETP researchers in 1985 learned that 64 percent of the boys and 51 percent of the girls at the subject schools had a computer at home. These computers were used overwhelmingly by boys and fathers. Compared to the boys, girls were three times as likely to say they did not use their home computers at all.
- In a survey of parents at one of the CETP field test schools, it was found that while parents considered computer knowledge "essential" for school and work for their daughters as well as their sons, they were more likely to buy computers for sons, used computers more with sons, and discussed computers and computer careers more with sons.
- In 1983, researchers Miura and Hess found not only that boys were twice as likely as girls to use their home computers, but that boys used them for longer periods of time than girls (1983).

Computer Camps

In the same study, Miura and Hess also reported on their survey of summer computer camp directors. They learned that girls' enrollment in the computer camps decreased with:

- Age: 30 percent in primary grades, 26 percent in middle grades, and 24 percent in high school grades.

- Curriculum difficulty: 27 percent for beginning and intermediate programming, 5 percent for assembly language.
- Cost: 32 percent for camps costing under $100. 15 percent for those costing more than $1,000 (1983).

At Work

In 1984 women were 35 percent of programmers and 30 percent of systems analysts (Epstein & Green, 1985). According to the National Alliance of Women in Communications Industries, women hold only 11 percent of the middle and upper management high technology positions.

Other Places

The next time you are near a newsstand, browse through the computer magazines. Only 20 percent of the pictures in four large-circulation computer magazines for adults were of women or girls (Sanders, unpublished research, 1984). What's more, some of them were not even shown at a computer; they were gazing adoringly at the men who were. And almost all the faces were white, by the way. Of the articles in these magazines, 76 percent of them were written by men and 12 percent by women. (The rest of the authors had unisex first names or initials.)

You can take a look at your local video arcade. It is not so long ago that kids called video games "computer games," which of course they are. Chances are the only girls you see are there to watch the boys play the games.

There are also computer stores. Are the salespeople male or female? The technical staff? The customers? Women bought only 2 percent of the microcomputers sold in early 1983. By contrast, they bought 45 percent of the cars sold then.

Finally, attending a computer trade fair is a consciousness-raising experience; attendance appears to be about 90 percent male.

The computer gender gap is society-wide; although schools may reinforce it, they do not cause it. It should be a familiar pattern: the same female avoidance behavior appears in relation to math and science.

WHY THE COMPUTER GENDER GAP MATTERS

In the short run, the computer gender gap matters educationally. The computer is a valuable educational tool that enables students to learn better and more: think for example of a computer simulation of a volcanic explosion, something that few of us would want to teach any other way in our classrooms. The computer allows students to do their work more accurately and more attractively: students take more pride in their writing, for example, when it looks professional thanks to a word processor and a printer. Using a spreadsheet to process numerical relationships, students avoid getting bogged down in arithmetical errors and are free to concentrate on the concepts involved. (Arithmetic is another lesson entirely.)

And in the long run, it also matters occupationally. The U.S. Department of Labor says that half to three-quarters of tomorrow's jobs will involve computers in some way, from simple button-pushing to jobs in sales and service, design of hardware and software, the development of computer applications in many fields, and especially millions of jobs in which people use computers to process information in the normal course of the day, as did the author of this chapter.

On the whole, these computer-related jobs pay well. Some pay extremely well, and paychecks are extremely important to women. Occupational segregation, or the division of the labor force into "women's" jobs and better-paying "men's" jobs, results in women earning about 60 cents for every dollar men earn. But did you know that nine out of ten of today's schoolgirls will work for pay? They will spend an average of 29 years working, more time than they'll spend raising children. More than half the mothers with children under age six are now working outside the home. More than two-thirds of the women who work do so out of economic necessity (U. S. Department of Labor, 1986).

The percentage of American families today that consists of a wage-earning father, a homemaker mother, and two children (the dog is optional) is less than 5 percent. The others are families with more or fewer than two children, single-parent families, and especially families with working wives. The typical American family isn't typical any longer.

So women are working because they have to support themselves and/or their families. The money they bring home affects not only the quality of their own lives but their children's as well. Economic advantage achieved in one generation tends to be passed on to the next, making women's paychecks an important long-range consideration.

Carol Edwards, Director of Project MiCro in Atlanta, points out that computer skills may well become tomorrow's "job marker," as is a college degree or standard English today, whether or not the job requires these skills. Girls who avoid the computer today are going to have a rough time of it in the job market tomorrow.

THE CAUSE OF THE COMPUTER GENDER GAP

So if there's no "No Girls Allowed" sign on the school computer or any of the other places where the computer gender gap can be found, why are girls avoiding the computer? Oddly enough, the evidence is the cause.

Girls live in the same world you and I live in. They look around and see Daddy at the computer at home, boys in the computer room in school, boys in the video arcade, and men in the computer ads. They notice that computer hackers are almost invariably male. They see boys responding in droves to the thrill of computerized weaponry and war.

When girls reach puberty, these observations begin to matter. At the middle-school age, they're sorting out what it means to be a woman in this society: what is appropriate behavior? what are appropriate interests? It is hardly surprising, given what girls see in the world around them, that they conclude computers are not quite the proper thing for a real girl to do.

This is why you don't have to hang a sign on the computer to account for the lopsided figures you read earlier in this chapter. Girls mentally place it there for themselves. Educators who are bothered by girls' computer avoidance often try to overcome it by being scrupulously evenhanded, but this rarely works. A catalog description of the COBOL elective that starts out "Boys and girls who take this course will..." isn't very likely to have a larger impact on a girl than the anticipated negative reaction of her girlfriends. And then there's the reinforcing effect of all those educators and parents who find it normal that mostly males use computers; they are hardly the ones to challenge girls' computer avoidance.

HOW WE ACHIEVED COMPUTER EQUITY

But computer equity can be achieved. The Computer Equity Training Project sponsored by the Women's Action Alliance was carried out on a grant from the Women's Educational Equity Act Program, U. S. Department of Education. The object was to find out what causes the computer gender gap and to develop, test, and publish strategies that educators can use to close it in schools.

After researching the issue in the literature, workers talked to many observant teachers to find out what they thought might be causing girls to avoid the computer. Researchers worked for a term with teachers, counselors, librarians, administrators, parents, and others in three middle and junior high schools to design computer activities and approaches that might appeal to girls (See Notes). Many of them did in fact turn out to be appealing, since girls' computer use rose substantially. This information, augmented by the computer equity suggestions of dozens of teachers and administrators across the country, was compiled in a book entitled *The Neuter Computer: Computers for Girls and Boys* (Sanders and Stone, 1986).

In a five-school, five-month field test for The Neuter Computer, data on students' optional computer use was collected at all five schools (See Notes). Three experimental schools received an in-service session on computer equity from project staff, *The Neuter Computer,* and biweekly progress conferences by phone. A team of faculty members at each of these three schools planned, carried out, and evaluated four to six computer equity strategies they chose from the book. A control school received the inservice session and the biweekly calls, but no book and consequently no strategies. A control school received only data-collection headaches.

During the term, girls' computer use at the experimental schools rose an average of 144 percent. Girls were 26 percent of the optional computer users at the beginning of the term and 48 percent of them at the end. In contrast, the attention control school increase was only 14 percent and no change at all at the control school. The results are described and analyzed in *The Neuter Computer: Computers for Girls and Boys* (Sanders and Stone, 1986).

The Neuter Computer has 56 computer activities that girls and boys like: ways to use graphics, databasa programs, spreadsheets, telecommunications, word processing, and others. The book also contains 96 computer equity strategies that teachers and staff, administrators, parents, and students themselves can use to persuade girls to do these interesting and educationally sound computer activities. Here is a representative sample of computer equity strategies that you can carry out in a classroom, in a school, or by reaching out into the community in order to close the computer gender gap.

HOW YOU, TOO, CAN ACHIEVE COMPUTER EQUITY

There are two absolutely essential and rather sensible ingredients to computer equity success, from which flow a wide variation in individual strategies.

Computer Equity Strategies for Teachers and Staff

1. Focus Specifically on Girls

Subtlety just will not work. You have to say, "G–I–R–L–S," loud and clear. Remember that when it comes to computers, girls translate "students" or even "boys and girls" to mean "boys." Moreover, target girls in groups and not individually. A girl cannot decline a computer invitation because she is worried about her girlfriends' negative reaction if her girlfriends are right there in the computer room with her. Invite her friends to bring other friends. Girls repeatedly told us that it is not the presence of boys in the computer room that discourages them from entering: it is the absence of their girlfriends. Make the adolescent herd instinct work *for* you, for a change.

2. Stress Usefulness

Girls and boys seem to approach the computer differently. Boys tend to enjoy playing around with a computer just to see what it can do: the computer as end versus means, so to speak. They happily spend hours playing an adventure game or working on a program for its own sake, not because they need it for something. Girls, on the other hand, tend to want the computer to do something useful for them: the computer as means versus end. This means that to attract girls to the computer, there has to be a point to the software you propose, a purpose to the result. Make it clear that a given computer activity will enable them to do something they consider important or desirable.

3. Schedule Optional Computer Use

First come, first served means that boys in their enthusiasm for the computer usually get there first. Change the rules. You can allow only even numbers of boys and girls to use the computers at any one time. You can schedule the sign-up process alphabetically: only students whose names start A to D can sign up today, E to H tomorrow, etc. You can reserve optional computer time to the 7th grade (or certain 7th grade classes) this week, with 8th grade next week. You can require that anyone who used a computer this week must wait until next week to get another crack at it. And then actively and personally invite girls (in friendship groups!) to sign up.

4. Start a Girls' Computer Committee

Identify the girls who are the leaders, the popular ones who set the trends. They will not necessarily be the best students, but you know who they are. Invite them to a meeting and ask for their help in making sure girls get a fair share of the computer. (Remember the power of the word "fair" to adolescent ears.) Give them the student chapter of *The Neuter Computer* for ideas, or watch them invent strategies of their own to hook girls' computer interest.

5. Offer Computer Graphics Sessions

Be sure you have something interesting and useful for girls to do in the computer room once they get there, or else they will not come again. An after-school or lunchtime session in computer graphics is just the thing: many girls love to use graphics software for making party invitations, personalized stationery, banners, and greeting cards. (Boys like it, too.) A spontaneous display of these things at the bus stop of one of our field test schools was an impressive recruitment technique. You can offer more sophisticated computer graphics in a mini-course after school.

6. Student Computer Teachers

Having students (especially girls) help other students use computers is a triply smart move: help for you, appealing to them, and role models for everyone else. You can make this strategy as formal or as informal as you like, but the girls will have to be taught first to ensure that they are reasonably computer-competent. Repeat, "reasonably": they do not have to be an experts.

7. Hold a Computer Career Fair

Invite as speakers and demonstrators people from the community who use computers in their work. Leaf through the Business Yellow Pages for innovative contact ideas to avoid having to rely once again on the same old insurance company down the street. Make sure a good number of your imports are women, and that all of them, women and men, stress what good fields these are for women to enter.

Several of these strategies involve graphics, while there are others you can carry out that involve word processing (producing the school newspaper, for example, or a literary magazine, via the computer). These strategies carry a risk: that of appealing to the most stereotypically feminine interests.

While I confess I would rather see girls making full use of a computer's capabilities by means of higher-order thinking skills or advanced programming, the truth is that simple graphics can often be more effective in getting girls' fingers on the keyboard. There are two ways to avoid the sexist trap that looms up. The first is that if "Print Shop" or the equivalent proves attractive to your girls, use it to establish their computer interest firmly, and then as soon as you can, move them on to more advanced uses. The second is to remember that some girls will be bored silly by "Print Shop" but would be fascinated by programming. Don't assume that *all* girls like "Print Shop" because they are girls.

The computer is an inherently interesting and useful machine, as most girls (and boys) discover when they get close enough to one. Your job is to get them close enough, and then to make sure they take full advantage of a wide range of applications and uses.

Computer Equity Strategies for Administrators

There are school strategies that only administrators, by virtue of their position, can carry out. Here are a few:

1. Low-Key Education About Computer Equity

We in the education business sometimes forget that in the history of the human race, adults did occasionally learn new things before the invention of the in-service workshop. As the administrator, you can ask faculty members to drop by the computer room when it is not being used for classes to see for themselves which kind of student is in there. You can ask them to take the Computer Neutrality Self-Test (a mini-diagnostic device in *The Neuter Computer*) and report on the results at a faculty meeting. You can put copies of articles about computer equity in everyone's mailboxes. You can bring the subject up at faculty meetings (note the plural) by asking for relevant observations and comments. You can make it clear in the dozens of ways you have at your disposal that a computer gender gap in your school is important and is not acceptable.

2. Expanding Faculty Access to Computers

Some faculty members seem to be even more wary of computers than some kids are. Teachers and staff who will not go near a computer are not terribly likely to sing its praises to girls or anybody else. One way you can help them discover that the computer will not bite them and that it's moreover enjoyable and useful is to institute an evening or weekend loan program. Many people are more willing to get to know a computer in the privacy of their living rooms than in the publicity of the computer room.

Be sure, though, that the faculty's new computer competence is followed up by actual classroom use with both girls and boys. I have noticed a new wrinkle on the Graduate Student Syndrome (which is to read and read and read in order to put off the awful moment of beginning to write the dissertation). Some faculty members delay using the computer with students until they feel they're expert at it, and, of course, that may be never. Let them know that something less than total computer expertise will be quite good enough for the classroom.

3. Build Computer Equity into District Policy

Most school districts now have or are developing computer education policy and curriculum goals. All districts have sex equity policy goals. Few districts make the connection between the two. You point it out and do what needs doing to make computer equity for girls an explicit district goal. This means defining the term "computer equity," what it plans to do to achieve computer equity, and by when.

To achieve a goal of no wider than a 60/40 male/female ratio in free time computer use and in computer elective enrollments, particularly the advanced courses, use these strategies and others in *The Neuter Computer*. Within a maximum of three or four years you should have the problem solved with only minor reinforcement needed at the beginning of each school year thereafter to make sure the new students understand that computers in your district are for everyone. And while you're at it, take a look at other computer gaps that may exist in your district: white/minority students, nondisabled/disabled students, higher achieving/lower achieving students, academic/vocational students, high income/low income neighborhood schools. These inequities also need to be addressed.

THE COMPUTER GENDER GAP
WILL NOT DISAPPEAR SOON

Some think that it would be smarter to wait out the computer gender gap rather than go to all this trouble to correct it, because they believe that it will disappear by itself before long. They give four reasons for their belief, each of which is arguable.

The first is that the computer gender gap should disappear when the quality of the computer education curriculum improves. Better computer education (goes this theory) serves all students, and since girls are half of them the problem will soon be solved. It won't. Even in schools with excellent computer education, a good many girls decline it. The reason, of course, is that girls come into school with the "computer equals male" equation in their minds. Even plus odd equals odd: equal computer education offered to unequal computer attitudes leads to unequal computer behavior. Put another way, the absolute number of computer-using girls will probably rise with better computer education, but the relative number (as compared with boys) will probably not.

A second argument is that the computer gender gap should disappear when today's kindergartners reach the upper grades. The theory is that since these children will be the first to have computers as an ordinary component of their early childhood years, the girls as they get older will continue to see them as ordinary female interests. Well, some of them may, but some of them may not. The "computer equals male" equation will hardly have disappeared from the adult world that was born too early to have a unisex approach to computers: advertisements, computer stores, video arcades, the workplace, and especially teachers and parents. As a result, many girls at adolescence may decide it is time to outgrow their childish interest in computers in favor of something a bit more feminine.

A third point is that since women seem to be flocking to adult education computer courses (often in greater numbers than men), the computer gender gap will disappear when today's adolescent girls reach adulthood and see the need for computer skills. At that point they will learn them. Not necessarily. Today's adult women did not have a negative emotional attitude towards computers at that time. Their decision to learn computers as adults is therefore based on somewhat more rational considerations than interference from adolescent emotional associations permits. When today's adolescents grow up and notice that a lot of good jobs require computer skills, many of them may respond not by signing up for a course but by saying, "I guess this job isn't for me, or this one, or this one . . ."

Finally, some people deny there is any computer gender gap now: "We have lots of girls!—in our word processing course." These people conveniently tend to forget about the advanced programming course, which rarely has lots of girls. The value of word processing cannot be denied, but a career in word processing is simply an updated version of a secretarial career. Female word processing specialists cannot be expected to be content with $20,000 a year while male systems analysts earn $40,000 a year.

Obviously, one cannot say that all these gloomy predictions will come to pass for every single girl. They will not. But they will come true for enough girls to make us take the computer gender gap very seriously today. It is much easier to fix something that's a little broken now than it is to wait and try to fix it when it is really in terrible shape later on.

WHAT THE ISSUE REALLY IS

When you step back a bit, computer equity for girls is the tip of a very large pedagogical iceberg that can be problematic for educators: how do we distinguish between those educational choices students have the right to make for themselves, and those we have the obligation to make in their behalf?

These two positions are the extreme points of a wide spectrum. Few educators would dispute the legitimacy of elective courses in high school. Even fewer would leave first graders free to choose between recess and reading. Between the two extremes, however, it's not always easy to achieve the right balance, and computer equity falls into the middle of the spectrum. When girls say "No thank you" to the computer, what should our response be? "Fine with me"? "Too bad, you have to"? Something else?

It seems to me that the examples of elective courses and reading vs. recess provide the guidance we need to determine the best response. We let students choose electives in advanced art vs. advanced chemistry, let's say, not only because both are good for them but because the absence of one or the other is not harmful to their futures. The fact that some kids choose to avoid advanced art is acceptable, because in choosing advanced chemistry they may be preparing a future in which chemistry is important.

And we have no qualms at all about not letting first graders choose recess over reading, as they surely would if given the choice. We as adults know that good reading skills are far more important to their futures than good ball-throwing skills. We also know that first graders cannot possibly know what the adult world will require from them, so they cannot evaluate the alternative consequences. We adults must therefore make the choice for them.

In my opinion, computer equity is more similar to recess vs. reading than to elective courses, in that the lack of computer skills is likely to be harmful to the future of most students. If this is so, if we as professional educators can legitimately say that computer knowledge will be valuable to most adults and essential to a good number of them in years to come, then it follows that we have an obligation to do all we can to ensure that girls do not remove themselves from the benefits of computer education opportunities.

The logic of this argument leads to the position that proficiency in computer applications (spreadsheets, telecommunications, graphics, data-base managers, etc.) should be required for all students, just as proficiency in math and reading are. Until the American educational system agrees that computer proficiency is important, individual educators must try to achieve the same goal by persuasion and encouragement.

You have chosen to be an educator because you care deeply about children's futures. If you can look into the future and see computers in it, and if you can communicate the reality that girls and computers do, indeed, go together, then you will have made a powerful contribution to the lives of your female students, and through them, to their children and their children's children.

NOTES

The pilot test schools for the spring 1984 term were: Franklin Junior High School, Whitewater WI 53190; Waldport Junior High School, Waldport OR 97394; and Mt. Hebron Middle School, Upper Montclair NJ 07043.

In the spring 1985 field test there were three experimental schools: Alfred Nobel Junior High School, Northridge (Los Angeles) CA 91324; Gering Junior High School, Gering, Neb. 69341; and Camel's Hump Middle School, Richmond VT 05477. The control school was Lamar-at-

Trenton Middle School, McAllen TX 78501. The attention control school was Cumberland Middle School, Cumberland RI 02864.

REFERENCES

Albuquerque Public Schools, Division of Instructional Research, Testing, and Evaluation. A.P.S. Computer Education Pilot Project Evaluation. Report #2: Implementation, December, 1984, 39–40.

Anderson, R.E., Welch, W., & Harris, L.J. Inequities in opportunities for computer literacy. *The computing teacher,* April 1984, 10–12.

Epstein, R.K., & Green, G.P. *Employment and earnings,* January 1985, *32* (1), 176–80.

Kolata, G. Equal time for women. *Discover,* January 1984, 24–27.

Lipkin, J., & Martin-McCormick, L. *Microcomputers in the classroom: Are girls getting an even break?* Washington, D.C.: Project on Equal Education Rights (PEER), 1984.

Miura, I., & Hess, R.D. *Sex differences in computer access, interest, and usage.* Paper presented at the American Psychological Association, Anaheim, California, August 1983.

National Center for Education Statistics. *Digest of education statistics, 1983–84.* Washington, D.C.: Government Printing Office, 1984, 114.

Sanders, J.S., & Stone, A. *The neuter computer: Computers for girls and boys.* New York: Neal-Schuman Publishers, 1986. Available from Women's Action Alliance, 370 Lexington Avenue, Room 603, New York, NY 10017.

Women's Bureau. *Facts on working women.* United States Department of Labor, 1986.

The following statements are designed for the exploration of personal reactions to the chapter, as well as for the review of the contents of the chapter. Emphasis in discussions should be on exploring issues in depth, rather than on determining the correct or appropriate responses.

FOR DISCUSSION:

1. Respond to the statement: "Once you know how to look (for the computer gender gap), you see it all over the place."
2. What are the long term effects of the "computer gap"?
3. Is focusing specifically on girls (as the author recommends) perpetuating sex bias?
4. Why are "paychecks extremely important to women"?, and how are paychecks tied to the computer "gender gap"?
5. Discuss the author's recommendation to organize an after-school or lunch time session in computer graphics.
6. Review the availability, level of access, and use of computers in your institution. Discuss your observations in terms of computer equity.
7. Discuss the teacher as role model (including your own role as an educator), in eliminating the computer "gender gap."
8. Is the author's statement that "... proficiency in computer applications (spreadsheets, telecommunications, graphics, database managers, etc.) should be required for all students..." a solution to the computer "gender gap"?

SUGGESTIONS FOR FURTHER READING

Center for Educational Equity-American Institutes for Research. *IDEAS for equitable computer learning.* Palo Alto, California, 1986.

Davis, S. *Free and inexpensive resources for promoting math and science participation and computer equity.* Trenton, New Jersey: Math EQUALS Connections, 1986.

Equal Play Resource Magazine. *Computer equity.* New York, New York: Women's Action Alliance, 1983.

General Electric. *What's it like to work with computers?* Fairfield, Connecticut: Education Communications Programs, 1982.

Hartmann, H., Kraut, R., & Tilly, L. (Eds.). *Computer chips and paper clips: Technology and women's employment.* Washington, D.C.: National Academy Press, 1986.

Lipkin, J., & Sadker, D. *Sex bias in mathematics, computer science, and technology: The report card #3.* Washington, D.C.: Mid-Atlantic Center for Sex Equity, 1985.

Project on Equal Education Rights. *Debugging the program: Computer equity strategies for the classroom teacher. Everything you ever wanted to know about computers in education but were afraid to ask.* Washington, D.C., 1984, 1985.

Susquehanna University. *P.C. squared—programming computers, planning careers.* Selingsgrove, Pennsylvania, 1986.

Chapter 14

THE DIFFERENCE DIFFERENCE MAKES:
SEX EQUITY IN URBAN SCHOOLS

WALTEEN GRADY TRUELY

INTRODUCTION

"If we can get her into a program that has day care, then maybe she'll stay in school."

The process of implementing sex equity policies and practices in an educational system becomes even more challenging in large urban environments. Issues that are often relevant in smaller school districts are of paramount importance in the major cities. Concerns such as race desegregation, youth unemployment, adolescent pregnancy, effects of poverty, changes in family structure, and English language proficiency all impact on attempts to provide an equitable education to thousands of students in one school system. In most cases, the urban demographics and economic trends in the cities result in large, urban schools with complicated management systems having multiple equity needs. For example, young minority males face the strong possibility of dropping out of school and long-term unemployment. Young minority females face "double jeopardy," experiencing both race and sex discrimination. Teen parenting, or employment opportunities can become the dominant themes in attempting to achieve gender equity in a city school system. In addition, significant urban issues such as transportation, crime, health, and poverty influence the establishment of educational priorities.

Policymakers and administrators in urban schools must not only recognize the number of variables that influence the achievement of sex equity in urban education, but must know the most effective means of utilizing their complex educational system. They must be sufficiently knowledgeable about the characteristics of the population of the city's schools. It is only possible to devise an appropriate sex equity plan if the needs and experiences of the students are fully comprehended. It is only possible to implement the plan if the administrators are cognizant of the system's hierarchy, politics, and decision-making process.

Once gender equity is understood as an overriding issue in urban education, then problems of the cities can be tackled via policies and programs that stress equal treatment of students and expanded educational opportunities. Walteen Grady Truely discusses the issues affecting the achievement of sex equity in urban schools.

175

THE DIFFERENCE DIFFERENCE MAKES:
SEX EQUITY IN URBAN SCHOOLS

Profound changes have taken place in education since the societal commitment to promoting equality was made, signalled by *Brown v. Board of Education*, 1954 and followed by the passage of the Civil Rights Act of 1964. For educators the mandate of the Supreme Court decision and subsequent legislative action (Fishel and Pottker, 1977) was to develop policies, programs, strategies and activities to overcome historical inequities on the basis of race and color towards the realization of full democracy through the public school systems of the United States. Just as other social movements for equality were sparked by the movements to abolish slavery and to achieve civil rights of the nineteenth and twentieth centuries, the period following *Brown* saw the advent of efforts within education to develop strategies and activities to promote equity on the basis of gender, disability, national origin and language. Viewed together the goal of these efforts towards equity in education has been the promotion of full human rights in our society. An ongoing challenge to educators committed to equality in education has been to find ways to promote strategies which address equity concerns as integral to each other and to the realization of excellence in education.

It is within that context that this chapter discusses efforts to promote sex equity in education in urban school systems. Because of the complex demographics of cities and the impact that the stark economic realities of urban life have had on the structure of the family, educators working in urban school districts face special challenges in implementing quality and equity in education, including devising and implementing strategies to promote sex equity. Many strategies, activities, and materials designed to promote the implementation of sex equity do not reflect an awareness of diversity and its implications for urban school populations or for the society as a whole and therefore fail to acknowledge the multiple equity needs of our students (Morgen, 1985). In so doing they reinforce other forms of inequity. This chapter will describe key aspects of the diversity found in urban schools using New York City as an example of some of the special challenges inherent in implementing sex equity in an urban school system. The elements and processes being practiced to achieve equity on the basis of gender will be identified and described and future needs and directions will be outlined.

Urban Demographic and Economic Trends

Estimates of the percentage of the nation's total public school population who attend urban schools range from 30–45 percent (Williams, 1987; Woo, 1987). Urban schools, as "the port of entry to the American dream," (Spillane, 1985) have been most sharply effected by economic demographic and sociological changes that have taken place during the past twenty years. These changes are having a tremendous impact on the composition of the public school population nationwide. They include structural changes in the economy, the continuing exodus of middle class whites to the suburbs, higher fertility rates for minority women and immigration from Asia and Latin America.

Demographic Profile of Urban Schools

Urban schools are increasingly made up of students whose families are headed by single females, who live in poverty, who are from racial minorities and who are from non-English speaking backgrounds. According to the Center for Education Statistics of the U.S. Department of Education, nationwide the proportion of minority students, particularly Asian and Hispanic students, has been increasing. Poor children and children from single parent families represent growing proportions of the nation's school children (Kaufman, 1986). In large urban districts, such children are already the majority. Thus class, race, national origin are central issues in any educational planning and analysis in urban education (Oakes, 1986).

Class

Increasing poverty is a pervasive fact of urban life. In New York city the poverty rate has grown from 15 percent in 1969 to almost 25 percent today. Changes in New York City's economy mirror the nation's shift from basic manufacturing to retail sales, service, finance, real estate, insurance telecommunications, and information processing. The decline of manufacturing is particularly critical because it has historically been a source of employment for unskilled workers. Almost half of the manufacturing jobs in New York City are held by black and Hispanic workers (Wagner, 1987).

Forty percent of New York City's children live in poverty. A black or

Hispanic child is three times more likely than a white child to be raised in a family with only the mother present. Many children are raised in households lacking both parents. One out of eight black children, one out of 12 Hispanic children, and one in 25 white children live with neither parent.

Single parent families constitute twelve percent of the city's households, (38% of families with children), almost 90 percent of which are headed by women. Only 17 percent of white families with children are headed by women, 51 percent of black and 44 percent of Hispanic families are headed by women. Sixty percent of these families live in poverty. These families average only one-quarter of the income of families with both parents present.

The predominance of poor female-headed families can be explained by a number of factors including the limited availability of quality affordable child care which serves to keep women out of the workforce, lack of pay equity (Dill, 1987), low wages in traditionally and/or predominantly female occupations and lack of access to and training for more highly paid nontraditional occupations. Sex equity in education is an important tool for addressing the educational needs of these women.

Unemployment rates for black and Hispanic males are twice that of white and Asian males, and have been for some time. Issues of male poverty, particularly poverty of minority men have been ignored or underestimated (Tobier, 1984). The political salience of sex equity in an urban, multi-racial context may be increased to the extent that proponents of sex equity in education examine differential treatment of students of both genders and their access to quality academic, vocational, and technical training. An economic trend with clear sex equity implications is the extent to which the nature of much of the country's and the city's new jobs has changed from areas of work traditionally seen as masculine to work traditionally seen as feminine.

Race

From 1970 to 1982 the proportion of minority enrollment in the nation's schools has been growing rapidly: in Seattle it grew from 20 percent to 48 percent, in San Diego from 25 percent to 50 percent and in Portland, Oregon from 12 percent to 27 percent. In Boston the proportion of minority enrollment nearly doubled from 36 percent to 70 percent. Minority enrollment in Los Angeles grew from 50 percent to 78 percent in 1982. By 1982 Atlanta; Washington, D.C.; Newark; and San Antonio had minority enrollments of over 90 percent.

Minorities are more heavily represented in the schools than they are in the total population of the city. In the 1985–86 school year the almost one million students of the New York City public schools were 38 percent black, 33 percent Hispanic, 6 percent Asian, 23 percent white, and less than .1 percent American Indian. In 1980 the overall population of New York City was 24 percent black, 20 percent Hispanic, 4 percent Asian, and 52 percent white (Quinones, 1986). The Commission on the Year 2000 predicts that by that year nonwhites and Hispanics will account for about 60 percent of the city's population (Wagner, 1987).

National Origin

The number of Asian and Hispanic students as a percentage of urban school populations is growing. Many of these students come from homes where English is not the primary language. Many of these students have limited English proficiency (LEP). Projections developed in 1981 by the U.S. Department of Education show the total number of LEP children ages five to fourteen increasing almost 42 percent between 1980 and 2000. New Mexico, Texas, California and Arizona will continue to have the highest number of non-English language background children. New York, New Jersey, and Connecticut have high proportions of such children.

The Gender Factor

Paralleling the geometric rise in poverty in single female headed households is the fact that the city has fewer young black and Hispanic men in the age groups most responsible for forming families. In New York City, for example, for every 100 black women aged 20 to 24, there are 78 black men. For every Hispanic woman aged 20 to 24 there are 79 men. No gender gap in life expectancy exists for whites until age 45. The gender gap for blacks and Hispanics is due to such varied causes as their higher participation rate in the armed forces as well as higher rates of homelessness, mortality, and incarceration. Other sources cite the high rate of death and disability of Afro-American men as a result of poor health care, disproportionate death from war and more dangerous work conditions, as well as many other stressors of poverty (Tobach and Rosoff, 1980).

The report of the Commission on the Year 2000 for New York City highlights the symmetry between male joblessness and female headed households among blacks and Hispanics indicating that the rise in the proportion of black and Hispanic males either unemployed or not in the labor force has consistently been matched by the rise in the proportion of nonwhite families headed by women (Wagner, 1987). While the sex equity issues involved in adolescent parenting have begun to be explored, the dynamics of the male sex role particularly for blacks, Hispanics, and Asians need further examination.

The sum total of the factors described above or any one of them place children served by urban public school systems at risk of being trapped as adults by the same circumstances that impact on them today. A commitment to educational equity is a commitment to provide a quality education in the context of the real needs of these students.

Sex Equity and the New York City Public Schools

The passage of Title IX in 1972 and the issuance of the final implementing regulations in 1975 coincided with the transition of the New York City public schools from a centralized system to a quasi-decentralized system. One aspect of the source of the energy that led to decentralization was concern about the racial composition of the school administrators, supervisors and teachers in the system. Struggles around this issue overwhelmed efforts to implement Title IX (Bordier and Menaham, 1984).

Following the passage of Title IX of the Education Amendments of 1972 two key measures were taken at the national level to provide financial support to local education agency efforts to implement sex equity. The Women's Educational Equity Act (WEEA) and Title IV of the Civil Rights Act both provided funding to local districts. New York City utilized both forms of technical assistance.

Title IV Sex Desegregation Assistance Center were funded, one to meet systemwide needs and one to serve a community school district. These centers conducted training workshops, provided technical assistance to teachers, guidance counselors, and administrators, and distributed sex fair materials and resources. WEEA funding was sought and won to support projects which addressed sex equity issues in the areas of math, computer equity, elementary social studies/language arts, and bilingual career education. Countless workshops were conducted and resources developed and distributed. Analyses were conducted regarding sex equity issues in employment as well as educational programs (Poll, 1979). The main limitation of these early efforts to achieve sex equity was their limited long-term institutionalization. The mainstream administrative processes ran into difficulties as well.

The first step of the implementation process of Title IX, the self-evaluation, was met with some difficulties because of the decentralized administrative structure of the school system (Bordier and Menaham, 1984). In 1976 the Office for Civil Rights of the Department of Health, Education and Welfare issued a letter of findings stating that the New York City Board of Education was not in compliance with both Title VI and Title IX in terms of staffing. A Memorandum of Understanding was signed in 1977 by the Board of Education, making the commitment to increase the percentages of minority and women in administrative, supervisory, and instructional positions. Implementation of the Memorandum particularly with regard to affirmative action steps in hiring blacks and Hispanics were challenged by a number of community school districts and Jewish organizations. Once a federal district court overruled these objections, the slowness in carrying out the first step of the agreement led the Office of Civil Rights to rule the New York City Board of Education ineligible for ESEA funds. In the ensuing legal actions the debate over race equity assumed predominance over the sex equity issues. The authors attribute this to the lack of internal or external constituencies for sex equity in New York City. They suggest that future federal equity policy initiatives should be based on providing support for advocates and local school system constituencies in their efforts to develop and strengthen coalitions. These forces, they contend, can be more effective than education officials in implementing equity policy.

The experience of this writer with current ongoing efforts to implement sex equity since 1983 highlight different concerns, and both challenges and supports the perspective and analysis cited above. The activity of an organized New York City-based multiracial coalition of sex equity advocates, which included the publication of reports documenting concerns regarding sex discrimination in employment and in educational programs (Women's City Club, 1978, 1983 Friedman and Untermeyer, 1983). Friedman and Huling, 1982) combined with the activity of advocates within city government (Friedlander, 1983; Friedman and Untermeyer, 1983), the issuance by the State Education Department (Jabonaski, 1983) of a letter of findings of sex discrimination in ten of the city's vocational and technical high schools and a number of central offices, and the appointment of a conscious and committed schools Chancellor led to the formation in December 1983 of a Chancellor's Task Force on Sex Equity.

The group was composed of a broad spectrum of advocates for sex equity from organizations outside of the Board of Education and Board of Education administrators. The Task Force focuses on six areas of concern: Administrative/Supervisory Employment, Athletics, Adolescent Pregnancy and Parenting, Curriculum and Instruction, Guidance, and Vocational Education. Systemic and specific area recommendations focus on such needs as:

- funding full-time site-based equity coordinators in order to institutionalize the carrying out of ongoing needs assessments, initiate long and short-range planning to address sex equity needs at the local level, and provide technical assistance, training, and resources on an ongoing basis.
- institutionalizing ongoing staff development training in equity concepts.
- institutionalizing ongoing review of curriculum and instructional materials to ensure equity.
- procuring increased resources to implement equity at all levels of the school system.
- strengthening both the internal and external constituency for sex equity in the school system.
- infusing sex equity awareness in the development of all agency plans, policies, programs, strategies, and activities.

Current efforts to carry out staff development training and to analyze practices and policies for sex equity are limited by the paucity of information on black, Hispanic, and Asian students with regard to this issue (Klein, 1985; Burgos-Sasscer, 1987). Such efforts would be aided by the existence of data and models normed for multiracial, multilingual working class and poor, urban school populations. Unfortunately, only a fraction of the sex equity materials and sex roles research have been developed with these students in mind (Diamond, 1975; Grant, 1984; Scott-Jones and Clark, 1986). Notable exceptions include work developed by the Project on Equal Education Rights (Crocker, Deluth, and Tucker, 1982) and a number of projects funded under the Women's Educational Equity Act Program. Also noteworthy is Schniedewind and Hall's *Open Minds to Equality* (1983). The class perspective of much of the research that is available does not reflect the reality of the vast majority of working class and poor white students in urban school systems.

Important strategies to include in efforts to implement equity in urban schools are the following:

- identify and communicate regularly with the person with the commitment/assignment of implementing equity in each key responsibility center in the school system administrative structure.
- involve these individuals in any planning efforts.
- consult and share resources with them on a regular basis.
- develop an outreach program to constituents and allies to maintain and strengthen the constituency for equity in the system.
- include elected officials in outreach efforts; such support is critical to receiving the kind of funding resources needed to carry out meaningful programs.
- reach out to area colleges and universities with women's studies and black and Puerto Rican studies curricula to maintain contact with a variety of perspectives on this issue.
- regularly survey the research to maintain currency on all the skills and content areas needed to perform competently as an equity specialist, including but not limited to: women's studies, ethnic studies, the sociology of the family, organizational development and change, managerial skills, equal opportunity law, marketing ideas, conflict management, group process, community organizing, office politics.

A great deal remains to be done to meet the challenge posed by the goal of achieving sex equity in education. Planning and implementing efforts to promote sex equity in education represents the latest lap in the relay race towards the goal of educating people to achieve full human rights in a democratic society. With the inspiration accorded by history and the strength and stamina provided by broadening coalitions who will actively work to achieve equity, failure is impossible.

REFERENCES

Bordier, N. & Menaham, M. Urban politics and federal equity policy: Title IX and employment in New York City public schools. *The urban review,* 1984, *16,* 87–101.
Burgos-Sasscen, R. Empowering Hispanic students: A prerequisite is adequate data. *Journal of educational equity and leadership,* 1987, *7,* 21–36.
Crocker, E. V. *The report card on educating Hispanic women.* Washington, D.C.: Project on equal education rights (PEER).

Crocker, E., Deluth, K. & Tucker, J. *A new frontier: Black women in a high tech world.* Washington, D.C.: Project on equal rights (PEER), 1982.

Diamond, E. E. (Ed.) *Issues of sex bias and sex fairness in career interest measurement.* Washington, D.C.: Department of Health, Education, and Welfare, National Institute of Education, 1975.

Dill, B. *Pay equity: An issue of race, ethnicity and sex.* Washington, D.C.: National Committee on Pay Equity, 1987.

Fishel, A. & Pottker, J. *National politics and sex discrimination in education.* Massachusetts: Lexington Books, 1977.

Friedlander, M. Sex equity in New York City Public Schools, report of the New York City Council Committee on General Welfare—Subcommittee on the status of women. New York: City Council, 1983.

Friedman, R. & Huling, T. *Their "proper" place: A report on sex discrimination in New York City's vocational high schools.* New York: Full access and rights to education coalition, center for public advocacy research, 1982.

Friedman, B.S. & Untermyer, N. *Five year follow-up survey: Women in administrative and supervisory positions in the New York City public schools, 1978-1983.* New York: Women's City Club, Committee on the Status of Women, 1983.

Grant, L. Black females "place" in desegregated classrooms. *Sociology of education,* 1984, *57,* 98–111.

Jabonaski, C. Correspondence to Anthony Alvarado, Chancellor, New York City Board of Education. Albany: State Education Department, November, 1983.

Kaufman, P. *The condition of education.* Washington, D.C.: Center for Education Statistics, Office of Educational Research and Improvement, 1986.

Klein, S. S. (Ed.), *Handbook for achieving sex equity through education.* Baltimore: Johns hopkins university press, 1985.

Maxwell, M. Correspondence to Anthony Alvarado, Chancellor, New York City Board of Education. New York: New York City Commission on the status of women, February, 1983.

Morgen, Sandra. *To see ourselves, to see our sisters: The challenge of re-envisioning curriculum change.* Memphis: State University Center for Research on Women, 1986.

Oakes, J. Teaching, inequality, and the rhetoric of reform: Why schools don't change. *Journal of education,* 1986, *168,* 60–80.

Poll, C. *Beyond role models: The significance of a sponsor-protege relationship in becoming a school administrator,* unpublished manuscript, 1980.

Quinones, N. *Changing schools for changing needs: The chancellor's plan for New York City public schools.* New York City Board of Education, 1985.

Ravitch, D. *The great school wars.* New York: Basic Books, Inc., 1974.

Rochman, B. & Grady, W. *Annual report, Chancellor's task force on sex equity,* New York City Board of Education, 1985.

Schniedewind, N. & Davidson, E. *Open minds to equality.* Englewood Cliffs: Prentice-Hall, 1983.

Schulzinger, R. & Syron, L. *Inch by inch: A report on equal opportunity for young women in New York City's vocational high schools.* New York: Full Access and Rights to Education Coalition, Center for Public Advocacy Research, Inc., 1984.

Scott-Jones, D. & Clark, M. L. (1986). The school experiences of black girls: The interaction of gender, race, and socioeconomic status. *Phi delta kappan, 67,* 520–526.

Spillane, R. R. Urban schools: A port of entry into the American dream. *Equity and choice,* 1985, *1,* 19–24.

Stafford, W. *Closed labor markets: Underrepresentation of blacks, Hispanics and women in New York City's core industries and jobs.* New York: Community service society of New York, 1985.

Syron, L. *Discarded minds: How gender, race and class biases prevent young women from obtaining an adequate math and science education in New York City public schools.* New York: Center for public advocacy research, 1987.

Tobach, E. & Rosoff, B., (Eds.). *Genes and gender,* Staten Island: *Gordian Press,* 1980.

Tobier, E. *The changing face of poverty, trends in New York City's population of poverty: 1960-1990.* New York: Community Service Society, 1984.

Wagner, R. *New York ascendant: The report of the commission on the year 2000.* New York: Office of the Mayor, 1987.

Williams, D. Telephone interview with the author. Connecticut: Market Data Retrieval, May, 1987.

Women's City Club of New York. *Survey of women in executive positions in New York City government. Part I women in administrative and supervisory positions in New York City public schools,* New York, 1987.

Woo, R. Interview with author. New York: New York City Board of Education, May 1987.

The following statements are designed for the exploration of personal reactions to the chapter, as well as for the review of the contents of the chapter. Emphasis in discussions should be on exploring issues in depth, rather than on determining the correct or appropriate responses.

FOR DISCUSSION:

1. What are the major economic and social issues affecting the major cities in your state? How are they related to the achievement of gender equity?
2. How do policies and programs in urban schools affect activities in smaller school districts and vice versa?
3. Is this chapter relevant to educators in non-urban settings?
4. How do the multiple equity needs of city schools affect national educational priorities?
5. How does the achievement of sex equity help to reduce the problems of teen parenting, dropout prevention, and youth unemployment?
6. Discuss the author's statement: "Many strategies, activities, and materials designed to promote the implementation of sex equity do not reflect an awareness of diversity and its implications for urban school populations or for the society as a whole . . . "
7. What role does the teacher have in institutionalizing change in policy in a large urban district?
8. How can coalitions of advocates affect the achievement of sex equity in education?

SUGGESTIONS FOR FURTHER READING

Academy for Educational Development. *Survey of primary pregnancy prevention activities for early adolescents in six cities: A report to the Ford Foundation Office of Urban Poverty.* New York, 1985.

Cetron, M. *Schools of the future: How American business and education can cooperate to save our schools.* New York: McGraw-Hill Book Company, 1985.

Fisher, P. *Steppin' up and moving on: A career education program for the urban, noncollege-bound student.* Newton, Massachusetts: EDC/WEEA Publishing Center, 1982.

Kumagai, G. *Multimedia curriculum aids for teaching about minority women.* St. Paul, Minnesota: Urban Affairs Department–St. Paul Public Schools, 1986.

Mid-Atlantic Center for Race Equity. *Color our children carefully.* Washington, D.C., 1983.

National Association of State Boards of Education. *Female dropouts: A new perspective.* Alexandria, Virginia, 1987.

Oakes, J. *Keeping track: How schools structure inequality.* New Haven, Connecticut: Yale University Press, 1985.

Tiedt, P.T., & Tiedt, I.M. *Multicultural teaching: A handbook of activities, information, and resources.* Boston, Massachusetts: Allyn and Bacon, Inc., 1979.

Weiner, R. (Ed.). *Teen pregnancy: Impact on the schools.* Alexandria, Virginia: Capitol Publications, Inc., 1987.

Chapter 15

MIRROR, MIRROR ON THE WALL:
BIASED REFLECTIONS IN
TEXTBOOKS AND INSTRUCTIONAL MATERIALS

Marylin A. Hulme

INTRODUCTION

"Put her in a pumpkin shell and there he kept her very well."

From the earliest months of a child's life, nursery rhymes, sing-song games and Mother Goose begin to relay messages to children about their options in life. Tales of fantasy become translated to mean possibilities for a girl or boy, man or woman. Preschool books, full of charming, entertaining fiction, inspire young children to envision how they will tackle life's experiences. Then come textbooks, workbooks, and other instructional materials. As students, children now read and absorb the direct and indirect messages about what life can be like for them. The literature that surrounds them serves to teach them about what is expected for boys and expected for girls.

Are children really that gullible? Are they so impressionable that *Sleeping Beauty* becomes "some day my prince will come!" and *The History of Man* means "only men make history?" Do they really apply the world of fiction and nonfiction to their personal world, drawing conclusions about their opportunities as girls and boys? It appears so.

The influence of the written word (let alone the influence of media) is always up for debate. Volumes of biased reading material for children influences their thinking about self-esteem, family life, career goals, and emotional well-being. They depend on assigned and "free" reading to find out about the world. What they read is often just part of the real picture.

Take, for example, a child who is living in a single-parent household. Or a child whose mother and father are both employed outside the home. (More than likely children come from either one of those settings.) The dominant reading material depicts an employed father, at-home-in-an-apron mother, and children who have never been on their own after school, or in an after-school daycare program. It is not surprising that the child may begin to wonder whether his or her situation is "normal." Is my home "broken"? Why does my mother have to work? How come dads are never shown hugging in books? It's embarrassing that my mom fixes our car; if we had a dad she would not have to do it herself!

Children's literature and textbooks are often used by children to give them perspective. However, if what is depicted in the literature is exclusionary, not based on reality, or even discriminatory, then students get a limited, warped perspective. They need reading to expand their view of life. Too often, the view is limited rather than expansive.

The topic of bias in instructional materials is a sensitive one. It is difficult to create materials that are up-to-date, fair, and effective in the classroom. Discussions about educational policy, purchasing, and censorship will continue as old materials are evaluated, and new resources are written. Marylin Hulme discusses the issue of bias in instructional materials, as well as strategies for providing students with equitable resources.

MIRROR, MIRROR ON THE WALL:
BIASED REFLECTIONS IN
TEXTBOOKS AND INSTRUCTIONAL MATERIALS

The girl came and jigged on one foot behind her father who was preparing lunch. "So, how did it go today," he said; how could the second day at Kindergarten go except well, he thought naively. "Well," she replied, "I got it all wrong". "Really?"—all wrong at that age? She went on. "We had some pictures. We had to draw lines from the Daddy and the Mummy to the things they were using—you know—things." The things were ordinary everyday tools used around the house and the garden: vacuum cleaner, lawn mower, stove, hose, iron, and so on. "What did you do?" he said, trying to appear calm; how could one's own bright eager child fail on only her second day in kindergarten? Hopping from one foot to the other, and relieved to be in a place where she could move freely, she said, "I joined all the things to the Mummy *and* to the Daddy." She added triumphantly, "'Cos Mummy mows the lawn and you cook!" Most certainly, he thought, as he made his way to the Principal's office (*Up We Go,* 1970).

This true anecdote illustrates clearly one aspect of the impact of bias in school materials. The student, puzzled by the lack of congruity between her home and her school book, senses failure in the classroom right at the beginning of her schooling. Her father, who is working to eliminate sex role stereotyping in the home, finds to his dismay that he had to tackle the school system as well. Everyone loses.

Bias-Free Instructional Materials

Educational materials are ubiquitous at every level of the school, comprising a major component of the educational process. In fact, 90 percent of student learning time is spent using them, whether they are textbooks, workbooks, library books, supplementary, or audiovisual materials (Scott and Schau, 1985). School boards spend a considerable amount of their resources on educational materials and some states are required to have a procedure in place for evaluating bias and discrimination before purchase.

With changing social mores comes the demand for change in materials

189

to reflect the reality of everyday life. Not only are these changes necessary to eliminate conflict in lives of students; they also affect students'
potential achievement. (Examination of achievement differences shows
the effects of differing expectations for boys and girls on the part of
school and society.)

In the areas of reading and mathematics, studies of sex differences
have tended to find male superiority in mathematics and female superiority in reading/language arts (Klein, 1985; Brody, Fox, and Tobin,
1980). Materials that include women and men in a variety of jobs allow
children to view more jobs as appropriate for both women and men, and,
by extension, appropriate for themselves (Klein, 1985, Scott, 1980). Reading about successful women has been found to cause girls to have higher
expectations of female success, an important component of achievement,
as is knowing that there is a historical perspective to achieving women.
Indeed, after hearing stories about a member of their own sex achieving,
both boys and girls have been known to spend more time on school tasks.
This "time-on-task" is one of the most important components of achievement (McArthur and Eisen, 1976). Equitable materials encourage both
girls and boys to learn.

The Civil Rights and the Feminist movements were instrumental in
bringing about change in educational materials, primarily by responding
strongly to the procedures and products of major textbook publishers.
Historians interested in women's and minorities' issues pushed for representation on textbook writing committees, thus influencing the structure
and content of the textbooks. Publishers issued guidelines on "bias-free
publishing"; McGraw-Hill's *Guidelines for Equal Treatment of the Sexes*
(1974), originally designed for use internally by their own staff, was
enthusiastically received by the educational community and widely disseminated as a training tool. These *Guidelines* were gradually expanded
to include sex, race, ethnic origin, and most recently handicap, and, at
the same time, supported change to inclusive language and illustration.
Other publishers followed suit, resulting in a tremendous amount of
activity towards eliminating bias in textbook publishing during the late
1970s. This was particularly noticeable in social studies materials, where
the contributions of women and minorities were beginning to be included.

The legal foundation for eliminating discrimination and bias in education as a whole was *Brown v. The Board of Education of Topeka, Kansas*
(1954) when it was decided that separate was not equal. Practical support
for integration and desegregation was funded by Title IV of the Civil

Rights Act of 1964, which made available training and technical assistance projects throughout the country. These projects began producing equitable materials for classroom use. The Desegregation Assistance Centers and other training components were, and still are, required to provide assistance in sex, race and national origin to any school district requesting help. The Federal Title IX of the Education Amendments of 1972 required the elimination of discrimination based on gender.

Since the mid 1970s, federal funds have supported projects to develop and publish materials to encourage equity in education. Two programs in particular, the Women's Educational Equity Act Program and more recently the Carl Perkins Act, are good sources of equitable materials.

Identification of Bias

The seminal work which laid the pattern for much of the examination of textbooks to come was produced by a group of women in Princetown, New Jersey. *Dick and Jane as Victims; Sex Stereotyping in Children's Readers* by Women on Words and Images analyzed elementary readers for the sex of the main character, numbers of girls and of boys portrayed and, most importantly, what the male and the female characters were doing and how they were rewarded. They found that girls were passive, concerned about their looks and getting dirty, fearful, and lacking creative interaction with others and with their own environment. Boys on the other hand tended to be heroic, physically strong, clever, and seemingly able to control their environment. In addition, adult role models provided a vast range of choices for boys, but little other than wife and mother for girls. Choice was not an issue, there was none for the female. This sorry state of affairs was traced through social studies and science textbooks, and basal readers (Weitzman and Rizzo, 1976), career education and foreign language materials (Women on Words and Images, 1976) and, somewhat earlier, though not in the same format, civics textbooks (McLeod and Silverman, 1973).

This was the "counting time." The study of bias in books produced statistics on jobs portrayed by females and males which might have been amusing if the implications had not been so serious. Britton and Lumpkin (1977) found that elementary materials portrayed females more frequently as fantasy figures (queens, princesses, and witches) than as real people, working at a variety of jobs with a variety of roles. Mothers who were in the labor force making a contribution to their families economic well-being received short shrift, usually shown as working in low-paying traditionally female positions, such as a retail clerk, secretary, teacher, or nurse. Men were depicted as workers without opportunities for emotional expression or family interaction. Role models for nontraditional jobs with opportunities to support their families and for advancement in the job market for either sex were invisible.

The forms of bias found in instructional materials fall mainly into the following types:

Invisibility. Certain groups are underrepresented in curricular materials. The significant omission of women and minority groups has become so great as to imply that these groups are of less value, importance, and significance in our society.

Stereotyping. By assigning traditional and rigid roles or attributes to a group, instructional materials stereotype and limit abilities and potential of the individuals in the group.

Imbalance/Selectivity. Textbooks perspetuate bias by presenting only one interpretation of an issue, situation, or group of people. This imbalanced account restricts the knowledge of students regarding the varied perspectives which may apply to a particular situation. Through selective presentation of materials, textbooks distort reality and ignore complex and differing viewpoints.

Unreality. Textbooks frequently present an unrealistic portrayal of our history and our contemporary life experiences. Controversial topics are glossed over and discussions of discrimination and prejudice are avoided.

Fragmentation/Isolation. By separating issues related to minorities and women from the main body of the text, instructional materials imply that these issues are less important than and not part of the cultural mainstream.

Linguistic Bias. Curricular materials reflect the discriminatory nature of our language. Masculine terms and pronouns, ranging from "our forefathers" to the generic "he," deny the participation of women in our society. Further, occupations such as "mailman" are given masculine labels that deny the legitimacy of women working in these fields. Imbalance of word order and lack of parallel terms that refer to females and males are also forms of linguistic bias.

Awareness and understanding of the negative "-isms" which pervade and color the tone of the textbooks and other materials is crucial to a comprehension of bias and prejudice, and how to counteract them. The following are some of the most frequently encountered forms of bias:

Sexism: an attitude, action or institutional structure which subordinates or discriminates against an individual or a group because of their sex. Sexism usually discriminates against the female, as most institutions have been run by and for the white male.

Racism: an attitude, action or institutional structure or practice which functions to subordinate a person or group because of their color. Most institutions are controlled by whites in American society. The control of institutional power distinguishes racism from individual prejudice.

Handicapism: an attitude, action, or institutional structure which functions to subordinate or limit people with disabilities. Physical structures, as well as mental attitudes, have until recently ignored the needs of the disabled.

Agism and other biases such as elitism, materialism, and ethnocentrism: all of these areas can be the basis of discrimination and bias. Individuals or groups are shut out or ignored, to their detriment as individuals, as well as that of society.

Stereotyping carries sexism, racism and the other "-isms" into materials; it is the vehicle by which characteristics, abilities, and expectations are arbitrarily assigned to an individual solely on the basis of their relationship to a group, with total disregard for the individual's attributes as a unique person. Certain images and assumptions come to mind in response to certain images: for example, "senator," "doctor," "secretary" each produce images of one sex only. The word "coal miner," "truck driver," "business executive," "member of congress" have been found to conjure up male images in the classroom; similarly, "secretary," "teacher," "librarian" female ones.

Bias and stereotyping can be identified and remediated in all subject areas; here are some pointers towards identification.

History and Social Studies

Social studies has moved to include social history during the last few years, using this branch of history to bring in the experiences and contributions of women and minorities. At first, parallel to that which already existed in the mainly political history being published and taught, famous women were slotted into the appropriate chapters: Queens Isabella of Spain and Elizabeth I of England as supporters of the exploration of the "New World"; Susan B. Anthony and Elizabeth Cady Stanton as leaders of the Suffrage movement. Frequently, a paragraph or illustra-

tion of famous women appeared at the end of a chapter still isolating
them from the mainstream of history. The exploration and settlement of
the American continent by Europeans has been presented in ethnocen-
tric terms, that is from the viewpoint entirely of the Europeans. The
most famous example of this is the sentence "Columbus discovered
America." Not only was Columbus *not* the first European to arrive on
American shores (the Scandinavians were), but America was already
populated by the Native Americans who had their own complex social
organizations, linguistic families, customs, and beliefs.

The Afro-American experience was one of the most poorly presented
topics. Recent research and the impact of the civil rights movement have
remedied some of the distortion and omissions, but linguistic bias in
terms of describing the black experience, especially after the Civil War,
has been constant. Illustrations were frequently caricatures, or white-
shaped faces with a brown wash. The same criticism can be addressed to
the treatment of other minority groups such as Asians, Hispanics, and
Native Americans. From the illustrations and text commonly found in
elementary textbooks on Native Americans, it would appear that they all
belonged to the Plains Indian tribes/nations, to judge from their customs and appearance (CIBC, 1970).

Mathematics and Science

Math and science have often been thought of as neutral. Can formulas
and numerals be biased? This is an area where the subtleties of bias
create an unsupportive atmosphere which does not encourage females,
nor for that matter many minorities, to pursue the study of math and
science. Although research shows that girls perceive math and science as
a masculine domain starting in the middle school, and that they internalize their failures in these subjects, textbooks by omission reinforce these
negative aspects. Word problems relate to male experiences, especially
sports experiences; male proper names are used in word problems; and
the scenarios themselves of the word problems do not engage females.
Female mathematics and scientists (except for the omnipresent Marie
Curie) are omitted; illustrations show obviously male hands demonstrating equipment and running experiments; the textbooks frequently use
the generic "he" (more recent ones have used the direct "you") and fail to
recognize the presence of women in the history of science. Some recently
published textbooks series, especially in the physical sciences, have

instituted some corrections by referring to the work of female scientists, by including brief biographies of women as well as men, and by showing women and men working together on experiments. The image of the lone, mad, male scientist is still portrayed in many supplementary materials and also in the media; the reality today is that most science is performed as a collaborative, group endeavor.

Home Economics, Industrial Arts and Vocational Education

Women make up 54 percent of the workforce, and are increasingly found in many different jobs, moving slowly into areas once predominantly male. Law school students are now over 50 percent female, the number of women engineers has increased, as has the numbers of women in accounting, business, and medicine. By contrast, women still only make up 1 percent of carpenters, 1 percent plumbers, and 13 percent engineers. Instructional resources generally refer to men in these professions. In turn, men are rarely depicted as nurses, cosmetologists, or child care workers.

Vocational education remains one of the areas most resistant to change, and this is also reflected in the textbooks and course descriptions. Not only do males predominate in shop and technical courses, illustrations of males predominate in vocational texts. Real life photos of jobs show male supervisors, male apprentices in areas such as masonry, diesel mechanics, carpentry, and plumbing. Females are shown as aides, secretaries, and observers. In some areas, such as graphics and electronics, females have made some progress. Even a manual on beauty culture, surely a female dominated field, the generic "he" was used throughout the text, and the salon owner illustrated was a male. When role models for women and minorities are needed, they must be located in supplementary materials, and multimedia products such as *Just Between Sisters* (Consortium, 1987), a poster set and videotape which shows black and Hispanic women in nontraditional technical jobs.

Home economics is where the most change has been accomplished. In many states considerable efforts have been made to create coed classes, especially at the middle school level, where home economics and industrial arts have been integrated to form practical arts, and to design innovative curriculum to interest both female and male students. Many middle school textbooks reflect those changes. Students now have the opportunity to learn techniques through activities that interest them, rather than those imposed by the system. Making outdoor clothing, woodworking projects that can be taken home and used, and cooking real meals are now pursued by both girls and boys working together in the classroom.

Language Arts, English, and Literature

Used at all grade levels in English and literature classes, anthologies contain mostly short stories by white, male authors. Stories by women and people of color are very infrequent, as are stories with girls and women as the main characters. Too often when females are portrayed, they are frequently portrayed in secondary, weak roles, stereotyped by action and language. Publishers are responsible for anthology collections and should be held accountable for stereotypical choices. Teachers of English have been increasingly sensitive to issues of gender-biased language. Unfortunately the grammar book publishers are lagging behind; terms of address in letter writing, the use of "he," "his," and "man/men" to refer to and to represent all people are still common in the textbooks though are changing in practice.

The one area where changes cannot be made in language, literary style and content is in the classics, and in literature in general. Historical settings and influences, social mores and constructs must be put into context. (In one class, Romeo was roundly blamed for the tragedy which befell him and Juliet; he should have hired 2 horses and taken Juliet with him to Mantua.)

Printed materials are not the only educational materials susceptible to bias and stereotyping. Audiovisual materials (films, videos, filmstrips, slide shows, and audiotapes) are equally susceptible and can be carriers of the same disease. In terms of subject areas, much of what has been described previously applies equally to audiovisual materials. There are, however, some additional characteristics to look for. Is the commentary appropriate to the subject matter? Is the voice-over male or female? Are women portrayed as serious contributors to the subject of the film, or are they merely token and decorative? How are they addressed? How are interactions between females and males depicted? Are minorities included? One of the most incongruous match-ups of film and commentary was the narration by Ricardo Montalban for the National Science Foundation film *Space for Women*. This visually beautiful film, created to stimulate girls' interest in science and mathematics, had a very much lessened impact, as the audience connected it immediately with Fantasy Island.

Censorship

The complex issue of censorship of books used in schools has been highlighted recently by an Alabama textbook case, which represents the extensive efforts by traditional conservatives to halt the expansion of inclusivity in educational materials.

In 1976, Island Trees school board removed books from the school libraries because they were "objectionable"; the books which included *A Reader for Writers* (with pieces by Jefferson and Madison) and *Slaughterhouse Five* by Kurt Vonnegut were described as "anti-American, anti-Christian." The case went to the Supreme Court which finally ruled in 1982 that school boards are not constitutionally permitted to remove books from school libraries simply "because they dislike the ideas contained in those books" (National Coalition against Censorship, 1985).

The general bias against specific trade books has a parallel movement against textbooks. The textbook publishing companies, greatly influenced by the conservative requirements of the large states which make statewide adoptions for all school districts (such as Texas and California), found themselves hurrying to revise their textbooks in an effort to keep their markets.

According to every major source of data on censorship activity, in 1982 many attempts were made to remove a wide variety of textbooks, library books, instructional and supplementary materials and even portions of the curriculum from public schools in order to conform with the thinking of the conservative fundamentalist right. Materials encouraging independent thinking, inclusion of hitherto neglected populations, and the discussion of conflicting ideas and values were, according to the suits, to be excised from the public school system. Due in part to the success of those wanting to correct previous biases and omissions, this reaction to the work of the "expansionists" centered on those states with statewide adoption policies. The Texas Adoption Process, in particular, influenced the development of teaching materials used nationwide because of that state's demands for revisions, coupled with its economic muscle. Books listed on the Texas approved list were guaranteed a market. During the early 1980s, hearings of the Texas State Textbook Committee were closely scrutinized by interested parties (publishers, educators, curriculum developers, parents around the country), to understand the philosophy and demands of people objecting to the contents of textbooks. High on their list of the topics to be rejected as objectionable was Evolution, with equal time being claimed for Creationism.

Two specific cases show that censorship is still alive and well in relation to public school education, and that the argument is taking on more religious depth. In Church Hill, Tennessee, a group of fundamentalist parents successfully defended their right to control and select their children's reading matter in school. They claimed that the school's reading series (Holt basals) promoted "the religion of secular humanism" and violated their traditional values. Included in the list of rejected materials was *The Wizard of Oz* (because of witchcraft) and a reader showing a family pursuing nontraditional roles (Mozart v. Hawkins County Public Schools, TN, 1986).

By the time that the movement reached the Alabama courthouse in 1987, secular humanism had been declared a religion by the presiding judge in the case (Judge Hand), who ruled that the state remove some 44 textbooks from its approved list and immediately out of the schools. Included were home economics, social studies, and career education texts. At the time of writing, the Court of Appeals has stayed the judge's order pending the appeal. This means that the students' educational process can continue with the same materials until the end of the school year (*Education Week*, March 11, 1987).

Censorship efforts are not limited to modern books in school libraries, and to textbooks; classics, notably by such authors as William Shakespeare (Romeo and Juliet—sex and drugs) and Mark Twain (Huckleberry Finn—racism) have come under fire. Efforts to create inclusive, better informed, and balanced textbooks, which mirror more closely the realities of the society we live in, have resulted in opposition to change and in the intrusion of religious issues into public schooling.

Strategies

- Two fourth-grade teachers in a semirural school district, appalled to find out how poor their students' general knowledge about women was, searched out biographies and supplementary history materials to rectify the situation.
- An administrator responsible for coordinating equity concerns in his school district organized a district-wide affirmative action com-

mittee with one representative from each building to meet and examine materials and curriculum on a regular basis.

- A Title IX coordinator decided to obtain as many free and inexpensive equitable materials as possible from education organizations, professional societies and equity centers; she then publicized these materials as being available in her office to all teachers.
- A school librarian gathered posters of women athletes for a big display to celebrate the Los Angeles Olympics; the display was so successful that others followed featuring women in different walks of life.
- A parent, member of a district-wide *ad hoc* committee on family life education, ensured that information and materials on sex roles and stereotyping were included in the curriculum, and obtained samples from the local Desegregation Assistance Center.
- Board of Education members ran as a team to defeat a conservative right wing candidate, whose platform included equal time for Creationism and the elimination of certain materials and topics from the curriculum.

These few examples, all of which had an impact on educational materials from an equity perspective, have been chosen from many, demonstrate general strategies which can be used by all members of the educational community, who have recognized bias and have responded by taking positive action. Through their involvement, they also came to understand more fully the effects of bias, discrimination, and stereotyping and were able to decide to obtain assistance from outside sources when necessary. Among these sources of help are the Desegregation Assistance Centers, located throughout the country, which provide training to school districts and can give sources and samples of equitable materials. Most Centers maintain libraries where these materials can be reviewed and borrowed. Another source of equitable materials is the Women's Educational Equity Act Publishing Center in Newton, Massachusetts; this center makes available a wide range of inexpensive equitable materials developed by funded projects (handbooks, curriculum outlines, self-evaluation manuals, and some audiovisual materials). The Feminist Press, an independent small press in New York City, specializes in publishing literature by women and has produced a range of classroom materials with accompanying teacher guides. The Council for Interracial Books for Children, also in New York City, publishes a bulletin with review articles on biases in different areas of the curriculum and features book reviews of children's literature. (Additional organizations are listed in the back of the textbook.)

Accentuating the Positive

When reviewing textbooks, library books, periodicals, audiovisual materials and other supplementary materials for selection, educators must include equity evaluation as a key area, along with the other parameters familiar to textbook review committees. In the previous section on identifying bias and stereotyping, negative issues in different curricular subjects were pinpointed; now it is the turn of the positive ones.

History and Social Studies

There are many well-known women who have made significant contributions to society in the United States and in many other countries; part of the mainstream of history, their stories must be interwoven into the text and not isolated or segregated into boxes at the end of chapters. Third World women must also be included in the text and illustrations when dealing with world history and geography. It is important that movements or episodes where women have taken a leading position are depicted in a serious manner, for example, the Abolition movement in the U.S., or the Suffrage movement in England. Potentially controversial issues, such as the women's rights movement and the Equal Rights Amendment, must be clearly described in a balanced account. Social history promotes the history of people's everyday lives and their membership of various subgroups; look for the many classes of women whose history has largely been ignored up to now, such as slave women, pioneer women, and immigrant women. Differing cultural backgrounds are an integral part of history, too; minority women (black, Hispanic, Puerto Rican, Chicana, Native American, and others) must be included. It is also important to integrate the discussion of the family, the changes it has undergone. Of special interest are those materials which document the erosion of rigidly traditional sex roles in sociology, psychology, and anthropology books.

Language Arts, English, Literature

Literature can be a very fruitful subject for the discussion of social customs, views, and differing perspectives. Include discussion of images of women in literature and media, such as film and television; anthologies which contain women authors and a variety of writing styles which give students a wider view of literature. With younger students, in particular, it is crucial to show positive images of girls and boys; make sure that girls are main characters in the story, or, if they are not, they at least should not be shown in stereotypical roles. Female characters should show initiative and leadership, and be depicted cooperating with boys and men in unusual and nontraditional situations. Male characters should be able to show emotions and display caring behaviors, especially in relationship to their children. Remember that mothers have lives outside the home, in the world of work, in politics, and as active community members. Search out newly published collections of folk and fairy tales which show strong, active girls as decisive characters who make decisions and in a fun role reversal even rescue princes!

Mathematics and Science

Teachers need access to mathematics materials that recognize and deal with the problem of math anxiety and its remediation; there are some particular works on this subject which should be part of every school's professional collection. In the textbooks and workbooks, word problems should include girls and women in nonstereotyped roles; these images should also be reflected in the illustrations, as should women participating at all levels of the scientific and technical world. Wherever possible, the contributions of women in the history of mathematics and science should be integrated into the text. Some recently published science textbooks portray real people working in scientific jobs at the ends of chapters as part of career information; check that both men and women are included and that there is a wide variety of jobs being performed by both males and females.

World of Work and Careers

Women are working in a wide variety of jobs, both traditional and nontraditional, and in greater numbers than ever before, particularly in the professions. Not only should they be portrayed in a wide variety of jobs, but also at different levels; entry, supervisors, executives, bosses of a mixed workforce. Women and men should be shown working together as equals on technical projects, in traditional and nontraditional areas. Women should also be shown working with a variety of tools, machinery and indoors and out. Both women and men should be shown as having the choice of working part-time, shared-time or flexitime to be able to spend time with their families; parental leave for both sexes should also be portrayed.

Language

Language must be used in a nonsexist, unbiased manner. Beware of the use of the generic "he," "his," "him" and of "man," and "mankind" to refer to all people; this essentially ignores the presence and contributions of women. It is particularly prevalent in areas such as science, technology, industrial arts, and careers. Ensure that job titles are nonsexist; firefighter, police officer, member of Congress, chairperson. Check that instructions in activities and games refer to both sexes or use the plural.

Activating the School District: Some Strategies District-Wide

School Board Policy

Every school board should have a policy on textbook examinations and selection procedures, affirmative action and parental access. A similar policy should be developed for library materials. These policies should include a statement on nondiscrimination; in some states with their own strong equal education laws (PEER, 1987), school boards are required to adopt and approve courses of study, instructional materials, and programs designed to eliminate discrimination, and promote understanding and mutual respect. Moreover, districts can promote policy to evaluate those courses and materials already in use, to supplement where necessary, and to replace them according to curriculum planning and budgetary constraints.

School boards should also include publishers and other suppliers of educational materials when informing their vendors of compliance requirements of nondiscrimination, and should also actively support and require the administration to develop equitable procedures and regulations emanating from board policy. It is particularly important to have comprehensive, well-thought-out procedures when dealing with sensitive issues, and any community involvement, such as ad hoc committees appointed to advise on areas such as family life education or affirmative action.

District Organization

In the best of all possible worlds, the scope and sequence of the curriculum is established first to suit the needs and requirements of the district and its students, and then materials are sought to support the curriculum. In states where lists of approved textbooks are maintained, such as Texas, California, and Alabama, districts must choose from those lists accordingly. Elsewhere, in New Jersey and New York for instance, schools are free to solicit materials for evaluation from publishers directly, and concomitantly have the responsibility for forwarding complaints and comments directly to the publishers when textbooks are inappropriate or biased. All members of the textbook evaluation committee must be trained in the evaluation and selection of equitable materials. They should also consider purchasing materials from alternative sources and presses, such as the Feminist Press, Women's Educational Equity Act Publishing Center, and others.

A sex equity committee composed of parents, teachers, and community members who have been trained to review and advise on the *equity* issues concerning materials selection can be particularly helpful. In one particular case, where the two-tier system existed, an Affirmative Action Committee agreed to approve the textbooks only if supplementary materials were also advocated. Here, further examination of materials and curriculum revealed that revisions which had been suggested but never implemented would have obviated the whole situation. Numerous evaluation instruments are available to these committees; a selection, *Checklists for counteracting race and sex bias in educational materials* (1982), is published by the Women's Educational Equity Act.

Before discussing student and classroom involvement, one must not overlook another very valuable resource. School librarians are, in fact, in a unique position to promote the evaluation, selection and use of equitable sex and race fair materials. They can serve as a resource to teachers in curriculum planning and as sources for the materials themselves. The most direct strategy is for the librarians to ensure that supplementary materials, such as biographies, fiction, posters, films, and videos which promote the roles and contributions of women and many minorities, are readily available to teachers. Periodically, librarians can compile new acquisition lists and highlight those which present positive images of females and nonstereotyped ones of males for distribution to the building faculty. The professional collection could include lesson plans and classroom activities about stereotyping and activities to integrate gender and ethnic studies into the classroom. Checklists for racism and sexism, and textbook analysis forms should be available.

Bulletin boards and display cases are valuable tools for disseminating information; posters, news clippings, and book jackets can be combined to create timely biographical or newsworthy bulletin boards of famous and not-so-famous women and men who are either in the news or have made varied contributions to society. These can be planned to coincide with birthdays, famous events, holidays, proclamations (such as Special Education Week), or any event in the school calendar.

Thematic displays, such as women and men working together in sports, science, politics, or scenes from family life, can provide interesting projects for students, involving the use of artifacts as well as print items, and introducing research concepts. One librarian inspired a class to dress small dolls (referred to as "models"!) to create historical tableaux with an accompanying narrative on a cassette tape. Another, determined to assess the high school library's audiovisual collection for sexism and racism, organized a committee of students, selected an evaluation form, and trained this cadre of students to review and evaluate films and videos. A rating system was developed to alert teachers to the level of bias in the materials.

Information tables and special exhibits can be organized for Back-To-School nights, Career Days, and at faculty and other school-based meetings, to present an integrated image of women and men, from a wide variety of backgrounds in a wide variety of roles and activities, some nontraditional and some conventional.

Naturally, both female and male students should be encouraged to participate in all library-based activities; gone are the days when the AV equipment squad was entirely male.

Student and Classroom Involvement

One very effective way in which to counteract bias in educational materials and also to teach about bias and discrimination in a wider context is to involve the students themselves. This can be done as a special project or as a classroom activity. Some suggestions follow:

- Teach the students to evaluate the textbooks themselves; by comparing the pictures and text with their own realities and using evaluation instruments appropriate to their level, students will begin to recognize stereotyping. Write letters to publishers giving them the results of those studies.
- Use all forms of media, such as television, films, magazines, and advertising, as fruitful fields for identifying bias and stereotyping.

One class, after examining ads for detergents, wrote to one company recommending that people wearing shirts should wash their own necks!

- Design student research projects to be inclusive; make sure that books by writers other than white males are included in reading lists and recommendations.
- Include women and men, minority and white, when assigning biographical reports.
- Develop a classroom collection of nonbiased reading materials and encourage students to read something different.
- Help students identify books for leisure reading that will give them enjoyment, expand their horizons, and introduce them to other cultures and societies.
- Encourage students to write stories and/or reports which directly counteract some of the biased books that they have read.
- Include a section on language and linguistic bias in all subjects. Discuss the diminution of individuals when they are subsumed into another group, as women are when included into the generic "he" and other male terminology. Examine such demeaning phrasing as "The pioneer moved west with his family and household possessions loaded on an ox-drawn wagon." Discuss the diminutive "-ette" and "-ess." For instance, consider the difference in image between "major" and "majorette," "poet" and "poetess," "steward" and "stewardess." In a far-reaching policy change, the *New York Times* recently announced that women would be able to choose their courtesy titles: Ms., Miss, Mrs. Until then the only choices had been Mrs. or Miss.
- Ask the students to write or rewrite their own versions of biased passages or problems. One elementary class created their own math word problems, using the concepts of addition and subtraction. Instead of Mrs. Smith's eternal apple pie ingredients, students created problems of interest to them, using multiple situations and characters, and, at the same time, improving their understanding of the concepts.
- Use posters and photographs of both sexes to illustrate jobs, social situations, stories, folktales and legends, history and other sections of the curriculum; ensure that minorities are represented.
- When using magazines that are frequently found in schools, make sure that all students' interests are catered to by subscribing to a magazine in the same field focusing on another clientele; for example,

Sports Illustrated, common in many schools, could be balanced out by subscribing to *Women's Sports.*

- Balance the use of limited textbooks with supplementary materials.
- Invite role models in jobs nontraditional for their gender to speak to the students, both for classroom visits and also for career days and assembly programs. By having the opportunity to talk to and ask questions of these visitors, students begin to understand not only the variety of myriad occupations available, but also how multiple roles (e.g., parent and worker) can be maintained. Neither Prince Charming nor Cinderella are appropriate role models for the late twentieth century.
- Prepare speakers by giving them guidelines on how to talk to young people if they are not accustomed to it, and also by asking them to model equitable behaviors and to use nonsexist language.

These are but some strategies which can be easily used in schools, with students, with teachers, with the whole school community. Many of them will probably be refined, lead onto new ideas and create other activities.

REFERENCES*

Britton, G., & Lumpkin, M. *A consumer's guide to sex, race and career bias in public school textbooks.* Corvallis, Oregon: Britton Associates, 1977.

Brody, L., Fox, L., & Tobin, D. (Eds.). *Women and the mathematical mystique.* Baltimore, Maryland: Johns Hopkins University Press, 1980.

Council on Interracial Books for Children. *Stereotypes, distortions, and omissions in U.S. history textbooks.* New York, 1977.

Klein, S.S. (Ed.). *Handbook for achieving sex equity through education.* Baltimore, Maryland: Johns Hopkins University Press, 1985.

McArthur, L.A., & Eisen, S.V. "Achievements of male and female storybook characters as determinants of achievement behavior in boys and girls", *Journal of personality & social psychology,* 1976, *33,* 467–473.

McLeod, J., & Silverman, S. *You won't do: What textbooks on U.S. government teach high school girls.* Pittsburgh, Pennsylvania: KNOW, 1973.

Mozart v. Hawkins County Public Schools, TN as reported in *Education week,* November 5, 1986.

National Coalition Against Censorship. *Books on trial: A survey of recent cases.* New York, 1985.

---

*Note: *Just between sisters* is available from the Consortium for Educational Equity (address listed under General Resources).

PEER Project on Equal Education Rights. *Title IX: A state by state guide to legislation.* Washington, D.C., 1987.

People for the American Way. *Attacks on the freedom to learn, 1985–86.* Washington, D.C., 1986.

People for the American Way. *As Texas goes, so goes the nation: A report on textbook selection in Texas.* Washington, D.C., 1983.

Scott, K.P. "Sexist and non-sexist materials: What impact do they have?", *Elementary school journal,* 1980, *81* (1), 74–82.

Smith v. Board of School Commissioners of Mobile County, Alabama, as reported in *Education week,* March 11, 1987.

Up we go (Pupils activity book for Kindergarten). Oklahoma City, Oklahoma: The Economy Company, 1970.

Weitzman, L., & Rizzo, D. *Biased textbooks* and *Images of males and females in elementary school textbooks.* Washington, D.C.: Resource Center on Sex Roles in Education, 1976.

Women on Words and Images. *Dick and Jane as victims: Sex stereotyping in children's readers, Help wanted: Sexism in career education materials,* and *Sexism in foreign language texts.* Princeton, New Jersey, 1975, 1976, 1976.

Publishers That Have Issued Guidelines for Eliminating Bias & Creating Positive Images in Textbooks

Silver, Burdett, Morristown, NJ
South-Western Publishing, Cincinnati, OH
Scott, Foresman, Glenview, IL
Random House, New York, NY
McGraw-Hill, New York, NY
Houghton Mifflin, Boston, MA
National Council of Teachers of English, Urbana, IL
Puerto Rico Department of Education (in Spanish)
National Center on Educational Media and Materials for the Handicapped, Reston, VA
Women on Words & Images, Princeton, NJ

The following statements are designed for the exploration of personal reactions to the chapter, as well as for the review of the contents of the chapter. Emphasis in discussions should be on exploring issues in depth, rather than on determining the correct or appropriate responses.

FOR DISCUSSION:

1. Other than written content, what other information does a student learn from textbooks?
2. Should traditional nursery rhymes be changed?
3. Select textbooks (or other instructional resources) that exemplify the six types of bias described in the article.
4. Can formulas and numerals be biased? Explain your responses.
5. Review the texts used regularly in your classroom for stereotyping and bias. How can biased materials be used in an unbiased manner?
6. Should biased instructional materials be removed from school shelves?
7. What is the stated policy of your educational institution about the selection and purchase of unbiased textbooks?
8. How can sex fair instructional materials improve students' level of understanding of sex equity issues?

SUGGESTIONS FOR FURTHER READING

Bracken, J. *Books for today's young readers: An annotated bibliography for ages 10–14.* New York: The Feminist Press, 1981.

Center for Sex Equity Instructional Materials Laboratory. *Sex-fair artwork: A sourcebook of reproducible line art.* Columbus, Ohio, 1986.

Columbia University Graduate School of Journalism. *Censorship or selection: Choosing books for public schools.* New York, 1982.

Cotera, M. *Checklists for counteracting race and sex bias in educational materials.* Newton, Massachusetts: WEEA Publishing Center, 1982.

Council on Interracial Books for Children. *Embers: Stories for a changing world.* New York, 1983.

Council on Interracial Books for Children. *Guidelines for selecting bias-free textbooks and storybooks.* New York, 1981.

Council on Interracial Books for Children. *Identifying racism and sexism in children's books.* New York, 1978.

Newman, J. *Girls are people too! A bibliography of nontraditional female roles in children's books.* Metuchen, New Jersey: Scarecrow Press, 1982.

Sadker, D., & Sadker, M. *Now upon a time: A contemporary view of children's literature.* New York: Harper and Row Publishers, 1977.

Shaffer, S.M., & Gordon, B. *Resource notebook.* Washington, D.C.: Mid-Atlantic Center for Sex Equity, 1980.

Tyler, K.B. *Promoting educational equity through school libraries.* Newton, Massachusetts: EDC/WEEA Publishing Center, 1978.

Chapter 16

ISSUES IN PHYSICAL EDUCATION
AND ATHLETICS

DOROTHY B. MCKNIGHT

INTRODUCTION

*"The girls and the boys are too shy and don't like
to be in the gym together"*

It is "gym period" for the seventh grade girls, 1963. The gym "shorts" are the regulation uniform. The girls line up for "basketball practice" which consists of dribbling across the width of the gym, passing the ball, and taking a break. A game is organized. Players can dribble the ball three times, taking no more than six steps, then they must pass the ball. The girls who are tall play as guards.

Obviously, the scene in a contemporary junior high gymnasium has changed. American society has become more health conscious, and has attempted to increase efforts to make children physically fit. Game rules have been revised and upgraded. Teams in a variety of sports, particularly for girls, have blossomed. Athletics have always been a strong component of the school program, but today demand attention from more students, parents, and staff than ever before. Opportunities for physical activity have increased dramatically since the President's Physical Fitness Program and since the implementation of Title IX.

One of the guidelines in the Title IX regulations (Section 86.34) specifically states that physical education programs cannot be divided on the basis of sex. Although there are allowances for specific skill levels and contact sports, classes are to be coeducational. Boys and girls are to work, play, and train together.

The initial reaction on the part of physical education instructors (and parents, teachers, and students) to Section 86.34 was resistance. But teachers who complied with the regulations soon found anticipated problems not as difficult as predicted. Sensitive teachers recognized that it is often uncomfortable for students, particularly adolescents, to appear in gym clothes and demonstrate skill (or lack of skill) in front of peers. So alternatives were provided, and instructors concentrated on establishing a climate of comfort. (One school encouraged loose sweat suits, any color, as the regulation gym outfit.)

Instructors began to offer a variety of sports to all students, including leisure/lifetime sports. They began to see boys and girls jogging and playing tennis together. Skilled students, either gender, spent more time with peers

209

who needed assistance, rather than isolating themselves into select groups. Attendance at games (both as participants and viewers) increased as students learned more about the sport, recognized their classmates, and developed a supportive spirit.

Not so obvious was the development of an understanding of the style, communication patterns, and attitudes of the other sex. Students began to play together just as they worked side by side in their other classrooms.

Younger children today, assuming that there was compliance with the initial Title IX legislation, have never experienced segregated physical education. They accept, indeed expect, a variety of choices and experiences in the gym and on the playing field. Dorothy McKnight discusses the critical effects of equitable physical education and athletic programs on the achievement, self-esteem, and physical well-being of students.

ISSUES IN PHYSICAL EDUCATION AND ATHLETICS

The purpose of this chapter is to delineate those issues of sex equity related to the subject area of physical education and the extracurricular activity of interscholastic athletics. Many student experiences in these areas are closely related to necessary psychomotor, cognitive, and affective life skills. It is important for all educators to understand the student skills developed in these programs along with the role of physical education and athletics in the total education of children.

For example, recruiters for management training programs and other positions in the corporate world will enlist varsity athletes of both genders before nonathlete students when their other qualifications are similar. The experience of working closely with others to form a team striving toward the same goal is felt to be irreplaceable.

The development of physical fitness along with the understanding of human movement are essential tools in many careers. In a well-planned and well-taught physical education program, students will have the opportunity to fully prepare themselves for a variety of job situations.

Differences Between Physical Education and Athletics

Programmatic. The physical education program is part of the academic curriculum of a school. It can be either a required or elective course, and various units within the course may be either required, elective, or a combination of both. All courses and all units must be open to all students except in instances where schools can offer several levels of one unit, i.e., beginning tennis, intermediate tennis, and advanced tennis. It is legitimate, in this instance, to judge people's skill and assign them to sections on the basis of skill. However, the opportunity to participate in *a* tennis class is offered to all.

In contrast, the interscholastic athletic program is an extracurricular activity, and as such, it does not provide every student an opportunity to participate. Student participation is based upon the ability to play the game or perform in the activity. Schools which understand the value of this type of participation will offer many levels such as varsity, junior varsity, "eighth grade team," and so forth. However, the determination of whether students will play or not will always be based on their skill level.

Title IX. The Title IX Guidelines attend to the innate differences between these two programs. In Section 86.34, Access to Course Offerings, the Guidelines prohibit a recipient from providing any course separately on the basis of sex; physical education classes are specifically mentioned in this paragraph.

In Section 86.41, Athletics; paragraph (b), Separate teams, the Guidelines allow a recipient to sponsor separate teams for members of each sex "where selection for such teams is based upon competitive skill or the activity involved is a contact sport," (contact sports include boxing, wrestling, rugby, ice hockey, football, and basketball).

Gender-Related Physical Differences and Similarities

Overlap. The only absolute physical difference between males and females is in the structure and function of the reproductive system. All other differences in physical characteristics must be stated in degrees based upon the "average" female and the "average" male. The range of the "average" of both genders is quite large; as a result, these differences can be observed almost as much within the data of one gender as between the sexes. Because of the large overlap of like physical attributes, it *cannot* be generalized that all males have a biological advantage which results in better motor performance than all females. The classic example to illustrate this statement is the defeat of Bobby Riggs by Billie Jean King in the much publicized tennis match.

Average. The following information is *not* in complete contradiction with the preceeding statements as it might seem. It is vital that both men, women, girls, and boys be given opportunities based on their individual needs and skills. However, to understand particularly the guidelines concerning athletics, it is necessary to look at the "average" physical characteristics of both genders with the warning that these differences must *not* be used to restrict opportunities for participation by any student.

Skeletal Differences. The average skeletal structure of men differs most widely from women in size and proportion. Bones of men tend to be longer with greater diameter and density than those of women. The proportion of arm and leg length to trunk length is less for the average woman than the average man. Greater size and proportion usually favor a performance which requires strength, power, and speed.

Aerobic Capacity. Aerobic capacity refers to the ability of an individual to continue delivering the amount of oxygen demanded by working muscles. On the average, men have a larger body size which includes a larger heart and lungs which gives them a larger "stroke volume" (more blood sent from heart for each beat). The most important fact is that the differences in aerobic capacity are reduced with training.

Muscle Mass and Fat Percentage. It is in this physical aspect that the greatest differences occur between the "averages" of each gender. Estrogen, the female hormone, stimulates the increase of adipose or fat tissues, while the male hormone, testosterone, causes an increased growth of muscle tissue. The obvious result is that women have a greater amount of fat and men have a greater amount of muscle mass. The average female body contains 20% to 25% fat and 23% muscle; the average male body contains 40% muscle and 10% to 15% fat. Therefore, the ratio of strength to weight of average males is 33% greater than average females. This difference affects performance capacity in areas of strength, speed, and power.

Training Effects. Through well-planned training programs, women can substantially increase their cardiorespiratory efficiency and their muscular strength along with decreasing the percentage of body fat by as much as 7 percent to 15 percent. Strength gains of as much as 35 percent have been reported; it seems easier for women to gain strength in their legs rather than their upper bodies.

Some interesting comparisons between time and distances achieved by women in the Olympics follow: 800 meters run was won in 1928 with a time of 2 minutes, 16.8 seconds, and in 1984 the winning time was 1 minute, 57.6 seconds; this was an increase of approximately 86 percent. The long jump was won in 1948 with jump of 18 feet, 8.25 inches and in 1984 with 22 feet, 10 inches for an improvement percentage of 82 percent. Other percentages of improvement from 1928 to 1984 are 100 meter run—90 percent, discus—57 percent, high jump—80 percent; from 1948 to 1984, the shot put performance improved 61 percent. From 1964 to 1980, the 400 meter run improved 76 percent; and in 1932, Babe Didrikson Zaharias threw the javelin 143 feet, 4 inches, while the 1984 winner's distance was 228 feet, 2 inches for a performance improvement of 63 percent against one who has been revered as the greatest American woman athlete. Training methods have improved, and when women take part in excellent training procedures, obviously, their scores will improve also. It is interesting to note that the improvement percentage in the throwing events using the upper body is less than in the running and jumping areas which substantiates the research findings (Staff, 1981).

The usual trap is to compare women's scores to men's scores which perpetuates the use of only one measure—bigger, faster, etc. is best. This concept has always been detrimental to women's athletics; a common statement heard by many women coaches over the years, "you'll get more money when your team plays as 'well' as the men's." "Well" is here defined as winning in head to head competition. However, one comparison seems applicable; in 1984 Joan Benoit won the first women's marathon ever held in the Olympics in 2 hours, 24 minutes and 52 seconds. She would have won the men's (and only) marathon in 1956 by 8 seconds (Staff, 1981).

Myths About Physical Activity for Women. The most influential myth about active participation by girls and women is the belief that the jumping, running, and subsequent jarring of the body is harmful to the reproductive organs of females. In reality, female reproductive organs are better protected than those of males because they are internal. The muscular strength developed through activity gives even greater support to the reproductive organs. The stronger abdominal musculature and greater cardiorespiratory endurance of trained athletes often leads to easier pregnancies and childbirths with shorter delivery time (Arrighi, Hult, and McKnight, 1982).

Lifting weights produces good muscle definition in males and certainly improved lines in women. However, bulging muscles will not occur in most women who lift weights in a reasonable program. Those women who have a more mesomorphic body type will show more muscle definition as will those on a heavy weight/body building program. The real difference in muscle definition between males and females is caused by hormones particularly testosterone. As was stated previously, testosterone causes an increase in muscle tissue or mass.

The belief that prolonged activity during menstruation and training for long distance running are harmful are myths of long standing. Taken to the extreme with a lot of overdistance work and a severe drop in fat percentage, some women will cease menstruating at all. This is a situation which is not normal and should not continue for long periods of time. The knowledgeable doctors now believe that this cessation is not harmful if it is only months in duration. The last months of training for the Olympics might be an example.

Sex Role Stereotyping/Socialization and Skill Performance

Basic Areas. The effects of sex role stereotyping can be seen in physical education and athletics as in other aspects of life, and most probably, they are more limiting. Sex role socialization and the concomitant stereotyping affects physical skill performance particularly in the following areas: achievement, self-esteem, and physical well being.

Achievement. The four major factors which are influenced by stereotyping and which affect achievement are: (1) Opportunities to perform and to lead a group: males are given many more opportunities with more recreational and Little League programs and also greater numbers of chances to demonstrate skills and be captain in coed situations. (2) Encouragement to perform skills: males are expected to participate in physical activities and are encouraged by all to do so, while praise for female athletes comes from small groups of people but not from society as a whole. (3) Expectations for achievement: this is perhaps the aspect over which the teachers and coaches exert the most influence. People of all ages are prone to strive to only that level expected of them; males are expected to achieve reasonable levels of performance in "appropriate" (often meaning contact) sports, and as a result, they are supported and instructed in their attempts to improve. Females, on the other hand, are rarely encouraged to achieve high levels of physical skill; if they are, it will most often take place in a "sex appropriate sport" such as figure skating, gymnastics, or tennis. Some research involving the observation and recording of verbal feedback given by teachers to improve the skill performance of students has shown that females most often receive comments of praise of performance but rarely receive prescriptive feedback which would give them the information necessary to improve their performance. What that says to the students is that the teacher thinks that level of performance is the best the female student can accomplish. In contrast, the males were given primarily prescriptive feedback which says to them that the teacher has higher expectations for them, they can get better and this is how. (4) Recognition of achievement: the rewards of awards, spectator interest, and financial gain for athletes are far greater for the men than for women. Some people are discouraged if they cannot see recognition for their efforts in the immediate future (Arrighi, Hult, and McKnight, 1982).

Self-Esteem. Self-esteem of both females and males can be adversely influenced by the stereotyped expectancies held by society in general. A male is expected to be aggressive and like contact sports; if he does not participate in those activities or is poorly skilled in them, he loses peer acceptance and ultimately self-esteem. Because active participation in physical activities and sports by women is not generally accepted in society, women who are active and excell in sports also find rejection and subsequent loss of self-esteem.

Physical Well-Being. Because of the societal expectations, females and unskilled males are likely to avoid participation in sport activities and as a result become physically unfit. Besides the physical benefits derived from successful participation, those who avoid activity also never know the satisfaction of performing skills and the joy of movement.

Physical Education Issues

Coeducational Classes

Values. When the dust settled from the original Title IX Guidelines, the change which touched all students and physical education teachers was the regulation that physical education classes would be taught in a coed organizational pattern. It is important to understand the advantages of coed classes to both girls and boys.

Simulated Work Place. The playground and similar activities are the work places of children. Giving boys and girls the opportunity to play and learn together in a more informal setting allows them the chance to know each other as friends, teammates upon whom they depend for certain input, and as classmates with whom they share a like experience. These relaxed opportunities for sharing activities and responsibilities help students develop an appreciation for the other gender without sexual overtones. So often if a child has a friend of the other sex, adults tend to make a girl friend or boy friend into a girlfriend or boyfriend. So even at an early age, the idea of relationships with members of the other gender carries sexual innuendos.

The give and take necessary to work as a member of a team is excellent training for similar actions as a member of a faculty, corporation, staff, or any other working group. There are chances to lead and make decisions, times when one must let others lead and give up one's own ideas, and opportunities to negotiate differences of opinion. Some might argue that these opportunities favor the young women as they enter the work force in greater numbers than before; however, because most men will now be working with women employed at the same level, their ability to understand and work with their female colleagues will be an important ingredient to success. Both genders and their employers will benefit.

Physical Skill. Because of a wider range of physical skill found in coed classes, teachers are forced to make allowances for these skill differences if learning is to occur. Therefore, the only logical way to deal with the situation is to divide the class into smaller groups based upon their ability and provide learning experiences which challenge each group. Observation and some research has discerned that in boys' classes where the teaching and practice opportunities were keyed to one level, the boys who were poorly skilled were not attended to or given the opportunity to learn skills at their level; as a result, these young men never reached a satisfactory performance level and shied away from physical activities from that point on. In the girls' classes the situation often seemed to be the lack of a challenge to the better skilled girls along with the aforementioned lower performance expectancy held by the teachers. If teachers of coed classes provide skill challenges appropriate for each skill level, both girls and boys of all abilities will benefit.

Implementation Problems

Teachers' Training. One of the greatest hurdles to overcome in the implementation of the coed classes lies in the differences between the training and experience of female and male physical educators; for the most part, the majority of current teachers graduated from sex-segregated teacher training programs. Many women were trained to be a "Jill of all trades/sports" with little depth of knowledge or experience in game situations or strategy; this manifested itself in a preoccupation with the execution of skills without the incorporation of these skills in the activity for which they were intended. Part of the reason for this was the lack of an interscholastic and intercollegiate athletic program. There was no avenue for the major students to perfect their skills and game play while in college and no reason as teachers to push their students toward greater excellence even if they had the necessary knowledge. The only obvious advantage of this situation is the fact that women teachers planned their class lessons more completely because the classes were the most important responsibility of the day.

Male physical educators usually have been highly skilled athletes who were involved in coaching interscholastic teams at the end of the day. As a result of their own abilities, they assume quick learning on the part of all their students and often neglect the practice steps required by the lesser skilled. Their involvement as a coach in planning for practices and games takes away from their concentration in the class situation, and the result is the teaching mode known as "throwing out the ball"!

Changes in Teacher Attitudes. The teaching approaches described above will not be successful in coed classes any more than they were in the single-sexed ones. The better skilled students will be bored if they never have a chance to participate in game-like activities, and the lesser skilled will never learn to perform the necessary skills if practice time with "achievable" tasks is not provided. The barrier to changing the teachers' attitudes is the natural resistance to change, especially in something as close to one as teaching style. It seems that experienced teachers view an attack upon their teaching approaches as an attack upon their personalities. There are highly successful ways to effectively teach classes with wide ranges of skill. These changes must be "sold" to the current teachers and to those in training.

Another teacher attitude which must be changed is the adherence to gender-based expectations. Teachers of both genders seem to expect less of girls in class as evidenced by their comments, nonverbal behavior, and assignments. Conversely, they expect all boys to perform with excellence. Change must occur so that teachers expect all students to succeed within their range of ability (Klein, 1985).

Coed classes are a great success in schools where the teachers believe in them and teach with a positive attitude and successful approaches. Schools with wonderful programs and happy, well-adjusted students and teachers can be found within a mile of a school with the same aged students in which the teachers say that "the girls and boys are too shy and don't like to be in the gym together." It seems logical to assume that children are not that different, but that the teachers' attitudes are what set up the contrast (Klein, 1985).

Program Improvement

Administration. It is imperative that administrators in individual schools as well as those in the school system's central administration assume a firm stance and commitment to sex equity and coed classes as that is manifested in physical education. Coed classes must be scheduled, and the teachers must know that the classes must be taught as scheduled. Because school administrators have been vague, many teachers have believed that they will never have to teach coed physical education classes. Therefore, they have not adjusted their methods or curriculum. Academic freedom seems to mean that "I will teach what I want to whom I wish"!

After the *Grove City* decision (See Chapter on Title IX) many administrators thought that they need not insist upon coed classes. With so many teachers wanting to return to single-sex classes, administrators have allowed this to happen. The unfortunate aspect, besides the illegality, is that if there were coed classes for a period of time, the teachers did not succeed in using them for positive experiences. Those teachers whose classes were successful never want to return to sex-segregated ones.

Inservice Training. It is imperative that time be set aside for inservice sessions to train the teachers in new ways to present material and practice skills. In order to accommodate the range of skill levels in one class, Title IX permits and good sense requires that teachers group students on the basis of their ability and assign tasks which will challenge them at their various levels. At the present time, most teachers teach one skill and have all students in the class practice that skill in the same way, at the same level of difficulty. and for the same length of time. This does not allow for the fact that some students know how to execute the skill, and others may never have seen it before. This "inclass ability grouping" and accompanying different approach to presentation and practice will require the teachers to carefully separate increasingly more difficult skills and ways to learn and practice them; progressions will be extremely important.

Another helpful approach is to use better students to help lesser skilled classmates by teaching the skilled ones how to analyze movement and skill improvement; they will gain also through the new knowledge that will help make them even better performers. Any approach which allows students much activity or practice time at their proper level of difficulty must be far superior to the usual command style/teacher directed manner used by most physical education teachers.

Curriculum Revision. In all too many cases, the curriculum for the coed classes was a combination of the boys' and girls' curricula used previously. Where teachers found difficulty in believing that both girls and boys should learn certain activities such as wrestling for the girls and modern dance for the boys, those activities either became a very sex-biased "choice" or were eliminated entirely.

It is essential that various activity units be analyzed to determine the value they add to the program. Through the contributions of appropriate units, the basic tenets of the school's philosophy and the specific goals of the physical education program should be reached. The reasons for including any activity must go beyond, "we've always taught that"!

Interscholastic/Intercollegiate Athletic Program Issues
Historic Programmatic Differences

Girls' and Women's Programs. Tracing the history of girls' and women's athletic programs since the end of the nineteenth century is a trip through barren deserts, lush single-species forests, and back again to the desert. Opportunities for girls and women to compete have varied by decade, by geography, by sport, and by intensity. In the first half of the twentieth century, the emphasis in the physical education teacher training programs for women was a wide range of activities primarily for the instructional program; this approach of training women to be "Jills of all appropriate sports and Mistresses of none" did not permit the indepth understanding necessary for coaching competitive athletic teams. Because the women trained in this manner in sexsegregated departments were the people responsible for girls' and women's programs in educational institutions, there were few programs other than intramurals and play days.

There were exceptions, of course. In areas of the east, field hockey has been very competitive in high schools and colleges from the time the sport was introduced at Harvard in 1901 by Constance Applebee. Miss Applebee had come from England to study at Harvard Summer School and was appalled at the lack of vigorous exercise available to women. The girls' basketball programs in rural areas, especially in Iowa, is another example of single sport programs in specific geographic areas. This program remains virtually unchanged in the high schools, as Iowa is the only state which still uses the six player (three forwards/three guards) rules of play. Nationally, the game has had many intermediate "rules stops" which have been designed to provide ever increasing challenges to the participants (Hult, 1987).

Major Beliefs. In her review of the historical literature of the period 1900–1950, Joan S. Hult identified five major beliefs operating within the environment of girls' and women's sports and influencing the direction of these programs in educational institutions. These beliefs are as follows: (1) "A sport for every girl and every girl for a sport" was the belief and programmatic support of the Division for Girls and Women in Sport of the American Association for Health, Physical Education, and Recreation. The type of program based upon this belief would obviously support large numbers of girls learning sports as opposed to funneling resources to a few girls striving for excellence; (2) vigorous sport was unfeminine and led to the development of both physical and psychological traits which are normally considered to be male-like. Examples are aggressiveness, competitiveness, and "masculine" postural positions necessary to succeed in sport activities; (3) physically demanding competitive athletics were harmful to the female athlete and would interfere with childbearing which was viewed by society as the number one role for women; (4) women should be responsible for the girls' and women's programs so that the previously mentioned beliefs could be an integral part of the program organization and implementation; (5) highly competitive programs led to the exploitation of athletes (Hult, 1987).

Boys' and Men's Programs. Historically, boys and men have had a variety of interscholastic and intercollegiate sport teams on which they could play. In smaller schools and poorer areas, the choice would not have been as wide; however, the pattern was to support at least three teams, one team per season such as football, basketball, and baseball. The emphasis was on team sports partially because the male teachers and coaches would have received more intense training in these activities but also because facilities and equipment was more readily available and there were more playing opportunities for more people.

Like the girls' programs, there were and still are pockets of great interest in specific sports in certain geographic areas. Some sports are east coast, midwest, or west coast related, while others are more aligned with a rural or urban setting. The critical difference between the history of boys' and girls' competition is that there have always been some interscholastic and intercollegiate sports for boys in all areas of the country.

Growth of Girls' and Women's Programs—1960-1985

The growth of opportunities for girls and women to compete in interscholastic and intercollegiate athletics began slowly in the 1960s and picked up steam in the early 1970s. The latter years of the 70s decade saw an explosion of athletic programs for girls and women prompted, of course, by the implementation of Title IX. Growth continued in the first few years of the 1980s but by 1985 had leveled off in almost all geographical areas and educational levels.

NAPECW Conference. In April 1966 at its National Conference, the National Association for Physical Education of College Women included a program entitled, "Competitive Sports for College Women." Members of the organization were interested in exactly what type of programs were being conducted. They . . . "wanted to know whether or not colleges and universities were allowing more competition for women or whether this was just a passing fad." To prepare for this program, a survey was conducted. A quick look at the results reveals the following information about competitive programs for women in the colleges: Eastern District—65 of 71 schools or 92 percent conducted programs. Central District—47 of 52 schools or 90 percent conducted programs. Midwest District—two-thirds or 66% conducted programs. The Western Society (west coast schools) reported that there was limited varsity competition supported by its schools, but that these programs were growing (Ley, 1966).

Commission Established. In March 1966, the Commission on Intercollegiate Athletics for Women was founded by the Board of Directors of the then American Association for Health, Physical Education, and Recreation. This Commission was charged to develop organizing plans for events, establish standards for competition, sanction events to which four or more teams were invited, and as the need became apparent, sponsor national tournaments (Ley, 1966).

Although the terms, "varsity" and "championship," are glaringly absent from the language, the establishment of this Commission was the first sign of approval for competitive athletics from the professional organization to which most physical educators belonged. As was noted earlier, the women physical educators were the people who coached and conducted those programs that existed. This was a far more influential event than the Commission's charge might indicate.

High Schools. At their 1964 Conference, the National Federation of State High School Athletic Associations passed a resolution that if and when competitive events for high school girls were initiated they should be controlled by the existing State Athletic Association. It seemed as if most parties were ready for the growth and changes to come (Ley, 1966).

Numbers of Teams and Participants. The results of a survey cited by J. J. Coakley placed the number of girls playing on high school varsity teams at fewer than 300,000 in the AY 1970–71. The contrasting figure is 1.8 million high school girls participating on athletic teams in 1983–84 (Lehr and Washington, 1987).

Coakley gives the figure of 16,000 college women participating in intercollegiate athletics in the 1970s. The staff of the publication, *Athletic Purchasing and Facilities,* reviewed varsity sport programs in 1976 and determined that 1006 senior colleges sponsored some programs for women. Dividing the 6220 total number of teams cited by the 1006 colleges, an average number of sports/college is 6.18. However, the total number of senior colleges which supported men's programs is 1152; it is unlikely that there were 146 more colleges which admitted men than women so the difference in numbers most likely represents those schools which did not support women's programs at all. If the higher number of colleges is used, the average number of sports per college becomes 5.39 which is closer to the 5.61. The men's figure is about 7.0 sports per college. The contrast in junior colleges in 1976 is even more severe; 792 junior colleges reported that they support 4,196 sports for men or 5.3 sports/school, and 479 junior colleges support 1,824 women's sports for average of 3.8 sports per school. However, again the discrepancy between the numbers of junior colleges supporting programs for both genders is very large, 313 schools. It is doubtful that there are 313 more junior colleges for men only, so the answer has to be that most of these 313 schools simply do not support sports for women (Lehr and Washington, 1987).

In 1980, the same number, 792, of junior colleges reported supporting men's programs while the number offering women's programs grew to 620. The per school average number of sports were 4.92 for the men and 4.06 for women.

In this same survey, the senior college statistics revealed that in both 1980 and 1981, the men's average number of supported sports was 7.38 sports/college, and the women's average was 5.56 sports/college. The results of this survey seem to indicate a leveling off of the growth of new teams in the colleges.

Budgetary and Support Aspects

Impact of Recession. The reduction of available funds and the rather extreme increases in costs of various aspects of athletic programs were two forces which worked to stop the enlargement of the girls' and women's athletic programs. True equality had not yet been reached, but programs were clearly headed in that direction. In the early 1980s it was necessary for both high schools and colleges to cut back on the support directed into the interschool athletic programs. In some states and local communities, the propositions passed by the taxpayers forced the schools to abandon some programs, charge students to participate, raise money through parent and community organizations, and generally use very creative means to subsidize the sport activities.

The colleges and universities were in the same financial bind with the added burden of earning the necessary scholarship money with tuition, room, and board costs constantly on the rise. They, of course, have far greater ability to earn money through the intercollegiate athletic program.

A further result of the budget crunch to the present time is that most coaching staffs remained constant in numbers and salary costs, travel schedules in the colleges particularly were cut back and teams traveled together. Junior varsity or "second teams" were discontinued in many high schools and colleges; these were teams which gave more young people an opportunity to play and enjoy interschool athletics and also gave late developers a chance to learn the sport with proper coaching. The junior varsities were especially valuable to the young women who still do not have the wide range of community opportunities to learn sports as are available to the young men.

Loss of Governance and Leadership Positions

On July 1, 1972, the Association for Intercollegiate Athletics for Women began its operations as the governing body for women's intercollegiate athletics. This organization grew out of the Commission on Intercollegiate Athletics for Women mentioned earlier in this chapter. There were 278 charter member schools, and by AY 1979–80, the membership totaled 970. The vast majority of the voting representatives of this organization were women, and as a result, the opportunities were great for those representatives to lead and to grow in leadership abilities as well as to establish networks of women in similar institutions with like problems.

By June 30, 1982, two years after the high point of membership and ten years after its beginning, AIAW and its duties were taken over by the NCAA, National Collegiate Athletic Association. The NCAA had governed the men's programs for years, and to many college presidents, two organizations providing the same services seemed excessive. Because most Athletic Directors who held the "purse strings" were men and were familiar with the NCAA, that is the organization which survived. Lawsuits followed, and some settlements were made, but the chance for significant numbers of women to make the decisions about the girls' and women's programs in the colleges was lost.

Coaches. Carolyn Lehr (Lehr and Washington, 1987), reports that in 1973, 92 percent of women's intercollegiate sports teams were coached by women. It was found that the percentage has dropped to 50 in 1986. Lehr also reports some figures about high schools which did not come from a national sample but included a number of states; in 1972, approximately 88 percent of the girl's interscholastic teams were coached by women, and by 1983, this figure was 46 percent. It is truly amazing that as opportunities to play sports have increased for the female students, the chances for women to coach and officiate in the interschool program have diminished very significantly. The concomitant loss of role models for the young women athletes is even more disturbing, because they will see no long-term role for themselves in the sport arena.

Summary

It is safe to say that physical education and athletic programs in schools and colleges are more sex equitable in the late 1980s than they were fifteen years earlier. Opportunities for young women to challenge their abilities have increased considerably. Society's acceptance of women exhibiting the more aggressive behavior necessary for success in competitive sports has increased; greater acceptance extends in some quarters to the young men who opt for a less traditional activity such as dance or gymnastics. Title IX has caused the movement experiences of both girls and boys to be enhanced.

So what is the problem? The problem is that insidiously, as the ocean takes back "its land," forces in society continue to work toward "getting things back to 'normal.'" Normal is also known as "the good old days" with boys playing football while girls cheer them on and men playing in the "Men's Gym" (the one with the bright lights and shiny floor) whenever they want and the women never leaving the "Girl's Gym" (the one with dull lights and no scoreboard or stands). Society members who care must constantly monitor local situations. If this appears to be an extreme or alarmist viewpoint, those who question must seek out and bring to a halt the quiet inroads of program deterioration since the Supreme Court's *Grove City* decision.

REFERENCES

Arrighi, M.A., Hult, J.S., McKnight, D.B. *Project missing link: A focus on instruction — participants' workbook & leader manual.* Chevy Chase, Maryland: Educational Sport Institute, 1982.

Arrighi, M.A., McKnight, D.B. *Instructional strategies for coed physical education* (2nd ed.). Chevy Chase, Maryland: Athletic and Sport Consultants, Inc., 1981.

Hult, J.S. Different AIAW/NCAA eligibility rules: Tip of the iceberg? *Athletic purchasing and facilities,* 1979, *3,* 12–16.

Hult, J.S. Personal interview: Historical reflections, 1987.

Klein, S.S. (Ed.). *Handbook for achieving sex equity through education.* Baltimore, Maryland: The Johns Hopkins University Press, 1985.

Lehr, C.A., & Washington, M.A. Beyond women's collegiate athletics: opportunity to play for pay. *Journal of physical education, recreation & dance,* 1987, *58* (3), 28–32.

Ley, K. Widening the scope of women's sport activities. *Proceedings of the fall conference: Topic—intercollegiate competition.* State College, Pennsylvania: Eastern Association for Physical Education of College Women, 1966.

Staff. (1977, April/May). College sports programs for men and women. *Athletic purchasing & facilities,* April/May 1977.

Staff. Fourth annual college sport participation survey. *Athletic purchasing & facilities,* August, 1981.

Staff. *AIAW directory—1980-1981.* Association for intercollegiate athletics for women, 1980.

The following statements are designed for the exploration of personal reactions to the chapter, as well as for the review of the contents of the chapter. Emphasis in discussions should be on exploring issues in depth, rather than on determining the correct or appropriate responses.

FOR DISCUSSION:

1. What are the "student skills" developed in physical education and athletic programs?
2. Discuss the author's statement: "The range of the 'average' of both genders is quite large; as a result, these differences can be observed almost as much within the data of one gender as between the sexes."
3. Discuss personal observations of how athletic opportunities affect achievement and self-esteem in boys and girls.
4. What is the "trap" of comparing women's scores to men's scores?
5. The author states: "Giving boys and girls the opportunity to play and learn together in a more informal setting allows them the chance to know each other as friends, teammates upon whom they depend for certain input, as classmates with whom they share a like experience." How are these opportunities utilized in adult life?
6. Discuss your physical education and athletic experiences as a child, focusing on how they affected your life as an adult.
7. What should be the objectives of in-service training for physical education personnel?
8. What should be the objectives of in-service training for athletic trainers and coaches?

SUGGESTIONS FOR FURTHER READING

American Alliance for Health, Physical Education, and Recreation. *Complying with Title IX of the education amendments of 1972 in physical education and high school sports programs.* Washington, D.C., 1977.

Arnett, C. *A.C.T.I.V.E.: Sex equity in elementary school physical education.* Newton, Massachusetts: WEEA Publishing Center, 1980.

Clement, A. *Equity in physical education.* Newton, Massachusetts: EDC/WEEA, 1980.

Cole, D. & Coyle, V. *Guide to implementing a girls' and women's sports commission.* Newton, Massachusetts: EDC/WEEA Publishing Center, 1978.

Equal Education Opportunity Center. *Tips and techniques: Ability grouping and performance evaluation in physical education.* Springfield, Illinois: Illinois State Board of Education, 1985.

ERIC Clearinghouse on Urban Education. *Physical education and athletics: Strategies for meeting Title IX requirements.* Arlington, Virginia, 1979.

Florida State University. *Decisions about physical activity.* Newton, Massachusetts: EDC/WEEA Publishing Center, 1983.

Griffin, P., & Placek, J. *Fair play in the gym.* Andover, Massachusetts: The NETWORK, 1983.

Uhlir, A. *Physical educators for equity.* Newton, Massachusetts: EDC/WEEA Publishing Center, 1981.

Chapter 17

SEX EQUITY IN VOCATIONAL EDUCATION

BARBARA A. BITTERS

INTRODUCTION

"In two years, I can guarantee you a job."

All teachers are vocational educators. Contemporary economic concerns require educators to provide students with the necessary skills to be productive citizens *and* to be prepared for a lifetime of at least part-time employment. All educators, whether they are employed in a vocational education institution or not, are involved in readying students for a vocation.

The field of vocational education has always focused on training students for potential employment. Yet this critical component of the educational program is often overlooked and misunderstood. At worst, it is regarded as less significant than the traditional educational process. Students pursuing business, carpentry, nursing, and other trades are often viewed as receiving a level of education that is secondary to the college preparatory curriculum.

Recently, vocational education has commanded more attention because of the profound societal emphasis on the need to prepare *all* students, girls *and* boys, for future careers. Although four-year college is still regarded as an essential conduit to successful employment, secondary and postsecondary vocational training institutions are gaining more credibility among all educators. Job satisfaction, utilization of skills and interests, and monetary incentives are influencing teachers, guidance counselors, and students when educational programs are selected.

The advent of the Carl Perkins Vocational Education Act, a reauthorization of the 1976 Vocational Education Act (VEA), caused equity issues to become an integral part of the vocational education process. Emphasis on career education, nontraditional options, servicing adult populations, and equitable school environments generated from the VEA legislation. All states participate at some level in carrying out the sex equity requirements of the legislation. Although the law provided the impetus for sex equity programs and activities, large numbers of educators carry the concepts into the entire educational setting.

Barbara A. Bitters reviews the role of sex equity in vocational education. Her discussion of pertinent legislation is especially important for educators interested in legal support for sex equity activities.

229

SEX EQUITY AND VOCATIONAL EDUCATION

Nowhere is the cost of sex bias, sex role stereotyping, and sex discrimination more compelling, concrete, or clear than in the area of occupational aspiration and choice, vocational education and training, and the resulting employment, economic self-sufficiency, and job satisfaction of females and males.

What is Vocational Education?

Vocational education is defined as educational programs directly related to the preparation for work, paid and unpaid, and is the link between school and the world of work. It covers instruction for all jobs that do not require a B.A. or high degree (this is 4 out of 5 jobs). Students of vocational education prepare for thousands of diverse occupations and careers encompassed in seven major program areas or disciplines: agriculture and agribusiness, marketing and distribution, health occupations, home economics, business, technical, and trade and industry.

In the broadest sense, vocational education prepares students for the dual roles of earning wages and maintaining a household and/or family. It provides students the opportunity to formulate a clear picture of work, work systems, and work rituals; to explore different work choices through "hands on" activities or through work experience programs outside the school; to develop general employability skills and attitudes such as how to fill out employment applications or interview for a job; and to develop specific competencies for a chosen occupation. Career awareness, exploration and development activities are an integral part of vocational education.

Vocational educators pride themselves on the fact that vocational education is student centered, practical, "real life" focused. Vocational education methodology expands the classroom through cooperative education (part time supervised placement with an employer), simulation (turning the classroom into a business/industry environment) and other work experience programs (job shadowing, community service or paid work). Vocational student organizations (VSOs) are an integral part of the instructional program and facilitate learning beyond the classroom. Vocational student organizations emphasize leadership development and civic responsibility in addition to refining occupational skills and knowledge. Finally, vocational educators have a long tradition of working in partnership with local advisory councils composed of business and community leaders designed to keep the curriculum "on target."

The vocational education enterprise is a federal, state, and local partnership with respect to policymaking and funding. Local delivery systems vary from state to state, but generally students' first access to vocational education occurs in middle or junior high school and is exploratory in nature. Senior high school vocational education provides continued exploration, vocational skill acquisition, and training for specific occupational competencies. Postsecondary vocational education emphasizes occupational competencies, advanced skill training, retraining for career changers and displaced workers, tailored training programs for local employers, and avocational course offerings.

What Are the Sex Equity Issues in Vocational Education?

Historically, vocational education enrollments have been highly sex segregated. Schools heavily reinforce traditional sex role stereotypes in course offerings, curriculum materials, and counseling and guidance programs which serve to reflect and perpetuate outdated, limited occupational and family roles for both females and males. In fact, prior to the mid-70s, females were still encouraged to prepare solely for the role of full time homemaker or were led to believe they would work only a few years in a low-paying, dead and "female" occupation. Verheyden-Hilliard wrote in 1975 that girls in vocational education were being prepared for "Cinderellahood" rather than jobs (Verheyden-Hilliard, 1975).

The goals of vocational sex equity are aimed at changing the following conditions in vocational education:

1. **Access to Vocational Courses or Schools.** Access to nontraditional courses and to some vocational schools was legally and practically denied to females and males prior to Title IX of the Educational Amendments (1975) and the Vocational Education Act (1976). Many schools had policies requiring completion of different vocational courses by males and females prior to graduation. Courses like "Bachelor Living" and "Powder Puff Mechanics" maintained the separation of the sexes in vocational education. Females' access to work study, job placement, cooperative and apprenticeship programs was limited and/or stereotyped. Membership in certain Vocational Student Organizations was restricted to members of one sex. (The Future Farmers of America voted to allow female members in 1969.) In 1974, almost 50 percent of all female students in vocational

education were in consumer home economics, training for the unpaid work of maintaining the family. Another 29 percent of females were training for entry level clerical occupations (Verheyden-Hilliard, 1975). Male students were concentrated in agriculture and industrial education.

Administrative and vocational staff patterns still reflect traditional sex distributions in instructional areas. Across the country males hold a substantial majority of positions in the program areas of Agriculture, Marketing, Technical, Trade and Industrial, and Industrial Arts. Females hold a similarly sizeable majority of positions in Health Occupations, Home Economics (Wage-Earning and Consumer) and Business. Administrative staff positions are held predominantly by males. The lack of nontraditional teacher role models acts as a barrier for students who are unable to see someone like themselves succeeding in a nontraditional vocational area.

2. **Sex Biased Attitudes.** Attitudes of educators, students, parents, and employers reflect outdated and inaccurate information about labor force participation and a clear belief that there are "men's" jobs and "women's" jobs. These attitudes limit students' career aspiration and occupational choice. Frequently traditional attitudes about the "proper" role and abilities of females contribute to a hostile learning environment for females who have made nontraditional vocational choices. More recently, sexual harassment of young women in vocational classrooms and labs nontraditional for their sex is being recognized as an important issue to be addressed.

Boys are discouraged from pursuing programs in cosmetology, nursing, and other fields nontraditional for their sex. Assumptions are made about the financial aspirations of boys and questions about their sexual preference are often raised.

3. **Vocational Guidance and Counseling.** Prior to Title IX and the Vocational Education Act of 1976, practices, materials, and assessment tools reflected traditional sex role stereotypes, with different scales used to measure interests and aptitudes of females and males. Research in the 1970s revealed that adolescent males were aware of a greater number of occupations, had higher occupational aspirations, and expected to achieve them. Adolescent females were aware of a limited number of occupations, and had lower aspirations and expectations of career achievements (Farris, 1978). Many counselors have not kept pace with the changing labor market or the changing roles of males and females, and few have actively incorporated this information into their counseling practices.

4. **Support Services for Females.** Lack of support services in the educational setting act as barriers to female participation in vocational education. This is particularly true for low income women, older women returning to school after many years, minority women, single parents, and women seeking nontraditional occupations. Support services needed include: Child care, transportation assistance, financial aid, flexible class scheduling, special counseling and guidance, remedial classes, role models, peer support groups, community role models and mentors, prevocational assessment, job development, and placement classes.

5. **Unequal Opportunities in and Benefits from Vocational Education.** Manifestations of sex bias in the teaching/learning environment create unequal educational opportunities. Even in coeducation classrooms, sex bias is visible in vocational texts and instructional materials that not only reflect, but exaggerate traditional, stereotyped roles and a "traditional" division of labor; curriculum which is geared to the interests and needs of only one sex; instructional practices which divide students into single sex groups; student evaluations which use different criteria for grading males and females; teacher expectations which differentiate between male and female students' unequal funding for equipment, labs, and student projects in female intensive vocational programs; and a higher ratio of students to teachers in female-intensive vocational programs.

One study of co-ed practical arts classes (Klein, Richardson, Thomas, Wirtenberg, 1978), found sexist behavior in teachers of both sexes such as: interacting more with boys than girls, admonishing girls to act like little ladies, asking boys to do heavy work, and seating girls and boys on opposite sides of the room. The work by the Sadkers and Grayson has shed additional light on unconscious gender differences in student-teacher interaction patterns in the classroom.

The conditions and practices in vocational education outlined above pose a stark contrast to the changes relating to women's participation in the paid labor force taking place from the 1960s up to the present day. Testimony presented before education committees of the U. S. Congress from 1970–1984 emphasized the gap between preparation in vocational education and the reality girls and women face after graduation. Deep-rooted and enduring social and economic changes have occurred during the last twenty years. These changes require vocational educators to broaden their perceptions of the educational needs of male and female students of all races and various mental and physical abilities so that these students are better prepared to survive and thrive in a society characterized by changing conditions and expectations.

Inequality between male and female workers is reflected in and partially created by the sex segregation, sex bias, role stereotyping, and discrimination present in vocational education. Even after workforce and social changes are well known, few vocational educators and counselors are informing all students that these changes will affect their life/work plans.

What is Vocational Sex Equity?

The term *sex equity* describes an environment in which individuals can consider options and make choices based on their abilities and talents, not on the basis of stereotypes and biased expectations. It brings about freedom from favoritism based on sex. The achievement of sex equity enables women and men of all races and ethnic backgrounds to develop skills needed in the home and in the paid work force, skills which are best suited to an individual's needs, informed interests, and abilities. It opens economic, social, and political opportunities for all people. It fosters mutual trust because persons of both sexes are unrestricted in their roles. The promotion of sex equity in vocational education involves creating an educational environment which allows students to *choose* vocational programs and careers, to *enter* those programs, to *participate* fully in, and *benefit* from those programs without regard to their gender.

During the last twenty years, efforts have been undertaken to increase educational opportunity and eliminate discrimination. Federal and state governments have seen the need for legislation to expand educational opportunities and to improve economic self-sufficiency for all people through changes in the educational system. The focus of early equity efforts centered on removing the overt barriers to equal access, treatment, and educational opportunity.

While compliance with nondiscrimination laws and removal of overt barriers to all courses of study and occupations is necessary, it is not sufficient to create an environment promoting educational equity and supporting expanded choices. Role stereotyping, bias, and lack of information about the impact of large social and economic trends perpetuate old patterns and old ways of thinking, feeling, behaving, and preparing for the future.

Achieving Equity Through the Vocational Education Curriculum

Programs and activities which are designed to overcome sex bias and stereotyping in vocational education should be based on the premise that sex bias impacts males as well as females and that both stand to benefit from sex equity. Programs also need to begin where people are, not where we think that they ought to be, recognizing that all of us carry biases and stereotypes with us to some degree or another. Sex equity activities and programs must be carefully planned and evaluated, based on local needs assessment and have clear goals with measurable objectives.

Frequently staff development activities must be provided which focus not just on awareness but on development of the knowledge and skills required to create enduring individual, institutional, and educational changes. Sex Equity activities must reach out and involve all groups (board members, administrators, instructors, counselors, students, parents, and employers) in the school and community.

Student programs must provide: awareness of the negative effects of sex role stereotyping and bias; skills to recognize and neutralize bias and role stereotyping; opportunities to explore, enroll in and complete nontraditional vocational education programs; and support services such as special counseling and encouragement, child care, transportation, job placement, and skill remediation.

In order for vocational educators to develop a curriculum free of sex discrimination, they must be able to recognize sex bias and sex role stereotyping in curriculum materials and in the classroom. Educators must devote consistent and informed attention to the goals of equity and to how those goals can be achieved at the very core of the teaching-learning processes; the learning environment, teacher-student interaction patterns, and the curriculum.

Strategies for achieving equity through the curriculum have evolved from the "checklist approach" of the 1970s, designed to address the goal of nondiscrimination, to more sophisticated strategies designed to weave equity into the fiber of each vocational course. The idea of student equity-related competencies as an integral part of curriculum objectives is new. Each of us must take conscious, planned, and active steps to include equity-related concepts and skills in the curriculum at each stage of its development.

There are at least four stages which must be considered in an attempt to ensure that a particular curriculum supports the goals of educational equity, as illustrated by the following figure.

FOUR STAGES OF ACHIEVING EQUITY

			Stage 4
		Stage 3	Reconstructing the curriculum to develop
	Stage 2	Revising an existing curriulum and seek-ing to attract and	new knowledge and skills based on changing roles,
Stage 1	Neutralizing stereo-types and bias in	meet the needs of both male and female	responsibilities and conditions.
Complying with the letter of the law.	existing instruc-tional materials.	students.	

1. Complying with the Letter of Nondiscrimination Laws.

At this stage, the policies and practices of the entire school district and each staff member must be reviewed. Federal and state laws prohibit discrimination in admission to any course or activity and prohibit sepa-rate courses for students on the basis of sex, race, or handicap. A review of course descriptions, counselor practices, the effect of prerequisites on enrollments, how the master schedule stifles or encourages nontraditional exploration, and many other access-related issues are investigated and changed.

2. Neutralizing Stereotypes and Bias in Existing Instructional Materials.

At this stage, one should review instructional materials, one's own language, course objectives and activities, and Vocational Student Orga-nization (VSO) activities, to determine if they are based on, rely on, or communicate stereotypes or traditional biases which "attribute behaviors, abilities, interests, values, and roles to a person or group of persons on the basis of their sex, race, national origin, ancestry, creed, pregnancy, marital or parental status, sexual orientation or physical, mental, emo-tional, or learning disability." (This definition of stereotyping comes from Wisconsin Administration Code, PI 9, on Pupil Nondiscrimination.)

3. Revising an Existing Curriculum and Seeking to Attract and Meet the Interests and Needs of Both Females and Males.

At this state, positive and ongoing steps should be taken to identify and meet, through revision or supplementation of the curriculum, the interests and needs of the student who has not traditionally enrolled in a particular course.

In reaching out to the nontraditional student, a troublesome paradox appears; in order to attract a nontraditional student, one needs to appeal to their interests, which are frequently based on stereotypes and bias. Without intervention and redirection by educators, there is a danger of reinforcing and perpetuating the very stereotypes and bias that should be neutralized. Specific strategies used by educators in this phase include the following:

- Recruitment strategies, aimed specifically at nontraditional students which increase their knowledge of certain occupations, opportunities, and skills which have been considered appropriate only for "traditional students" in the past.
- Provision of role models in a variety of nontraditional occupations including entry level and advanced jobs.
- Review and change of the classroom environment to eliminate "one sex only" images and promote messages that encourage participation by nontraditional students.
- Supplementation of the curriculum concerning the changing roles of females and males.
- An examination and neutralization of the forms of sex bias, especially communication/linguistic bias, by both teachers and students.

4. Reconstructing the Curriculum to Develop New Knowledge and Skills for Students Based on Changing Roles, Responsibilities, and Conditions.

This stage represents a conceptual shift, or redefinition of each course, by including new instructional objectives and activities which embrace equity concepts and goals for both female and male students. While some courses lend themselves more directly to discussing equity ideas, the entire program and curriculum must embrace and support new equity-related knowledge and skills.

A great deal of research on gender differences and similarities, on women, on men, on changing roles, and on equity has been conducted in the last fifteen years. Equity-related instructional objectives and activities must be gleaned from this research. At this time, there are few actual models of reconstructed curriculum to draw upon. Therefore, each educator must carefully examine assumptions underlying the current or projected curriculum. Some of the questions one needs to be concerned with include the following:

- Has the new body of knowledge on changing roles and gender role stereotyping been incorporated into the curriculum?

- Will the curriculum give students skills for the future, or will it establish expectations for the gender and occupational roles and responsibilities of a bygone era?
- Do instructional objectives facilitate critical thinking about the impact of major social and economic changes on the individual, the family, and on work?
- Will students truly be prepared for the dual roles of "work of the family" and work in the paid labor force?
- Will both female and male students have a greater respect for traditional "women's work?"
- Will both female and male students be prepared for the work partnerships of the future labor market?
- Will the curriculum build trust between the sexes leading to greater teamwork and productivity on the part of future workers?
- Will the new curriculum lead to greater understanding and appreciation of both women's and men's experiences, needs, perspectives, values, and futures in the rapidly changing world of work?
- Will instructional activities lead students to broader, more flexible definitions of masculinity and femininity?
- Will students feel free to enroll in courses nontraditional for their gender and be prepared to accept and support nontraditional coworkers in the future?

Federal, State, and Local Agency Initiatives to Promote Sex Equity in Vocational Education

In addition to classroom-based activities, the goal of promoting and achieving sex equity in vocational education involves policy changes, provision of incentives, and implementation strategies at the federal, state, and local level.

Federal Level

Since the 1970s, policy changes at the federal level in vocational education have been initiated by Congress through passage of legislation. Title IX of the Education Amendments of 1972 is the basic civil rights protection against sex discrimination in any education program or activity receiving federal financial assistance. The provisions regarding recruitment, access to classes, and counseling are particularly relevant to vocational education.

The Women's Educational Equity Act of 1974 provided for the development of model programs to meet the letter and intent of Title IX. Since 1976, several WEEA grants have produced materials relevant to vocational education. In 1977, the Career Education Incentive Act included the elimination of bias and stereotyping as one of its overall goals. In 1979, the Office for Civil Rights (OCR) issued *Guidelines for Eliminating Discrimination and Denial of Services on the Basis of Race, Color, National Origin, Sex, and Handicap in Vocational Education Programs.* These guidelines require state education agencies to establish a civil rights compliance program to monitor and provide technical assistance to ensure nondiscrimination in vocational education programs. The Carl Perkins Vocational Education Act of 1984 and its predecessor the Vocational Education Act of 1976 (VEA) represent the most comprehensive effort to date to infuse sex equity into an educational program, by requiring positive action to end bias and stereotyping as well as ensuring nondiscrimination.

The provisions of the VEA required for the first time that each state hire at least one full-time person to coordinate and infuse sex equity throughout the vocational education system. The law recognized the need for special programs or efforts for certain target groups and required states to spend some of their federal allocation on programs for displaced homemakers, single heads of households, people who want a nontraditional occupation, and part-time workers who want to work full time. It required states to offer incentives to local districts to develop model programs to encourage nontraditional enrollments. The law mandated fair representation of women, minorities, and the handicapped on local and state advisory councils for vocational education. It required states to address sex equity in state plans and accountability reports, and required public hearings for citizen participation in identifying needs and designing programs and activities to improve vocational education. The law encouraged, but did not require, states to spend money on support services for women, care for students' children, grants to overcome sex bias, grants to promote sex fair counseling practices, research on sex bias, curriculum revision and development, inservice training on sex equity and other professional development activities. The Vocational Education Data System (VEDS), established by the Act, required uniform collection and reporting of enrollment data and outcomes by sex, race, and handicapping conditions.

The Carl Perkins Vocational Education Act of 1984 retained and expanded upon the key sex equity provisions of the 1976 Act. States are required to assign one person full-time responsibility for fulfilling seven mandated functions. In contrast to the 1976 Act, however, the Carl Perkins Act provides the financial resources necessary to meet the vocational education needs of women, to encourage nontraditional enrollment and placement, and reduce sex stereotyping and bias in vocational education. The Act accomplishes this through two setasides in Title IIA; one for Single Parents and Homemakers (8.5% of the Basic Grant), the other for Young Women and Sex Equity Programs (3.5% of the Basic Grant). The responsibility to administer these programs rests with the sex equity coordinator. This represents an important shift in the role of the coordinator, from a direct provider of training and technical assistance to an administrator of programs, services, and activities. Fifty percent of the funds available for Adult Training and Retraining must be spent on single parents and homemakers and 20 percent of the Guidance and Counseling funds are to be used to eliminate sex, age, and race bias.

The setasides have provided the first opportunity for school districts in many states to take planned steps, based on local needs, over a period of time to address equity issues and provide for greater economic self-sufficiency for girls and women through vocational education programs and activities.

Federal policy is based on legislation but refined by regulations and actions of administrative departments. Federal incentives include both "carrots" (usually money) and "sticks" (usually requirements and sanctions). State agencies are motivated to comply with the provisions of the Carl Perkins Act and the OCR Guidelines so that they remain eligible to receive uninterrupted federal funding for their vocational programs. The effectiveness of federal incentives depends on the monitoring of state compliance by federal administrative agency staff. In summary, federal policy to promote sex equity in vocational education has two main thrusts: compliance with federal civil rights laws, and programmatic infusion of sex equity throughout the educational delivery system.

State Level

State Education policy is created by state constitutions, state legislatures, state regulations, administrative codes, and by administrative boards such as State Board of Education. The responsibility for implementing state education policy is usually vested in the State Education Agency; however, some states have a separate state agency which acts as the sole state agency for vocational education.

Two recent studies of state laws and policies in the area of sex equity in education have been completed by the Council for Chief State School Officers (Bailey, 1982) and the Project on Equal Education Rights (PEER, 1987). The Council surveyed the fifty states, the District of Columbia, Puerto Rico, and the Virgin Islands. Thirty-two states have some kind of state law ensuring nondiscrimination on the basis of sex. In eleven of these states, a state Equal Rights Amendment affects the issue of sex equity in education. Thirty-eight states, the District of Columbia, Puerto Rico, and the Virgin Islands have educational policies or regulations concerning the provision of sex equity in education.

Most state laws, regulations, and policies have been proposed and enacted in the decade from 1975–1985. The diversity of state policy issues and approaches represented include:

- laws and policies requiring equal educational and employment opportunities, nondiscrimination, affirmative action and local equity plans
- teacher certification requirements for knowledge of civil rights
- sex fair and multicultural, nonsexist curriculum, textbooks and materials
- equal athletic opportunities
- fair counseling and pupil appraisal
- laws which require the State Education Agency to provide technical assistance to local schools
- policies supporting women in educational administration

Implementation activities at the state level are initiated, coordinated and administered by the sex equity personnel required by the Carl Perkins Act. The sex equity coordinators act as educational change agents within the state education agency and externally with local school districts, individuals and groups concerned with sex equity in vocational education. Sex equity coordinators seek to facilitate both state and local institutional change, to assist in the development or revision of vocational programs, and to develop the capacity of state and local staffs to promote sex equity.

Local Level

The support or nonsupport of local school administrators for equity policies is crucial in the attainment of educational equity. Where administrators and school board members are knowledgeable and supportive the greatest gains toward educational equity can be made.

Local implementation strategies have focused on eight major areas:

1. **Revision or Development of Administrative Policies, Procedures, and Practices.** This includes review of existing policies and development of new policies consistent with Title IX and the Carl Perkins Act. It includes district activities to ensure nondiscrimination in employment and affirmative action efforts. It may include revising procedures such as scheduling to allow more flexible and equitable access to courses or programs. For example, offering home economics and technology education courses during different class periods rather than during the same class period, or offering semester-long courses rather than year-long courses, increase flexibility and the potential for nontraditional course selection.

2. **Equity Evaluation, Vocational Program Evaluation, and Planning.** In some states local districts have been required to conduct equity self-assessments and to submit equity plans to the State Education Agency as a result of Title IX or the Carl Perkins Act. All schools are required to participate in some form of vocational program evaluation and develop local long range plans under the Act.

3. **Staff Development.** Staff development activities range from awareness raising to intensive skill-building workshops. Retraining of vocational educators who teach in a traditional program area so that they can teach in nontraditional program areas is another staff development strategy.

4. **Curriculum Supplementation and Revision.** One of the main purposes of curriculum revision is to ensure that the interests and needs of all students are met in the curriculum. This activity initiated for equity purposes has often led to greater excellence in the teaching/learning process. As discussed earlier the inclusion of equity-related student competencies in each vocational course and program represent the newest curricular strategies aimed at achieving sex equity.

5. **Counseling and Guidance, Recruitment, and Support Services.** Revision of counseling procedures and practices has been initiated in many schools. This involves the use of new sex fair materials and tests, new counseling strategies such as developmental guidance or peer counseling, and active promotion or consideration of higher-wage careers. Many vocational educators are working more closely with counselors and taking more responsibility for encouraging or recruiting nontraditional students.

6. **Student Awareness Activities and Programs.** Across the country, Vocational Student Organizations and other student groups in and outside of

school are involved in programs and activities which directly raise awareness of equity issues and expanding career options. Nontraditional role models and speakers outline the advantages of nontraditional careers. The focus is on how to recognize bias and discrimination and how to combat it and/or cope with it. More recently, schools are teaching new skills students enrolled in traditional occupational areas need to survive and thrive in a rapidly changing future. These skills include sensitivity to the rights of nontraditional workers, assertiveness, management skills, stress management, networking, life-work planning, upward mobility skills, recareering skills, and adapting to change skills.

7. **Business and Industry Partnerships.** Currently the entire educational community is seeking to develop and nurture partnerships with business and industry. Vocational education has the longest history of working with business and industry to create a skilled workforce. A few school districts have enlisted the support of employers to promote equity ideas and consideration of nontraditional employment. In the past educators have assumed that employers were not "ready for" or "open to" employing nontraditional workers and employers have bemoaned the fact that schools are not training any nontraditional workers. Opening communication channels between schools, business and industry on equity related issues allows for misperceptions to be resolved.

8. **Community and Parental Awareness and Monitoring of Equity in Vocational Education.** In several states, local community coalitions have formed to monitor sex equity in vocational education. These community groups are working successfully to achieve sex equity by meeting with school boards and other groups that can affect school programs and practices. These groups also educate the local community as to the need for equity in the schools and help build the consensus and support needed for schools to achieve sex equity.

After just a few short years (1977–1987) it is difficult to assess and measure the effectiveness of the above institutional change strategies. Several studies suggest that wherever the Vocational Education Act of 1976 provisions for sex equity were implemented well they worked (Wells, 1982). Sex equity efforts and activities under the Carl Perkins Act have not been studied to date on a national basis. Most states are just closing out the second year of projects funded under Carl Perkins. It is clear that many more equity projects, programs, services, and activities are occurring in every state as a result of the set-asides.

Enrollment trends are changing; females made the largest gains in "mixed" programs, vocational programs where women comprise 25.1 percent to 75 percent of the enrollment (Institute for Women's Concerns, 1980). The Sex Equity Coordinators have taken an active role in promoting awareness of the issues and increasingly provide the catalyst for positive and corrective changes in vocational education (Vocational Education Equity, 1981).

Recommendations

There are still a number of issues that sex equity in vocational education has not adequately addressed. Vocational Equity as a specialized area of expertise is in its infancy. Equity professionals are in the process of developing more sophisticated methods and practices. The measures of success for equity efforts and activities must be clarified. To date the only measure of success has been more balanced vocational education enrollments. More emphasis on assisting students to free themselves of limiting stereotypes about masculine and feminine traits and roles is needed in equity programs. Sex equity efforts must increasingly be directed at students not just toward educators. Staff development activities must focus much more on developing skills and knowledge to create and sustain educational change rather than on awareness of the issue.

Positive role models in high visibility positions are critical to students' entry into nontraditional fields. More effort must be directed to increasing the number of female and male instructors in nontraditional fields and increasing the number of women in vocational education administrative positions.

There is still too little recognition for the economic contribution and experience of homemakers. Mechanisms for giving credit for homemaking and volunteer activities must be improved and disseminated. Single parents and homemakers have a great need for access to short-term skill training. They often have only two to six months to get a job. This subject is discussed in greater detail in the chapter on adult women.

Additional emphasis should be placed on training women for entrepreneurship. This is a particular need for rural women, but should not be limited only to them.

Support services for women, most notably child care and transportation, so essential to their success in vocational training, are still inadequate. These services must be developed as integral parts of sex equity programs.

All vocational education programs, but sex equity programs especially, must continue to focus on areas of expanding occupational opportunities and on the enormous potential being created by the technological and computer revolutions.

Clearly, vocational education is off to the right start in bringing equality and fair treatment to females and males in our country and in recognizing the need to involve women in a more productive work force, but there is still a long distance to travel. This was best expressed by a vocational school principal who said: "All these initial energies (resulting from the 1976 law) have been spent cracking the wall. The same amount of energy applied now will be to seal up that initial crack and thus waste all of that initial effort" (League of Women Voters, 1982).

REFERENCES

Bailey, S., & Smith, R. (Eds.) *Policies for the future.* Washington, D.C.: Council for Chief State School Officers, 1982.

Farris, C. J. *Expanding adolescent role expectations.* Ithaca, New York: Cornell University, 1978.

Institute for Women's Concerns. *Increasing sex equity.* Washington, D.C., 1980.

Klein, S., Richardson, B., Thomas, V., & Wirtenberg, J. *Sex equity in American education.* Educational leadership, January 1981, 311–319.

League of Women Voters Education Fund. *Achieving sex equity in vocational education: A crack in the wall.* Washington, D.C., 1982.

National Center for Educational Statistics. *The condition of vocational education.* Washington, D.C., 1979.

Verheyden-Hilliard, M.E. Cinderella doesn't live here anymore. *Womanpower,* November 1975.

Vocational Education Equity Council and State Sex Equity Coordinators. *Sex equity in vocational education: A policy paper for reauthorization,* 1981.

Wells, J. (Ed.) *A good start: Opportunities for women under the vocational education act.* Washington, D.C.: Lawyers' Committee for Civil Rights Under Law, 1982.

The following statements are designed for the exploration of personal reactions to the chapter, as well as for the review of the contents of the chapter. Emphasis in discussions should be on exploring issues in depth, rather than on determining the correct or appropriate responses.

FOR DISCUSSION:

1. Are schools supposed to prepare students for careers?
2. What vocational education programs are available to your students?
3. How can elementary students be prepared for future selection of careers?
4. Are girls in your educational institution still being prepared for "Cinderella-hood"?
5. Who in your educational institution is responsible for activities related to the Carl Perkins Vocational Education Act, and what activities have been carried out?
6. Review the goals of vocational equity. Are they the same goals of your educational institution?
7. Discuss the author's statement: "Programs also need to begin where people are, not where they think they ought to be . . . "
8. Discuss the author's list of recommendations.

SUGGESTIONS FOR FURTHER READING

Education Development Center. *Resource guide for vocational educators and planners: Helping displaced homemakers move from housework to paid work through vocational training.* Newton, Massachusetts: EDC/WEEA Publishing Center, 1980.

Department of Occupational Education and Technology Research Coordinating Unit. *Making home economics relevant to males.* Austin, Texas: Texas Education Agency, 1980.

Illinois Office of Education. *Building sex equity in vocational education: An inservice training program.* Springfield, 1980.

Koltnow, J. *The sky's the limit in math-related careers.* Newton, Massachusetts: EDC/WEEA Publishing Center, 1982.

National Center for Research in Vocational Education. *Professional development programs for sex equity in vocational education.* Columbus, Ohio: Ohio State University, 1986.

National Center for Research in Vocational Education. *Vocational education sex equity strategies.* Columbus, Ohio, 1978.

Ruina, E. *What can counselors and teachers do to encourage young women?* New York, New York: Committee on the Status of Women in Physics, American Physical Society, 1981.

Shields, L. *Displaced homemakers: Organizing for a new life.* New York, New York: McGraw-Hill, 1981.

State of Delaware. *Achieving sex equity in business and office education.* Dover, Delaware: Bureau of Archives and Records, 1980.

Tittle, C. *Careers and family: Sex roles and adolescent life plans.* Newbury Park, California: Sage Publications, 1981.

Veres, C., & Carmichael, M. *Expanding student opportunities in occupational education: Methods to reduce sex-role stereotyping in program choice.* Ithaca, New York: Institute for Occupational Education, Cornell University, 1981.

Wider Opportunities for Women, Inc. *The Carl Perkins vocational education act: A sex equity analysis.* Washington, D.C., 1985.

Wood, C., & Johnson, J. *Tomorrow's training today: A guide for introducing young women to technology.* Boston, Massachusetts: Women's Technical Institute, 1981.

Chapter 18

CHART: EXPLORING CAREER CHOICES
WITH YOUR CHILD

Does Your Daughter Know That . . . *

- The chances are high that she will be in the paid work force for a significant part of her life? (40 years if she is single, 30 years if she marries and has no children, and 15–25 years if she has children.)
- The chances are also high that she will be working for pay out of economic necessity to support herself and her family.
- Young women must select and train for work which suits their interests and needs, work which can provide them economic security and personal satisfaction. Some of these jobs have traditionally been stereotyped as "men's jobs." Young women should also make certain that they gain some of the basic home maintenance skills they may need as independent workers or as heads of families.

Does Your Son Know That . . .

- The chances are high that, if he marries, his wife will work for pay outside their home.
- As more and more women are working outside their homes, increasing numbers of men are called upon to assume responsibilities for child care, food preparation, and home maintenance. If he is the one man in every three whose marriage ends in divorce, or if his wife becomes ill or disabled, this responsibility may be total.
- Young men should prepare now not only for work outside the home, but also work within the home and family.
- Equal employment opportunity now allows young men to move into jobs traditionally stereotyped as "women's jobs" if these jobs suit their interests and abilities.

---

*(The above information was adapted from An Equal Chance, a publication of the Indiana State Advisory Council on Vocational Education; and from Cabinets, Carrot Seeds, and Computers, a publication of Michigan Department of Education.) Reprinted from the VOICE Newsletter, New York State Education Department.

Together, you and your child can start to focus attention on jobs in many ways, right near your home:

- Invite your child to visit you at work now and then. Demonstrate what you do, what your supervisor does, or what your secretary or helper does.
- Point out what relatives and neighbors do at their jobs. Urge your child to talk to these familiar people about their work.
- Explore the work of others when you take a vacation or visit unfamiliar settings. Ask about the duties involved in jobs, and what people like best about them.
- Watch your neighborhood, the newspapers, and television for people who are pioneering in jobs that are not traditional for their sex. Call your child's attention to them because they increase their options.

You can also help your child take advantage of the school's assistance in exploring occupational choices:

- Encourage your child to find out what Vocational Education Programs are offered at school.
- Urge her/him to see a counselor and ask for details about the programs and their varying requirements.
- Suggest talking to the teachers of programs which seem interesting.
- Remind your child that the librarian at the school or public library would be happy to help find printed or audio-visual material about different jobs and careers.
- Talk with teachers and counselors yourself about the kind of guidance given students in making career choices.
- Finally, and most important, help your child understand how vital good school work will be to final work choices. Reading and math, for instance, are needed in almost any job, as well as in job preparation programs.

Chapter 19

THE ACTIVIST COUNSELOR: MAKING A DIFFERENCE

Mary Ellen Verheyden-Hilliard

INTRODUCTION

"Do you realize how hard chemistry is?"

Anyone who interacts with students is a guidance counselor. Teachers are often approached by students for advice about course selection, careers, personal difficulties, and other problems. Administrators often guide students who require discipline, family counseling, or special recognition.

But it is the school guidance counselors who are expected to be a personal resource for every student assigned to them. They are expected to be able to keep attendance, plan schedules, advise students about their programs and their future, as well as to be up-to-date on colleges and the job market. If there is even time to tackle those tasks, personal counseling is usually impossible to accomplish.

Equitable guidance counseling can become an integral part of the numerous tasks assigned to the guidance department. It does not have to be yet another thing to learn about, share, or monitor. After completing some initial steps (such as quickly surveying the office for obviously biased materials), the process of becoming an equitable counselor can be carried out as the regular job is done.

The key is self-consciousness. As students are advised, guidance counselors (or anyone counseling a student) should be aware of language employed, subtle body language messages, and verbal reactions. Is the advice equitable? Does the voice say, "Of course, boys can enroll in the nursing program" when the crossed arms and slight smile say something more powerful?

Are the materials that are disseminated quickly checked for sex fair language, and photos of both sexes? Are class schedules planned for a look at the future, rather than for boys only or girls only? Is a little extra time spent on encouraging students who are hesitating (or daring) to pursue more math, home economics electives, nontraditional vocational education, and other programs that are not the traditional path? Most important, is information provided in counseling sessions based on the student's *personal* attributes and interests?

As each work day progresses, slight changes can be made in the counseling approach. Occasional research may be required, just as it would be when new occupations appear on the horizon or new courses are offered. Counselors who are up-to-date and knowledgeable are also tuned in to the negative effects of biased counseling.

The "activist" counselor, described in Verheyden-Hilliard's article, is someone who recognizes the need for equitable guidance, and becomes known to the students as the counselor who treats them as individual people, even if time is often at a premium.

THE ACTIVIST COUNSELOR: MAKING A DIFFERENCE

Counselors are harried, hurried, and harassed educational professionals. Doing only what is required typically takes all day and suggestions on how to add to the day's work load are not generally appreciated, or paid much attention to. So, a word of advice to save busy people time: this chapter does not contain a wonderful checklist of what-to-do-Monday to quickly persuade all girls and boys to give up the gender based educational and career limitations they have unknowingly imposed on themselves. Just turn the page; it isn't here. What is here are some reasons for being an activist counselor known for your ability to support and encourage students to explore nontraditional career options. The "known" part is very important.

Surrounding yourself in your role as counselor with a special aura that makes you a key person in your school who knows about nontraditional educational and career options, and who is known for helping students explore those options can be rewarding for you as well as your students. The atmosphere the activist counselor creates extends well beyond Monday and will, I believe, do more good than any checklist. Anyone who thinks being an activist counselor is an impossible combination of words should also just turn the page.

A decade ago, when my daughter entered a new school, a junior high school, she walked around the halls wondering what this new place would be like, what the teachers and counselors would be like. When she came home that first day she told me about one office where the door was open as if someone had just stepped out and on the wall was a poster. "You know the one," she said, "it says 'A Woman's Place is in the House . . . and in the Senate.'" It turned out to be the counselor's office (an activist counselor in my opinion) one who left clear messages for any passer-by to read. It was a message that told students that this person might be especially willing to help with certain kinds of questions, who would not make fun of your high-falutin' ideas about yourself, who wouldn't laugh if you were a girl who wanted to be a carpenter, a president, or, anyway, something different.

To those still reading, my first suggestion for gender-free counseling is that you forget some of your training, or, at least, hold it in abeyance with regard to career counseling. Almost everyone trained to be a counselor has been lectured on the disasterous results of imposing one's own ideas on those who come for assistance. It is a wise counselor who knows the difference between not imposing and taking the easy way out. Helping girls and boys explore those occupations in which they have expressed an interest sounds like reasonable counseling behavior, but is, in most instances, totally inadequate if expanding career options beyond the stereotypes is your goal.

For example: the vocational school of a major east coast school system participated in a career exploration program sponsored by a local women's group. The group asked junior high school girls about their career interests and then arranged for visits to workplaces where the young women could meet and talk with people who worked at the jobs in which they had expressed interest. The community group commendably wished to encourage the girls to remain in school by showing them what education could lead to. However, the places the young women expressed an interest in visiting were almost entirely stereotypical. The workplaces of beauticians and executive secretaries, for example, were high on the list of the places the young women wanted to visit. When asked why the girls were not encouraged to use this wonderful opportunity to find out about nontraditional occupations about which they had no information, leaders of the program replied that the purpose of the program was to help the girls explore their interests, not to impose others' views of what education made possible. What that project needed was an activist counselor who would see to it that the girls saw not only what their limited experience taught them was available to them as young women who planned to go to work right out of high school, but what other higher-paying jobs were also possible.

Intervention Payoffs

The busy counselor may wonder if the effort to show students what nontraditional careers are like is really worth the effort. It is. The research tells us that the noninterventionist stance, such as the one taken by the vocational project, no matter how well-intentioned, is a mistake. Student attitudes about the appropriateness of nontraditional jobs for women and men can be changed by exposure to workers in nontraditional jobs. Ninth-grade students given an opportunity to actually explore nontraditional jobs in the community were significantly less stereotyped in their view of the world than were those in the control group who did not have that experience. Viewing role models at work in nontraditional occupations had a positive effect on reducing students' sex-typing of occupations and broadening personal occupational choice (Dunlap, 1979; Humberg, 1980; Green, 1982). Most importantly, the research supports the idea that direction intervention with personal efforts to increase enrollment in nontraditional career exploration course gets good results (Ott, 1980). Some may call that imposing the adult's values. What it really is, however, is making use of your education for the benefit of your students; your letting them know not only that nontraditional careers exist, but that it is all right for them to explore those careers. Making it all right, by lending the support of your backing to nontraditional exploration may prove to be the most important thing you can do for your students.

When Sally Ride's junior high school science teacher encouraged her in science, there was then, for most, no concept that women could be astronauts. Yet without the push that teacher provided, Sally Ride might never have pursued the science courses which were the prerequisites for her Ph.D. in astrophysics—the degree that was a major contributing factor in her selection for the NASA astronaut training program from which she went on to become America's first woman in space (Verheyden-Hilliard, 1985). Encouraging girls as well as boys to consider careers in science is not so unusual now. As technology increasingly infuses every aspect of society, it is a rare counselor who would dismiss the idea of girls taking mathematics and science because, as used to be said just a few years ago, girls will just get married and only need checkbook math.

Getting Rid of the Math-Science-Computer Gender Discrepancy

Still, the Center for Educational Statistics (1986) reports that boys are almost twice as likely as girls to take physics in high school, and almost 33 percent more likely to take trigonometry or calculus. And what does it matter that equal mathematical preparation is still an unattained goal? The Center for Early Adolescence at the University of North Carolina reports that the differences sometimes seen in math achievement scores of boys and girls as they grow older do not represent the difference in innate ability but the difference in the number of math courses taken. When one does badly on achievement scores, teachers, parents, counselors, and the students themselves rarely see that subject as something to pursue intensively, and the excuses to drop math multiply.

Why should there continue to be this overall discrepancy in advanced math and science courses taken by boys and girls? Again, a large component of the answer is in the differential messages, spoken and unspoken, delivered to boys and girls. Some studies have found that neither girls or boys, on average, are terribly interested in math. But somehow more boys than girls get the message that they are expected to study math, like it or not, in order to enhance their future educational and career opportunities (Verheyden-Hilliard, 1984).

In some sense, mathematics has become a show of intellectual machismo, a difficult proving ground that upward-bound boys, but not girls, learn they must get through. With regard to science, Jacobowitz (1982) has shown that gender was the strongest predictor of science as a career preference among black female and male students in an inner city junior high school Choosing or not choosing science as a career was not related to realistic assessments of mathematical or scientific achievement, but to sex role considerations.

In such a situation it could make a difference if activist counselors offered support, encouragement, and long-view explanations to the girl whose high school course plan skips the nonrequired math and science courses because, she believes, such learning is irrelevant to her life now or in the future. Too many girls apparently get at least passive agreement with their shortsighted view of their future, It's OK if you don't want to struggle with advanced math and science, you probably won't need it anyway (is the checkbook syndrome still alive and well after all?).

In a related aspect of school life these days, counselors find computers taking an increasingly important place in the curriculum starting in the earliest grades. And some educators have reported the resistance of girls to dealing with computers. However, recent studies are showing that girls really like computers. What they don't like is arguing with the boys about whose turn it is at the keyboard. When teachers literally intervened and set up time-sharing rules, the girls spent as much time on the computer as the boys. Like "math anxiety," the myth that girls have some innate dislike of computers is dangerous and can force girls to begin to behave the way they see adults expect them to behave. When the headlines blare "Why Can't Johnny Read?," the following article does not assume he was born with "reading anxiety." It assumes that something has gone awry with the process of teaching him to read and suggests what can be done to bring him up to the mark. If teachers tell you of their troubles in getting girls to use computers, be an activist counselor with suggestions for a little scheduling of computer time and a lot of insistence that math taken now, like it or not, will pay off later. If we can do it for boys, we can do it for girls.

Athletics Are Important for Everyone

Another area of extreme importance is athletics. Most counselors probably do not think of building physical fitness and athletic skill as a priority concern for girls as much as for boys, but perhaps they should. Physical fitness is a requirement in the apprenticeable trades. Nationally, preapprenticeship training programs for adult women spend hundreds of thousands of dollars teaching women the math, basic vocational skills, and physical fitness they will need to be accepted as apprentices, all of which could have been learned in school. The teamwork athletics can teach is now recognized as a very important asset in the corporate world as well as in other fields (Duquien, 1982).

The astronaut, Dr. Sally Ride, played football in elementary school and had the potential to be a world-class tennis player. Knowing how to be a team player turned out to be important to her not only on the playing field but in the space capsule. Another important reason for girls to pursue physical fitness and athletics is to be found in the college athletic scholarships that Title IX has now made available to young women as well as to young men. The activist counselor should keep in mind that athletic scholarships are stepladders to higher education for girls as well as boys. And, interestingly, college female athletes, on average, do much better academically than do male athletes.

Course Selection and Placement Adds Up To Money

Of course, not all stereotypic behaviors and outcomes are so clear as those dealing with math, computers, and athletics. Like breathing, some are critical but unnoticed. One of the main reasons the overall average wage gap between men and women continues to hover around $1.00 to 60 cents is that most women who enter the labor force out of high school, or reenter at a later date, enter into low-paying "women's work" where, no matter how important the work is, there is little opportunity for advancement or for significant pay raises. Yet if there were just one more slot left in the electronics class do you know counselors who would automatically skip over the next girl on the list because they don't know many girls who have gone on to become electricians? Do you think they would fill the slot with the next boy on the list because they believe he is more likely to make use of the training? Would it make a difference if they know the girl had scored high on a mechanical aptitude test? Why does the girl have to "pass" a test and the boy does not? The other side of that gender stereotype of who is expected to be interested in what affects boys. Somehow we continue to expect all boys to "know" about cars, have an interest in electronics, and possess a genetic indisposition to classes on child care. And those expectations often force boys to limit their choices rather than face negative reactions.

The activist counselor (or, indeed, any counselor) must eliminate all gender-related arguments against putting any girl or any boy in any class, if for no other reason than it is illegal to do so under Title IX of the Education Amendments of 1972. It is also bad counseling because it limits students' opportunities to freely learn and explore while still in school, opportunities that will never be so "free" again.

In 1974 the National Institute of Education gathered counseling professionals from around the country to establish guidelines for gender-fair counseling that would be in compliance with Title IX. One of the adopted guidelines reads as follows:

> Within the context of career guidance, sex bias is defined as any factor that might influence a person to limit—or cause others to limit—his or her consideration of a career solely on the basis of gender. (U.S. Department of Health, Education and Welfare, 1974)

Selecting one sex over the other for class placement, thus limiting exploration on the basis of gender expectations, would fall under this definition of sex bias.

Fairness aside, there are very practical reasons for encouraging boys to take nontraditional courses, for example in child care and home economics. If marriages are to survive, tomorrow's men need a better understanding of what will be expected of them in a world where the majority of women no longer work only in the home. Girls need to be encouraged to use the courses offered in school, such as electronics, to explore the possibility of nontraditional careers. The apprenticeable trades pay, on average, three to five times more than the traditional female jobs. Furthermore, apprentices are paid while they learn; like a college scholarship this can be a critical factor to young women with limited financial resources (From Here To There, 1983). In the apprenticeable trades that do not require college, such as electrician, less than 10 percent of the job holders are women. One of the reasons some young women are not accepted into apprenticeship training programs is because their educational background shows no interest in the field—they did not take any related courses in high school. Under those circumstances, denial of an apprenticeship slot when they enter the workforce is not altogether unreasonable. Harvard, afterall, does not give scholarships to study science to someone who did not bother to take any science classes in high school.

The activist counselor who understands that there are "prerequisite" courses that will help students just out of high school be competitive in the job market—just as there are courses which help college admissions officers make decisions—can make a real contribution. In both situations, some of these courses are technical in nature and some are basic, or should be, to any high school graduation. Business in the United States is increasingly teaching its workforce to read, write, and compute. The student who comes with those basic skills well in hand has indeed got a head start on employment.

Activist counselors have an opportunity here to encourage nontraditional vocational training in the same way they would encourage math and science as a prerequisite to many different kinds of future careers. The fear that some blue collar jobs are disappearing is certainly well grounded, but millions remain. Among those that remain, the pay is typically much better than among most pink collar jobs. For example, according to the Department of Labor there are, nationwide, about 542,000 people employed as electricians. The top 10 percent earn approximately $675 a week. If half of that top 10 percent were women there would be 27,000 more women working at jobs which pay them approximately $35,000 a year. And that is only one of the apprenticeable trades.

Helping the Pioneer Student

In career fields that require college, many have no doubt heard a version of the lament of the physician/mother whose small daughter, when asked what she wants to be when she grows up, declares she will be a nurse. When asked why not be a doctor, she tells her physician/mother that everybody knows only boys can be doctors. The story, I regret to say, is not apocryphal. Why does it sometimes happen that what seems so evident is not so evident to a child? I think the phenomenon puts a new spin on an old saying well-known to parents: Do as I say, not as I do. And on another even older saying: The exception proves the rule.

The number of women who are becoming doctors is growing rapidly. That does not mean, of course, that across the nation children are yet seeing anything like 50 percent women as physicians either when they need medical attention, when they read books and magazines, or when they watch television. In the real world of most children, although they might not articulate it this way, the physician who is a woman is the exception that proves the rule. So putting a new spin on the saying "Do as I say not as I do" becomes critical, as Spaulding recognized:

> Professors don't have to make it a specific point to discourage their female students—society will do that job for them. All they have to do is fail to encourage women students. (1974)

Those words were written about higher education, but the message is just as important for those who work with elementary and secondary students. The research tells us that students need talk, discussion, messages, encouragement that tell them it is all right for them to be pioneers who break with tradition to explore nontraditional career choices.

Since the implementation of Title IX of the Education Amendments of 1972 which forbids discrimination on the basis of sex in educational institutions, many girls and women have been able to take advantage of newly opened educational opportunities as more gender-integrated classrooms were opened in secondary school and higher education. But a young woman's entry into a classroom or course of study that was previously considered to be "for men only" did not always ensure that the struggle was over, and still does not. The activist counselor needs to be aware that support and encouragement is still desperately needed for the pioneer student. Wirtenberg (1980) found that whether in sexdesegregated home economics or industrial arts classes, both male and female teachers interacted more with boys than with girls and continued to treat both sexes stereotypically.

If the teachers are unable to provide an unbiased setting, an activist counselor who understands the situation could make the difference by encouraging a girl to take a long-range view and stick it out in the industrial arts course. Perhaps the counselor could even have a word with the teacher, who often does not even realize the difficulties that unintentionally biased actions are causing students. Classic examples of this attitude can be seen in the fact that teachers are more likely to jump in to help girls, while encouraging boys to do more of the problemsolving themselves. The result, however well meant, is that boys are more likely than girls to get the ego reinforcement that comes with having figured something out for themselves.

Interaction of Disability and Gender

Nowhere is the early intervention of an activist counselor more needed than with disabled girls who, the 1980 census statistics reveals, drop out of elementary school five times more often than nondisabled girls. Among disabled males and females of all racial and ethnic groups whose disabilities do not prevent them from working, disabled girls are less likely than disabled boys to complete even eight years of school. One major result of the disasterous dropout statistics is that disabled women are less likely than disabled men to be employed. When they are employed, disabled women, like nondisabled women, are clustered in the low-paying, traditionally female occupations in the service and clerical fields. Disabled men, on the other hand, are employed in a wide range of occupations (Bowe, 1981).

A disabled girl in elementary school is in desperate need of an activist counselor because the research reveals that a disabled girl receives less career encouragement in school than does a disabled boy; she is viewed more negatively than disabled males; and educators have long been transmitting negative messages to the disabled girl (Baker and Reitz, 1978; Corbett and Weeks, 1980; Fine and Asch, 1981; Gillespie and Fink, 1974). As a result she is more limited by the perceptions of others than by her own disabilities. For example, disabled girls with a mobility impairment which requires sitting down tend to be counseled into those "sit down" professions that are lower paying, bookkeeping, for example, rather than the higher paying "sit down" professions which require advanced education (for example, science.) More than one researcher found that, given little support and seeing no alternative, disabled girls, more often than disabled boys, subscribe to negative images of themselves and have lower aspirations based on stereotypes rather than capability. It is a vicious circle that grows to encompass employment. Disabled men average 60 cents for every dollar earned by nondisabled men. Nondisabled women average 64 cents. Disabled women, however, average 35 cents, not only less than what is earned by nondisabled men and women, but less than the earnings of disabled men.

If education does not prepare disabled girls to take as much financial care of themselves as possible, the statistics indicate that marriage cannot be expected to take up the slack—not because they are disabled, but because they are disabled women. Census statistics reveal that disabled women are less likely to be married than are disabled men. Those who do marry are more likely than disabled men to be separated, divorced, or widowed. Hispanic disabled women, for example, are three times more likely than Hispanic disabled men to be divorced (Bowe, 1981). This means that the disabled woman's 35 cents on the dollar is unlikely to be supplemented by a husband's contribution. Disabled women are among the most economically disadvantaged.

Without access to role models of achievement and with little encouragement from others, it is very difficult for the young disabled girl to see the connection between staying in school and better future possibilities. Because research indicates that disabled females identify primarily with the disabled, they can be greatly helped by the activist counselor who makes sure that career days and career fairs and career materials include role models who are disabled women. Some school systems have arranged for disabled women, and men, to come into the classroom to talk with both the disabled and the nondisabled students about their life and their achievements. If your proposal of that idea gets a less than enthusiastic reaction at first, you should be aware that in school systems where this is now an on-going and important experience, some teachers had at first declared that their students would be uncomfortable in such a situation. However, it proved to be the teachers who were expressing their own discomfort, for once the program began, the students, both disabled and nondisabled, were very accepting and interested in learning about disabilities. The role models can help all students gain a greater appreciation of the disabled student's potential. This, as the research has told us, is particularly critical for disabled girls, perhaps particularly at the elementary level where the dropout rate of disabled girls is five times that of nondisabled girls. Finding disabled women role models who are doing well in their careers could be a priority for an activist counselor in a school system that is mainstreaming its disabled students.

Hidden Stereotype Fallout in Long-Range Decisions

In higher education, sex desegregation seems to be moving apace. According to the Center for Educational Statistics, women now comprise more than half the undergraduate population and earn 50 percent of the master degrees. But a close look behind the statistics reveals some relentlessly stereotypical figures. As with the high school situation where male and female students graduate but more males have prepared themselves with advanced math courses, a breakout of master's degrees shows gender stereotyping in full flower. For example, of all the M.A.'s awarded to women, 39 percent are in education, 2 percent in engineering, .004 percent in chemistry, and .001 percent in physics. Compared to the even lower rates of participation of a decade ago, these are steps forward. But clearly, women are not well represented in the male-dominated fields of study.

For counselors involved in the day-to-day activities of elementary and secondary schools, questions of which student will get into an apprenticeable trade or who will get a doctorate may seem matters of some distance and no pressing relevance. But they are.

In a review of achievement motivation in girls, Celka (1981) found that girls and young women make long-range decisions about their lives based on perceived and internalized stereotypes[.] Without early intervention and support to explore nonstereotypic possibilities, the stereotypes which limit girls' lives, because it is all that they know, will prevail. Thus, early encouragement in nontraditional educational paths that can lead to nontraditional careers is critical to all girls.[] Interviews with women mathematicians have shown that they became interested in math at an early age. Junior high school girls who are not counseled about the long-range danger of taking as little math as possible will skim through the last six years of school and end up having foreclosed an increasing number of college majors. And young women who leave high school without strong backgrounds in math, science, or technology, have no leverage on the better paying jobs that do not require college.

Counseling Carefully for the Future

As new career opportunities for women become available and more and more women work outside the home, it has become fashionable in the media to discuss women's "dual career roles." Counselors are often encouraged to take up this topic as well. It seems a step forward, suggesting that women should prepare to work outside the home as well as in it. In reality, the discussion too often becomes an opportunity to reinforce the traditional female responsibility for the care of home and children.

In 1976, now almost a dozen years ago, in a speech at the American Association for the Advancement of Science's Bicentennial Symposium on Women (Verheyden-Hilliard, 1976), I said that there were three kinds of counselors: traditional, liberated, and radical. The traditional counselor suggests to a girl with high scores in math and science that she might be a high school science teacher because that would allow her to be home by three o'clock when her children come home. The liberated counselor suggests a career as a brain surgeon because the girl could be a pioneer in the field, make lots of money, and set her own schedule so she could be home at three o'clock when her children come home. The radical counselor suggests a career as a brain surgeon because the girl could be a pioneer in the field, make lots of money, and set her own hours. Period.

To suggest to girls and young women in school that they must worry about menu plans for meals that can be prepared in 15 minutes upon their return from work for husbands they do not have, or how they will find baby sitters for children they also do not have, before they can plan a career is, in my view, indefensible. Why should that burden be placed on girls? Where the question needs to be raised is with each boy who, if he thinks about marriage in relation to his career at all, is very likely to still expect his wife to be there to take care of his home and his children leaving him free to pursue his "single career." A very enlightening career counseling session might be held by an activist counselor with a group of boys on the question of their approaching "dual careers" and how they are going to find baby sitters and cook quick nutritious meals for their families. In the lively discussion that is sure to follow, insist that the word "help" be eliminated. How to *share* home responsibilities, not "help" with them is what boys need to be learning. The Women's Bureau of the U.S. Department of Labor in Women in Nontraditional Careers (1984) provides formats for excellent workshops and handouts on this and other related topics.

Helping boys deal with their stereotypes about themselves and about girls is a serious matter. The literature reveals that boys and young men are more traditional in their view of gender roles than their female peers. Again, what the boys learn in school about acceptable behavior will have an impact in their later attitudes as men on the job. Boys allowed to grow up believing that certain careers "belong" to them are unlikely to become men who are accepting of women moving into nontraditional fields. While girls need encouragement to explore nontraditional careers, boys need encouragement to understand that girls have every right to do so.

It is often in counseling or classroom discussions about expanding opportunities that a sexist "joke" will come into play about the girl or boy who wants to break out of gender-related career stereotypes. If that should happen, ask the group if a similar "joke" would seem funny when said about a minority group member. Girls and boys need to understand that sexist remarks are as unacceptable as racist remarks and will not be tolerated. From a career counseling perspective, it is probably never too early to make clear that in the workplace verbal sexual harrassment is against the law and can bring grave consequences to the harrasser.

The importance of strong adult support for eliminating gender stereotyping of roles and careers cannot be overestimated. In an attempt to develop a model to reduce gender-stereotypical attitudes of students in several elementary and secondary classrooms, teachers were given a short training period, some gender-fair materials, and techniques to use in the classroom. After the intervention period of six weeks, the posttest showed that the teachers had indeed been able to reduce the stereotypical expectations the children had expressed in the pretest, except in one classroom. In the classroom the posttest showed children to be more gender-stereotypic in outlook after the intervention program than before.

In reviewing what had happened in that classroom, the researchers found that the teacher, when challenged by some male students on the nonstereotypical options and attitudes being presented, had backed down. Having gained the impression that alternatives to traditional beliefs could not be upheld by the authority figure, the boys' biases were strongly reinforced and they were able to bring the rest of the class to their point of view. Young girls were unable to do what the teacher had not been able to do, to stand up for a gender fair approach to education and careers. The tragedy is not so much that those who did not want to change did not, but that girls and boys who may have wanted to explore new options, did not find the support they needed to do so. If the authority figure gives way, or does not encourage gender fairness in the first place, how can youngsters be expected to do so?

Allowing children, as well as colleagues and parents, to see that you are aware of stereotypes and take their limiting effects seriously is the most important thing you as an adult can do to help children avoid the damaging effects of the stereotypes that bombard them and that will, if accepted without question, permanently affect their lives.

Activist Counseling is Successful Counseling

Taking an active counseling role does not mean forcing your career ideas on anyone. It does mean being willing to be the one to take the first step to open a dialogue on the subject, to explain the new options to students and colleagues, to disallow sexist jokes (do you allow racist jokes?), and, most importantly, to uphold the right of any girl or boy to explore nontraditional educational opportunities with a view to pursuing nontraditional careers.

Your personal and open commitment can be reinforced by prominently displaying gender-fair career materials in your office, by bringing in nontraditional role models for girls and boys during career week, by arranging for students to visit nontraditional worksites, and by using Women's History Month to engage teachers and administrators in creating a school-wide and year-long aura for expanding options for girls. But nothing will be as important as your personal commitment if it is known to those who can benefit from your help.

Three decades ago Blau's research on Children's development spelled out the importance of keeping choices open for all young children:

> Occupational choice is a developmental process that extends over many years . . . There is no single time at which young people decide on one out of all possible careers. But there are many crossroads at which their lives have taken decisive turns which narrow the range of future alternatives and thus influence ultimate choice of an occupation. (1956)

The activist counselor who has made a serious and ongoing effort to let students know that she or he exists, will experience the reward of being asked questions when students are at those "crossroads." Then, having established a reputation for good information and strong support, you will be in a position to guide students away from the narrow lanes of limited job choices and onto the wide-option career highways.

REFERENCES

Baker, L., & Reitz, H. Altruism toward the blind: Effects of sex of helper and dependence of victim. *Journal of Social Psychology*, 1978, *104* (1), 19–28.

Blau, P. Occupational choice: A conceptual framework. *Industrial and labor relations review*, July 9, 1956, *9* (4), 531–543.

Bowe, L. *Disabled adults of hispanic origin.* Washington, D.C.: The President's Committee on Employment of the Handicapped, 1981.

Bowe, L. *Disabled women in America.* Washington, D.C.: The President's Committee on Employment of the Handicapped, 1981.

Celka, R. Achievement motivation and the vocational development of adolescent women. A review and Application of Achievement Motivation Research to Vocational Development Theory, March 1981. ERIC Document Reproduction Service No. ED 203 244.

Center for Educational Statistics. *Earned degrees conferred, 1985.* Washington, D.C.: U.S. Department of Education, forthcoming data.

Center for Educational Statistics. *Digest of educational statistics, 1985–86 edition.* Washington, D.C.: U.S. Department of Education, 1986.

Corbett, K., & Copolo, A. *No more stares.* Berkeley, California: The Disability Rights Education and Defense Fund, 1982.

Corbett, K., & Weeks, C. *What happens after school? A study of disabled women and education.* San Francisco, California: Women's Educational Equity Communications Network, 1980.

Dunlap, L.J. Role of television models in children's career decision-making. Unpublished Master's thesis, Washington State University, 1979.

Duquien, M. The importance of sport in building human potential. *Journal of physical education and dance,* March 1982, *53* (3), 18–20, 36.

Fine, M., & Asch, A. Disabled women: Sexism with the pedestal. *Journal of sociology and social welfare,* July 1981, *8* (2), 233–248.

Gillespie, P., & Fink, A. The influence of sexism on the education of handicapped children. *Exceptional children,* November 1974, *41* (3), 155–162.

Green, A. Attitudinal effects of the use of role models. *Information about sex typed careers,* June, 1982.

Guttentag, M., & Bray, H.J. *Undoing sex stereotypes.* Cambridge, Massachusetts: Harvard University Press, 1975.

Hoffman, L.W. Childhood experiences and achievement. *Journal of social issues,* 1972, *28* (2), 129–155.

Humberg, R. Occupational sex-role stereotyping: Effects of a ninth grade experience-based career education program on occupational sex role stereotyping. Paper presented at National Experience-Based Career Education Conference, February, 1980.

Jacobowitz, T. Factors associated with science career preference of black junior high school students. *Research on education,* July, 1982.

Ott, M. The identification of factors associated with sex-role stereotyping. *Occupational education,* March, 1980.

Shepard, W., & Hess, D. Attitudes in four age groups toward sex role division in adult occupations and activities. *Journal of vocational behavior,* 1975, *6,* 68–73.

Spaulding, J. *What does education do to women? Sounds of change: A report in counseling and programming for women's career opportunities.* Los Angeles, California: University of California, 1974.

U.S. Department of Health, Education and Welfare, National Institute of Education, Education and Work Groups. *Guidelines for assessment of sex bias and sex fairness in career interest inventories.* Washington, D.C.: Government Printing Office, 1974.

Verheyden-Hilliard, M.E. *Cinderella and science: Career counseling for girls.* Paper presented at the Bicentennial Conference of the American Association for the Advancement of Science, Boston, Massachusetts, 1976.

Verheyden-Hilliard, M.E. (Ed.) *From here to there: The apprentice to journeyworker career ladder.* Bethesda, Maryland: The Equity Institute, 1983.

Verheyden-Hilliard, M.E. *Scientist and astronaut, Sally Ride.* Bethesda, Maryland: The Equity Institute, 1985.

Verheyden-Hilliard, M.E. The drops that fill the glasses: Teachers and students, one on one. In *Equal play.* New York: Women's Action Alliance, 1984.

Wirtenberg, J. Paper Presented at Annual Conference of American Psychological Association, September, 1980.

Wilson, J., & Daniel, R. Effects of a career options workshop on social and vocational stereotypes. *Vocational guidance quarterly,* June, 1981, *29* (4), 341–349.

Women in nontraditional careers (WINC): Curriculum guide. Washington, D.C.: Women's Bureau, U.S. Department of Labor, 1984.

The following statements are designed for the exploration of personal reactions to the chapter, as well as for the review of the contents of the chapter. Emphasis in discussions should be on exploring issues in depth, rather than on determining the correct or appropriate responses.

FOR DISCUSSION:

1. What is the role of the "activist counselor" in providing "non-traditional education"?
2. Discuss the author's statement: "Surrounding yourself in your role as counselor with a special aura that makes you a key person in your school who knows about nontraditional education and career options, and who is known for helping students explore those options can be rewarding for you as well as your students."
3. How can a counselor become recognized as the "activist" counselor described in the article?
4. How can a counselor become recognized as the "activist" counselor who promotes sex fair guidance for boys as well as for girls?
5. Consider your interactions with the guidance counselor(s) in your institution. Discuss how you can assist each other in providing sex fair counseling.
6. Review the visible evidence in your institution that informs students of the availability of sex fair guidance counseling. Discuss additional information that could be promoted.
7. Review the counseling information in your institution that is available specifically for disabled students.
8. The author states: "Helping boys deal with their stereotypes about themselves and about girls is a serious matter." Why? How does this statement relate to sex fair guidance?

SUGGESTIONS FOR FURTHER READING

Catalyst. *It's your future—Catalyst's career guide for high school girls.* Princeton, New Jersey: Peterson's Guides, 1984.

Center for Sex Equity in the Schools. *Tune into your rights: A guide for teenagers about turning off sexual harassment.* Ann Arbor, Michigan: University of Michigan, 1985.

Choices and challenges instructor's guide, Choices: A teen woman's journal for self-awareness and personal planning, and *Challenges: A young man's journal for self-awareness and personal planning.* Santa Barbara, California: Advocacy Press, 1983, 1984.

Council of Chief State School Officers—Resource Center on Educational Equity. *Achieving equity in education programs for disabled women and girls.* Washington, D.C., 1986.

Delany, H., & Nickel, P. *Working with teen parents.* Chicago, Illinois: Family Resource Coalition, 1985.

Girl Scouts of the USA. *Careers to explore for Brownies and Junior Girl Scouts* and *From dreams to reality.* New York, 1977.

Interracial Books for Children. *Issue on homophobia and education, 14* (3,4), 1983.

Massialas, B. *Fair play: Developing self-concept and decision-making skills in the middle school.* Newton, Massachusetts: WEEA Publishing Center, 1983.

Pfiffner, K.J. *Choosing occupations and life roles.* Newton, Massachusetts: EDC/WEEA Publishing Center, 1983.

Till, F. *Sexual harassment: A report on the sexual harassment of students.* Washington, D.C.: National Advisory Council on Women's Educational Programs, 1980.

Tittle, C.K. *What to do about sex bias in testing.* Syracuse University, New York: ERIC Clearinghouse on Tests, Measurements, and Evaluation, 1979.

Women and Disability Awareness Project. *Building community: A manual exploring issues of women and disability.* New York: Educational Equity Concepts, Inc., 1984.

Chapter 20

EXPANDING NONTRADITIONAL
PROGRAM OPTIONS

LYNN M. GANGONE

INTRODUCTION

"Son, first you join the Army, then *you can teach kindergarten."*

S uppose that you are a young man who is about to meet with his guidance counselor about scheduling for the upcoming school year. The selections that you make will determine not only your academic goals, but possibly a career choice as well. You are fifteen years old, everyone is giving you advice, and the time has come to make some serious decisions.

Suppose that, as that same young man, you have observed your mother's profession, nursing, and have been intrigued by the work that she does. She has discussed her patient cases with enthusiasm and has included you in her nursing activities. She has shared her feelings of frustration, accomplishment, and satisfaction as she pursues her career. You welcome the challenge of nursing, recognizing your own strong nurturing and decision-making skills, and admire those in the profession. You decide that you, too, want to be a nurse.

Suddenly you are "nontraditional," a "pioneer" in a vocational program. You have selected a field of work that has been traditionally dominated by women; a "helping" profession. Just as a girl who selects programs nontraditional for her gender (e.g., technology, automotive mechanics, machinery operation, electrical/carpentry trades), you are risking negative reactions and lack of support from peers, parents, and others. Somehow pursuing a field of choice because it matches interests and abilities (and not gender expectations), is cause for teasing, mockery, questioning, even rejection.

Not everyone will react with surprise and/or disdain. Not everyone will question the motivations of a "nontraditional" student, including low self-esteem and sexual preference. (Aren't all male nurses gay? Isn't she pursuing a trade because she's a tomboy? Doesn't he just want to meet more girls—doesn't she just want to be one of the guys?) Not everyone will fail to see the match between personal skills and vocational choice.

But because "pioneers" are still so unusual, it is not surprising that students do not even consider nontraditional program options. First, they have to be aware that the options are open to them. Second, they need recognition of their skills, and encouragement in their investigation of an occupation. Third, they need support in their nontraditional choice.

Once students can overcome the obstacles in making the choices, then they need the stamina to survive in the program. Daily reminders of being "different" can often discourage students who made it in but need support to stick it out. Nontraditional students have reported incidents of missing tools, isolation, ridicule, even sexual harassment. If they have an instructor who is a positive role model, and, better yet, a "pioneer peer," then finishing the program becomes easier. If an extracurricular support group exists, then students can grin and bear it.

Pioneer students often demonstrate that extra ounce of fortitude that it takes to pursue a path that is not the traditional route. They often become the class leaders, the top student, or the spokesperson in support of the field of occupation. When it comes time to seek work, they must, once again, call on that perserverance to land a job and stay in the profession.

The young man who decides to be a nurse, or the young woman who chooses carpentry, needs adult (and peer) support during the recruitment/selection process, the training process, and the employment process. Educational institutions that already establish an environment that supports the pursuit of programs that match needs, interests, and abilities, will be likely to see more student pioneers. Lynn Gangone discusses the concept of nontraditional choices, as well as strategies for providing expanded program options for all students.

EXPANDING NONTRADITIONAL PROGRAM OPTIONS

The question posed to members of a nontraditional student support group was: Do you foresee any difficulties being one of the few young men or women in your chosen occupation? "Hey lady, this is the eighties!" was the response of a young man who was enrolled in the licensed practical nurse program. "Those kinds of things don't happen anymore, no one would treat me any differently because I'm a guy and I'm a nurse . . . it's the eighties, things have changed."

For that student, life has changed. He was enrolled in a nontraditional occupational program and doing well. He was a member of a nontraditional student support group that met regularly. He had continual access to a vocational counselor that was committed to expanding nontraditional options for all students. He was part of a vocational technical school headed by a principal who understood the need for additional programming for nontraditional students and who gave the vocational counselor the "go ahead" to implement recruitment and retention services for nontraditional students.

Yes, this is the eighties, but does every school district provide special support services for nontraditional students? Are there efforts specifically designed to encourage students to pursue any occupation, regardless of gender? Do all schools provide the extra services required to retain nontraditional students? Are all faculty and staff supportive of expanding options for students, and do they understand this population's special needs? Do most educators even know what the term "nontraditional" means?

This chapter will explore the concept of nontraditional options for students, dispel myths associated with nontraditional choices, and provide examples on how to recruit and retain students in programs nontraditional to their gender. In between the definitions and strategies lie exciting opportunities for new and innovative educational programming that can make nontraditional options part of the everyday choices of each student.

During the past decade, the term *nontraditional student* has been used in a variety of ways. For the purpose of this chapter, the term nontraditional refers to any vocational or professional program in which fewer than 25 percent of the students are either male or female (Sanders, 1986). A "nontraditional student" is a student enrolled in a nontraditional program, and is considered a member of a special student population. It is not too difficult to name which programs are male dominated (automotive mechanics, electrical construction, and maintenance) or female dominated (cosmetology, licensed practical nurse). Because we rarely meet a female heavy machine operator or electrician, or a male nurse, we grow up believing that such people do not exist, or, if they do, that they are exceptions to the norm. Growing up in a world in which it is "normal" for men to be truck drivers and women to be nurses, has an impact on how we, as educators, encourage our students to make career and life choices. Parents, employers, community members (everyone who is a part of our contemporary society) are affected by who we see employed in various occupations. What we see helps to create our attitudes which, in turn, affect how students make their career and life choices.

Sex role socialization and bias determine gender-appropriate behavior from the moment a girl or boy is born. Gender-appropriate behavior, and the social reinforcers of that behavior, influence skills development and career aspirations at extremely early ages. By the ages of four and five, most children can tell us which jobs are "male" jobs and "female" jobs. The language that we use to describe occupations (fireman, policeman, mailman) are interpreted by young students as meaning that a man occupies those positions. Even titles that do not indicate a specific gender (doctor, nurse, secretary, truck driver) conjure images in our minds which specify gender. These kinds of images cannot be changed overnight! Educators must go beyond simply stating that all courses, thereby all careers, are open to all students. "Affirmative action" or more simply, extra efforts, must be made to assure that both female and male students are choosing from the widest range of career options possible.

The need to expand our conceptions of the occupations and careers our students can pursue is critical. Opening our minds, and our educational programming and curricula, to the possibilities that emerge from the consideration of nontraditional occupational areas for our students is the necessary "first step" in redefining the norm of the world of work. This alternate view also provides educators with the opportunity to create and implement new and innovative programming to meet the needs of nontraditional students and, ultimately, to expand career options for all students.

Many educators find the term nontraditional a cumbersome and negative one. Since it is highly unlikely that the average student would choose to define herself/himself as a nontraditional student, alternative terms have been suggested. Many experts choose to use the term "pioneer" student, since these students are breaking new ground, moving into unfamiliar territory, and making the way easier for those who follow. Others (such as Mindy Bingham, author of the highly acclaimed *Choices and Challenges* series of career and life exploration journals for young teens) use the terms *higher paying, higher control* to define many nontraditional careers. These terms let students know that certain jobs will provide them with greater economic rewards and, therefore, greater control over their life choices and commitments. Although nontraditional jobs for men are not necessarily higher paying, they do offer opportunities for men to pursue careers that are potentially more rewarding and self-satisfying and that allow greater individual freedom and control. Regardless of the terminology that is used, educators need to determine the best way to communicate these career options to students.

For many men and women, pursuing a nontraditional occupation is a choice just because it is different from the average, everyday choices that people make. For others, a nontraditional occupation allows them to utilize skills which were introduced at an early age; as barriers to what girls or boys can and cannot do continue to disintegrate, many children are learning skills that had previously been restricted to only one gender. However, there are also different incentives for men and women to make nontraditional career choices.

For girls and women, an economic incentive is primary; jobs which are nontraditional for women simply pay more money than traditional female occupations, such as secretaries or clerks. For example, 1985 median annual earnings (based on weekly median earnings) was $14,508 for secretaries (98% female) and $25,740 for electrical equipment repairers (92% male) (National Commission on Working Women, 1986). According to current socioeconomic trends, nine out of ten women will work outside the home sometime in their lives; 49 percent of married women with children under the age of six work outside the home; 61 percent of divorced, widowed, and separated women with children under the age of six work outside the home; 45 percent of women with children under the age of one are now working outside the home (U.S. Department of Labor, Women's Bureau, 1986). These statistics, and others like them, make it clear that contemporary female students will participate in the paid labor force. It is imperative that educators provide these young women with choices that ensure economic self-sufficiency, as well as personal reward and satisfaction. Nontraditional jobs for women can provide the economic self-sufficiency so vital to today's students and allow them to develop expertise in new and exciting skill areas.

Boys and men choose nontraditional occupations for the freedom to pursue jobs which utilize skills not often encouraged in the males in our society. Many men are discovering rewarding careers as nurses, elementary school teachers, and other so-called "helping professions." Due to the nature of sex role socialization and bias, men have avoided nontraditional careers. Such careers have been undervalued both economically and professionally. However, as contemporary men discover the freedom of choosing from a range of characteristics wider than those dictated by the good old "macho" stereotype, they are finding that nontraditional occupations offer a feasible alternative to the traditionally male dominated careers. It is not unusual to find many "older," post high school men choosing nontraditional careers. These men note that as they got older and developed self-confidence, they were able to counteract any pressure from their peers, families, and others to pursue "traditional" male careers. They also report that they find job satisfaction they previously had not experienced.

Both genders share a list of barriers to overcome as they begin to consider nontraditional areas of study. Among the most critical are those that flow from peer and parental pressures, coupled with school counseling, which continues to steer students into traditional curricula (Hagerty, 1985). Adolescent nontraditional students challenge basic gender-appropriate norms at an age when gender-appropriateness is the key to a student's popularity and success. A girl auto mechanic? A boy in a beauty culture program? How would you feel if your child came home with such an announcement? How would your child's peers react? How would you react if a friend chose a nontraditional occupation? There are countless stories in which students receive little or no support, and even blatant discouragement, from the significant people in their lives. In choosing a nontraditional occupational area, students face an additional series of barriers, including the isolation of being the only male or female in the classroom, lack of faculty support or understanding, sexual harassment, and the general strain that results from choosing a "different" path.

Through their choices, nontraditional students require us to look beyond our own scope of the world and reassess the variety of career options available. Nontraditional students provide concrete evidence that students can and will choose from the vast realm of career possibilities. The success that nontraditional students can achieve is dependent on the support of educators, parents, and employers. It is clear that we, as educators, must educate parents, students, employers, and our peers to sensitize them to the needs of nontraditional students.

Although some of the motivations for choosing nontraditional careers are different, strategies to recruit and retain both male and female students into nontraditional vocational areas are quite similar. Most experts agree that extra effort on the part of educators is required to interest students in nontraditional occupational areas. The band-aid approach to the issue—one counselor recruiting students on a part-time basis with no assistance from the faculty, one bulletin board displaying nontraditional workers, casual comments to a student in a guidance interview that "other" options are available just does not work! The downfalls of a typical school's effort to recruit nontraditional students include the ideas that one or two short-term strategies can address the issue, that there can be a recruitment effort without follow-up strategies for retention, and that there can be retention without any preparation for student placement.

A successful nontraditional recruitment and retention program requires a long-term, district-wide effort which includes the participation of administrators, faculty, counselors, parents, students, and community and business members. The following factors are present in every successful nontraditional recruitment and retention program:

1. The educational staff have received inservice training in sex equity, providing them with an understanding of and a commitment to their students future economic and personal self-sufficiency.

2. Key educational administrators in the school district insist that all educators be 100 percent committed to sex equity. Ideally, that commitment includes a staff member in the district who is responsible for equity on a full-time basis.

3. Nontraditional role models, particularly former students who have graduated and have succeeded in pioneering fields, are provided to show students that success and job satisfaction is possible.

4. The faculty, particularly those who teach "gatekeeping" courses (introduction to vocations, industrial arts, etc.), have learned to understand and accept nontraditional students in their classrooms.

5. Prospective students are given special attention and allowed the time to try out any machinery, tools, crafts, etc., that are required of a particular trade or occupational area, so that what is foreign and unfamiliar becomes familiar.

6. Solid linkages are created and maintained throughout the community: with parent/guardian groups to ensure the support of significant others in the student's life; with the business/industry community to ensure that programming meets local industry and employment needs so that the level of student employability is high.

7. The educational staff "mainstream" special programs for nontraditional students so that services for pioneering students become the rule and not the exception.

The Vocational Equity Project headed by Armenia Smith of the Ysleta Independent School District in El Paso, Texas, provides a successful equity program model (Smith, 1986). Under the direction of Ms. Smith, Yselta has created a number of low-cost, successful vocational equity programs; a higher percentage of both their male and female students are choosing nontraditional occupational areas. The programs include the following:

1. Eighth grade students are given tours of the vocational high school, complete with a peer tour guide who, ideally, is enrolled in a nontraditional occupational area. The faculty at the vocational school participate fully and are prepared to discuss courses, job skills, and

employment information particular to their specific area of training.

2. A "Futures Week" exposes students to nontraditional jobs through integrating nontraditional career information into already established curriculum. Writing, reading, science, and math classes sponsor Futures Week activities. Field trips to local government offices and business and industry centers are conducted, allowing students to observe nontraditional workers on the job and speak with employers. Vocational teachers sponsored a Parent Night to illustrate the advantages of nontraditional careers and to encourage parents to take a more active role in their children's education. A Career Day, featuring all types of professional and skilled craft workers, was the final activity of the week.

3. An "Open House" program was established and publicized through each vocational counselor and to every participating school. Women and men from nontraditional areas are featured and highlight their experiences in the world of work. Parents/guardians are invited to accompany students during the Open House, and open dialogue between all participants is encouraged throughout the program.

4. Students already enrolled in vocational programs participated in a job visitation program. They are placed at a worksite for one full day. Educational personnel request that the businesses assign a nontraditional worker from their company so that the student can "shadow" the worker for the day. Ysleta staff discovered that each company was impressed with the quality of students participating and agreed to help in the job placement of vocational graduates.

5. Programs have been targeted specifically to parents, including a questionnaire, a community outreach program which enables vocational educators to speak to various civic groups, and brochures.

6. A series of linkage conferences have been established. These conferences bring together vocational educators and business and industry members (particularly nontraditional workers). The conferences provide invaluable information regarding current job training/opportunities in the field, and contacts for future programming, role models, etc.

7. Finally, a series of inservice training workshops and conferences are offered on a continual basis through Yselta's Sex Equity Program. These sessions help keep faculty and administrators current on the facts and figures of vocational education and provide strategies to help them communicate to students the advantages of vocational training.

The benefits of such a low-cost, comprehensive program are clear. With a full-time coordinator leading the way, student enrollments are stabilized or increased, faculty are more enfranchised in the educational process, businesses have access to a qualified and prepared pool of applicants, and female and male students become well-trained and are able to develop the skills that lead to personal and economic self-sufficiency.

There is a misconception throughout the educational community that gender equity is a pursuit which falls outside the current movement for excellence in education. Programs designed to achieve sex equity in education actually open up opportunities for all students, regardless of gender, race, or physical abilities! As a result of examining the issues relevant to the recruitment and retention of nontraditional students, we examine all our recruitment efforts and examine all interactions that we have with students, and we discover new and innovative strategies to achieve educational excellence.

Each state, by federal mandate through the Carl Perkins Act P.L. 98-524, has a statewide equity coordinator. This coordinator is a liaison between educators and funded projects which provide training, technical assistance, and resources to aid in implementing nontraditional recruitment and retention services. Contact your state department of education for information on specific services available.

Yes, this is the eighties, and we have made some progress. We have increasing numbers of nontraditional workers who can serve as role models. We have educators who have begun to implement affirmative programming. We have the Perkins legislation which provides training, technical assistance, resources and direct student service programs. We have employers who have begun to seek out nontraditional workers. But, we have much more work to do. Only through the continued efforts of all educators will future students have the support, information, and opportunities to succeed in any occupation, regardless of gender.

REFERENCES

Hagerty, S.C. The bottom line: Non-traditional jobs. *Vocational education journal,* October, 1985, *60* (7), 36.

National Commission on Working Women. *Pay equity — A fact sheet.* Washington, D.C., 1986.

Sanders, J.S. *The nuts and bolts of NTO* (Second Edition). New Jersey: Scarecrow Press, 1986.

Smith, A. *Sex equity: Keeping the drive alive! A guide to promoting sex equity in your school district.* El Paso, Texas: Yselta Independent School District, 1986.

Women's Bureau, U.S. Department of Labor. *Twenty facts on women workers.* Washington, D.C., 1986.

The following statements are designed for the exploration of personal reactions to the chapter, as well as for the review of the contents of the chapter. Emphasis in discussions should be on exploring issues in depth, rather than on determining the correct or appropriate responses.

FOR DISCUSSION:

1. Are nontraditional careers "higher paying, higher control"?
2. How often do students in your educational institution get the opportunity to interact with adult nontraditional role models? How can the situation be improved if necessary?
3. Describe your impression of various careers that have been dominated by one gender (e.g., trucking, child care, machinery repair, construction, cosmetology). Could you encourage a student to be a pioneer in the professions that you have described?
4. How is the low number of "pioneers" tied to the issue of homophobia?
5. Why do men seem to return to school later in life to pursue professions such as nursing and elementary school teaching?
6. Respond to the author's question: "How would you feel if your child came home with such an announcement (to pursue a nontraditional career)?"
7. Are there efforts in your educational institution specifically designed to encourage students to pursue any occupation, regardless of gender? What additional efforts can be made?
8. Should students be aware of the possible negative reactions that they may experience in the classroom and on the job?

SUGGESTIONS FOR FURTHER READING

Consortium for Educational Equity. *Futures unlimited: Real people, real jobs and how to encourage girls to select and to stay in nontraditional courses (The recruitment and retention challenge)*. New Brunswick, New Jersey: Rutgers University, 1985.

Gilbert, M. *Choices/changes: An introduction of alternative occupational role models.* Newton, Massachusetts: EDC/WEEA Publishing Center, 1982.

Jaffe, N. *Men's jobs for women: Toward occupational equity.* New York: Public Affairs Pamphlet No. 606, 1982.

The National Center for Research in Vocational Education. *Unlocking non-traditional careers—four training packages.* Columbus, Ohio: The Ohio State University, 1981.

Project on the Status and Education of Women. *Looking for more than a few good women in traditionally male fields.* Washington, D.C., 1987.

Ricci, L. *High-paying blue-collar jobs for women.* New York: Ballatine Books, 1981.

Riley, S. *A fair shot/an equal chance.* Billerica, Massachusetts: Department of Education, 1980.

Verheyden-Hilliard, M.E. *From here to there: Exploring the apprentice-to-journeyworker career ladder with girls and boys in grades 1–9.* Bethesda, Maryland: The Equity Institute, 1983.

Wider Opportunities for Women, Inc. *Overcoming barriers to nontraditional training for women and girls: A resource bibliography.* Washington, D.C., 1985.

Chapter 21

ADMINISTRATIVE POLICY: RELATING EQUITY POLICY TO PROGRAM DEVELOPMENT

Eleanor Linn

FOSTERING SEX EQUITY IN PUBLIC SCHOOL SYSTEMS: THE IMPORTANCE OF LOCAL PLANNING AND POLICYMAKING

Charles B. Vergon

INTRODUCTION

"But we've already done sex equity!"

It is often difficult for an educator on the lower rungs of the institution's hierarchy to initiate and implement district-wide equity policy and practice. Although there may be tacit support on the part of administrators, equity issues can appear to be just another requirement or yet another task. The checklists are completed, the programs surveyed in a cursory manner, and obvious discriminatory practices changed. Ongoing programmatic revision as well as proactive strategies are rarely conducted on a routine basis.

Even administrators who are most sensitive to the value of achieving equity in education, are often confused about the steps necessary to make it an integral part of the educational process. Efforts frequently appear to be "add-ons," special short-term activities, one-time staff development, or a quick perusal of programs and resources. Unless a grievance arises, sex equity appears to be supplemental to the curriculum, if it is regarded at all.

Yet, as stated in the September 1986 newsletter published by the Council of Chief State School Officers Resource Center on Educational Equity:

'Educational equity' should not consist of a finite set of discrete programs and people operating under Title IV of the Civil Rights Act or comparable civil rights funding provisions. Rather the promotion of educational equity should be a priority in every activity and at every level of the educational system. (Issue XVIII, p. 2)

283

A number of concerned individuals may need to get involved in the process of institutionalizing sex equity policy and programs. Teachers, parents, guidance counselors, students, and administrators may be able to create an equitable district if they work together.

The administrators, however, are the key personnel in seeing that equity is actually achieved and maintained. Principals, curriculum supervisors, athletic directors, and superintendents can best recognize appropriate strategies to maneuver proposals through the system. They can eliminate barriers to implementation, whether the hurdles be individuals, existing policies, lack of information, or institutional politics. They are in a pivotal position to make changes in education if they are motivated, can garner appropriate support, and use their authority effectively.

Once educators with less clout team up with supportive administrators, the change process can be conducted, particularly if the suggestions outlined in Eleanor Linn's chapter are followed.

Charles B. Vergon presents an effective systems approach for local policy makers who are responsible for translating legal mandates into sex equity policy in the public schools.

ADMINISTRATIVE POLICY: RELATING EQUITY POLICY TO PROGRAM DEVELOPMENT

This chapter addresses the role of school administrators in translating equity policy into actual programs, though the material also may be useful to board members, community advocates and teachers. Readers who are not administrators can use this information to teach, guide, or pressure administrators into playing a more active role regarding equity in their schools, but only those in administrative positions will be able to carry out change in the ways described here. Although this message may be disheartening to some equity advocates, it may also be a relief to others, who may expend enormous amounts of energy trying to achieve changes that their role does not allow. Knowing the strengths and limitations of your particular role is one of the most important aspects of planning for any change in an organization. Understanding hidden roles and agendas is essential in bringing about an equity change.

Administrative practice in sex equity shares many characteristics with administrative practice in other areas. Abstract goals must be made increasingly concrete, tasks delegated, timelines kept, and outcomes monitored. The administration of equity, however, must differ from other forms of administrative practice because equity roles do not carry the same power and prestige inherent in mainstream administrative positions. Equity power, therefore, must be borrowed from other roles that are seen as more legitimate by the organization, either through the support of other people who are not directly affiliated with the equity effort, or through other roles held by the equity administrator.

Many administrators working in equity are surprised when their efforts are thwarted in this area, especially when they are usually successful in their administrative activities. They attribute their loss of power to personal failings, poor timing, lack of interest, or the incompetence of others. In observing a large number of diverse school districts, and seeing the same power issues arise, it has become apparent that this problem of discounting authority is the central issue in equity administration. Although played out in many ways, it exists in one form or another in all organizations, and must be recognized and counteracted by equity administrators in order to be effective.

285

Equity administration is feasible, and ultimately rewarding, for it gives us the satisfaction of being able to make our organization supportive of all of its service recipients. Finding your own most effective way to overcome the discounting of your authority will be your main task in the successful administration of equity. It will involve your acquiring a collection of strategies that work in your organization, and making the best use of your particular strengths. It will also help if you are very knowledgeable in the content of equity. The information in this chapter is intended to give you beginning guidelines and suggestions.

I. Understand Your Role in the Organization

A candid and detailed understanding of your role is crucial to developing an equity strategy of maximum impact. If you work in the central administration, you have control over different aspects of the organization than if you manage a school building. If you work primarily in staff development, your equity initiatives will be quite different from those that you would use if you manage the district's business affairs. If your district has a tightly controlled centralized authority, you will devise different practices than if authority is delegated on a short-term basis, or if authority is widely distributed throughout the organization. If rules and responsibilities are narrowly defined and distinctly separated, your successful administrative strategies will be different from those in a district that displays a good deal of formal or informal role overlap. The size of the district, financial situation, previous history of change in other areas, and relationship of the board to the administration are all factors that will influence the development of successful administrative strategies in fostering sex equity.

Central Office Roles. Ideally, the central coordination of the process of translating board policy into administrative practice should take place in the Superintendent's office. Its authority over all functions of the organization makes it an obvious choice. The Title IX Coordinator reports directly to the Superintendent, using the authority of that office to develop standards, assess needs, and monitor progress throughout the district.

In reality, however, this is rarely the case. The Superintendent, having been bestowed the symbols of success in the current system, rarely has the level of personal energy commitment toward the gender issue that is needed to set the example. Does the Superintendent attend as many sexual harassment workshops as football games? Does the Superintendent know the President of the Project on Equal Education Rights (or another local equity organization) as well as the President of the Rotary (or another local civic organization)? The Superintendent's visible support of equity sets the tone for the organization. If you are the Superintendent, set that example of commitment.

The real power of the Title IX Coordinator is another factor that the Superintendent controls. Does the Title IX Coordinator have the authority and budget to mandate projects and guidelines? Is the Title IX Coordinator's authority based primarily on that person's other, or former job responsibilities? A Title IX Coordinator who can gain cooperation from Curriculum Directors, but not from Principals (a common complaint in equity circles) probably does not have the Superintendent's full support. Otherwise, the Superintendent is not really the central power of the school district. It may be necessary to find the real power and get its support. Even a Title IX Coordinator who is knowledgeable and committed to equity will at times need visible borrowed authority from the Superintendent, or other authority. For the Title IX Coordinator who has other high level responsibilities, (such as an Assistant Superintendent), the issues will often focus around the need to demonstrate knowledge and commitment to sex equity in order to be a credible and useful authority. Showing your commitment, your knowledge, and your willingness to learn will be very important to your furthering your equity goals.

The Title IX Coordinator's responsibilities usually are:

1. Assuring that the policy from the board is translated into a number of concrete goals;
2. Seeing that district standards for each of the goals are set;
3. Making sure that goals are monitored throughout the district;
4. Assisting school buildings, departments, and other subgroups in planning and implementing activities that will have a positive impact on their goals;
5. Setting equitable procedures for allocating resources needed to meet equity goals;
6. Recommending rewards, encouragement or sanctions for departments in relation to their level of equity and commitment to change.

The district with a Title IX Coordinator who has the knowledge, commitment, and authority to perform these functions has a good chance of achieving greater equity.

If your Superintendent and Title IX Coordinator carry out the responsibilities listed above, your job is to bring greater specificity to how district goals are enacted in your program in terms of gender levels of participation, balance in types of activities and encouragement, fairness in the allocation of resources, and consequent equity in the distribution of rewards. You need to take a more detailed look at the data that the Title IX Coordinator asks you to collect, and identify where inequities may exist, spot possible causes and suggest possible remedies.

If, for example, you are asked to report the enrollment in science classes by gender, you should know the levels of gender balance or imbalance in each building, grade and course, set the standard of acceptability and identify where balance is improving, and where it is deteriorating. You need to be familiar with procedures and activities that could be implemented to improve the situation, know what has been done, and ascertain whether improvement is indeed documented in the programs that were affected by change efforts. The difficulty of your task depends in large part on the amount of already published material on gender differences in your particular area of responsibility. Section II of this chapter will discuss substantive areas in greater detail.

The key difficulty if your role is in the central office, will be in enlisting support from others in your organization. Your authority over employees you supervise may be tested as you request certain tasks of them. Peers or higher level administrators with other areas of responsibility may start making claims on your "territory," or expressing opinions about your initiatives. You may find that such acts of resistance undermine your self-confidence, or make you feel that advocating for equity is not worth the hassle. This behavior, though unnerving, is normal in an organization threatened with a profound examination of values such as gender equity. Expect the resistance and try to prepare for it. Here are some hints.

1. Some people will want to test the seriousness of your convictions. Think about your commitment to equity before others can put you on the spot. Know what issues you are ready to stand up for, and which ones you consider extremist, unfeasible, or remnants of biased values that you continue to hold. Decide which views you will reveal in public. You don't have to be 100 percent pro-equity to help further its cause, but you do have to support your particular issue.

2. Include possible disrupters in your planning process. It may take longer to arrive at a plan or a generally recognized standard, and it may

be more diluted than you originally wanted, but it has a greater chance for success. Develop an advisory committee from the start and use them for making and confirming decisions.

3. Obtain a written mandate from your supervisor giving you authority to develop plans and make decisions in this area. Ideally your supervisor will assign and apprise peers of other equity responsibilities at the same time. Use your mandate as a source of authority with those you supervise. Treat this area of responsibility with the same seriousness that you treat other important areas. Expect follow-through, and enforce assignments.

4. Try to foresee possible objections. Identify individuals or groups who may be hurt by your programs and initiatives, or who may not have been aware of their long-held and unrecognized privileges. Explore the best ways of appealing to them, by relating goals to aspects of their own self-interest, or to their concern for helping others. Find opportunities for educating them in a nonconfrontational way. Remember, people are more acutely aware of injustice *against* them, than of privilege from which they have benefited. More specifically, white male administrators rarely see the advantages they have had. They usually ascribe their success to their own individual ability, and hard work. They are keen to notice the advantages of other white males, however, who attended more prestigious schools, or had more support from those in power. (Appealing to their aspirations for their daughters often helps them see equity issues more clearly.)

5. Know your organization's power problems and ambiguities. Try to resolve them in another context, so that equity is not used as fuel for a different confrontation. If you can't solve surrounding problems, devise schemes that work around them, but keep those findings to yourself. No one gives rewards to the person who announces that the emperor is wearing no clothes.

6. Assess the level of real support that you have from your superiors and the amount of autonomy you have for implementing equity initiatives. Your "equity leash" may be shorter than your latitude on other aspects of your job. Find safe ways to test what is possible before embarking on a grand plan. In most cases, you will accomplish more by taking small steps successfully, than by forcing a major crisis.

Building Level Roles. The Principal's real or assumed authority over curriculum content, materials selection, equipment acquisition, and staff hiring, evaluation and training varies greatly by school district and by school. The size of the school, presence of department chairs, grade levels taught, power of the central office, power of unions and associations, level of teacher autonomy, gender composition of building staff and leadership, and principal's leadership style are all factors that influence building level initiatives in sex equity. If you have control over curriculum, materials, hiring, or evaluation, learn more about equity issues in these aspects of your role and devise procedures and programs to address them, working with the central office staff or other school officials with whom you share power. School climate, however, is the factor most likely associated with building level control and most likely for you to be able to change. Principals, therefore, have greatest responsibility and success in implementing procedures and supporting programs related to promoting equity in student treatment and fostering a positive learning environment.

Principals also have authority over discretionary funds that should be audited for sex equity. How much of the fund is used for activities that primarily benefit one gender? How much of the fund is used to address problems more common to one gender? Is it used in conjunction with organizations that focus on one gender? Discretionary fund activities should include some programs that promote equity and counteract bias. A principal can easily fund an equity library, classroom-based research and material development projects, internships or training to encourage staff members who aspire to positions that are not traditional for their gender, and equity-related extracurricular activities that may not otherwise be self-supporting.

Principals usually have greatest success if they work along with a building level equity committee made up of a representative group of teachers. The committee may also include noncertified staff. Often in an elementary school, the fact that a male principal leads a predominantly female teaching staff is the major barrier to further equity implementation. The principal may find staff who are more knowledgeable or committed to gender issues, and may feel pushed or threatened by them. Discussion and awareness of gender differences in patterns of communication, expectations, motivation, problem-solving styles, expressions of respect and praise are necessary in such a school to build greater gender trust. Learning to share power with staff members who have greater expertise in this area may help. Attempting to lead in an area where you are not the leader, only reinforces gender conflict. Recent work in social psychology and group process can be of assistance to educators in understanding gender differences in communication and in helping forge new patterns, without prying into staff members private lives.

Aides, cafeteria workers, custodians, bus drivers, and secretaries are often overlooked as important contributors to school climate concerns. Their frequent interactions with students convey important messages about school values. Their omission from most school training programs and decision-making processes leaves them more dependent on their personal reactions to gender issues. Changing work and family patterns in their own lives leave them confused about how to best help children develop all their abilities. Whether your building level gender equity committee includes noncertified staff depends largely on the extent that you intend to address school climate, rather than curriculum issues. It can also depend on whether a combined committee will yield a more gender-balanced group. If you do not combine groups, then establish a separate structure for dealing with equity issues in the support staff.

Principals also play a significant role with parents and the community. You can support proactive community equity groups with resources and information. Provide them with strategy suggestions, listen to their concerns, respect their leadership, and where feasible, implement their requests.

You will inevitably also hear a number of complaints against equity initiatives. Make sure that you have documented any new procedures, informed people about them, and implemented them fairly. Assess whether a complaint is a result of a single displeased individual, or whether it reveals an unforeseen unfairness in the system. Handle it with procedures set out for managing complaints, and if need be, borrow authority from elsewhere in the system. If conflicting requests invoke the same equity principles, assess the prevalence and severity of each, explore options that can include all parties involved, and seek help from officials who can clarify and apply district level policy.

Exploring Administrative Links to the Advisory Committees and the Board. Sometimes, because of inaction of others, you may wish to spur mandates or activities that are beyond your own job responsibilities. The best way to accomplish this goal is by serving on other people's committees or by encouraging community members to do so. If, for example, you want to see the district take a stronger stand against sexual harassment, you could request clarification about the current code of conduct, inform the committee that hears such complaints about inadequacy of blanket "professional behavior" language, and volunteer to serve on a fact-finding or policy-drafting committee. You could suggest that a policy contain guidelines and timetables for dissemination, training, sanctions, and staff responsibility. Although you may not be responsible for administering that program, you have helped make it more likely that a concrete program will be implemented. Administrators can strengthen or instigate policy. School boards make policy.

At other times you may be barred from participating in a committee, or your participation may involve a conflict of interest. Encourage appropriate colleagues to take on the needed role, or speak with community members who share your view. For example, as School Business Manager, you may not have access to the committee that will write interview questions for the High School Principal position, though you would like to see some new questions included that could highlight female candidates' student discipline skills. You suggest that a community member you know with excellent personnel credentials be invited to join the personnel advisory committee, or be a citizen observer on the administrative committee. You ask that person to volunteer their services and voice your concerns. You explain the need for new questions and see if they agree. You provide encouragement and support for the person's committee participation.

Setting Priorities. No one person would have the time or energy to embark on all the initiatives that are recommended to achieve educational equity. If your major job responsibility is in equity, you may be able to accomplish five goals each school year. Otherwise, targeting one or two goals is more realistic.

First, look at any areas that may involve district liability. Especially if you are the Superintendent, act on these first. If you have another role, inform those responsible of potential liability.

Then, look at which goals are likely to be accomplished. They are probably tied in to initiatives in this year's major policy statement, and will already have a number of supporters. In the long run, you will effect more change by directing several small initiatives, than by insisting upon one issue. Make sure, however, that the issues you choose seem worth your energy. You'll lose your self-respect and that of others, if you support a seemingly insignificant cause.

Also, look at the severity, prevalence, and persistence of the issues you would like to address. Do some of them lend themselves to definition within this year's new policy initiatives? Can concrete steps be outlined and set in a reasonable timetable? Can part of them be accomplished successfully?

Talk over the possibilities with colleagues and staff who you will need to involve in the projects that you are considering. Note which projects elicit their energy. Talk with your counterparts in other districts, or with professionals in sex equity. They may help you find a logical sequence of initiatives, or give you confidence in taking the risks involved.

Finally, make your decision, even if it seems a little arbitrary. More harm can be done by not deciding on a strategy at all, than by having to start again, but don't be so rash as to risk your job.

II. Substantive Issues in Sex Equity Administration

The Equity Administrator must be knowledgeable in the specific equity content of her or his program responsibilities. Educational policies are often written in quite broad language, which is positive in allowing for flexibility of implementation, but which also risks leaving their implementation too general or vague. The expansion of gender research into an increasing number of diciplines has provided us with more precise information about how sex bias affects individuals in all aspects of their lives. The more definite your equity goals and program design, and the more closely you monitor their actual implementation, the greater the likelihood that your program will indeed make a difference.

It is not possible to describe every area of sex equity in schools in one article, or one book, but a brief review of major policy areas with related program goals may be helpful for you to identify important indicators of equity and interventions that may lead to equity improvement. This list is neither complete nor definitive. Each year new research, programs, and discussion uncover unnoticed areas of concern and strategies for success. The best advice is to keep up with new findings in your field.

Student Classification and Treatment

Policies relating to fair treatment of students may often address such issues as access to courses and extracurricular activities, selection processes for honors and special services, discipline codes, complaint procedures, sexual harassment, and a host of behaviors often associated with positive school climate.

If your responsibilities lie within one of these areas, you should first develop a system for assessing the current level of equity and set an approved standard of acceptability. If this standard is not generally accepted in advance, you will expend enormous amounts of energy trying to convince people that there is indeed a problem. Then learn as much as you can about specific programs that have been designed to counteract bias in this area. Think about what factors could make a difference in the equity outcome in your specific situation. Make time to talk with others about how your program could influence that factor. Plan a series of tasks to bring about change. Monitor the change, and modify your program accordingly. Table 21-1 may help you start planning your equity initiatives in areas related to student treatment and placement.

Curriculum and Educational Materials

Many school districts pass policies stating that the curriculum should be free of gender and race bias, but fall far short of implementing the policy because of lack of detailed knowledge of gender issues in the given content areas, or because of undue reliance on standard textbooks.

An important issue for the equity administrator is first identifying experts in gender issues in the particular subject area in question. The curriculum expert may or may not be the equity expert in that field. Find the person or people who can lead you to the information and resources you need to consider. Value their expertise. Find out about the contributions of women to the field in question. Is there research about aspects of the field that influence women and men differently? Does that research imply a change in content or teaching techniques? Are there assumptions about previous skills and experiences needed to understand key concepts, which are really only familiar to one gender? Are the jobs that use these skills stereotyped by sex? Is there information for students about women who use these skills in their work? Is the motivation in lessons linked to a gender-related reward system? Are cultural values and communications patterns of both genders respected and used in the instructional process?

After you gain a beginning knowledge of gender issues in the field, then begin to assess the scope of your curriculum, the fairness of your print and nonprint instructional materials, the actual content of classroom activities (as opposed to what is set out in either the textbook or curriculum), and the relationship of learning objectives to future career needs. You may decide to implement more stringent equity review before textbooks can be adopted, or supplementary materials selected. You may devise programs to further relate the curriculum to career

Table 21-1.
Student Treatment and Placement

Policy Area	Possible Goal	Possible Indicators	Possible Interventions
Access to courses	Equal enrollment by gender in all courses, especially upper level math and science, computer programming, skilled trade programs, home economics, child care, health care, business practice.	Analyze district level enrollment data for differences in gender. Make on-site visits to key classes to observe participation of girls and boys. Gather information from teachers and dept. chairs about numbers of boys and girls in classes. Ask them to explain differences in enrollment. Survey students about why they take certain classes. Compare reasons given by girls and boys.	Student awareness and recruitment programs. Run publicity campaigns to emphasize why girls or boys would want to take a given course. Change course titles to make them more interesting to both genders. Change course location to a place where both genders feel more comfortable. Change teaching techniques to include more cooperative and peer learning. Change funding levels to make a new course more appealing.
Access to extra-curricular activities	Equal enrollment by gender, especially in sports programs, community service programs, and the arts.	Survey student advisors about reasons students of each gender participate in activities. Survey students about their reasons for participating in activities. Make on-site visits to activities and observe level and type of interactions between students of each gender.	Run student recruitment campaign. Change advisor training techniques to make them more aware of gender needs and differences. Appoint advisors of the other gender. Change funding level of activity. Change time, seasons, publicity.

Table 21-1. Continued

Policy Area	Possible Goal	Possible Indicators	Possible Interventions
Fair distribution of honors and awards.	Equal number of female and male students receive any given award over a four-year period.	Collect list of awards and award recipients. Compare number of males and females who received each award. Document publicity, value, and location of awards. Compare visibility and worth with number of females and males that receive them.	Change award ceremonies to include broad range of activities. Change award criteria to make it more likely that both genders are eligible. Educate award committees to solicit nontraditional nominees. Campaign for funds/publicity for certain undervalued awards. Choose role models of both genders to give out awards.
Fair discipline	No students of either sex act in violation of the school discipline code. A small, but equal number of girls and boys act in violation of the code and have equal consequences.	Compare number of boys and girls involved in disciplinary actions. Document time, place, reason for discipline violations to assess different gender patterns. parents, staff.	Review school discipline code for possible gender differences. Form gender balanced school discipline team to hear com- Encourage nuturing male roles in students,
Prevention of sexual harassment and fair handling of cases	No cases of sexual harassment exist in the district. Those incidents that do occur are identified and resolved fairly.	Disseminate district policy and complaint procedure to staff, students, community. Keep records on the number of complaints and their outcomes. Compare number of complaints to amount of education on the issue.	Develop a district policy. Train complaint managers. Publicize the policy and complaint procedure. Resolve any cases brought. Discuss sexual harassment with students, staff, community.
Teachers/ Student Interactions	Teachers give females as much positive attention, encouragement, and constructive criticism as they give males.	Observe classrooms for equal levels of probing, eye contact, physical proximity for both genders.	Implementation of awareness training and observation programs such as TESA, GESA, and Intersect.

education, or to train teachers in gender issues in the field. You may evaluate teachers and administrators for their inclusion of equity content, change course requirements to mandate courses selected more often by students of one gender, change test content to influence the teaching in a particular course, or analyze achievement test scores by gender to point out specific content areas that need to receive greater amounts of class-room time. You may try an experimental elective course on women's issues in a particular field, an extracurricular support activity, or a faculty study group on a given issue. You may decide to present frequent reports on the status of equity in your field, to key policy makers and administrators, or to document the progress of steps being undertaken.

The extent of your efforts may well depend on your level of knowl-edge and commitment, the resources you have for equity change, and the support you have in the organization. It may also depend on the extent of overlap between your curriculum area and others, giving you greater or lesser flexibility and credibility in the field, the amount of time students spend in your classes, the power of national organizations in your field either to initiate equity programs and standards or to remain rigidly against them, and the presence or absence of standardized tests and accountability procedures. Some subject areas definitely have more freedom of flexibility than others. Some educators believe they have less flexibility than they actually do. Inform yourself about equity efforts in your field before you fall back on an excuse for not changing. Use that information to counter resistance from others. Chances are your curricu-lum and materials could use a good deal of equity improvement.

Table 21-2 outlines a few content initiatives in four curriculum areas.

Personnel Administration

Far fewer people in a school district have responsibility for administering personnel policies than for administering curriculum or student treat-ment aspects of education. This small group of people is also more predominantly male than the district as a whole and has at its command fewer ready models for gender equity auditing and change. The bulk of the material in school personnel initiatives must be borrowed from government and industry, drawn from fair employment legislation, class action litigation, and various initiatives from women's advocacy groups.

Most important among personnel issues, is the monitoring of job incumbents by race and gender and the implementation of a plan to achieve equal levels of employment. The more narrowly defined the job

Table 21-2.
Fair Curriculum

Content Area	Possible Goal	Possible Indicators	Possible Interventions
Language and Literature	Gender fair language used in all writing and speaking.	Student and staff communications checked periodically for gender fairness. Use of biased language reported publicly.	Teach gender fair language in formal curriculum.
	Literature selected uses gender fair language, or bias, if present, is subject of discussion. Literature themes reflect major life experiences of traditional and non-traditional male and females.	Gender equity review of textbook, library, and supplementary reading. Observation of classroom discussion when biased materials are used. Review of course syllabi, student reading selections with theme analysis.	Correct gender bias in written and spoken communications. Make sure all district official communication is in gender fair language. Institute equity review for purchasing new materials and only approve materials that pass review or have documented extenuating circumstances.
	Equal representation of female and male authors.	Review of syllabi and student reading selections.	Run in-service programs or sponsor tuition at University courses on women's literature, feminist criticism, and sex fair children's literature.
Math	Equal enrollment by gender in all level math courses.	Compare enrollment levels of girls and boys particularly in Algebra II, Calculus, Computer Programming, and remedial math.	Carry out the goals listed.
	Equal achievement scores at all levels for boys and girls.	Compare achievement level of boys and girls in math, particularly in high school.	
	Tutoring, support groups, special classes for all students needing skills or confidence in math.	Compare availability of math support services for girls to reading support services for boys.	Set up special programs. Get funds allocated, use peer tutors or community groups.

Table 21-2. Continued

Content Area	Possible Goal	Possible Indicators	Possible Interventions
	Use female and male role models in math related careers each month in classrooms at all grade levels.	Monitor number and gender of career role models, particularly in middle school grades.	Work with career and education program, local industry, community service groups to bring nontraditional role models to school.
	Place priority on teaching skills for which girls are school dependent: spatial relations, multistepped problems, statistics and probability, use of tools.	Assess amount of time teachers spend on each of these topics. Compare results over time to see if it is increasing.	Provide administrators and teachers with good activities in these areas. Support staff who use them well. Encourage adoption through workshops, handouts, newsletters, modeling.
	Universal adoption of cooperative rather than competitive problem solving strategies, behaviors.	Observe learning strategies in key classrooms.	Workshops, discussion, modeling, subject of evaluation.
Social Studies	Equal representation of the accomplishments of women and men in the past.	Use of instructional materials that include public accomplishments of women and men in equal numbers.	Workshops, handouts, newsletters, supplementary materials about women's lives and accomplishments of women.
	Equal discussion of the influence of public events on the lives of men and women.	Syllabi, homework questions, test questions, discussion questions that address influence of events equally on women and men.	Special women's history week/month celebration.
	Equal portrayal of the lives of women and men in different cultures.	Use of supplementary materials, and interviews, artifacts to gather info. about women's lives.	Rename your school, put different pictures on the wall, rename awards and clubs for women of note.
	Use of quantitative problem solving skills in formulation of ideas.	Lesson plans and student reports reflect quantitative analysis.	Honor roll models as graduation speakers, special award recipients.

Table 21-2. Continued

Content Area	Possible Goal	Possible Indicators	Possible Interventions
Science	Implement math goals in science classes. Draw all lesson motivation from real life experiences common to both genders.	Number of analysis to competitive sports, munitions, and dangerous activities should decrease each year in classroom discussion.	Rework motivation and application of traditional course materials.
	Students cooperate in lab partnerships.	Both partners should be observed actively doing experiments.	Change partners frequently, discuss how to be partners, break up couples working together, try single sex partnerships.
	All students are comfortable with use of equipment.	Lessons in curriculum on equipment use. Student appraisal on equipment use.	Assess level of equipment anxiety. Use simpler equipment. Stress safety, not possibility of accident.
	Emphasis on observation and thinking skills.	Test questions, reports that stress process rather than memorization of facts.	Change tests, student evaluation criteria. Change judges of science contests. Make projects less competitive.
	Every student can name positive role model who uses scientific methods or concepts of science.	Prevalence of career info., race and gender balanced role models, discussion of balance of work and family for both genders, discussion of science as promoter of place and well-being.	Set up shadowing programs, mentor programs, use visitors to classroom, films, stories. Assess curriculum content for peaceful uses of science.
	Increased emphasis on peaceful uses of science, contributions of women to science, scientific studies of female as well as male of species. Reconciliation of science and health curricula.	Development of new curriculum materials, adaptation of new research to K–12 use.	Workshops, materials, discussion of new aspects of science.

category, the more likely you are to find gender disparities. For example, the number of female and male administrators in your district may be equal, but females will predominate in lower-paying curriculum and special consultant areas. Look carefully at how you plan to collect and analyze your employment data. Rather than grouping jobs, you may assess how many of your job titles are imbalanced by gender. You may take mean salaries of female and male teachers, administrators, supervisors, and noncertified staff. Your job in personnel-related issues will be to help the district set goals, foster potential nontraditional candidates, and advocate for their hiring.

If you supervise staff, you are in a position to mentor nontraditional employees and recommend them to others. Remember to include nontraditional workers in your informal discussions about how things really work and what may be happening in the future. Share staff development opportunities and possible job openings with them. Tell them about the usual career ladders in your area. Collaborate with them on important projects. Assign them tasks that will enhance their skills and give them greater exposure. Mention their strengths to top level administrators. Confront any stereotypic statements or behaviors you see focused on them and confront any attempts to discredit you as a mentor of a nontraditional worker.

You will also need to assess the gender impact of a broad range of personnel policies and programs, recommend revisions, and carry out ensuing changes. Do policies on leading extracurricular activities give salary and advancement advantages to one gender over another? Does seniority accrue during leaves taken by one gender more than by another? Are certain informal responsibilities considered the training ground for higher level positions? How are employees informally and formally selected for advancement? Are interview questions standardized? Who receives formal evaluations? Who is reviewed by peers? Who by supervisors? Who serves on search committees? Are there rules about nepotism, child care, geographic proximity, work schedules, or fringe benefits that have a disparate impact on women and men?

If your life has been influenced by one of these factors, you will be acutely aware of the differences. If these are not personal issues for you, you will probably need to discuss them with employees who have been affected by them, or review employee records to assess the prevalence of such issues. The data you collect will help you influence others about the need for implementing fair employment practices. Skills in data analysis and presentation will be a definite advantage for you. If you do not have the resources to carry out a study, try getting outside support from an association or a university. An equity study group in your district may also be an important help. Should you have the resources, you should consider doing a comparable worth study in your organization. Your efforts at changing personnel procedures must be focused at the people who have power to change them, or you must redefine responsibility for those decisions. Personnel areas take a long time to change.

Resource Allocation

Like the area of personnel administration, centralized resource allocation responsibilities are usually held by a small number of administrators, who usually have not been affected personally by past biased practices. Although the fair use of funds is essential to creating an equitable environment, very few guidelines and prepared programs exist for assessing, remedying, and ensuring equity in this area.

Administrators should all examine the extent to which they do have control over resource allocation and the extent to which this bias influences the equitability of services that their programs can provide. Ideally an administrator can devise an estimated program expenditure per male and female student, taking into account the cost of special education programs, equipment, supplies, special facilities, coaching, tutoring, and transportation that benefit primarily one gender, or compensate for needs that are unique, or more common to one gender than the other. In-kind services and gifts that are targeted to one gender, or tend to benefit one gender more should also be assessed.

A budget of expenditures for counteracting sex stereotyping can be estimated and compared to the budget for continuing traditional activities. For example, what is the expenditure for equitable supplemental materials, as compared to the budget for traditional materials that have not gotten equity committee approval? What is the comparative budget for predominantly female extracurricular activities to predominantly male ones? How much is spent on remedial reading programs, primarily used by boys, as opposed to remedial math programs, more frequently needed by girls?

Are employee training, travel, and leave benefit expenditures equal throughout the district? Do job categories that have more employees of one gender enjoy greater rewards in any of these areas? Are insurance policies free of bias, or are there differentials by gender in annuity payments, health coverage and survivors' benefits? Is accident insurance coverage equal?

Are nonmonetary privileges distributed on an equitable basis? Who gets secretarial support? Who has professional organization dues paid?

Whose discretionary funds may be used for community activities, travel, or entertainment? Do these rewards come more frequently to jobs held by members of one sex?

Who uses discretionary funds to advance equity? Are there funds that you can use to advance equity? Is there a professional library of equity-related materials? Is there money to sponsor equity training, an assessment study, or to compensate for a biased tradition?

How are decisions made about resource allocation? Is there a gender balanced committee that hears requests? Is the Director of Finance knowledgeable in the workings of hidden discrimination? How can the financial managers of the district be taught more about the importance of equity in resource allocation? To whom are they accountable for equity? How is that information communicated?

A fair school district allocates its funding fairly. You can ask for equity budgetary reports, or equity implications in expenditure decisions. Your decisions about how to spend money reveal your values and priorities.

III. Learning From Others

The following examples of administrative strategies that have helped advance gender equity in other districts may assist you in devising plans that will work in your school. They are drawn from real life, but have been simplified substantially. They are intended to illustrate issues of discounting of equity authority; institutionalizing equity process; redefining goals; and distinguishing between policy, program monitoring and training.

Case A: Institutionalizing a Women's History Week Project

A high school principal in a midsize urban school district was very pleased to see a committee of teachers work hard to put on an ambitious women's history week celebration. Over the next three years, even though she increased the discretionary budget allocation from $50 to $100, interest in the project was lagging. Here are some of the things she decided to try.

1. Ask a community committee to pick up some of the work the teachers did in past years.
2. Sponsor the teachers to present their project at a professional organization and bring back new ideas from others.
3. Recommend one of the teachers for a sabbatical to find more women's history materials and present them to colleagues.
4. Recommend that the school board proclaim women's history week

city-wide and volunteer on a committee to disseminate sample materials throughout the system.

Her goal was to institutionalize a special event and to bring professional rewards to staff who took the initiative.

Case B: Strengthening the Textbook Review Process.

The Director of Curriculum in a large urban school district established a textbook equity review committee to assess educational materials under consideration. His budget allowed for two days training for the six committee members drawn from five major subject areas. The training session evaluations were positive, but attendance was low at subsequent committee meetings. Here's what he decided to try.

1. Add committee approval as necessary to the acquisition procedure. Books cannot be bought without their recommendation.
2. Have advocates and opponents of selected titles make presentations in front of the committee. Public discussion increases the perceived importance of the decision.
3. Speak to committee members individually about their assessment of the problem, and send out an anonymous questionnaire. Address issues of the group as a whole by making changes and appoint new people to the group, if individual problems cannot be addressed.
4. Subdivide the committee into curriculum area task forces. Participants reported feeling unable to make decisions about other curriculum areas.
5. With the help of equity experts, evaluate how much committee members actually know about substantive equity issues in their fields. Provide additional training and discussion to build their skills and confidence.
6. Incorporate textbook review in a rotating curriculum review process and focus on only one area each year. This goal was to put greater value on textbook equity decisions by creating more public attention and discussion, and by relating consequences directly to the groups' decisions.

Case C: Giving Authority to Complaint Managers.

The Title IX Coordinators and Assistant Superintendent of a large urban school district worked effectively with the Superintendent to introduce and have the board pass a policy on sexual harassment. After training of building level complaint managers and dissemination of the grievance procedure to students and staff, she was dismayed to find a number of relatively minor complaints that were unresolved at the building level, and had to be handled in her office. Her immediate reaction was to provide an additional day of training for complaint managers. After some thought she decided to:

1. Make herself available for complaint management consultation, while complaints were at a building level.
2. Develop a network of complaint managers, so that they could provide support and consultation for each other.
3. Mount a publicity campaign in the professional community and the community at large about the concept of complaint management and the state-of-the-art training that district managers had received.
4. Develop a list of criteria for the selection of appropriate complaint managers, discussed criteria with principals, and reassigned people where necessary.
5. Print buttons and small posters designating complaint managers.

Her goal was to give more authority to complaint managers so that their recommendations would have greater likelihood of acceptance. She also saw the need to use her time to handle the most serious complaints.

Case D: Redefining the Target Group.

The Director of Guidance in a small school district was frustrated with the slow change in gender enrollment patterns in elective courses. Few boys chose secretarial courses and few girls chose machine repair, even though the district had run several nontraditional career fairs. He decided the best tactic would be to change the school rather than the students, by getting beginning word processing in the writing curriculum and beginning machine repair in the required science curriculum. He started the effort by:

1. Talking with the Director of Curriculum, a long-time friend, to secure cooperation and ideas.
2. Establishing a school/industry advisory group including potential donors of equipment and advocates of the project.
3. Encouraging several outspoken community members in favor of the idea to talk to teachers, curriculum committee members, and school board members.
4. Gathering preliminary information about available resources for training teachers in these skills.

His goal was to redefine the problem and enlarge support for it, using his legitimate role as career advisor. His greatest potential danger was a territory issue, which he felt confident of overcoming because of his long-term friendship with the Director of Curriculum.

Summary

This chapter has outlined a number of considerations for school administrators to weigh in deciding how to translate sex equity policy into actual school programs. Many of the strategies suggested focus around counteracting the discounted authority, or lowered status, of the administrator who becomes an equity advocate. Understanding roles in the organization and borrowing authority from channels perceived as more legitimate is one main route. The other is by becoming an expert in the substantive aspects of sex equity. Setting reasonable goals, finding the best models and resources, expecting results, carrying through on consequences and rewarding yourself and your colleagues should help lead your program to effective sex equity change.

REFERENCES

Moody, C.D., Sr. On becoming a superintendent: Contest or sponsored mobility. *The journal of negro education*, 1983, *52* (4), 383–397.

Center for Sex Equity in Schools, University of Michigan. *Title IX line.* Issues on sex equity in public policy (Spring, 1984), *4* (3); Sexual harassment (Fall, 1983), *4* (1); Women in literature: Historical images of work (Spring, 1985), *5* (2); Fostering sex equity in math (Winter, 1986), *6* (1); Women's history: Women and work (Winter, 1984), *4* (2); Women in administration (Spring, 1983), *3* (2); Comparable worth (Winter, 1985), *5* (1).

University of Michigan. Effective schools. *Breakthrough,* Winter, 1982, *10* (2).

University of Michigan. Equity and the change agent. *Breakthrough,* Spring, 1985, *13* (1).

The following statements are designed for the exploration of personal reactions to the chapter, as well as for the review of the contents of the chapter. Emphasis in discussions should be on exploring issues in depth, rather than on determining the correct or appropriate responses.

FOR DISCUSSION:

1. What points from this article would you share with superordinates? How would you relay the information?
2. What does the author mean by the statement: " . . . only those in administrative positions will be able to carry out change in the ways described here"?
3. The author states: "It may be necessary to find the real power (in the institution) and get its support." Review your institution and determine who in the hierarchy has the interest and the power to institutionalize change.
4. Identify key personnel in your institution and community who can be visibly supportive of attempts to provide sex fair education.
5. What barriers specifically related to your institution are not discussed in this article? What support exists in your institution? How can the support eliminate the barriers?
6. Compare Cases A and B to the process of decision-making and program implementation in your institution.
7. Compare Cases C and D to the process of decision-making and program implementation in your institution.
8. Review the tables provided in this article to determine where you may provide assistance.

SUGGESTIONS FOR FURTHER READING

Denbo, S. *A school principal's guide to incentives to promote educational equity for girls and boys.* College Park, Maryland: Ellis Associates, Inc., 1981.

Grayson, D. *The equity principal.* Los Angeles, California: Los Angeles County Office of Education, 1986.

Guthrie, E., & Miller, W.C. *Making change: A guide to effectiveness in groups.* Minneapolis, Minnesota: Interpersonal Communication Programs, Inc., 1978.

Kanter, R.M. *Men and women of the corporation.* New York: Basic Books, 1977.

Kaser, J. *Count me in! Guidelines for enhancing participation in mixed gender groups.* Andover, Massachusetts: The Network, 1985.

Pennsylvania Department of Education. *Self-study guide to sexism in schools.* Harrisburg, Pennsylvania, 1977.

Project on the Status and Education of Women. *Guide to nonsexist language.* Washington, D.C.: Association of American Colleges, 1986.

Sarason, S. *The culture of the school and the problem of change.* Newton, Massachusetts: Allyn & Bacon, 1982.

Vetter, L., Burkhardt, C., & Sechler, J. *Vocational education sex equity strategies.* Columbus, Ohio: The National Center for Research in Vocational Education, 1978.

Vocational Education Equity Program. *For your civil rights information.* Pennsylvania Department of Education, 1986.

FOSTERING SEX EQUITY IN PUBLIC SCHOOL SYSTEMS: THE IMPORTANCE OF LOCAL PLANNING AND POLICYMAKING

Although periodic debates concerning the need, purpose, and appropriate setting for educating males and females can be traced to the very beginnings of organized education in this country, gender equity is a relatively new policy concept in American public education. This policy, which emerged in the mid 1960s and early 1970s within the context of a broader feminist and civil rights movement, has expanded in scope in the ensuing decade. It has been furthered by constitutional interpretations, legislative enactments, and administrative regulations originating at both the state and federal level.

The substance of this policy has been shaped by the concept of equal protection found in the Fourteenth Amendment and the Equal Rights Amendment adopted in numerous states. It has also been influenced by the principles embodied in Title IX and the Vocational Educational Amendments enacted by Congress in 1972 and 1976 respectively, as well as the administrative regulations promulgated by the U. S. Department of Education in conjunction with both laws.

The Equal Pay Act adopted in 1963 and the Equal Employment Opportunity Act enacted the succeeding year, both of which were extended to school districts and other governmental employers in 1972, also have served to explicate the meaning of gender equity, as has the Pregnancy Discrimination Act of 1978. Numerous judicial interpretations of these laws and those alluded to previously, have further clarified the legal obligations of educational agencies. Finally, in recent years a number of states have amended or supplemented their civil rights laws to bolster protections against discrimination based on gender. At least a dozen states have enacted laws specifically designed to apply to public school districts and guarantee sex equity in the provision of educational services and activities (Project on Equal Educational Rights, 1987).

Yet, within our governmental system, the actual provision of equitable educational opportunities and services depends primarily on local school system policy and the extent to which educators implement it at the district, building, and classroom level. The practice of sex equity policy at these levels, more than a generation after its articulation, is both encouraging and discouraging.

It is encouraging that significant progress has been made in increasing educator awareness of the issue and in promoting greater access to certain educational opportunities regardless of student gender. Substantial progress has been made, for instance, on the playing fields of our nation's schools where the number of females participating in interscholastic athletics increased by more than 570 percent between 1970 and 1978 (U. S. Commission on Civil Rights, 1980). Yet even in areas where considerable progress has been made, substantial discrepancies persist between male and female representation, participation, and achievement. Even in the area of athletics, where the number of females participating rose dramatically in the 1970s, the proportion of males playing interscholastic sports still exceeded the proportion of females by a margin of three to one at the end of the decade. Nor did the expansion of athletic opportunities diminish the patterns of sex segregation reflected in high school competition with fewer than 10 percent of all teams being coeducational and 7.7 percent of all athletes participating in coeducational competition in 1980 (U. S. Department of Education, 1982). In some areas of schooling the most recent generation of students has witnessed only miniscule progress, and in some cases even the erosion of prior levels of sex equity.

Within the vocational education curriculum, seven of nine occupational training programs had enrollments that were predominantly (70 percent or more) of one sex as recent as 1980. Not only were seven of the nine programs gender-identifiable, but 79 percent of all female students were concentrated in only two of the nine programs, those preparing students for office occupations or homemaking. Correspondingly, high proportion of males were concentrated in training programs for agricultural, industrial arts, technical and trade and industrial occupations (U. S. Department of Education, 1981).

Patterns of employment in public education have also changed little since the enactment of equal opportunity laws. Today's workforce is still largely stratified and substantially segregated along gender lines. Although representing over 60 percent of all professional educators, females constitute only about five percent of all superintendents, 15 percent of the nation's principals, and fewer than one in 20 of the craftworkers employed by school districts in 1980. Males were correspondingly overrepresented in these job classifications and underrepresented among the ranks of elementary teachers (16.7%), librarians (12.7%), and clerical workers (2.4%) (U. S. EEOC, 1981).

As these statistics suggest, sex equity continues to pose challenges to both local policymakers and those charged with implementing such policy in elementary and secondary school systems. The purpose of this chapter is to briefly explore how policymakers and implementors may respond to the challenge of translating the new legal mandate for sex equity into local policy and practice. In doing so, it addresses the following questions: What factors influence policy compliance, implementation, and impact? What are the components and characteristics of effective school district policies and implementation plans? How can such policies and plans be developed? And, what approaches and strategies can district and building level administrators employ to enhance the implementation of equity policies?

Factors Influencing Compliance, Implementation and Impact

A variety of factors may influence organizational compliance, policy implementation, and the ultimate impact of federal and state sex equity policies. An understanding of these factors will help us appreciate not only the obstacles to attaining sex equity, but also the approaches and strategies that may be most effective in furthering this public policy goal.

Before examining some of these factors, however, it is important to define several important concepts associated with translating any new policy into practice. These include the concepts of compliance, implementation, and impact. For our purposes, "compliance" refers to the decision of a school district or individual to either ignore or conform to the mandates of the new policy. "Implementation" refers to the series of activities that a school district or educator engages in to translate policy goals and directives into meaningful programs and practices. "Impact" refers to both the intended and unintended effects that implementation activities have on the attainment of policy objectives.

An appreciation of these concepts suggests the complexity of using federal or state policy as a vehicle for organizational change. Numerous decisions, consciously or unconsciously made at various times and junctures, will affect the extent and rate of progress in achieving sex equity. The lack of progress, for instance, may be attributable to the decision of school officials not to comply with the policy, or to do so on a selective or gradual basis. Even in those districts that embrace the policy enthusiastically, progress may not be evident, because no programs or activities have been designed to promote the policy, or those that have been designed have not been adequately implemented. Nor, however, is a decision to comply and implement planned activities a guarantee that the impact of the policy will coincide with intended outcomes. The implementation approach or activities, whether dictated by the federal or state policy or chosen by the local school district, may simply be inappropriate or inadequate to overcome the conditions which the policy seeks to correct. These concepts of compliance, implementation, and impact may thus also be useful in assessing the plausible explanations for the lack of progress in realizing intended policy outcomes within any organizational context.

While there may be little agreement among those engaged in policy research regarding the relative importance of various factors, or the most appropriate theory to explain the relationship of such factors, a common core of variables has emerged as important determinants of policy compliance, implementation, and impact. They include: (1) the nature of the problem; (2) the characteristics of the policy; (3) the capacity and legitimacy of the policymaking agency; (4) the nature of the implementing organization; (5) the disposition and ability of local implementors; and (6) the societal setting and environmental conditions in which both the policymaking and implementing agencies operate (Baum, 1980; Boyum et al., 1972; Dolbeare & Hammond 1971; Gardiner, 1977; Gross, 1971; Milstein, 1980; Pressman and Wildavsky, 1973; Sabatier and Mazmanian, 1979; Van Horn and Van Meter, 1977; Williams, 1982).

For purposes of this chapter, the nature of the problem is the traditional translation of sex role stereotypes into actual practice in an educational setting. The characteristics of the sex equity policy as designed by the policymaking agencies at the state and federal level translated by school districts into meaningful local policy include the clarity of the policy and the basis or rationale underlying it, the nature of the charge mandated and the degree to which implementation standards and responsibilities are set out, and the extent to which the policy provides new resources to facilitate compliance and/or penalties and enforcement mechanisms to discourage noncompliance.

In terms of clarity, implementation is generally enhanced if the policy includes a clear and unequivocal statement of its goals or purpose, clarifies the organizations to which and individuals to whom it applies, and emphasizes the obligatory nature of the responsibilities set out in it. Compliance and implementation are further enhanced to the extent that the policy articulates a rationale for its adoption which is compatible with the ideology or prior policy of the implementing organization, or else is supported by a substantial body of consistent educational research or authoritative legal precedent (Bullock, 1980; Grossman, 1972; Krislov, et al., 1972; Becker and Feeley, 1973).

In addition, environmental conditions may influence not only the formulation and content of the policy, but also its implementation and impact. Such conditions include changes in the nature or magnitude of the problem that the policy is designed to address; advances in research or technology regarding how the problem may be resolved; and shifts in the law on which the policy is predicated; or in the relative priority accorded the policy by the public agencies responsible for its enforcement, as well as its implementation. Changes in the level and intensity of public support or opposition to the policy and variations in the size, cohesion, and resources of special-interest or beneficiary groups may also have a substantial effect on policy implementation. Finally, fluctuations in the economy may expand or contract public resources available to support the policy, thereby necessitating a thorough reevaluation of the feasibility, relative priority, manner and rate of policy implementation (Sabatier and Mazmanian, 1979; Van Horn and Van Meter, 1977).

The Implementing Organization

The characteristics of the organization charged with implementing the policy may also affect the manner and extent to which it is implemented (Gross, Giacquinta, and Bernstein, Van Horn and Van Meter, 1977). Traditionally, many organizations, including school systems, are considered bureaucratic in nature, characterized by a hierarchial structure, a highly specialized division of labor, and strict routines governing the work of lower level officials. In such organizations, new policy mandates announced by the leadership are integrated into organizational practice by adapting and adjusting work routines to ensure compliance.

While this approach may be appropriate and effective in certain organizations, research indicates that school systems are far from bureaucratic in their operation. Instead they are characterized by the semi-autonomous nature of each school unit and the substantial discretion afforded each building administrator and the classroom professionals over which they exercise general supervision. This characteristic of schools contributes to limited organizational control. Consequently, even where there is a relatively unambiguous policy, ensuring conduct that complies with policy expectations throughout such a loosely-coupled organization is often exceedingly difficult (Milstein, 1980; House, 1974; Meyer, 1978; Weatherly and Lipsky, 1977; and Weick, 1976).

Thus for example, although a district has adopted an affirmative action plan and charged the personnel director with its implementation, in many districts principals are commonly afforded substantial decision-making authority over the hiring and assignment of personnel to their respective buildings. Their exercise of what constitutes a choice among a prescreened set of applicants may serve to undermine district progress in achieving affirmative action goals. Secondary department chairs, while under the direct authority of the building principal may also be supervised by and responsible to a district-level curriculum coordinator, an arrangement that serves to insulate the chairperson from the complete control of either with potential negative implications for sex equity initiates originating at the district or the building level. Coaches function under a similar arrangement, nominally under the supervision of the principal, but also subject to the authority of the district athletic director. To the extent that the personnel director and the principal, or the principal and the curriculum coordinator or athletic director, have varying perceptions of organizational goals or the importance of various policies and practices, such an organizational structure permits and may even promote noncompliance or the lack of policy implementation.

The Implementors

The skills and disposition of those charged with carrying out the policy have a significant effect on the degree to which policy is implemented and the extent to which intended outcomes are realized. While this is true irrespective of the nature of the organization, the disposition and skill of the implementors may be particularly important in loosely-coupled organizations where professionals enjoy considerable discretion as the result of control and accountability mechanisms that are poorly developed or infrequently exercised.

Implementation of sex equity principles requires the affirmative approval of the local school board along with active administrative leadership. Even though their authority to effect change may be less than commonly presumed, the superintendent and other administrative staff must make a conscious decision that the organization will acknowledge the policy and work toward its implementation. To the extent that the policy is to be implemented at the building or classroom level, the attitudes of principals and teachers toward compliance are also important. Their disposition toward the new policy may revolve around whether the policy coincides or conflicts with fundamental personal values or professional philosophies, reinforces or distracts from other organizational purposes and priorities, or facilitates or disrupts established work processes and methods considered effective by lower level implementors.

In reality, many lower-level implementors have a substantial say in determining whether a new policy is implemented at all, and if implemented, the form it actually takes in practice (Baum, 1980; Doig, 1978; Elmore, 1978; Weatherby and Lipsky, 1977). Naturally, the likelihood or extent of implementation is influenced strongly at this level by the problems the new policy poses to the unit's goals or method of work. The adoption of coeducational physical education classes, for example, may be resisted because it requires, or may be perceived to require, changes in how staff are assigned, the variety of activities incorporated in a course, the grading system employed, and even the method by which locker rooms are supervised. While these have not proven to be insurmountable problems, they may seem so, particularly where the individual teacher has personal reservations regarding the physical, social, and psychological advisability of such coeducational instruction or competition. Similarly, if teachers of advanced math and science courses feel their national merit scholar production will drop as the result of adopting a less competitive and more cooperative instructional approach in their classes, they may be expected to resist such approaches, even if their conduct has the effect of discouraging female representation in advanced courses.

Where the new policy is largely compatible with individual values and organizational priorities, it may nevertheless require new skills and abilities among those charged with its implementation. Secondary math and science teachers for instance may need to be familiarized with research on the differential effectiveness of various instructional techniques for male and female students and the means of implementing a variety of classroom approaches that are conducive to the learning styles of different students. Coaches of traditionally single-sex teams may need more information regarding the similarities and differences in psychological maturation as well as physiological development of male and female students and the implications of both on student recruitment, motivation, and appropriate coaching techniques.

New policies may require not only new technical knowledge and skills regarding the substantive aspects of the policy's implementation, but also new leadership skills in order to ensure the cooperation of those who are charged with actually implementing the new policy, including those who perceive compliance as antithetical to their interests or values. In this regard, superintendents, building principals, departmental chairpersons, athletic directors and others with substantial responsibility for ensuring the implementation of sex equity policies, may find it necessary to devise new leadership approaches and strategies to foster change among the individuals they supervise (Milstein, 1980; Chesler, et. al., 1978; Elmore, 1978). They may find it important for instance to adopt an organizational development rather than a bureaucratic approach to bring about certain types of change; or to engage in active negotiation with their subordinates and supervisors with respect to the prioritization of other competing goals and the reallocation of available resources. They may also find it advisable in some situations to emphasize the policy outcome and leave the precise means for attaining it to those charged with its implementation at the building or classroom level.

Characteristics of Effective Policies and Implementation Plans

Aware of the types of factors that may represent common obstacles to the full and effective implementation of state and federal educational policy, we next turn our attention to the characteristics of effective policies and some of the approaches and strategies that local officials may utilize to heighten the implementation of sex equity in their school districts. In order to be successful, school districts must face the dual challenge of first developing local policies governing gender equity and then devising strategic implementation plans.

The first challenge facing local school officials is to develop a clear vision and coherent policy concerning gender equity in the public schools. A cogent and persuasive educational rationale for pursuing it should also be established. A means must also be put in place to ensure that the policy is effectively communicated, not only to those responsible for implementing it, but also to those directly affected by it.

Because even a clear policy is not self-implementing, school districts must design and structure a process by which paper pronouncements are translated into meaningful practices. Thus, in addition to setting out a philosophy and principles to guide future action, policy must identify the components of a systematic plan of action that school officials will develop to facilitate the initial and continuing implementation of the policy. While the policy should leave specific implementation details to district officials, it should identify the administrative units or unit responsible for overall policy attainment, and clarify that local resources will be made available to support its implementation. Finally, the policy should ensure that a process is devised to provide on-going feedback regarding policy implementation and outcomes, along with a system of rewards and sanctions to encourage exemplary implementation efforts and discourage noncomplying conduct.

Such a policy provides clear organizational direction and a framework for facing the second major challenge, development of a detailed implementation plan for the period leading up to and through the initial cycle of policy implementation. The implementation plan serves to add specificity and an action-orientation to the district's policy by detailing a set of sequential activities that are to be undertaken in furtherance of the policy goals. Common components of implementation plans designed to compensate for inadequacies in federal and state equity policies are:

a. an expanded rationale for the policy;
b. explicit criteria to be used in organizational decision making;
c. operational standards to guide action;
d. specific approaches and activities that will be employed;
e. identification of the unit, role group, or individual responsible for each activity;
f. an explanation of the means of securing and coordinating resources; and the nature and frequency of evaluation and reporting with respect to implementation progress and policy impact; and
g. measures that will be used to evaluate accomplishment of the activity or achievement of the goal.

Local Policymaking: Process and Participants

Local school board policies afford one means of translating often abstract and sometimes ambiguous federal and state sex equity policies and principles into local practice. The need for such translation has been often overlooked entirely or else satisfied on a largely ad hoc basis. This is unfortunate since local school district policy serves a number of important purposes. The adoption of local policy heightens individual, organizational and community awareness of district goals and commitments. It also encourages the development of a well-thought-out educational philosophy of equity and provides a rationale to guide future actions. This philosophy may also permit the clarification of school and community expectations beyond what would otherwise be possible if definitions and principles were left to whatever the prevailing interpretation of applicable laws might be at any given point in time.

By clarifying goals, philosophies, and expectations, local policy facilitates efficient decision making and promotes consistency across various school units and among different school district officials. It also promotes continuity of district purpose and programs over time. Finally, policy adoption contributes to individual coordination and accountability, thereby enhancing overall organizational effectiveness, while at the same time decreasing the potential for disruptive litigation and costly school district liability. Because of the relatively recent emergence of gender equity as a policy, and the multiple sources and still evolving nature of legal precedent in this area, local sex equity policy takes on added significance. Yet the extent to which local policy serves these purposes and promotes the goal of sex equity is dependent on both the policymaking process and those who participate in it.

Process

The process used to develop policy recommendations will have a significant impact on their content. Historically, many school districts have practiced reactive rather than proactive policy development and adoption, resulting in piecemeal policies that are more responsive to a particular crisis than reflective of a carefully-thought-out educational philosophy or program. In order to develop comprehensive and considered sex equity policies, as well as in order to facilitate the involvement of participants with a broader array of perspectives and experiences, a more systematic policy formulation process is necessary. Figure 21-1 identifies the major steps in a policy formulation process, which is designed to encourage the development of comprehensive equity policy that incorporates the components and characteristics of effectiveness described in the preceding section.

Participants

The content and characteristics of a policy are also influenced by those who participate in its formulation. School boards are of course the legally-authorized policymaking bodies for local school districts. Increasingly, in the face of more complex issues and heterogeneous constituencies,

Figure 21-1
MODEL POLICY DEVELOPMENT PROCESS

Identification of Federal and State Sex Equity Policies
Determination of the Need for Local Policy Development or Revision
Identification of Persons to be Involved
Provision of Information & Training for Participants
Development of Proposed Policy
Submission of Policy to Others for Review
Revision & Preparation of Final Document
Submission to Board for Formal Adoption
Dissemination of Policy & Education of School Community
Implementation of Policy
Monitoring, Evaluation & Revision

school boards rely heavily on the superintendent and a small cadre of administrators to formulate policy recommendations for their consideration (Cistone, 1975). How does the composition of school boards and central administrative staff affect the content and adoption of sex equity policies? Given their general demographic characteristics, are boards and central administrators likely to be aware of sex equity issues? Sensitive to the causes for inequity? Familiar with remedial programs and strategies? Motivated to act decisively? Promptly?

While available data do not provide direct answers to these questions, the following profile of boards of education and school district administrative staffs may afford some insights into their respective orientations to the concept of educational equity. The average school board member is a married white male in his forties with children attending school in the system he serves. He has a college degree, is employed in a professional or managerial position and earns between $40–$50,000 annually. Women occupy two of the seven seats on the average board. They are overwhelmingly white, are married, and have school-aged children. Four of ten female board members are homemakers, while an equal proportion are employed as professionals or managers. As a group neither the males nor females on the average board are representative of the larger community they are elected to represent.

The organization of boards and their functioning may also reflect their orientation toward issues of gender and schooling. Before running for the board of education, three of four women report doing volunteer work at school and serving as an active member in the PTO/A. Only 35 and 50 percent of the male board members report similar prior volunteer work and PTO membership respectively. Not withstanding their greater experience in volunteer and PTO/A capacities, these female members are underrepresented in the highest leadership positions on their boards, constituting only 28.6 percent of all board presidents, although they comprise 36 percent of all board members and nearly 50 percent of the total populace. At the same time, females represent 55.1 percent of all those serving as board secretaries, a position which has historically been filled by females. Committee assignments also reflect traditional stereotypes of men's and women's work, with males overrepresented on subcommittees with responsibility for facilities, transportation, and budget, while females are overrepresented on board subcommittees overseeing textbook selection, curriculum, and public relations (Alvey, Underwood, and Fortune, 1986).

Women are also missing or substantially underrepresented among the ranks of administrative personnel most often involved in formulating policy recommendations. In 1980, females comprised only 20 percent of all district-level officials and managers (USEEOC, 1981). Even these female administrators were concentrated in a few substantive areas of responsibility such as curriculum and instruction, thereby further restricting the likelihood of their involvement in formulating policy recommendations across the full spectrum of district operations.

While the gender of participants in the policy recommendation process is an important reason for considering a more participatory model for policy development, it is not the only reason for doing so, nor necessarily even the most compelling one. In part, this is because there are not only substantial differences between males and females as groups but also within each group concerning the perceived importance of sex equity in the schools or the best way to achieve it. Consequently, the other, more compelling reason for broadening participation is its strategic importance in facilitating organizational change.

Conventional principles of planned change provide that anticipated change will be resisted to the degree that those affected by it have little or incorrect knowledge about the change, limited trust in those responsible for the change, and slight influence in controlling the nature and direction of the change (Bennis, Benne and Chin, 1969 and Corbett, 1984). Involving all members of the school community in policy development and in the planning, implementing, and monitoring of the policy helps reduce these common causes of resistance to change.

Participatory policy formulation represents an unusually effective forum for communicating the nature of problems associated with sex segregation and inequality and for increasing the knowledge of individuals about educational equity and its benefits. The participation of community leaders, parents, students, and educators in addition to district administrators may also facilitate better understanding between those ultimately charged with responsibility for policy implementation and those directly affected by it, thereby increasing the trust level and cooperation between these groups. The quality of plans may also be enhanced by wide participation, since more viewpoints and ideas may be presented than would be the case if responsibility was vested exclusively in a small group of school administrators and board members.

Participation also reduces the school community's feeling of powerlessness in controlling the change and thus lessens opposition to the form the final change takes. To the extent people perceive that their viewpoints are valued by school officials, even if not adopted, they will be more likely to consider the policy or plan their own, and advocate its adoption, and implementation. Involving people other than those employed by the district in promoting the policy and plan also serves a legitimizing function among other community members, while at the same time alerting district personnel to the existence of organized community concern regarding the implementation of the policy. In addition to adding valuable insights in the planning of appropriate programs, parents and community groups may provide a source of volunteers for facilitating policy implementation and monitoring.

For all these reasons, the use of a policymaking process that encourages and facilitates broad participation at the recommendatory stage may be advantageous, particularly in the formulation of sex equity policy. Naturally, responsibility for the final form such policy takes and its formal adoption must rest with the board of education.

Implementing Local Policy: Promising Approaches and Strategies

Even the adoption of a sex equity policy does not ensure its implementation or intended outcomes. There is simply no single solution to the gender differences and inequality that exist in the nation's public schools. As the Supreme Court has repeatedly acknowledged since 1954 with respect to racial segregation in the schools, "Full implementation of constitutional principles may require solution of varied local school problems..." including those associated with such factors as "administration, physical condition of facilities, personnel, modification of admissions policies, and revision of local regulations..." which may inhibit desegregation and educational equity (Brown v. Board of Education, II, 1955).

As has become increasingly apparent in the intervening years, the Court was accurate in determining that no uniform plan or approach can be superimposed on all districts in the nation, in one region of the country, or even in a single state. Consequently, school districts must focus on the implementation of equity policy not as a single act or even a static plan, but rather as a dynamic plan which is part of a continuing process. The objective of the process must be to elucidate, assess and find solutions to local problems that thwart the attainment of educational equity for all students.

An Approach To Policy Implementation

One approach I have found useful in working with school districts in addressing a variety of equity issues, is a phased-systems model for policy implementation. This approach, as I have employed it, consists of seven phases, each designed to alleviate a major pitfall in the efficient and effective implementation of equity policies. Briefly, these pitfalls include:

a. the lack of awareness and basic knowledge concerning the problem and its consequences;

b. the lack of comprehensive needs assessments to evaluate the nature and extent of the problem locally and the factors contributing to the existence of the problem;

c. the lack of experience in systematically developing both long- and short-range remedial plans;

d. the lack of technical knowledge and intergroup skills necessary to implement such plans;

e. the lack of systematic monitoring of the implementation and evaluation of the effectiveness of the plan and its component strategies; and

f. the lack of adequate information-sharing and dissemination regarding outcomes for the benefit of other buildings or similarly situated school districts.

The major steps or phases in implementing sex equity policies in school district settings coincides with overcoming the pitfalls identified above. These steps include building awareness, assessing needs, designing action plans and programs, developing organizational capacity and staff expertise, implementing the plans and programs, monitoring and evaluating their impact and effectiveness, and disseminating the results to other buildings or school districts. These steps or phases are set out in Figure 21-2, along with the objectives associated with each phase of the implementation process. This same phased-systems process may be employed regardless of whether a district is confronted with the development and implementation of a comprehensive gender equity plan or the resolution of specific discrimination problems, such as the sexual harassment of female students and employees or stereotypic counseling and placement of students in vocational education programs.

Strategies for Facilitating Policy Implementation

Given such a phased-systems approach, it is still necessary to identify strategies and specific activities that may be instituted to foster policy implementation at the district, building, and classroom level. While space precludes the enumeration of specific remedial activities pertaining to the myriad types of sex differences and inequalities that may be manifested in schools, it may be useful to briefly review some of the fundamental ways in which organizational compliance, implementation, and policy impact can be promoted. These include by means of not only policy, but also personnel, program, resources, and organizational rewards. Several strategies associated with each of these "levers for change" are set out in the accompanying inventory of illustrative implementation strategies (Vergon, 1984). School officials may draw from this catalogue of change strategies as they devise their own district or building level implementation plans. Even if the district has not adopted a comprehensive sex equity policy nor mandated the development of systematic implementation plans, individual administrators may find some of these strategies helpful for informally encouraging sex equity within the sphere of their responsibility.

Conclusion

Achieving sex equity in education represents a substantial and continuing challenge to school districts in the United States. Although meaningful progress has been made in many districts, much remains to be done. In some districts the lack of progress is attributable to a failure of compliance, in others it represents the failure to actively pursue implementation measures, and in still others it is the result

Figure 21-2.
A SYSTEMS APPROACH FOR IMPLEMENTING
SEX EQUITY POLICY IN THE PUBLIC SCHOOLS

Phase	*Objectives*
1.0 Awareness	To increase the awareness and knowledge level of school personnel and community members regarding (1) segregation and discrimination-related problems; (2) the implication of federal and state nondiscrimination laws for local policies, programs and practices; and (3) local sex equity policy and district goals.
2.0 Needs Assessment	To assist the district is systematically identifying segregation- and discrimination- related problems and contributing causes, as well as in evaluating the visibility of various alternative approaches to promote attainment of sex equity goals.
3.0 Implementation Planning	To facilitate development of district and building of departmental implementation plans to resolve identified sex equity problems. The plans should be devised in conjunction with affected parties as well as those responsible for implementing them. They should include specific steps and strategies, delegations of responsibility, timelines for the accomplishment of each step, and means of securing and coordinating necessary resources.
4.0 Preparation and Training	To develop in the school building or system the individual skills and the organizational capacity necessary to implement the sex equity policy and related implementation plan and programs.
5.0 Implementation	To implement the policy utilizing organizational structures and strategies embodied in the action plan and the heightened knowledge level and competencies of school personnel developed in the preceding phases.
6.0 Plan Monitoring, Evaluation and Follow-up	To institute a systematic monitoring process that both evaluates on an on-going basis, the effectiveness and efficiency of the plan in resolving the identified problems, and ensures the utilization of such information to bring about timely modifications in programs, plans and policies programmatic modifications as appropriate.
7.0 Model Dissemination	To disseminate to other school building districts as well as state education agencies the methods and models utilized to resolve sex segregation and discrimination related problems, along with an evaluation of their effectiveness.

of the failure to select appropriate approaches and effective strategies for bringing about the desired policy outcomes.

A number of factors may affect compliance, implementation and the impact of policy. These include factors associated with the problem, the policy, the implementing agency, the implementors, and the environment. One means of compensating for some of the deficiencies of federal and state sex equity laws is to translate them into local school district policy. This may be most effectively accomplished if a systematic and participatory process is used. The adoption of local policy, however, must be coupled with the development of a detailed implementation plan. In designing an implementation plan, school officials may find it useful to employ a variety of strategies including those focusing on policy, personnel, programs, resources and rewards. Such a plan should utilize these strategies to address various needs associated with planned organizational change, beginning with the need to develop awareness and concluding with the need to evaluate policy implementation and impact. A carefully formulated school district policy and a systematic implementation plan will contribute substantially to translating intergovernmental policy into the intended policy outcomes of educational equity for all students at the local school district level. A chart describing Strategies for Promoting the Implementation of Sex Equity Policy follows:

STRATEGIES FOR PROMOTING THE IMPLEMENTATION OF SEX EQUITY POLICY

I. Policy and Administrative Leadership

- develop or reaffirm district nondiscrimination policy statement.
- revise and expand policy statement to reflect affirmative commitment to sex equity and to clarify organizational expectations.
- emphasize and explain the importance of equity in public presentations and remarks before board, staff, community and civic organizations.
- place equity issues and status reports on the agenda of the board and administrative cabinet.
- create a district-wide advisory council on educational equity and ensure representative participation of females and males on it and all other district advisory committees.
- encourage females to run for the school board and leadership positions in professional associations.
- subscribe to, regularly read, and circulate one or more sex equity-oriented publications to maintain awareness.
- attend at least one sex equity conference annually to learn of new developments and innovative programs.

II. Program

- adopt equity as a priority goal for the district.
- initiate the readministration of the Title IX organizational self-assessment to determine areas of need.
- review complaints and grievances filed over the past twenty-four months to ascertain areas where attention may be needed.
- encourage the development of divisional and building level remedial or affirmative action plans as may be appropriate.
- establish a procedure for the review, approval and monitoring of these action plans.

III. Personnel

A. Sex Equity Coordinator

- assign or reassign responsibility for coordination of sex equity efforts.
- develop or clarify written job description and expectations associated with this position.
- upgrade the status of the position or assignment to reflect district commitment.
- expand the authority associated with the sex equity coordinator.
- increase the effort allotted or persons assigned to this function.

B. Other Personnel-Related Actions

- review all district policies, procedures and collective bargaining contracts, along with insurance and pension plans to ensure equal and equitable treatment of personnel irrespective of gender.
- conduct a workforce analysis and establish goals and timetables to correct underrepresentation of women and men in various work classifications.
- utilize demonstrated experience in and commitment to sex equity as a screening and selection criteria for new hires.
- introduce sex equity-related performance criteria into the instruments used to evaluate already employed administrators, teachers, and other employees.
- provide systematic opportunities for staff who demonstrate a lack of awareness to develop an appreciation for the educational importance of implementing equity programs and techniques.
- afford all staff periodic opportunities for staff development.

IV. Resources

- commit a reasonable and equitable amount of general fund dollars to support sex equity goals and programs.
- develop and submit proposals to various governmental and private foundation sources for supplemental monies to support major equity thrusts.
- promote cooperative projects with private business, labor, institutions of higher education and various public sector agencies that have ideas, materials, equipment, money, or staff resources and enthusiasm to contribute.
- establish, with the assistance of local foundations and organizations, an equity trust fund from which monies may be made available to support innovative programs developed by schools, individual teachers or community associations.
- establish and support one or more sex equity demonstration sites or projects to develop organizational capacity and human resources for subsequent districtwide programming.
- collect all the equity-oriented programs and activities developed by district personnel and publish them in an idea book for distribution to others across the district.
- create a sex equity resource center in conjunction with the existing instructional support office and media center.

V. Incentives/Reward Structure

- call public attention to equity activities taking place in your district.
- encourage the publication of positive press releases and feature articles that recognize innovative programs and the personnel responsible for them.
- utilize exemplary teachers and administrators as presenters and trainers in district-wide staff development programs.
- provide opportunities for equity sensitive employees to attend state, regional, and national conferences to further develop their leadership.
- establish an equity achievement award to honor a division, building, or individual student, employee, or community person for their outstanding contribution.
- provide monetary support for buildings and individual teachers for the development and implementation of equity projects.
- adopt and widely disseminate grievance procedures for discrimina-

tion and sexual harassment complaints as a means of promoting individual and organizational responsibility.
- thoroughly investigate complaints and take firm but fair action after a due process hearing against those who have been proven to have acted inappropriately.
- incorporate "equity awareness" and "commitment to program implementation" into district performance evaluation instruments.

REFERENCES

Alvery, D., K. Underwood, & J. Fortune. Our annual look at who you are and what's got you worried. *American school board journal,* 1986, *173,* 23–27.

Baum, L. The influence of legislatures and appellate courts over the policy implementation process. *Policy studies journal,* 1980, *8* (4), 560–574.

Becker, T., Feeley, M. (Eds.) *The impact of supreme court decisions.* New York: Oxford University Press, 1973.

Bennis, W., Benne, K., Chin, R. (Eds.). *The planning of change.* New York: Holt, Rinehart and Winston, 1969.

Boyum, K. Clark, J., Krislov, S., Shaefer, R., White, J. (Eds.). *Compliance and the law.* Beverly Hills: Sage, 1972.

Bullock, C. The Office for Civil Rights and the implementation of desegregation programs in the public schools. *Policy studies journal,* 1980, *8* (4), 597–616.

Center for National Policy Review. *Justice delayed and denied.* Washington, D.C.: Catholic University, 1974.

Chesler, M., B. Bryant and J. Crowfoot. Institutional changes to support school desegregation. *Law and contemporary problems,* 1978, *42* (4). 174–213.

Cistone, E. *Understanding school boards.* Lexington: Lexington Books, 1975.

Corbett, et. al. *School context and school change.* New York: Teachers College, Columbia University Press, 1984.

Doig, J. Police policy and police behavior: Patterns of divergence. *Policy studies journal,* 1978, *7,* 436–442.

Dolbeare, K. and P. Hammond. *The school prayer decisions.* Chicago: University of Chicago Press, 1971.

Elmore, R. Organizational models of social program implementation. *Public policy,* 1978, *26,* 185–228.

Gardiner, J. *Public law and public policy.* New York; Praeger, 1977.

Glazer, N. Towards an imperial judiciary? *The public interest,* 1975, *41,* 104–123.

Gross, N., J. Giacquinta and M. Bernstein. *Implementing organizational innovations.* New York: Basic Books, 1971.

Grossman, J. The Supreme Court and social change. *American behavioral scientist,* 1972, *13,* 535–552.

Guba, E. The effect of definitions of policy on the nature and outcomes of policy analysis. *Educational leadership,* 1984, *42,* 63–70.

House, E. *The politics of educational innovation.* Berkeley: McCutcheon, 1974.

Johnson, R. *The dynamics of compliance.* Evanston: Northwestern University Press, 1967.

Klein, S. A. Examining the achievement of sex equity in and through education. In (Klein, Ed.), *Handbook for achieving sex equity through education,* Baltimore: John Hopkins Press, 1985.

Krislov, S., K. Boyum, J. Clark, R. Schaefer & S. White (Eds.). *Compliance and the law.* Beverly Hills: Sage Publications, 1972.

Martin, W. *The American sisterhood.* New York: Harper and Row, 1972.

Meyer, J. (Ed.) *Organizations and environments.* San Francisco: Jossey-Bass, 1978.

Milstein, M. (Ed.) *Schools, conflict and change.* New York: Teachers College Press, 1980.

Pressman, J. & A. Wildavsky. *Implementation.* Berkeley: University of California Press, 1973.

Project on Equal Educational Rights. *Beyond Title IX.* Washington, D.C.: NOW Legal Defense and Education Fund, 1987.

Project on Equal Educational Rights. *Stalled at the start: government action on sex bias in the schools.* Washington, D.C.: NOW Legal Defense and Education Fund, 1976.

Sabatier, P. & D. Mazmanian. The implementation of public policy: a framework of analysis. *Policy studies journal,* 1980, *8* (2), 538–560.

Sabatier, P. & D. Mazmanian. The conditions of effective implementation. *Policy analysis,* 1979, *5,* 481–504.

Sorg, J. A typology of implementation behaviors of street-level bureaucrats. *Policy studies review,* 1983, *2,* 391–406.

Stockard, J. (Ed.). *Sex equity in education.* New York: Academic Press, 1980.

U. S. Commission on Civil Rights. *More hurdles to clear: women and girls in competitive athletics.* Washington, D.C., 1980.

U. S. Dept. of Education. *The condition of education: 1981 edition.* Washington, D.C.: National Center for Educational Statistics, 1981.

U. S. Dept. of Education. *National school civil rights survey.* Washington, D.C.: Office for Civil Rights, 1982.

U. S. Equal Employment Opportunity Commission. *Report of minorities and women in public elementary and secondary schools (1979).* Washington, D.C., 1981.

Van Horn, C. & D. van Meter. The implementation of intergovernmental policy. *Policy studies annual review,* 1977, *1,* 97–120.

Vergon, C. Administrative strategies for promoting sex equity. *Title IX line,* 1984, *6* (3), 9–12.

Wasby, S. *The impact of the United States supreme court.* Homewood: Dorsey Press, 1970.

Weatherly, R. & M. Lipsky. Street-level bureaucrats and institutional innovation: Implementing special education reform. *Harvard educational review,* 1977, *47,* 171–197.

Weick, K. Educational organizations as loosely-coupled systems. *Administrative science quarterly,* 1976, *21* (1), 1–19.

Williams, W. (Ed.) *Studying implementations: Methodological and administrative issues,*
    Chatam: Chatham House Publishers, 1982.
Yudof, M. Implementation theories and desegregation realities. *Alabama law review,*
    1981, *32,* 441–464.

The following statements are designed for the exploration of personal reactions to the chapter, as well as for the review of the contents of the chapter. Emphasis in discussions should be on exploring issues in depth, rather than on determining the correct or appropriate responses.

FOR DISCUSSION:

1. Who in your educational organization would be responsible for planning and implementing sex equity policy?
2. Review the author's chart on Strategies for Promoting the Implementation of Sex Equity Policy. Identify activities that are already being conducted in your educational institution.
3. Discuss the author's statement: "Implementation of sex equity principles requires the affirmative approval of the local school board along with active administrative leadership."
4. What role do teachers play in forming district-wide sex equity policy?
5. How is an educational organization protected by a strong sex equity policy?
6. What points could be emphasized to policy-makers in an attempt to encourage them to "adopt equity as a priority goal for the district."?
7. Discuss the author's statement: "The semi-autonomous nature of each school unit . . . contributes to limited organizational control."
8. What additional planning and policymaking variables should be considered for large urban districts and for small rural districts?

SUGGESTIONS FOR FURTHER READING

Bryant, B.I., Chesler, M.A., & Crowfoot, J. *Making desegregation work: A professional guide to effecting change.* Beverly Hills, California: Sage Publications, 1981.

California State Department of Education. *Summary of California education code statutes pertaining to sex equity in education in elementary and secondary schools.* Sacramento, California, 1986.

Council of Chief State School Officers-Resource Center on Educational Equity. *Equity training for state education agency staff.* Washington, D.C., 1986.

Council of Chief State School Officers-Resource Center on Educational Equity. *Policies for the future.* Washington, D.C., 1982.

Kane, R. *Sex discrimination in schools: Evaluating employment practices.* Newton, Massachusetts: EDC/WEEA, 1979.

Klein, S. (Ed.). *Handbook for achieving sex equity through education.* Baltimore, Maryland: Johns Hopkins University Press, 1985.

Sandler, B. *The campus climate revisited: Chilly for women faculty, administrators, and graduate students.* Washington, D.C.: Project on the Status and Education of Women, 1986.

Schmuck, P., & Charters, W.W. (Eds.). *Education policy and management: Sex differentials.* New York: Academic Press, 1981.

Sindelar, L. *Hiring procedures.* Newton, Massachusetts: EDC/WEEA, 1982.

University Council on Educational Administration. *Overcoming sex disequity in educational administration: Eliminating persistent barriers through the development of an instrument for department self assessment and a model for institutional change.* Tempe, Arizona, 1986.

Chapter 22

ILLUSIONS:
WOMEN IN EDUCATIONAL ADMINISTRATION

Jean R. Feldman
Margaret Jorgensen
Eve Poling

INTRODUCTION

"But how can she decide if the high school roof needs repair?"

A cursory observation of schools can quickly reveal that women teach and men run the district. Occasionally a woman will hold an administrative position, usually in middle management or at the elementary level. As progress is made towards equity in other educational domains, women continue to be shut out of positions of decision-making power. They have some authority over their students, but little to say about policy, budget, community relations, school philosophy, or programs.

There are those who assert that women cannot meet the qualifications of an administrator. In fact, some believe that women prefer the classroom and do not actively pursue experiences that may lead to positions of authority. Others claim that women put family first, or cannot handle "tough jobs" such as discipline, budget decisions, and building maintenance.

The facts refute many of the explanations. Women have the degrees and the experience. Their socialization often provides them with unique, effective problem-solving skills (even for the "tough jobs"). They aspire to move out of the classroom into the ranks of administration.

But the barriers to women are high and wide. Traditional images of women (poor leaders, indecisive, poor at math, and so forth) often cause employers such as school boards, consultants, and superintendents to demand more from women applicants. The "old boys network" limits employers' knowledge about potential candidates. Over and over again, women who even make it to the interview are ruled out in the end. The number of women in administration has not changed significantly in decades.

The implication is that men are in the positions to hire, and, therefore, men are intentionally keeping women out. Although cases of that nature may exist, it is a combination of factors that keep women in the classrooms. Men who are concerned about seeking out the finest employees work hard at gender blindness. They often are mentors for women who aspire towards administrative positions. They encourage women who demonstrate leadership, but who have not indicated an interest in moving up, to pursue administrative training.

Many women do not have the confidence to pursue higher level positions. They, too, have been told that women cannot handle the difficult decisions and demanding responsibilities of an administrator. Since role models are negligible, they are often unaware of their own potential and of employment possibilities.

Margaret Weber Jorgensen, Jean Feldman, and Eve Poling discuss strategies for increasing the number of women in the upper ranks of the educational system.

ILLUSIONS—WOMEN IN EDUCATIONAL ADMINISTRATION

The decade of the eighties promised a great deal for women seeking careers outside the home. Building on the legislative actions of the seventies and the momentum built from societal pressure for equity, women have made significant strides into previously male-dominated employment areas. Increasing numbers of women are entering previously male-dominated fields. Women are working on construction crews. Women are teamsters. They are successful politicians. And, of course, they are, as in the past, teachers. They are *not* educational administrators; women staff the classrooms, but they are not the decision-makers in education.

It is ironic that in education, one of the professional fields where women have dominated in sheer numbers, they have made *no* progress in gaining access to positions of power. Indeed, the opposite has happened. Women have constituted a majority in the teaching profession since the 1920s, but they have held proportionately fewer and fewer administrative positions.

As the 1990s approach and the decade of promise for women comes to a close, it is time to examine the reasons why women have not been successful in entering the power structure in education. What is it about educational administrations that makes it so resistant to attempts by women to gain access? What is it about women, their roles, and attributes, that makes administrative positions in education unattainable? Why has education been so resistant to change when other professions with deeper roots in male dominance, such as law and medicine, have been more responsive to equity concerns?

The 1980s seemed to set the perfect stage for women to move into administrative positions in education. Certainly there were many, many women with qualifications, and there was a growing pressure to change the educational system to accommodate increasing technological pressures for a different kind of literate society. The pressures for "Excellence in Education" are wide-spread and deep-rooted. The increasing demand to teach not only the basics, but to equip our youth with the skills to allow them to flourish in a technologically sophisticated world and to enable our nation to compete economically in world markets with an increasingly service-oriented base, places an enormous burden on the schools of this country. Seemingly, all was ready for women to take

335

control of the educational system, since the recent history of educational administration had failed to produce the outcomes demanded. Unfortunately, criticism of education frequently became criticism of women.

The apparent inability of the public school system as it is currently operated continues to reinforce the stereotype that women, even as managers of classroom learning, are ineffective. This criticism seems to extend into the administrative ranks; if women cannot produce in one classroom, certainly they cannot produce as a manager of many classrooms.

The focus of this discussion is to examine why women have made *no* progress in gaining proportional representation in educational administration, and to suggest how women might tackle the challenges persisting in the field and how they might succeed over new pressures introduced during the 1980s.

Historical Overview

During the period encompassing the two World Wars, the shortage of men in the labor force opened many administrative opportunities to women in education. In 1928, 55 percent of all elementary school principals were women. However, by 1948, men had returned in droves to enter the labor force and this percentage had declined to 41 percent. This decline has continued steadily.

Year	Percentage of Women Principals
1928	55
1948	41
1958	38
1968	22
1971	21
1973	20
1984	18

NEA, 1973; NEA, 1981; Educator Opinion Poll, 1985.

The lack of progress for women, in what should be one of the more accessible power structures, makes it clear that relatively impermeable boundaries exist which separate the world of the teacher from that of the administrator. Schmuck (1975) describes men as the gatekeepers to the profession of school management. The data from the seventies and early eighties certainly support her statement. In essence, the top echelon in education (the decision-makers, role models, and power-brokers) is drawn from only male teachers. Since males constitute approximately one-third of the population of teachers, females in the profession are clearly an underutilized resource. Despite increasing awareness in society that women must not be denied equal access, women who do seek careers in educational administration find that equality of the sexes is a legislated reality that becomes illusion in practice. The educational system in the United States is generally structured as a traditional home: men run the schools and women nurture the learners (Loomis and Wild, 1978).

Men not only dominate control of the school building but also other levels of the educational structure in this country. Men fill the majority of positions in state level departments of education. Men are the chief state school officers in nearly every state and they staff most school board positions. Programs to train educational administrators on college and university campuses are staffed by men at the 98 percent level (Silver, 1977), and men staff research agencies specializing in educational issues. In short, women remain the workhorses of the profession and men call the shots!

The disproportionate representation of women in administrative positions is found at all levels of education. The statistics vary slightly from source to source, but in fact the evidence is undeniable: women are a clear minority in educational management. Only 18 percent of school principals are women; fewer than 5 percent of all superintendencies are held by women (Educator Opinion Poll, 1984). Fauth's (1984) data is even more abysmal. She claims that overall, only 12 percent of all public school principals are women: 20 percent of elementary school principals are women and 4 percent of secondary school principals are women. Fauth claims that even when adding the number of women who hold assistant principalships, the overall percentage barely reaches 18.

Recent data from the U.S. Department of Labor indicates that 84.5 percent of the elementary teachers are female and 49.5 percent of the secondary teachers are female. But where are the women administrators? Can it be that there are so few women who are capable of managing a school? Can it be that there are so few women who *want* to manage a school? Do women enter the education profession only to teach?

The reasons for the persistence of low percentages of women in educational leadership positions are complex and, to a large degree, difficult to identify. Fortunately, the continuing press for educational reform gives incentive to examine the inequity in educational administration. During the last years of the twentieth century, educators are facing an unavoidable self-examination into management practices. Will the schools continue to be "sanctuaries for the imcompetent?" (Pipho, 1978), or will education as a profession reexamine its structure and effect change which will make equity meaningful? This is the optimism for women and for education.

Key Factors and Targets for Change

Before discussing the current environment and context for change, it is important to understand factors which may have inhibited women from assuming leadership positions. Certainly the psychological, societal, and political theories provide explanations for persistent and pervasive underrepresentation of women in positions of power in education.

This discussion will focus on these key factors and targets for change:

> Personal and Social Roles
> Aspiration Levels
> Personal and Family Constraints
> Discriminatory Employment Practices
> Attitudes About Administration

Personal and Social Roles

To understand why women have occupied primarily low-ranking positions in the field of education, one can look at the traditional female role. Sex roles are learned cultural prescriptions and they have social expectations. Desirable male adult traits include dominance, achievement, autonomy, and aggression. Such traits are also commonly associated with "leadership" (Maccoby and Jacklin, 1974). In contrast, accepted standards of behavior for adult women are those not generally associated with leadership, such as emotionalism, self-abasement, passivity, deference (Bach, 1976). Thus women are conditioned by societal expectations in ways which are antithetical to leadership roles.

Numerous research projects have identified at least a dozen statements of beliefs espoused by male administrators in education which testify to the persistence of these traditional role perceptions for men and women. Such statements include:

Women should mainly be responsible for their husbands and
   children.
Women can't handle discipline problems.
Women are too emotional.
Women should not be aggressive.
Women are indecisive. (Little, 1983)

Women also view themselves as having stereotypic characteristics which
inhibit them as managers. They often see themselves as less competent,
less independent, less objective, and less logical than men (Broverman et
al., 1972; Schmuck, 1975). Little (1983, p. 79) claims that "the female
educational leader is usually one who has overcome her acculturation
toward timidity and self-abasement . . . "

Case #1

Perhaps this accounts for the career path of Susan N. She taught for
fifteen years in primary and elementary grades, serving as Lead Teacher
for five, and coordinating district-wide curriculum committees. It was
not until her male principal resigned in the middle of the academic year,
leaving the school without leadership, that Susan N. became assertive
enough to point out to the local school board that she could effectively
manage the school for the remainder of the year. Undoubtedly, the
school board's willingness to give Susan N. the opportunity to assume
the principalship was as much motivated by convenience as anything
else. And her willingness to serve as principal was probably a result of
her emotional attachment to the school and her need to see it continue to
run smoothly. Susan's experience as an acting principal was positive but
when she applied for the permanent position, the experience quickly
became a nightmare. She competed in the traditional interview setting
and at least superficially won the support of the superintendent. However,
when the superintendent presented the motion to name Susan N. as the
new principal in a regular position, the motion died for lack of a second.
A man was appointed at the next board meeting.

The reality facing the women who choose to pursue a position in
educational administration is that men and women hold stereotypic
beliefs which inhibit women both internally and externally. Unfortunately,
traditional role perceptions seem to be more powerful than do research
findings on effective leadership.

Aspiration Level

Many studies suggest that women prefer to remain in the classroom. Niedermayer and Kramer (1974) describe this as the path of least resistance. There are noticeable differences in the aspiration levels of male and female beginning teachers. For example, men are far more likely than women to indicate at the outset of their career that they intend to go into administration (Mason, 1961; Fishel and Pottker, 1974; Educator's Opinion Poll, 1984). Schmuck (1975) also found that men were more persistent than women and that they tended to reapply for administrative positions much more frequently than women.

Men seem to seek advancement to positions of power in education because of internal motivations. In contrast, women are more likely to aspire to positions in educational administration because of the influence and persuasion of others (Schmuck, 1975). The likelihood of accepting leadership positions tends to decrease for women as the level of responsibility increases (McMillan, 1975). Further, women seem to be "place-bound," rather than "career-bound" (Carlson, 1972). This is clearly supported by the data from the 1984 Educator Opinion Poll, which shows that women tend to remain in the teaching field many more years before becoming administrators than do men.

Kanter (1977) identified three variables that can have an important impact on the aspiration and advancement of women in educational administration: structure of opportunity in the organization, structure of power in the individual, and the proportional distribution of people at different levels in the organization. None of these three variables is under the control of the individual. Constraints imposed by societal expectations and the effects of opportunity, power, and number require organizations, not people, to change.

Case #2

Do women "see the handwriting on the wall?" regarding their chances of successfully aspiring to positions in educational administration? Certainly that is the reality for Alice S. Her career goal during her undergraduate years was to be a master teacher. She believed strongly that her contribution to education was to be made at the classroom level. Alice's mother had been a teacher and her father had been a principal, and Alice knew the importance of high quality teaching. Alice's plan was to spend three years in the classroom and then return to complete graduate work on a part-time basis while she continued to practice her trade. Her graduate work was in curriculum, with a speciality in reading. She felt that these credentials would allow her to eventually become a resource teacher in reading. Alice lived her plan and became a reading resource teacher in 1979. However, in 1981, her district's budget was cut, and her position was eliminated. In 1982, Alice left education because she felt she had reached a "dead-end" and was no longer able to implement change.

Personal and Family Constraints

The traditional role for a woman is in her home, dedicated to her husband and children. A woman's career is often regarded as supplementary to her domestic role and to her husband's income. Even when the female in the household earns more than the male, this belief persists. Despite the fact that 70 percent of all adult women work (U.S. Census Bureau, 1986). Almost one-half (45%) of all mothers with children between the ages of 6 and 17 in a two-parent family work outside the home. One-third (32%) of the mothers with children between the ages of 3 and 5 are working and one-fourth (23%) who have children under the age of 3 work outside the home (Women's Bureau, Department of Labor, 1985).

Women must resolve conflicts among family responsibilities, career aspirations, and the perceived characteristics of leadership. For example, although the job of a teacher is socially compatible with the female role (Niedermayer and Kramer, 1974), it is traditionally considered to be a supplementary occupation. On the other hand, leadership positions are incompatible with the female role. Thus, a woman educator may feel that she must choose between an "acceptable" or "unacceptable" female job. Certainly, women in educational administration have resolved that conflict in a way that denies traditional options such as family.

Women who hold positions as principals are less likely to be married than are men in similar positions. Women are less likely to have young children than are men. So, women have made the choice. Either they delay holding administrative positions until the stress of raising a family has lessened or they choose career over family.

Competing demands between the professional role and the mothering role cannot be conveniently manipulated when the women's career status is traditionally secondary to the male's. In this case, the woman is twice victim to conflict: conflict exists within her roles as professional and mother, and between herself and mate in their respective parental and career roles. Even outside the context of the family, women are assumed to be playing the supplementary role and may be considered to be a less viable applicant for an administrative position because of this traditional view.

Psychological stress from such conflict may account for the results of studies reported by Krchniak (1978), Gross and Task (1976) and others. These studies report that most female administrators are single, and among those who are married, very few have children. These data tend to be opposite for males. The evidence here suggests that the "between" wife and husband conflict has been resolved by the majority of women administrators by self-denial of the status of wife, by foregoing motherhood, or by waiting to assume such positions after childbearing and childraising years.

Case #3

Barb M. is a typical case in point of the ambitious, competent teacher who aspires to positions of leadership in education. She completed undergraduate training in elementary education and quickly became a well-respected teacher in a progressive school system. Atypically, she was mentored by a seasoned male administrator in the same district. Following his direction and her own ambitions, Barb pursued graduate training in administration, completed an administrative internship, and became an effective principal in an elementary school in this same school district. Her job was her life. She devoted days, nights, and weekends to becoming an effective and "successful" school administrator. For Barb there was no juggling of career and family. Her school staff was her family. In her early forties, she reevaluated her priorities. She resigned and returned to the classroom realizing the lack of balance between her professional and personal life.

Discriminatory Employment Practices

Hoferek (1979) draws upon some lesser known history to impress the role of men as gatekeepers of power. She reminds us of John Adams' response to his wife Abigail's plea to him that women be remembered with more generosity and favor in the nation's new code of laws than in the past:

We have been told that our struggle has loosened the bonds of government everywhere; that our children and apprentices were disobedient; that our schools and colleges were grown turbulent; that Indians slighted their guardians, and Negroes grew insolent to their masters. But your letter was the first intimation that another tribe, more numerous and powerful than all the rest, were grown discontented. This is rather too coarse a compliment upon in we know better than to repeal our masculine systems (Butterfield, 1963, p. 382).

It is beyond argument to say that the gatekeepers to positions of power are white and male. White males have, and continue to control access to positions which lead to power and money in our social, political, and economic systems. Today's gatekeepers are, of course, more subtle than those of John Adams's day. But they are, nonetheless, as effective.

Women are not likely to find other women in large proportions enrolled as graduate students in departments training educational administrators. Ninety-two percent of all students in educational administration training programs are males (Cirincione-Coles, 1975). Nor are women encouraged to become principals or superintendents within the public education system. Instead, if they are encouraged to pursue advanced training, it is more likely to be in areas of guidance and counseling, curriculum, or special programs. This type of encouragement is. well supported in hiring practices. The proportional increase in women in administrative positions is found in areas of personnel and support, rather than in positions of decision-making and power (Lesser, 1978).

In the south eastern region of the country, however, there does appear to be a promising trend in the numbers of women being trained at the masters and doctoral level in educational administration (Cornett, 1983). Male dominance in the number of degrees awarded at these levels has dropped from 75 percent in 1973–74 to 55 percent in 1980. If this trend continues and becomes widespread, there will be more academically qualified women to serve in administrative positions. Whether this is sufficient to combat male dominance in positions of power remains to be examined.

John Adams's quote is manifest in the research of Krchniak (1978). These researchers found that male superintendents were unlikely to hire women as administrators even in the presence of written policies for equal opportunity. Indeed, in Taylor's study, sex was the only factor which had any significant relationship to the hiring decision. Other variables, such as age, length of experience, size of school district, background, and type of position had no relationship to the hiring practices.

The fact that women principals are older and more experienced than men clearly reflects discrimination. The average age for the career principal is 47 for women and 46 for men (Educator's Opinion Poll, 1984). Women principals also tend to have more than three times as much teaching experience as do male principals.

For superintendents, the average age is 49 (Educator's Opinion Poll, 1985) with superintendents in larger school districts being somewhat older. Women superintendents, scarce that they are, tend to be located in small (i.e., fewer than 300 students) and low-paying districts.

Perhaps the most persistent and pervasive discrimination barrier, and the one most resistant to change, is "cronyism," or the buddy system. Women have made inroads in reducing discrimination using formalized routes. They have succeeded in changing laws and heightening public awareness. But, women have not succeeded in breaking into the informal systems through which men mentor and encourage other men.

Case #4

Ms. V. applied for two administrative vacancies. The posting for the elementary principalship listed three qualifications: master's degree or equivalent, three years' public school experience, and the principal's certification. Ms. V. was one of thirty applicants. She was also one of ten individuals selected for possible interviews by the school board. The board selected an out-of-state male who did not have the specified administrative certificate and hired him. The posting for director of special education cited two qualifications: appropriate certification and three years' special education experience. Ms. V. was one of eleven applicants. The all-male screening committee interviewed all applicants and recommended that the district psychologist be hired and the board acted on that recommendation. Ms. V. was qualified for both positions and was rejected for each. The rejections were based on subjective evaluations, not on objective qualifications. Ms. V. filed suit in federal court alleging sex discrimination under Title VII of the Civil Rights Act. The Federal District Court who had jurisdiction in this case ruled in favor of the school board. The court held that subjective evaluation plays a legitimate role in the hiring decision. (Verniero v. Air Force Academy School District No. 20, 705 F. 2d 388 10th Cir. 1983.)

One might speculate that such subjective evaluations are based on the same-sex interactions, so-called "locker-room comradery," and the like. Discrimination against women does not appear to exist at the entry level into the education profession. However, patterns of discrimination emerge when differential rates of promotion and advancement, into the field are examined (Muhich, 1974, Blanchard, 1976). Methods of sex discrimination in hiring and promotion practices and policies are known as the "filtering methods." These methods subtly eliminate many qualified women applicants.

Another reason which does not appear in the literature with the frequency of those cited earlier is the suggestion that entry into educational administration positions is not contingent upon the acquisition of specific entry characteristics, credentials, experience, etc. Since the initial entry hurdles are not clearly defined, men can get jobs in a variety of ways and it is impossible for women to gain all of the possible criteria for those same jobs. Clements suggestion is plausible and perhaps it does account for some of the disproportionate representation of women in educational administration. It is certainly clear that although school systems may have quite formal mechanisms in place for hiring administrators, these practices are, in effect, overridden by the informal mechanisms where personal perceptions based on physical presence rule.

For example, because there are alternative paths to positions in educational administration, the necessary criteria for acceptance into this power body are not clearly communicated to women. If women come out of the ranks of teachers, i.e., women colleagues, they are not likely to know how to interact with men professionals beyond job specific responsibilities. Schmuck uses the term, "homosociality," the wish to meet and talk with someone like oneself. As one woman said, "Attending a principal's conference is like being at the Elk's Club" (Schmuck, 1979, p. 20). The important information communication among peers becomes a tremendous obstacle for women.

When the past twenty years are examined critically, one can see improvement in the representation of disenfranchised groups in many professions and occupations. The same cannot be said for women in education. It is time to be critical of explanations and recommendations offered in that period of time because they have not worked. Women are still, and in a way even more, disenfranchised from positions of power in education than they were five, ten, and fifteen years ago. And, this should not be a surprise. Medicine and law responded to the press for equal opportunity and access to the profession only after representational quotas were ruled illegal. Only after federal legislation were the restrictive barriers to women in these professions removed. There has been no parallel legislation in education. And, women in education should not expect the men in power to serve as advocates for women. Quite the contrary, there is a strong need to survive and maintain the status quo which operates to obstruct change. "Groups who hold predominate power typically do not welcome an increased number of competitors (Schmuck, 1979, p. 20).

With such pervasive psychological, sociological, and political obstacles to equitable representation of women in educational administration, it is apparent that change will be brought about only by an understanding of how these inhibitors can be reduced and eliminated in aspiring women, and how the informal pathway to leadership can be better defined for those aspiring leaders.

Attitudes About Administration

There has been a loss of public confidence in principals because the social expectations exceed the capabilities of the office (Mayhew, 1974). The principalship is one of the most demanding jobs, and the present training and certification of principals is not adequate (Higley, 1975). Many women do not seek leadership positions because of this negative image of the school administrator (Howard, 1981).

In addition to the negative image, there are many beliefs and myths regarding male and female principals which further account for the scarcity of women in educational leadership positions. Research literature and empirical evidence challenge these myths and assumptions.

One of the most popular rationalizations for more men than women in administration is that men are supposedly better suited for the principalship than women. However, studies comparing men to women suggest that women are as competent as principals as men and often make better administrators (Bottomley, 1977).

The Florida Leadership Project, involving both high school and elementary principals, reported that of the three types of authority structures examined, democratic, authoritarian, and laissez-faire, only the democratic structure elicited positive attitudes among pupils, teachers, and parents (Wiles and Grobman, 1955). This study also reported that women principals were observed as operating democratically 22 percent more often than their male counterparts and scored higher on most effective responses given to administrative practices. Parental approval was higher in schools with women principals. No differences were found in comparing pupil achievement. Teacher quality made more of a difference than the sex of the principal. A follow-up study one year later (Grobman and Hines, 1956) again showed women operating democratically more often than men.

Gross and Task (1976) conducted part of a larger National Principalship Study (NPS) begun at Harvard in 1959. Using a national cross-section of elementary school principals, they compared men and women principals. Major findings from both direct and indirect evidence indicated the performance of women principals to be superior. Women principals gave greater importance to the differences between individual students, placed more emphasis on the detection and helping of delinquency-prone pupils, and generally were more concerned for the students in their schools. They found no difference between sexes in the importance they attributed to the academic performance of pupils or in their emphasis on discipline. Women principals tended to exert more supervisory control and worry less than male principals. There was no difference between the sexes in attempts to involve parents in school affairs, support given to a teacher in a conflict with a pupil, and teacher morale. Schools run by women principals produced more capable students, regardless of socioeconomic levels.

It has been assumed that both men and women teachers prefer male principals. The attitudes of teachers toward women principals were analyzed by Barter (1959) and by Gross and Trask (1964). Men and women teachers differ in their views toward women principals, although they rated men and women principals as equal in both abilities and personal qualities. Women teachers favored women principals more than did men teachers. A teacher's age, marital status, tenure, and level of education were found not to be significant in determining the teacher's attitude toward women as principals. Both teachers who had the least and the most experience were the most favorable toward women principals. A revealing finding was that male teachers who had taught in a school under a woman principal were more favorable to women as principals than men were who had not had this experience. This reflects the emotional prejudice of male teachers toward female principals. Schmuck (1976) suggests that women administrators pose a "psychological threat" to men teachers. And, in 1980, McQuigg and Carlton concluded that research indicates that there is probably no reason to believe that women are less effective than men as elementary or secondary principals.

Effectiveness in administrative positions, i.e., principalships and superintendencies, is tied to certain skills and behaviors which are independent of sex:

> Problem analysis—date collection and analysis
> Judgment—critical evaluation and decision-making
> Decisiveness—acting when a decision is needed
> Organizational ability—planning and scheduling personnel and resources
> Communication—speaking and writing skills

(National Association of Secondary School Principals, 1985)

The American Association of School Administrators has published competencies for graduates of college programs for school leaders that include the ability to:

1. Design and establish a school climate with attainable goals (organizational, motivational, leadership, and interpersonal skills)
2. Understand and employ political skills for support of education (public relations, communication of position, and negotiation)
3. Develop a systematic school curriculum (understand cognitive development, and develop indicators for instruction)
4. Plan and implement an instructional management system (monitor student achievement)
5. Manage finances, materials, and human resources

"Clearly, a complex set of behaviors is necessary to be a good school principal. All of the studies point to a core of competencies that include basic knowledge about curricula, supervision, and evaluation of instruction, basic management skills, verbal and written skills, and the ability to interact with people in a variety of situations" (SREB, 1986). Nowhere does the research support the fact that males make better principals than females.

Targets for Change

Two unequivocable facts emerge from the research on women administrators in education. First, men are the gatekeepers to the profession. Second, women are not gaining ground in administration; representation of women in educational administration is on the decline at all levels of education. What remains, then, is to identify the critical "targets for change" if women are to gain equal access, equal participation, and equal rewards in educational administration.

The years ahead provide a stage for women to build upon the success of other minority groups and of women themselves in other career fields. But success will not come easily. The reasons for the decreasing number of women in educational leadership positions are complex. Psychological and sociological factors, compounded with institutionalized barriers to women in education and employment, appear to have created an atmosphere in which few women aspire to obtain administrative positions. The perpetuation of these barriers should be recognized and eliminated or the phenomenon of the vanishing female administrator will continue. Thus, women educators clearly face a challenge in the remaining years of the twentieth century if they aspire to move from the classroom into administrative positions.

The task of gaining access to administrative positions in education, however, should not be focused on attitude change. Men and women who support equal access to administrative positions need to be reminded that attitude change is slow and is more likely to result from changes in behavior, rather than cause behavior change. Thus, women educators need to increase the number of qualified aspiring administrators in their ranks. Specifically, more women must:

- Obtain credentials in educational administration
- Apply for positions in educational administration
- Encourage other women to aspire to positions in educational leadership
- Gain access to the informal networking of men in educational administration

These targets for change do not assume that sex-role stereotypes, family constraints, or discriminatory hiring practices are easily changed. We know that is not the case. They do, however, place the responsibility for action with the group that has the vested interest, women. Women must pursue administrative positions in education with the same commitment and vigor that they have pursued admission to other male-dominated professions. It is imperative that women become aggressive in pursuing administrative positions so that women will be proportionately represented in educational administration in the twentieth century.

There are many recommendations for promoting the equal representation of women in educational administration. The Equal Pay Act, Title VII of the Civil Rights Act of 1964, and Article IX of the Education Amendments of 1972 were designed to eliminate employment discrimination in the public schools. But laws alone, as has been shown during the past ten years, will not bring about change. Neither will resolutions, such as passed by the National Association of Secondary School Principals in 1975, which directs school districts to "recruit, employ, provide appropriate inservice education and promote women as educational administrators and to encourage qualified women to prepare for and to accept the challenges of administrative and executive positions..." (Barnes, 1976, p. 89).

Women who are interested in becoming educational administrators must know themselves and trust their abilities (Krohn, 1976). They must be courageous, seize the initiative, be prepared for obstacles, and project greater involvement. Women must have a willingness to learn and to work, to seek and to give. They must also turn a deaf ear to those who would dissuade them from leadership aspirations. Administrative positions will always exist and women must be persistent in applying for them.

Specific Recommendations

Individuals should

- separate from an orientation to children and teachers to develop a district-wide perspective.
- develop an ability to manage community groups.
- demonstrate an ability to manage crucial areas such as conflict, discipline, legal issues, finance, and maintenance.
- develop an ability to assertively draw attention to their own accomplishments (Marshall, 1985).

Local school districts should

- publicly identify the elimination of discrimination against women as a priority including examination of both written and unwritten policies
- analyze personnel policies which discriminate against women, including leave of absence policies for pregnancy and childbirth
- survey female personnel to determine the level of interest in administrative positions and design career ladders leading to administrative positions

- encourage women to prepare for administration by inviting them to participate in leadership activities
- announce administrative positions widely
- actively recruit women school board members
- review and revise curricula to eliminate sexist references (Schmuck, 1976; Cirincione-Coles, 1975).

State Departments of Education should

- identify the hiring of women for state administrative positions as a priority
- establish statewide policies and guidelines that set forth hiring practices to be employed in local school systems
- analyze alternative means for qualification as school administrators (Muhich, 1974).

Higher Education should

- recruit women for faculty positions in schools of education especially in the area of administration
- provide flexible registration and enrollment practices in degree programs
- actively recruit women students interested in educational administration
- offer placement activities for administrative internships
- encourage and assist prospective women teachers to develop and practice leadership skills.

REFERENCES

Bach, L. Of women, school administration, and discipline, *Phi delta kappan,* 1976, *57* (7), 463–466.

Barnes, T. America's forgotten minority: Women school administrators, *NASSP bulletin,* 1976, *60,* 87–93.

Barter, A.S. The status of women in school administration—where will they go from here? *Educational horizons,* 1953, *37* (3), 72–75.

Bikler, S.K., & Brannigan, M.B. (Eds.). *Women and educational leadership.* Lexington, Massachusetts: Lexington Books, 1980.

Blanchard, P.D. *The impact of sex discrimination in the recruitment of educational policy-makers.* Paper, Southeastern Conference on the American Society for Public Administration, Miami Beach, 1976, (ERIC Document Reproduction Service No. ED 128 856).

Bottomley, M. The case of the female principal: Sex role attitudes and perceptions of sex differences and ability. *Australian and New Zealand journal of sociology,* 1977, *13* (2), 68–73.

Broverman, I.K., Vogel, S., Broverman, D.M., Clarkson, F.E., & Rosekrantz, P.S. Sex-role stereotypes: A current appraisal. *Journal of social issues,* 1972, *28,* 59–78.

Butterfield, L.H. (Ed.). *The Adams family correspondence. Vol. 1, December 1761 to May 1776.* Cambridge: Belkap Press of Harvard University Press, 1963.

Carlson, R.O. *School superintendents: Careers and performance.* Columbus, Ohio: Charles E. Merrill Publishing Co., 1972.

Circincione-Coles, K. The administrator: Male or female? *Journal of teacher education,* 1975, *26* (4), 326–329.

Cornett, L.M. *The preparation and selection of school principals.* Atlanta, Georgia: Southern Regional Education Board, 1983.

Educator Opinion Poll. *Teachers and principals.* Arlington, Virginia: Educational Research Service, 1984.

Educator Opinion Poll. *School superintendents: Opinions and status.* Arlington, Virginia: Educational Research Service, 1985.

Fauth, G. Women in educational administration: Research profile. *The educational forum,* 1984, *49* (1), 2–8.

Fishel, A. & Pottker, J. Women in educational governance: A statistical portrait. *Educational researcher,* 1974, *3,* 4–7.

Grobman, H., & Hines V. What makes a good principal? *NASSP bulletin,* 1956, *40,* 5–16.

Gross, N., & Trask, A.E. *The sex factor and the management of schools.* New York: Wiley Press, 1976.

Heferek, M.J., & Scott, M.G. (Eds.). *Women as leaders in physical education and sports.* Iowa City, Iowa: University of Iowa Press, 1979.

Higley, J. Training and certification of school principals. *NAESP school leadership digest,* 1975, *12,* 1–8.

Howard, S. *Why aren't women administering our schools?* Arlington, Virginia: National Council of Administrative Women in Education, 1981.

Kanter, R. *Men and women of the corporation.* New York: Basic Books, Inc., 1977.

Krchniak, S.P. *Variables associated with low incidence of women in school administration: Towards the empirical understanding.* Paper presented at the annual meeting of the American Educational Research Association, Toronto, Canada, 1978.

Krohn, B. The puzzling case of the missing Ms. *Nation's schools and colleges,* November 1976, 32–38.

Lesser, P. *The participation of women in public school administration.* Paper presented at the annual meeting of the American Educational Research Association, Toronto, Canada, 1978.

Little, N. Why women make the best principals. *High school journal,* 1983, *67,* 77–80.

Loomis, L.J., & Wild, P.H. *Increasing the role of women in community college administration,* 1978, (ERIC Document Reproduction Service No. ED 181 943).

Maccoby, E.D., & Jacklin, C.N. *The psychology of sex differences.* Stanford, California: Stanford University Press, 1974.

Marshall, C. From culturally defined to self-defined: Career states of women administrators. *The journal of educational thought,* 1985, *19* (2), 134–138.

Mason, W. *The beginning teacher.* Washington, D.C.: U. S. Government Printing Office, 1961.

Mayhew, L. *Educational leadership and declining enrollments.* Berkeley, California: McCuthan, 1974.

McMillan, M. R. Leadership aspirations of perspective teachers: A comparison of men and women. *Journal of teacher education,* 1975, *26,* 323–325.

McQuigg, B.D., & Carlton, P.W. Women administrators and America's schools: A national dilemma. *High school journal,* 1980, *64,* (2), 50–54.

Muhich, D. *Discrimination against women in educational administration.* Paper presented at the annual meeting of the National Association of Women Deans, Administrators, and Counselors, Chicago, Illinois, 1974, (ERIC Document REproduction Service No. ED 114 937).

National Association of Secondary School Principals. *Performance-based preparation of principals—a framework for improvement.*

National Education Association. *26th biennial salary and staff survey of public school professional personnel.* Washington, D.C., 1973.

National Education Association. *Statistics for public schools.* Washington, D.C., 1981.

Niedermayer, G., & Kramer, V.W. *Women in administration positions in public education.* Philadelphia, Pennsylvania: Recruitment Leadership and Training Institute, 1974. (ERIC Document Reproduction Service No. ED 096 742).

Pipho, C. Minimum competency testing: Can the state legislate literacy? *Phi delta kappan,* 1978, *9,* 59.

Schmuck, P.A. *Sex differentiation in public school administration.* Arlington, Virginia: National Council of Administrative Women in Education, 1975. (ERIC Document Reproduction Service No. ED 128 966).

Schmuck, P.A. *The spirit of Title IX: Men's work and women's work in Oregon public schools.* Eugene, Oregon: Oregon School Study Council, 1976. (ERIC Document REproduction Service No. ED 128 966).

Schmuck, P.A. *Sex equity in educational leadership in Oregon public schools.* Eugene, Oregon: Oregon School Study Council, 1979.

Silver, P. Are women underqualified for leadership? *Phi delta kappan,* 1977, *59,* 207.

Southern Regional Education Board. *Effective school principals.* Atlanta, Georgia, 1986.

Verniero v. Air Force Academy School District No. 20, 705 F. 2d 388 (10th Cir. 1983).

Wiles, K., & Grobman, H.G. Principals as leaders. *Nation's schools,* 1955, *56,* 75–77.

The following statements are designed for the exploration of personal reactions to the chapter, as well as for the review of the contents of the chapter. Emphasis in discussions should be on exploring issues in depth, rather than on determining the correct or appropriate responses.

FOR DISCUSSION:

1. Should women be administrators of schools? Explain your response.
2. How did, as the authors state, "criticism of education frequently (become) criticism of women"?
3. Review your institution to determine the number of women in administrative roles, as well as the number of women aspiring to administrative positions. Describe the barriers as well as the encouragement for women to move up in the hierarchy of your institution.
4. Discuss evidence of bias and discrimination against women in administration in your institution. Create a list of suggestions for the institution so that discrimination does not occur, and the best candidate is hired. How would the board of your institution react to the suggestions?
5. Do women want to be school administrators? Compare your observations with evidence discussed in the article.
6. How does the "old boys network" fit into the points described in this article?
7. Does mentoring help or hinder women who desire to pursue positions in educational administration?
8. What would your advice to a women who aspires to be an administrator?

SUGGESTIONS FOR FURTHER READING

Biklen, S., & Branningan, M. *Women and educational leadership.* Lexington, Massachusetts: Lexington Books, 1980.

Gilligan, C. *In a different voice: Psychological theory and women's development.* Massachusetts: Harvard University Press, 1982.

Hart, B., & Dalke, D. *The sexes at work: Improving work relationships between men and women.* Lyons, Colorado: Leadership Dynamics, Inc., 1987.

Jones, E. Survey: *Attitudes toward women as school district administrators.* Newton, Massachusetts: EDC/WEEA, 1981.

Jones, E., & Montenegro, X. *Women and minorities in school administration: strategies for making a difference.* Columbia University, New York: Institute for Urban and Minority Education, 1983.

Loden, M. *Feminine leadership or how to succeed in business without being one of the boys.* New York: Times Books, 1985.

Shakeshaft, C. *Women in educational administration.* Newbury Park, California: Sage Publications, Inc., 1986.

Thorine, B., & Henley, N. (Eds.). *Language and sex: Difference and dominance.* Rowley, Massachusetts: Newbury House Publishers, 1975.

Timpano, D.M., & Knight, L.W. *Sex discrimination in the selection of school district administrators: What can be done?* Washington, D.C.: National Institute of Education, 1976.

Chapter 23

A MODEL OF INSTITUTIONAL
DISCRIMINATION APPLIED TO GENDER

GERALD PORTER

INTRODUCTION

"Because we've always done it that way..."

Each chapter in this text has emphasized that once sex bias and discrimination in education are recognized, strategies can be employed to rectify the inequitable situations. All of the writings focus on raising the awareness of educators so that they can value an equal education for all students and strive to achieve it in their own institutions. The theme has been combining understanding with action. Activities such as the evaluation of enrollments, observation of instructional interactions, and the establishment of administrative policy are all critical efforts towards the achievement of sex equity. There are a number of ongoing strategies that require continuous development, monitoring, and revision. In time, changes can become an integral, permanent part of the institutional structure.

But it is the baseline understanding of the institutionalization of inequities in education that can lead to the exterpation of the insidious problem of sex discrimination that permeates all institutions. Once the issues of inequity are raised and dealt with in some capacity, it becomes necessary to probe more deeply to learn about the sources and impact of sex role stereotyping, bias, and discrimination.

It may seem as if understanding the explanations of the sources of bias *after* reviewing the concerns of sex equity, is moving in reverse. Why implement strategies for change when the reason behind the problem is not fully comprehended? Isn't it enough to know that institutions perpetuate stereotyping, bias, and discrimination, and that those institutions can be changed from within?

The response is to look at the phrase "from within." All educators, parents, and students bring their personal and group socialization to school every day. They, purposefully or unconsciously, act out attitudes developed over years of interaction with other groups and institutions. Sex role stereotyping becomes learned. Sex bias becomes action. Sex discrimination becomes routine, "the way it always was." The psychology of sex equity, "from within," becomes the psychology of the institution.

Gerald Porter provides a challenging discussion of the institutionalization of sex discrimination. Strategies towards sex equity that can begin to dig deeper into the educational system are recommended.

A MODEL OF INSTITUTIONAL DISCRIMINATION
APPLIED TO GENDER

The model of institutional discrimination has gradually replaced an earlier "prejudice causes discrimination" model, which is still common currency for most people considering this issue (Feagin and Feagin, 1978). This chapter will explore the model of institutional discrimination with a special focus on sex discrimination. This will be a generic analysis of the institutional discrimination model which should apply equally well for any group traditionally excluded from full participation in American institutional life.

The model serves as a prototype for all forms of discriminatory practice and can direct our attention to the interplay of the fundamental issues of power, wealth, and justice that are the parameters of all societal discrimination.

This chapter is intended to be an essay on the origins, forms, and underlying processes of institutional discrimination. Many of the examples are currently in the process of change, either by eliminating the source of discrimination or by taking more subtle, covert forms. But a grasp of the institutional model provides the tools to discern discrimination in any of its many forms.

The psychological factors that occlude our objective vision of injustice and render us complacent will be discussed, as will the institutional features that isolate the individual from the pain of dehumanization that afflicts both the oppressor and victim.

Institutional Discrimination

Why do women earn only 62 cents for every dollar earned by a man?

This is a particularly awkward question when the vast majority of Americans support the principle of "equal pay for equal work." Most Americans would probably sincerely argue that they are not prejudiced against women and do not discriminate. But there is overwhelming statistical evidence that women as a class are victims of discrimination.

The *"prejudice causes discrimination"* model assumes that discrepancies in female and male earning power are the combined result of countless individual acts of discrimination against girls and women (Feagin and Feagin, 1978). Prejudice refers to an intolerant, biased, unfavorable, unfair, or negative attitude that motivated these discriminatory behaviors. But attitude commonly refers to our likes and dislikes, of which we are presumably aware. The implication, then, is that our attitudinally-derived actions are intentional. Yet, very few people deliberately wish to limit women's opportunities, which is implied by the prejudice model.

Instead, the source of discrimination appears to be beyond the intent of awareness of most people who harbor no deliberate desire to harm. The notion of *"institutional discrimination"* provides an explanation for this situation. The institutional model accounts for the often blatant discrepancy between attitudes advocating equal treatment and the tell-tale statistics that document the continuing vitality of sex discrimination in America. What becomes increasingly clear is that intent to harm nor awareness of the possible harmful effects of one's actions are necessary ingredients for discrimination.

The most significant features of the institutionalization of sex discrimination is that it is pervasive and invisible to those socialized within our society. Individuals tend not to perceive their harmful actions as such because these behaviors are defined by convention as appropriate and are not necessarily motivated by hostile feelings. Ironically, this includes the victims of institutional discrimination, who all too often attribute their failure to self-inadequacy. The most blatant signs of institutional bias to an objective eye are only natural to those socialized to accept differential treatment as an extension of obvious fact.

That "obvious fact" is merely a social construct or concensus of prevailing opinion. The prevailing social constructs that define social practice as normal are set by the dominant group to protect their privileged status. Thus, the hostile feelings that drive the prejudice model are secondary in the institutional context which views prejudiced attitudes as justifications for already established unfair situations. Institutional discrimination occurs on a comparatively large scale and tends to be ongoing and routinized.

To *discriminate* is to notice differences. In the behavioral domain, discrimination has its origins in the processes of perception and cognition (Geis, Carter, and Butler, 1982). In particular, the relationship between past experience, inference, and perception of new experience can suggest the underlying psychological mechanisms of bias on an institutional scale. Understanding how discriminatory practice has its roots in how we think and process experience can give us important clues to effectively intervene to counteract systemic bias.

The term *"institution"* applies to specific organizations such as a school or a corporation, but just as often institution is generalized to include large-scale combinations of smaller organizations. Institution can be specific and concrete or global, characterizing prototypical societal elements such as "the church," "government," "education," or "the economy." *Institutional discrimination* is defined as the incorporation of specific discriminatory practices against specific outgroups as a component of the organizational mechanisms for selection, resource distribution, and decision-making power within the institutional structures of society.

In the institutional model people are still the agents of harm, but the institution frequently validates those actions by prescribing practices that are carried out within an institutionally-sanctioned role. Similarly, the individuals sheltered within their institutional role may not be members of the dominant class but merely their agent. For example, most police officers are white and male. Few are more than nominal members of the ingroup, but even nominal status affords them additional privilege. Their societal role within the power structure provides even more privilege.

Discrimination can be either intentional and overt or more subtle, covert and unintentional. The most insidious form of institutional discrimination negatively affects subordinate groups through formal and informal organizational practices that are not deliberately motivated by prejudice or harmful intent. This type of discrimination can only be detected by careful analysis of the differential outcomes for dominant and subordinate groups following their encounter with the institution. For example, most women are more severely hurt economically by divorce than their ex-husbands. This is because of a complex interaction of factors including the fact that women on average are paid less and usually get custody of the children. The bottom line is an unintentional but selectively negative affect on women.

Sometimes, this selective process occurs because discrimination in one societal sector adversely affects outgroups in another. Women in the traditional societal role of primary caretaker for children, must take jobs with shorter and/or more flexible hours and are not as competitive in the employment sphere. Similarly, women who by social convention did not normally assume positions of authority in the past are still finding it difficult to get hired as high school administrators or corporate CEOs. Thus, past discrimination can establish informal practices that harm subordinate groups in the present.

The organizational structure of the institution selectively responds to different people based on their group membership. The differential treatment of ingroups and outgroups is validated by prejudicial assumptions about the value of the outgroup. Implicit in policies and procedures are value judgments about the people and context in which they will be applied. If the implicit assumptions upon which policy and procedures are formulated are stereotypical and biased, then this presumption of inferiority is built into the institutional structure and serves as a selective membrane favoring ingroup over outgroup members.

Discriminatory practice is installed into the action mechanisms of institutions by policy and procedure makers who are usually ingroup members who participate in the concensus assumptions that devalue outgroups and justify those in power. Again, actions may perpetuate discrimination unintentionally. These institutionalized practices appear fair because they reflect mainstream values and social assumptions implicit in the prevailing societal environment. But prevailing social assumptions are not necessarily impartial, and reflect outgroup stereotypes and collective ingroup self-interest.

It is important to note that everyone in society (including outgroup members) are socialized by the same set of norms (or implicit assumptions) but each learns to assume and identify with their assigned place in the social order. Each person internalizes the social expectations of their societal place and role as a result of socialization. This means that they learn to organize not only their behavior but their perception and subjective life experience to conform to the socially defined parameters of propriety and convention.

Segregation and Institutional Discrimination

Often the prejudicial attitudes that get translated into discriminatory institutional practice are based on misperception fostered by social and physical isolation. In the case of race in the United States, whites and blacks tend to live apart. There is very limited opportunity for blacks and whites to interact with each other even about issues of mutual concern. The traditional assignment of blacks to roles low in power and influence has been a principal tool in limiting their voice within existing institutional structures and simultaneously limiting opportunity to disconfirm stereotypes. Generally increased social exposure can break down prejudice given the appropriate conditions.

Research suggests that when people from different groups have an opportunity to get to know each other personally, prejudice is reduced. This is facilitated when the individuals involved have common interests or shared personal characteristics. Within an organizational setting intergroup harmony is fostered by support and encouragement downplaying intergroup competition and opportunities for conflict has been shown to be helpful.

Women are segregated from power and full institutional participation, but physical separation is neither desired nor necessary. In fact, women's close proximity to men obscures their actual powerlessness until circumstance forcefully illustrates their marginal access. For example, the case of displaced homemakers. Due to the divorce or death of a spouse, displaced homemakers frequently suffer significant loss of wealth and status which was previously derived from the women's close association and dependence on the man.

The apparent intimacy of women with men does not mean equal power but mere conformity to societally defined subordinate roles. Women's traditional confinement to the home can be viewed as a form of segregation since few other viable options existed. Even today most predominantly female occupations center around the home or are extensions of women's stereotypical role of familial nurturer and household custodian. The majority of working women are segregated into the "pink collar ghetto" in traditional jobs such as secretary or receptionist (Howe, 1978). In the typical American household, chores are stereotypically divided between women and men, segregating women into devalued jobs. Women with low incomes such as single mothers or displaced homemakers end up segregated to poor neighborhoods aggravating already limited access to quality medical care and education for their children (or themselves).

All men do not enjoy the same level of power and dominance exerted by other men, usually a small and select group, but all men as a dominant group derive benefit relative to their place in society. Males as an ingroup are subdivided by factors such as race, ethnicity, social class, educational level, parental income, or religion. One's status within any of these factors can significantly affect one's level of dominance and advantage even within the ingroups. Just as multiple outgroup membership can have a negative multiplier affect on one's life chances for societally acknowledged success, so multiple ingroup membership can substantially enhance one's life prospects. However, in societies where group membership is more salient (such as South Africa or the United

States prior to the dismantling of Jim Crow), racial identity overrides less valued variables such as social class or income. Clearly, minority women are hit hardest of all because they suffer double liability.

Frequently it is noted that changing economic conditions that have forced the majority of women into the workforce in itself has broken down institutional sex discrimination (BNA, 1986). And to the extent that meaningful contact between men and women in the workplace has counteracted implicit prejudice some real progress has been made. But all women are undercut by the assumptions of inferiority to men built into our institutional structures.

The Invisibility of Institutional Bias

The institutional model asserts that control over the distribution of resources is a means to maintain the status quo and control outgroup behavior. The ingroup holds control over institutional resource distribution by holding the positions that set informal and formal policy and procedures and make decisions. The effect of ingroup institutional control is the implementation of procedures implicitly biased in favor of the ingroup. Outgroups are given limited access to resources and no effective control within the institutional context. Individual outgroup members who violate role expectations either formally defined as law or informally by binding social expectations, face severe sanctions.

The imbalance in access of resources is accepted by both oppressor and victim alike because both perceive the situation as normal and natural. As a result no injustice is perceived. Although, poverty is certainly acknowledged, it is not typically associated with inordinately disproportionate distribution of wealth but rather to the poor's failure to work hard or to some implicit defect that renders them as "deserving" of their fate. Similarly, the rich or members of the ingroup tend to be regarded as the "best" and consequently "deserving" of their advantages and privilege.

This tendency to interpret events to justify the status quo, has been called by Lerner (1980), the *just "world" hypothesis*. If we allow ourselves to accept and see that existing conditions are unjust then we will have to bear the emotional distress that we typically experience when confronted with an inequity. If the injustice really penetrates our cocoon of complacency we may be compelled to alleviate this discomfort with action to right the wrong. But it is far easier to make the comparatively inexpensive psychological accommodation of not noticing any or even excusing an injustice.

Unfortunately, this justification process almost invariably leads to a dehumanization of the outgroup and to correspondingly degrading life conditions. Perhaps the most bitter aspect of the dehumanization of the outgroups, is the internalization and acceptance of this message by the outgroup members themselves. Not only does the outgroup bear the disgrace of inferiority, but each member builds their identity on this premise and, as a result, imposes self-limits. They are conditioned not to strive for the paramount societal ideal but to a degraded stereotype that severely limits opportunity for genuine personal fulfillment. The psychological limitations this places on outgroup members compounds the already effective external mechanisms of oppression and sets up conditions confirming the negative stereotypes.

Ingroup members internalize the same implicit assumptions that justify their privilege but their identities can be built on the assumption of superiority (relative to the outgroup) or at least of implicit self-worth.

Prejudicial assumptions about the outgroup are taught to children both directly and indirectly and are internalized as the factual basis of their perception and interpretation of raw events. For instance, children are sometimes told directly that women are not as intelligent as men. But more often, and more persuasively, children can observe prevailing social conditions where women do not assume societal roles requiring what society defines as intelligence. This is no indication of women's actual intellectual ability, but illustrates how misleading conclusions regarding the victim of discrimination are frequently drawn from observing only the debilitating effects. If girls and women are systematically excluded from science and math training, then they can hardly be expected to become scientists. If women are told explicitly and implicitly that science is not a feminine pursuit then all but the most intrinsically motivated women will be discouraged.

Most of us cannot test every stereotype for accuracy. Instead we rely on the collective wisdom passed on from those we trust, to be tested and true. Unfortunately, such collective wisdom is frequently no more than an explicit articulation of the prevailing concensus of reality or conventional stereotypes cloaked as homey aphorisms superficially validated by the outcomes of discrimination, rather than by its causes.

Institutions reinforce the already biased orientation children have acquired by the time they are old enough to function within institutional structures. In fact, the official institutional imprimatur validates the justifications of discrimination while relieving the individual of the burden for carrying overtly discriminatory actions except within a sanctioned societal role such as parent, teacher, police officer, or judge. *Institutionalization provides the advantage of removing the person from the immediate discriminatory act.* Hence, most individuals do not feel they participate in discrimination if they even acknowledge it exists or is valid. They do not perceive discrimination because the discriminatory act is veiled behind the expectations of the roles we all strive to fulfill.

It is not often appreciated that discrimination against subordinate groups also negatively impacts members of dominant groups. In the more abstract sense, if one denies the humanity of the subordinate group then one simultaneously denies that in oneself. For example, men who are highly sex-typed are far more likely to have difficulties expressing emotion than less sex-typed men or women. Unfortunately, a society which idealizes a macho emotionally repressed male stereotype devalues emotional frankness and ease of expression as "weakness" or "feminine." Men who attempt to live up to the macho stereotype end up rejecting their own so-called "feminine" qualities, with no recognition of the physical and psychological risks such defense mechanisms require.

Men are hurt by sex discrimination against women but are conditioned to overlook their pain or to project it onto objects society defines as weak. Society does not value what it takes from men (e.g., expression of emotion) and, as a result, men as a class do not miss what has been stripped from them and are not generally interested in sex role reform.

However, sex discrimination deprives women of highly valued societal objects such as wealth, power, and status. As a result, it is easier for women to see past the initial barrier of sex role occlusion and notice their deprivation. In a qualitative sense, both are harmed equally but in profoundly different ways which limit each's capacity for personal fulfillment through expression and cultivation of latent personal potential.

In the most practical sense, discrimination narrows the base of human talent available. Ironically, this limiting of the talent pool is precisely the intent of discriminatory practice which regards this as the advantageous reduction of competition. Implicit in the tacit acknowledgement of the subordinate as competition, is the negative affirmation of their value and humanity. If the outgroup were truly inferior then no external regulation would be required to hold them in their place, the outgroup's natural inferiority would impose internal limitations.

Also implicit in the rejection of the subordinate group is the fear that there are not enough resources for all to have an adequately comfortable life. As a result, the dominant group protects its privilege and its lion's share of the wealth. Unfortunately, this is perpetuating a continuing concentration of already disproportionately distributed wealth to an exclusive and small dominant group. This induces an artificially created shortage of wealth and resources.

Interventions: Reducing Institutional Discrimination

Traditionally, discrimination has been fought with the effort to change biased attitudes towards the outgroup. This strategy has met with limited success because even where positive attitude change has been demonstrated, new unbiased behaviors have not necessarily followed. The correlation between attitudes and behavior is consistently low (Deaux and Wrightsman, 1984). Attitude change has been the basic remedial tool of the prejudice model of discrimination. This approach has proven to be a limited strategy in counteracting systemic discrimination because it views attitude as too fixed and enduring a characteristic of a person.

Research suggests that specific discriminatory acts are more the result of compliance to the behavioral expectations a person perceives are required of them by salient others. Thus, discriminatory behavior is closely linked to situational factors and perceived social expectation rather than some consistent, relatively enduring attitude that reliably leads to predictable behavior.

This suggests that changing biased social expectations can lead to reduction in discriminatory behavior. This is where societal leaders from all quarters can be effective by vocally decrying sexism and by affirming policies aimed at reducing discrimination and its results. More importantly, women and minorities must have highly visible and credible opportunities to counteract traditional stereotypes by modeling nonstereotypical behaviors in leadership positions in business, government, and education.

Existing civil rights laws need to be expanded to include effective monitoring and tougher penalties for violations. Reasonable legislative appropriations are necessary to truly institutionalize civil rights reforms which can effectively break down implicit discrimination. Congress should set standards that enable enforcement agencies to objectively identify institutional discrimination by basing detection and remedial strategies on disproportionate outcomes. Incentives can be offered employers who voluntarily implement successful affirmative action programs that demonstrate tangible results. Such incentives could include tax benefits or credits to be applied to the awarding of government contracts for large businesses and government-subsidized employee health insurance for small business. School systems might be rewarded with increased state and federal aid for successful efforts at eliminating discrimination. Districts could be rewarded for significantly increased nontraditional enrollments with bonuses for each nontraditional student who successfully completes the course or program. All incentive funds should be allowed as general operating expenses to maximize the advantage to districts.

Affirmative action needs to be revitalized but with clear criteria specifying when equitable conditions will have been achieved and special remedial efforts can be terminated. Affirmative action must be based on analysis of the differential outcomes for dominant and subordinate groups. Remedial hiring strategies must be designed to minimize and distribute as broadly as possible any loss to dominant groups. Job qualifications under no circumstances should be lowered to increase the hiring of subordinate groups, although reassessment of the appropriateness of existing qualifications should be a necessary component of any institutional civil rights review.

The most immediate and effective site for institutional change is in ourselves. Personal change must go deeper than merely overriding our conditioned prejudices or attitudes. It must be based on a deeper understanding of self and society. One must come to consciously grasp how our perceptions and beliefs about gender are shaped by the socialization process, which consists largely of internalizing overt and implicit messages about the value and place of women and men. We must also recognize that until we directly see our prejudicial likes and dislikes operating within ourselves we can easily be drawn into unintentional harmful acts and continue to be insensitive to others suffering. We need to self-consciously observe where our beliefs and action are based more on biased social assumptions than objective fact and make the effort to accept that we have actually incorporated these biased assumptions into our view of the world.

This step is the greatest stumbling block for most people, even those who sincerely wish to change, because it is very difficult to grasp that admitting prejudice, that we barely know is even present, is the only way to be genuinely free of it. We cannot overcome the implicit bias instilled during our socialization without acknowledging that we have accepted the bias and become so identified with it that it disappeared from our view. However once one's personal bias is acknowledged the process of disconfirming our instilled prejudicial perceptions and impulses becomes increasingly easy and the realization enduring.

The collective effect of persons who have deliberately overcome their biased socialization is a significant factor in overcoming institutional discrimination because these are the people who can see that the emperor has no clothes. But as an institutional problem, discrimination must be countered on a larger institutional scale that for educators includes the classroom, the school or district level, and the greater society.

In the classroom, teachers can directly counteract stereotypes and avoid reinforcing any form of biased behavior including students verbal expressions of stereotypical ideas. Teachers can make efforts to systematically include all students in class activities. It is particularly important to be sure girls are included and made comfortable when engaged in nontraditional activities. The other side of inclusion is taking care not to inadvertently favor boys in traditional male domains. Care should be taken to take disciplinary action consistently and consequences should match the offense rather than our expectations of their culpability. Teachers are powerful role models and must act out the values they wish their students to accept, making compensatory affirmations that not merely deny the validity of biased assumptions but actively assert the value and worth of the outgroup. Related to compensation is teacher nontolerance of bias or discriminatory behavior.

Within a specific institutional setting such as a school or district, a detailed reassessment for systemic bias should be undertaken. Initially, this reassessment should consist of a careful and comprehensive analysis of all institutional policy and procedures (formal and informal). Particular attention should be paid to empirical indicators of systemic bias such as disproportionate enrollments or hiring practices.

Once the particular problems have been identified, strategies to counteract these weaknesses can be formulated and implemented. The interventions must include a systematic elimination of the biased selection features within the institution and frequently the simultaneous implementation of compensatory efforts to places with a longstanding history of discrimination. Also, when strategies are mapped out, clearly defined goals and objectives must be set to determine when genuinely equitable conditions have been reached. This step is particularly important for compensatory interventions such as an affirmative action hiring plan.

Progress should be monitored on a formative basis enabling programs to be finely tuned or modified as necessary. Ideally, there will be strong support from the top. Leadership should actively express support and provide explicit direction to their managers on a regular basis affirming organizational commitment to equity. Leadership should spearhead community involvement and educate their constituency as to the reasons for and efforts being made. Elicit community support by structuring regular and meaningful involvement in desegregation.

Training for staff and managers is another important feature of organization-level antidiscrimination efforts. Training programs should be balanced between voluntary and obligatory participation. A balanced training program might consist of the following:

1. Optional personal growth-oriented training targeting the staff most actively involved in the interventions. Such training besides the basic information should aim at fostering the personal change process discussed earlier.

2. Mandatory management training emphasizing equitable practice for all administrators.

3. Training aimed at facilitating growth in moral judgment following the theory and method of Kohlberg and Gilligan. Persons functioning at higher levels of moral reasoning are more committed to principled action and exhibit higher consistency between belief and behavior. Participation should be optional but strongly encouraged for all staff (including nonprofessional and support staff).

In general, the school or organizational atmosphere should emphasize interpersonal harmony and cooperation while deemphasizing individual performance and normative comparison especially between ingroups and outgroups. Coed teams that experience success are most likely to break down stereotypical thinking, action, and incidentally, maximize individual performance.

One final principle needs to be remembered when developing strategies to overcome institutional discrimination. While behavior may be only loosely caused by attitudes, it seems clear that attitudes will be accommodated to changes in behavior. Thus, policies that require equitable behavior change will over time likely result in more equitable attitudes. Particularly, if structural changes are introduced in concert with attempts to reduce threat and increase understanding. The most effective interventions at reducing institutional discrimination are structural changes and the most important structural changes occur at the site of evaluative processes aimed at individuals, groups, or their products.

But smaller organizations are part of larger national or even global institutions. Effective reduction and eventual elimination requires large scale intervention beyond the reach of local institutional structures. The most overlooked but intractable factor contributing to discrimination is the extraordinarily disproportionate distribution of wealth. As long as so few have so much while the vast majority scramble for the modest portion that remain, the continual threat of scarcity for subordinate groups and of loss for the dominant group will reinforce the self-interest that feeds bias and discriminatory practice. Outgroups can overcome their systemic disadvantage by collectively asserting their power, which comes from their integral if lowly role in the economic order. The progress of the fifties and sixties in civil rights demonstrates the effectiveness of the collective assertion of power by those traditionally denied power within society's official structures. The contemporary women's movement was ridiculed and trivialized during its first two decades but has resulted in significant strides in women's access to power and an acknowledged institutional role.

Beyond collective action aimed at structural change, the most significant factor in reducing institutional sexism on a societal level is a concerted campaign to root out the stereotypes that implicitly define women as inferior. An effective component of such a large scale effort would include an assault on male stereotypes that implicitly assert the validity of male dominance at the expense of women and that socially defined as feminine in men's lives.

In summary, effective response to institutional sex discrimination requires a multifaceted attack. The most fundamental and enduring changes will be structural rather than merely contentual or attitudinal. But systemic change cannot take root if the attitudinal soil has not already been prepared by providing individuals with opportunities to examine and modify their fundamental assumptions about gender. This process is facilitated by individual confrontation with organizational changes in policy and procedure that invest the process of values examination with urgency and relevance.

REFERENCES

Bureau of National Affairs, Inc. *Work & family: A changing dynamic.* Washington, D.C.: U.S. Department of Labor, 1986.

Deaux, K., & Wrightsman, L.S. *Social psychology in the 80's* (4th ed.). Monterey, California: Brooks/Cole Publishing, 1984.

Geis, F.L., Carter, M.R., & Butler, D.J. *Research on seeing and evaluating people.* Women's Educational Equity Act Program, National Institute of Education, Department of Education, 1982.

Feagin, J.R., & Feagin, C.B. *Discrimination American style: Institutional racism and sexism.* Englewood Cliffs: New Jersey: Prentice-Hall, 1978.

Howe, L.K. *Pink collar workers: Inside the world of women's work.* New York: Avon Books, 1978.

Lerner, M.J. *Belief in a just world: A fundamental delusion.* New York: Plenum Press, 1980.

The following statements are designed for the exploration of personal reactions to the chapter, as well as for the review of the contents of the chapter. Emphasis in discussions should be on exploring issues in depth, rather than on determining the correct or appropriate responses.

FOR DISCUSSION:

1. Are attitudinally-derived actions intentionally discriminatory?
2. Discuss examples in educational institutions that support the statement, "In the institutional model people are still the agents of harm, but the institution frequently validates those actions by prescribing practices that are carried out within an institutionally-sanctioned role."
3. What does the author mean by: "Each person internalizes the social expectations of their societal place and role as a result of socialization."
4. Is everyone biased?
5. How does women's "close proximity to men" obscure their "actual powerlessness"?
6. How and why does an outgroup impose self limits?
7. The author suggests increased funds to school districts as a "reward" for successful efforts at eliminating discrimination. Would such a reward system be effective?
8. How can one " . . . come to consciously grasp how our perceptions and beliefs about gender are shaped by the socialization process, which consists largely of internalizing overt and implicit messages about the value and place of women and men?"

SUGGESTIONS FOR FURTHER READING

Benokraitis, N., & Feagin, J. *Modern sexism: Blatant, subtle, and covert discrimination.* Englewood Cliffs, New Jersey: Prentice-Hall, 1986.

Bleier, R. *Science and gender: A critique of biology and its theories on women.* Elmsford, New York: Pergamon Press, 1984.

Citizens' Commission on Civil Rights. *Affirmative action to open the doors of job opportunity.* Washington, D.C., 1984.

Council on Interracial Books for Children. *Understanding institutional sexism.* New York, 1982.

Giddings, P. *When and where I enter: The impact of black women on race and sex in America.* New York: William Morrow & Co., Inc., 1984.

Hartmann, H.I., & Reskin, B.E. (Eds.). *Women's work, men's work.* Washington, D.C.: National Academy Press, 1986.

Lord, S.B. *The female experience in America.* Newton, Massachusetts: EDC/WEEA Publishing Center, 1982.

Project on Equal Education Rights. *Organizing for change: PEER's guide to campaigning for equal education.* Washington, D.C., 1982.

Ryan, W. *Equality.* New York: Pantheon Books, 1981.

SEX EQUITY ORGANIZATIONS

The following list of organizations provide newsletters, publications, and audio-visual materials on topics related to sex equity in education.

Access to Equity Project
Office for Disabled Students
Barnard College
3009 Broadway
New York, NY 10027

Action Against Sexual Harassment in
  Education and Employment
P.O. Box 1491
Madison, WI 53701

Advocacy Press
P.O. Box 236
Santa Barbara, CA 93102

The Association for Women in Science
1346 Connecticut Ave., NW, S. 1122
Washington, DC 20036

Association of American Colleges
Project on the Status and Education of
  Women
1818 R Street, NW
Washington, DC 20009

Cambridge Documentary Films, Inc.
P.O. Box 385
Cambridge, MA 02139

Catalyst Information Center
14 East 60 Street
New York, NY 10022

Center for Family Resources
384 Clinton Street
Hempstead, NY 11550

Center for Public Advocacy Research
12 West 37 Street
New York, NY 10018

Center for Sex Equity in Schools
The University of Michigan
School of Education
Ann Arbor, MI 48109

Center for Women in Government
Deaper Hall, 302, SUNY Albany
1400 Washington Avenue
Albany, NY 12222

Consortium for Educational Equity
Rutgers University
4090 Kilmer Campus
New Brunswick, NJ 08903

Constitutional Rights Foundation
1510 Cotner Avenue
Los Angeles, CA 90025

Council on Interracial Books for
  Children
1841 Broadway
New York, NY 10023-7648

Displaced Homemaker Network, Inc.
1010 Vermont Avenue, NW, S. 817
Washington, DC 20005

EDC/WEEA
Education Development Center
Women's Educational Equity Act
Publishing Center
55 Chapel Street, S. 200
Newton, MA 02160

Educational Equity Concepts, Inc.
114 East 32nd Street
New York, NY 10016

Educational Equity for Black Girls
  Project
National Black Child Dev. Institute
1463 Rhode Island Avenue
Washington, DC 20005

EQUALS
Lawrence Hall of Science
University of California
Berkeley, CA 04720

EQUALS in Computer Technology
American Institutes for Research
P.O. Box 1113
Palo Alto, CA 94302

The Equity Institute
4715 Cordell Avenue
Bethesda, MD 20814

Family Resource Coalition
230 North Michigan Avenue
Suite 1625
Chicago, IL 60601

Federal Education Project
Lawyer's Committee for Civil Rights
  Under Law
733 15th Street, NW, S. 526
Washington, DC 20005

Feminist Press
Box 334
Old Westbury, NY 11568

Helaine Victoria Press
4080 Dynasty Lane
Dept. NW
Martinsville, IN 46151

Home and School Institute
1201 16th St., NW
Washington, DC 20036

Journal of Educational Equity and
  Leadership
Sage Publications
2111 West Hillcrest Drive
Newburgy, CA 91320

Journal of the National Association for
  Women Deans, Administrators, and
  Counselors
Suite 210
1325 18th NW
Washington, DC 20036

Journal of Sex Roles Research
Plenum Publishing Company
233 Spring Street
New York, NY 10013

KNOW, Inc.
P.O. Box 86031
Pittsburgh, PA 15221

Lawyers Committee for Civil Rights
  Under Law
1400 I Street, NW
Washington, DC 20005

Lollipop Power, Inc.
Box 1171
Chapel Hill, NC 27514

Mathematics Department
Toronto Board of Education
155 College Street
Toronto, Ontario M5T 1P6

Math/Science Resource Center
Mills College
Oakland, CA 94613

Men's Studies Review
P.O. Box 32
Harriman, TN 37748

Mid-Atlantic Center for Sex Equity
Suite 310
5010 Wisconsin Avenue, NW
Washington, DC 20016

The Ms. Foundation
370 Lexington Avenue
New York, NY 10017

National Center for Research in Vocational Education
Ohio State University
1960 Kenny Road
Columbus, OH 43210

National Coalition of Women and Girls in Education
c/o PEER
1413 K Street, NW, 9th Fl.
Washington, DC 20005

National Commission on Working Women/Center for Women and Work
1211 Connecticut Avenue, NW, S. 310
Washington, DC 20036

National Committee for Citizens in Education
10840 Little Patuxent Parkway
Suite 301
Columbia, MD 21044

National Council of Administrative Women in Education
1815 Forth Meyer Drive North
Arlington, VA 22209

National Council of Teachers of Mathematics
1906 Association Drive
Reston, VA 22091

The National Organization for Changing Men
P.O. Box 451
Watseka, IL 60970

National Women's History Project
Box 3716
Santa Rosa, CA 95402

National Women's Law Center
1616 P Street, NW, S. 100
Washington, DC 20036

The Network, Inc.
290 S. Main Street
Andover, MA 01810

New Day Films
Box 315
Franklin Lakes, NJ 07417

New Ways to Work
149 Ninth Street
San Francisco, CA 94103

NEWIST/CESA #7
IS 1110
University of Wisconsin
Green Bay, WI 54301

New York State Sex Equity Technical Assistance Center
Project VOICE/MOVE
1015 Watervliet-Shaker Road
Albany, NY 12205

9 to 5: National Association of Working Women
145 Tremont Street
Boston, MA 02111

OASIS
15 Willoughby Street
Brighton, MA 02135

Organization for Equal Education of the Sexes
438 Fourth Street
Brooklyn, NY 11215-2902

PEER (Project on Equal Education Rights)
1413 K Street, NW (9th Fl.)
Washington, DC 20005

Project Pro-Ceed
Dept. of Education
Gallaudet College for the Hearing Impaired
Kendall Green
800 Florida Avenue, NE
Washington, DC 20002

Resource Center on Sex Equity
Council of Chief State School Officers
400 No. Capitol St., NW, S. 379
Washington, DC 20001

Resources for Change
67 Mount Vernon Street
Cambridge, MA 02140

TABS
74 Carroll Street, Dept. NW
Brooklyn, NY 11215

United States Dept. of Labor
Women's Bureau
Office of the Secretary
200 Constitution Ave., NW
Washington, DC 20210

United States Equal Employment
  Opportunity Commission
2401 E. Street, NW., Rm. 4202
Washington, DC 20506

Vocational Resources Center
Education Service Center Region II
209 N. Water
Corpus Christi, TX 78401

What's New in Home Economics
North American Pub. Co.
401 N. Broad Street
Philadelphia, PA 19108

Wider Opportunities for Women, Inc.
1325 "G" Street, NW (Lower level)
Washington, DC 20005

Women's Action Alliance
370 Lexington Avenue
New York, NY 10017

Women and Mathematics Education
c/o Education Department
George Mason University
4400 University Drive
Fairfax, VA 22091

Women's Equity Action League
Educational and Legal Defense Fund
(WEAL Fund)
805 15th St., NW, S. 822
Washington, DC 20005

Women's Hall of Fame
Box 335
Seneca Falls, NY 13148

Women in the World Curriculum
  Resource Project
1030 Spruce Street
Berkeley, CA 94707

Women on Words and Images
Box 2163
Princeton, NJ 08540

Women's Audio Exchange
Box 273
Cambridge, NY 12816

Women's Sports Foundation
195 Moulten Street
San Francisco, CA 94123

Work and Family Life
Bank Street College
610 West 112th Street
New York, NY 10025

Working Women's Institute
593 Park Avenue
New York, NY 10021

INDEX